HISTORICAL DICTIONARY

The historical dictionaries present essential information on a broad range of subjects, including American and world history, art, business, cities, countries, cultures, customs, film, global conflicts, international relations, literature, music, philosophy, religion, sports, and theater. Written by experts, all contain highly informative introductory essays of the topic and detailed chronologies that, in some cases, cover vast historical time periods but still manage to heavily feature more recent events.

Brief A–Z entries describe the main people, events, politics, social issues, institutions, and policies that make the topic unique, and entries are cross-referenced for ease of browsing. Extensive bibliographies are divided into several general subject areas, providing excellent access points for students, researchers, and anyone wanting to know more. Additionally, maps, photographs, and appendixes of supplemental information aid high school and college students doing term papers or introductory research projects. In short, the historical dictionaries are the perfect starting point for anyone looking to research in these fields.

HISTORICAL DICTIONARIES OF LITERATURE AND THE ARTS

Jon Woronoff, Series Editor

Science Fiction Literature, by Brian Stableford, 2004.
Hong Kong Cinema, by Lisa Odham Stokes, 2007.
American Radio Soap Operas, by Jim Cox, 2005.
Japanese Traditional Theatre, by Samuel L. Leiter, 2006.
Fantasy Literature, by Brian Stableford, 2005.
Australian and New Zealand Cinema, by Albert Moran and Errol Vieth, 2006.
African-American Television, by Kathleen Fearn-Banks, 2006.
Lesbian Literature, by Meredith Miller, 2006.
Scandinavian Literature and Theater, by Jan Sjåvik, 2006.
British Radio, by Seán Street, 2006.
German Theater, by William Grange, 2006.
African American Cinema, by S. Torriano Berry and Venise Berry, 2006.
Sacred Music, by Joseph P. Swain, 2006.
Russian Theater, by Laurence Senelick, 2007.
French Cinema, by Dayna Oscherwitz and MaryEllen Higgins, 2007.
Postmodernist Literature and Theater, by Fran Mason, 2007.
Irish Cinema, by Roderick Flynn and Pat Brereton, 2007.
Australian Radio and Television, by Albert Moran and Chris Keating, 2007.
Polish Cinema, by Marek Haltof, 2007.
Old Time Radio, by Robert C. Reinehr and Jon D. Swartz, 2008.
Renaissance Art, by Lilian H. Zirpolo, 2008.
Broadway Musical, by William A. Everett and Paul R. Laird, 2008.
American Theater: Modernism, by James Fisher and Felicia Hardison Londré, 2008.
German Cinema, by Robert C. Reimer and Carol J. Reimer, 2008.
Horror Cinema, by Peter Hutchings, 2008.
Westerns in Cinema, by Paul Varner, 2008.
Chinese Theater, by Tan Ye, 2008.
Italian Cinema, by Gino Moliterno, 2008.
Architecture, by Allison Lee Palmer, 2008.
Russian and Soviet Cinema, by Peter Rollberg, 2008.
African American Theater, by Anthony D. Hill, 2009.
Postwar German Literature, by William Grange, 2009.
Modern Japanese Literature and Theater, by J. Scott Miller, 2009.
Animation and Cartoons, by Nichola Dobson, 2009.
Modern Chinese Literature, by Li-hua Ying, 2010.
Middle Eastern Cinema, by Terri Ginsberg and Chris Lippard, 2010.

Historical Dictionary of Baroque Music

Joseph P. Swain

The Scarecrow Press, Inc.
Lanham • Toronto • Plymouth, UK
2013

Published by Scarecrow Press, Inc.
A wholly owned subsidiary of The Rowman & Littlefield Publishing Group, Inc.
4501 Forbes Boulevard, Suite 200, Lanham, Maryland 20706
www.rowman.com

10 Thornbury Road, Plymouth PL6 7PP, United Kingdom

British Library Cataloguing in Publication Information Available

Library of Congress Cataloging-in-Publication Data

Swain, Joseph Peter.
  Historical dictionary of baroque music / Joseph P. Swain.
    pages cm. — (Historical dictionaries of literature and the arts)
  Includes bibliographical references.
  ISBN 978-0-8108-7824-2 (cloth : alk. paper) — ISBN 978-0-8108-7825-9 (electronic)
1. Music—18th century—Dictionaries. 2. Music—17th century—Dictionaries. I. Title.
  ML100.S88 2013
  780.9'03203—dc23
                                                                          2013005104

Contents

Editor's Foreword

In music, as indeed in all the arts, fashions change, and what once appealed becomes dull and uninteresting and passes. This, indeed, is what happened to Baroque music, which reigned supreme from about 1600 to about 1750—these dates being very fuzzy. At any rate, about that latter date, new fashions gained ground, and Baroque music not only ceased being composed but also even being played by and large. Then, in the late 19th century and ever stronger during the early 20th, it was rediscovered and brought back to life, not only as an oddity but also as one of the strongest strands of what is usually called "classical music." If anything really needs explaining here, it is not so much why Baroque music has made a comeback but how the glorious music of Bach, Handel, Vivaldi, and many others could have been forgotten and some of it actually lost forever. Now that it is indeed back and being performed frequently and enjoyed enormously by many, we still do need to consider the period that produced it more closely to see, among other things, what the basic rules were then and how they were constantly revised and "improved" to the extent that one could already speak of a "*stile antico*" and a "*stile moderno*."

That is among the tasks taken on by the introduction, which gives us a very insightful look at the period that generated this music. The countless, essential details are then provided by the dictionary section, which among many other things acquaints us with the instruments, some of which have since disappeared while others were modified and are still with us; the forms of music, many of which (such as the opera and concerto) are familiar to all music lovers while others are a bit more distant; the centers of musical life at that time, basically an age when composers lived off the church or nobility; and last but not least, a plethora of composers, including not only the three above but also many others who are known and appreciated today and who shaped the music of that period. No less important are the many entries on technical terms that do require elucidation. Although that all happened long ago, the time sequence is important in following the course of events, and the chronology is most helpful in that respect. For those who want to learn more, the next step is obviously to follow the leads given in the bibliography.

The very first volume on music in this series is the *Historical Dictionary of Sacred Music* by Joseph P. Swain, who has also written this *Historical Dictionary of Baroque Music*. Obviously, the two are closely related in some ways, given the very prominent position of sacred music during this period. And Dr. Swain is a particularly apt choice for both, considering the fact that he has been teaching music history and theory for more than 35 years, directed Tapestry, the All-Centuries Singers for 19 years, and is now organist and director of music at St. Malachy's Church. This experience has resulted in a number of books along with the aforementioned historical dictionary, some of which are related while others show the breadth of his interests, in particular *The Broadway Musical*. Once again, he proves an excellent guide for those who are interested in Baroque music—and they are legion—and who want to know more, whether they are part of the general public or scholars.

Jon Woronoff
Series Editor

Preface

This *Historical Dictionary of Baroque Music* provides in one volume basic information about the most important traditions, famous pieces, persons, places, technical terms, and institutions of Baroque music, that is, the music of Western Europe dating from about 1600 to 1750. It also provides an extensive bibliography if the reader requires more information about any of the entries. It is intended for musicians at all levels and for readers with diverse interests—students and teachers of music history, students and teachers of the Western tradition, and above all for lovers of Baroque music who wish to inform their listening experiences. The dictionary assumes familiarity with the basic components of traditional Western music—musical notation, the violin, the concepts of melody, harmony, rhythm, and so forth—but at the same time offers entries for many fundamental terms of musical discourse—"key," "functional harmony," "meter," "violin," to name a few—which have particular meanings in the Baroque context.

The introduction presents the most important historical developments that characterize the entire period but are too broad or diffuse to capture with individual dictionary entries. It begins with a description of the invention of opera, the crucial event that provided composers with a new set of aesthetic goals transforming not only their art but also the entire musical culture and, to a degree, European society itself. From there, the essay proceeds to subsequent technical developments that assured, all at once, the long-term success of the operatic experiment, the synthesis of Renaissance techniques and genres into the new musical language, and the tremendous accomplishments of the instrumental forms of suite, sonata, and concerto.

Nearly one half of the entries are biographical, dominated by composers, of course, but also including other important personalities that affected the history of Baroque music: music theorists and critics who summarized ideas and compositional techniques in contemporary language, poets who wrote opera librettos, and a few remarkable 18th-century performers. Not included are modern performers or scholars of Baroque music. In a single volume dealing with such a vast subject area, it is best to keep the music front and center, and in any case, the bibliography should give a good picture of the state of scholarship.

Another fifth of the entries focuses on Baroque genres of composition (e.g., "concerto," "cantata," "*opera seria*") and describe their origins, developments, and principal composers. About one tenth of the entries defines technical terms peculiar to the Baroque, such as "figured bass" and "double dotting," as well as others that appear elsewhere in music history but have particular connotations in the Baroque, such as "cadence," "counterpoint," and "inversion." Other groups of entries include Baroque instruments (e.g., "harpsichord"), not omitting familiar modern instruments, such as "violin," that have unfamiliar characteristics in their Baroque versions or that play Baroque music differently; historically important cities for Baroque music; and finally some of the landmark compositions of the period, such as the *Well-Tempered Clavier* and *Messiah*.

Except where the most objective technical language allows the audible to be usefully communicated (e.g., "a solo singer with lute accompaniment" or "strophic forms in homophonic arrangements"), the entries do not attempt to describe the sound of the music. Objective facts—definitions, names, dates, places, techniques—make up most of the information. If this treatment of the music seems a bit cold, it allows a much greater coverage, and besides, no writing substitutes for the learning that comes from hearing the music itself.

In order to facilitate the rapid and efficient location of information and to make this book as useful a reference tool as possible, extensive cross-references have been provided in the dictionary section. Within individual entries, terms that have their own entries are in **boldface type** the first time they appear. Related terms that do not appear in the text are indicated in the *See also*. *See* refers to other entries that deal with this topic.

To name individual pitches, the dictionary adopts the system typically used in American music theory. Middle C is C^4, the octave above is C^5. The pitches between these are all superscribed with 4 (e.g., D^4, E-flat^4, etc.). The pitches of the next higher octave are superscribed with 5, those of the next lower octave with 3, and so on.

Names and musical compositions with 18th-century spellings are not consistent. In the case of a title of a unique work—*Rappresentatione di Anima e di Corpo*—the dictionary adopts the spelling used by the composer or publisher, except where usage within the work or set of works is inconsistent—*Pièces* and *Pieces*—in which cases the modern spelling is taken. In all other cases, modern spellings are preferred.

The compiler's problem with subject as vast as Baroque music is not the acquisition of information but rather deciding what to include and what to omit. Some entries may merit their places because of intrinsic worth, such as Claudio Monteverdi's *Vespers of the Blessed Virgin* (1610), a magnificent but unique composition without significant influence. Much more often, precious space is allotted to persons or events that affected the course of Baroque music history in some way, especially in regard to the minor biographies. Generally, the choice of what information to include was governed by the question of what would best inform the reader's experience of listening to Baroque music.

A number of friends and colleagues have generously given me their expert advice in various areas of Baroque music, without which I could not have finished the book. In particular, I would like to recognize the contributions of Ms. Laura Campbell, Mr. Ralph Dudgeon, Mr. Thomas Klenck, Fr. Jerome F. Weber, who expertly looked over the entire manuscript, and members of the NYS Baroque Ensemble. The photographs of Baroque instruments supplied by these people were edited by Joseph F. Swain and Cynthia Lee Swain. I must also recognize Jon Woronoff of Scarecrow Press, who offered me the project and offered much valuable advice along the way. And beyond the inestimable support of my wife Jan and our children, who played Baroque music with me on many occasions, I would like to remember members of my own family who unknowingly planted the seeds of this project decades ago: my sister Chris, who introduced me to *Messiah* one gray December; my brother Bern, who showed me that the Baroque was hardly limited to *Messiah*; and Katie and John, who tolerated my constant playing of Baroque music on the stereo in the house.

My deepest appreciation to all who supported this project.

Joseph P. Swain
Hamilton, New York

Chronology

1563 4 December: The Council of Trent promulgates its final document, upholding the plainsong and polyphonic traditions of liturgical music while rejecting certain characteristics of secular music as inappropriate for the Roman Rite.

1574–1589 The meetings of the Camerata in Florence.

1577 Antonio Gardano publishes the first printed score in Venice.

1580 Jan Pieterszoon Sweelinck appointed organist at the Oude Kerk in Amsterdam.

1582 Claudio Monteverdi's earliest publication, the *Sacrae Cantiunculae*.

1587 *Concerti di Andrea, et Gio. Gabrieli* published in Venice. Claudio Monteverdi publishes his first book of madrigals in Venice.

1588 Jacopo Peri, early opera composer, appointed singer at the Medici court, Florence.

1589 Performance of the play *La Pellegrina* with intermedi of Emilio de' Cavalieri, Jacopo Peri, and Giulio Caccini, all collaborators in the earliest operas, for the wedding festivities of King Henry IV of France and Catherine de' Medici.

c. 1590 Claudio Monteverdi appointed viol player at the court of Mantua.

1592 Antonio Naldi invents the theorbo, an important Baroque continuo instrument, in Florence.

1597 Giovanni Gabrieli publishes *Sacrae Symphoniae* in Venice.

1598 Performance of the first known opera, Jacopo Peri's *La Dafne*, during Carnival season at the Medici court in Florence.

1600 Pope Clement VIII's *Caeremoniale Episcoporum* ratifies the practice of substituting organ versets for plainchants at Roman Catholic liturgies. **February:** Performance of Emilio de' Cavalieri's *Rappresentazione di Anima e di Corpo*, often considered the first oratorio, at the Oratorio della

Vallicella, Rome. **6 October:** Performance of *Euridice*, the oldest surviving opera, with music by Jacopo Peri and Giulio Caccini, libretto by Ottaviano Rinuccini at the Medici court in Florence.

1601 **26 November:** Claudio Monteverdi appointed *maestro di cappella* for the court of Mantua.

1602 Publication of *Cento Concerti Ecclesiastici* ("One Hundred Sacred Concertos"), Ludovico Viadana's Opus 12, the first published collection of sacred music to include a figured basso continuo. Publication of Giulio Caccini's first volume of *Le Nuove Musiche*, significant collection of vocal monodies.

1603 Publication of controversial Book IV of Italian madrigals of Claudio Monteverdi.

1604 Giovanni Girolamo Kapsberger publishes his first of four volumes of guitar music, *Libro I d'Intavolatura di Chitarrone* in Venice. Michael Praetorius appointed *Kapellmeister* to Duke of Brunswick-Wolfenbüttel.

1605 Claudio Monteverdi publishes Book V of Italian madrigals, which required a continuo for the first time. William Byrd publishes his first volume of *Gradualia*, polyphonic propers for the Roman Catholic mass, London. Michael Praetorius begins to publish his nine-volume set of chorale arrangements, *Musae Sioniae.*

1606 Agostino Agazzari's music drama *Eumelio* performed during Carnival in Rome.

1607 Salomone Rossi publishes *Sinfonie e Gagliarde* for instrumental ensemble and continuo. **24 February:** First performance of Claudio Monteverdi's opera *L'Orfeo.*

1608 Girolamo Frescobaldi assumes the position of organist at the Cappella Giulia at St. Peter's, Rome, and publishes his first volume of keyboard music. **28 May:** Claudio Monteverdi's second opera, *Arianna*, performed to great acclaim.

1609 Publication of Monteverdi's *L'Orfeo*. Samuel Scheidt appointed court organist in Halle, Germany. Heinrich Schütz arrives in Venice to study with Giovanni Gabrieli.

1610 Publication of Claudio Monteverdi's collection of music for vespers and the *Missa In Illo Tempore*, altogether known as the "Vespers of 1610."

1611 Heinrich Schütz's book of Italian madrigals published as Opus 1.

1612 Michael Praetorius's *Terpsichore* dances published. Oratorio dei Girolamini inaugurated in Naples. **29 July:** Claudio Monteverdi dismissed from the court at Mantua. **August:** Giovanni Gabrieli dies in Venice.

1613 **19 August:** Claudio Monteverdi appointed *maestro di cappella* at St. Mark's Basilica, Venice.

1614 Medicean press in Rome publishes the revisions of Roman Catholic plainchant authorized by the Council of Trent. Michael Praetorius begins to publish his four-volume treatise, *Syntagma Musicum*.

1615 Heinrich Schütz appointed to the electoral court at Dresden, beginning a lifelong association. Appearance of Giovanni Gabrieli's *Canzoni et Sonate*, published posthumously. Girolamo Frescobaldi publishes *Recercari et Canzoni*. **21 May:** Johann Hermann Schein appointed *Kapellmeister* to the ducal court at Weimar.

1617 Hermann Schein publishes the *Banchetto Musicale*, an early collection of instrumental suites.

1618 Hermann Schein begins to issue his collection of sacred music, the *Opella Nova*.

1619 Giovanni Anerio introduces the Italian oratorio with *Teatro Armonico Spirituale*. Heinrich Schütz publishes his first volume of *Psalmen Davids*.

1620 Alessandro Grandi's reprint of *Cantade et Arie*, first known occurrence of the term "cantata."

1621 Dario Castello's first volume of solo instrumental sonatas appears. **15 February:** Michael Praetorius dies in Wolfenbüttel, Germany. **16 October:** Jan Pieterszoon Sweelinck dies in Amsterdam.

1622 Salomone Rossi publishes *Ha-Shirim Asher Li'Shlomo*, a set of madrigals on Jewish texts.

1623 Jehan de Titelouze publishes early French organ versets.

1624 Samuel Scheidt's *Tabulatura Nova* published, an important collection of early organ music.

1625 Heinrich Schütz publishes motets in *stile moderno* in *Cantiones Sacrae*.

1627 Alessandro Grandi appointed *maestro di cappella* at Santa Maria Maggiore in Bergamo, Italy.

1628 Girolamo Frescobaldi appointed court organist to the Duke of Tuscany, Florence. *Psalmen Davids*, 90 psalm paraphrases, published by Heinrich Schütz.

1629 December: Giacomo Carissimi appointed *maestro di cappella* at the Collegio Germanico e Hungarico, Rome. Juan Gutiérrez de Padilla appointed *maestro de capilla* at the Puebla Cathedral, Mexico. Heinrich Schütz publishes first volume of *Symphoniae Sacrae*. Heinrich Scheidemann becomes organist of the Catharinenkirche, Hamburg.

1630 Antoine Boësset's seventh book of *airs de cour* calls for a continuo, first instance in France.

1632 18 February: First performance of Stefano Landi's *Il Sant' Alessio*, an important early oratorio, in Rome. **December:** Franz Tunder appointed court organist at Holstein-Gottorp.

1633 12 August: Jacopo Peri dies in Florence.

1634 Performance of an early English masque, *The Triumph of Peace*, with music by William Lawes. Girolamo Frescobaldi returns to Rome and the Cappella Giulia.

1635 Girolamo Frescobaldi's most important collection of organ versets *Fiori Musicali* published in Venice. Ben Jonson writes earliest extant ode text "A New-Yeares-Gift Sung to King Charles."

1636 Heinrich Schütz publishes his first volume of *Kleine Geistliche Konzerte*.

1637 Carnival: First public opera theater, Teatro San Cassiano, opens in Venice with Francesco Manelli's *Andromeda*. **June:** Jakob Froberger wins grant to study with Girolamo Frescobaldi in Rome.

1638 Earliest known performance of *Britannia Triumphans*, an English masque including music of William Lawes.

1639 23 January: Francesco Cavalli appointed second organist at San Marco, Venice. **24 January:** Cavalli's first opera *Le Nozze di Teti e di Peleo* opens in Venice.

1640 Premiere of Pietro Della Valle's *Oratorio della Purificazione*, first instance of the word "oratorio" applied to a musical work. The term *lo stile recitativo* first appears in print, in Giovanni Battista Doni's *Annotazioni*. **Carnival:** Claudio Monteverdi composes his late opera *Il Ritorno d'Ulisse in Patria*.

1641   Good Friday: Thomas Selle's *Passio secundum Joannem cum Intermediis*, first known oratorio passion, performed in Hamburg.

1642   Francesco Cavalli's opera *Egisto* revived in Vienna.

1643   Carnival: first performance of Claudio Monteverdi's last opera *L'Incoronazione di Poppea*. **1 March:** Girolamo Frescobaldi dies in Rome. **Good Friday:** Premier of Giovanni Valentini's *Santi Risorti*, earliest known example of *sepolcro* in Vienna. **29 November:** Claudio Monteverdi dies in Venice; buried with full honors of the Republic of Venice.

1644   Barbara Strozzi publishes her first book of madrigals.

1646   Francesco Cavalli's *Egisto* performed in Paris. **February:** Jean-Baptiste Lully moves to Paris.

1647   Franz Tunder assumes post of organist at the Marienkirche in Lübeck, Germany.

1648   Francesco Cavalli composes opera *Giasone*. Heinrich Schütz publishes large-scale motets in *Geistliche Chormusik*.

1650   Giacomo Carissimi's oratorio *Jephte* complete. Athanasius Kircher's *Musurgia Universalis* published. The city of Naples sees its first opera, *Didone* (composer unknown). Heinrich Schütz publishes his last volume of *Symphoniae Sacrae*.

1651   Posthumous publication *Madrigali e Canzonette* of Claudio Monteverdi, in Venice.

1652   Henry Du Mont publishes his first motets in Paris.

1653   Juan Hidalgo composes the earliest surviving Spanish-language recitative in *Fortunas de Andrómeda y Perseo*. Matthew Locke composes first English recitatives for the masque *Cupid and Death*. **16 March:** Jean-Baptiste Lully appointed court composer by King Louis XIV of France. **9 April:** Louis Couperin appointed organist at St. Gervais, Paris.

1655   Matthias Weckmann appointed organist at the Jacobkirche in Hamburg.

1656   In Rome, Queen Christina of Sweden appoints Giacomo Carissimi music master in her household. Elector Johann Georg II of Dresden begins to reconstruct the Hofkapelle. *Les Galanteries du Temps*, earliest surviving ballet by Jean-Baptiste Lully, introduces his new orchestra Les Petits Violons. **September:** *The Siege of Rhodes*, the first English-language opera, is performed in London.

1657 Christoph Bernhard publishes theory of music and rhetoric in *Tractatus Compositionis Augmentatus*. Maurizio Cazzati appointed *maestro di cappella* at San Petronio, Bologna.

1658 Jean-Baptiste Lully's *Ballet d'Acidiane* presents the earliest known French overture.

1660 Earliest surviving full-length Spanish opera, *Celos aun del Aire Matan* of Juan Hidalgo. First oratorio performed in Vienna: *Il Sacrifizio d'Abramo*. Matthias Weckmann founds Collegium Musicum in Hamburg. **Spring:** Francesco Cavalli produces his opera *Ercole Amante* in Paris. **29 September:** Henry Cooke appointed Master of Children and begins to restore the Chapel Royal, London. **25 December:** Premiere of Heinrich Schütz's *Christmas Oratorio*, Dresden.

1663 **26 September:** Heinrich Scheidemann dies during the plague in Hamburg, and Johann Adam Reincken succeeds as organist of the Catharinenkirche.

1664 **29 January:** Jean-Baptiste Lully's *Le Mariage Forcé*, the first collaboration with the dramatist Molière, opens in Paris.

1665 Maurizio Cazzati publishes his first trumpet sonatas in Opus 35. Early cello sonatas appear in G. C. Arresti's Opus 4. **11 January:** Francesco Cavalli appointed first organist at San Marco, Venice.

1666 Earliest extant ode compositions in England. Heinrich Schütz composes three passions. **April:** Juan Bautista Cabanilles appointed first organist at Valencia Cathedral.

1667 **7 May:** Jakob Froberger dies in Héricourt, France.

1668 **11 April:** Dietrich Buxtehude chosen to succeed Franz Tunder as organist at the Marienkirche in Lübeck. **12 and 14 July:** Antonio Cesti's spectacular opera *Il Pomo D'Oro* creates a sensation in Vienna. **28 November:** Francesco Cavalli succeeds Giovanni Rovetta as *maestro di cappella* at San Marco, Venice.

1669 Appearance of *Pièces de Luth* of Denis Gaultier. In Genoa, Alessandro Stradella composes *Il Trespolo Tutore*, an early example of *opera buffa*.

1670 Arcangelo Corelli admitted to the Accademia Filarmonica, Bologna.

1671 The Teatro Tordinona opens in Rome. **17 January:** *Psyché*, last collaboration of Jean-Baptiste Lully and Molière, opens in Paris.

1672 Johann Philipp Krieger appointed *Kapellmeister* in Bayreuth, Germany, where he remains for 45 years and composes 2,000 church cantatas.

The oldest surviving zarzuela score, *Los Celos Hacen Estrellas*, by Juan Hidalgo. **March:** Jean-Baptiste Lully acquires royal privilege to produce French-language operas. **6 November:** Heinrich Schütz dies in Dresden.

1673 **April:** Jean-Baptiste Lully's *Cadmus et Hermione*, his first *tragédie lyrique*, opens in Paris.

1674 Pelham Humfrey contributes music for *The Tempest*. Giovanni Battista Vitali appointed *vice-maestro di cappella* to the ducal chapel at Modena. **12 January:** Giacomo Carissimi dies in Rome. **January:** After the success of Jean-Baptiste Lully's *Alceste*, King Louis XIV provides full support for the *tragédie lyrique*.

1675 Arcangelo Corelli begins a long residence in Rome.

1676 Nicolas Lebègue begins to publish three volumes of organ music. Heinrich Ignaz Franz von Biber composes the programmatic "Rosary Sonatas" at Salzburg, Austria. **1 January:** Tomás de Torrejón y Velasco appointed *maestro de capilla* of Lima Cathedral. **14 January:** Francesco Cavalli dies in Venice.

1677 **August:** Matthew Locke dies in London. **10 September:** Henry Purcell succeeds Matthew Locke as composer in ordinary to the king of England.

1678 Buxtehude expands the *Abendmusiken* in Lübeck to include oratorios and sacred concertos. Henry Purcell appointed organist at Westminster Abbey. **2 January:** Opening of the Gänsemarkt public opera house in Hamburg. **19 June:** Johann Pachelbel begins 12-year residency in Erfurt, Germany.

1679 Alessandro Scarlatti's early opera *Gli Equivoci nel Sembiante* premieres in Rome and achieves immediate notoriety.

1681 Publication of Arcangelo Corelli's trio sonatas Opus 1 in Rome. **5 January:** Giovanni Legrenzi appointed *vice-maestro di cappella* at San Marco, Venice.

1682 Antonio Draghi appointed *Kapellmeister* to the imperial court, Vienna. **14 July:** Henry Purcell appointed organist to the Chapel Royal.

1683 *Venus and Adonis*, a masque of John Blow, performed in London.

1684 Johann Kuhnau appointed organist at Thomaskirche in Leipzig. First sojourn in Naples for Alessandro Scarlatti. Arcangelo Corelli and Alessandro Scarlatti admitted to the Congregazione di Santa Cecilia, Rome. **11 August:** Friedrich Wilhelm Zachow appointed organist at the Marienkirche in Halle, Germany.

1685   16 April: Giovanni Legrenzi succeeds Monferrato as *maestro di cappella* at San Marco, Venice. **21 May:** Procurators of San Marco establish a regular ensemble of 34 players, one of the largest in Europe.

1686   Marin Marais begins to publish suites for viol and continuo.

1687   Elisabeth Jacquet de La Guerre begins to publish harpsichord works. **February:** Arcangelo Corelli leads an ensemble of 150 in music of Bernardo Pasquini at the Palazzo Riario, Rome. **22 March:** Jean-Baptiste Lully dies in Paris. **23 November:** Last *tragédie lyrique* of Jean-Baptiste Lully, *Achille et Polyxène*, premieres in Paris.

1688   Summer: Agostino Steffani appointed *Kapellmeister* to the ducal court at Hanover.

1689   Henry Purcell's *Dido and Aeneas*. Jean Henry D'Anglebert publishes his *Pièces de Clavecin*. Giovanni Battista Vitali publishes *Artifici Musicali*. **January:** Michel-Richard de Lalande appointed *surintendant de la musique de la chambre* by King Louis XIV.

1690   Georg Muffat appointed *Kapellmeister* of Passau, Germany. François Couperin publishes *Pièces d'Orgue Consistantes en Deux Messes*, his two organ masses.

1691   Giovanni Carlo Grimani and Apostolo Zeno found the Accademia degli Animosi to reform opera in Venice. **Late spring:** First production of Henry Purcell's very popular semi-opera *King Arthur*.

1692   Marin Marais publishes *Pièces en Trio*, one of the earliest collections of French trio music.

1693   Carnival: Antonio Lotti's first opera, *Il Trionfo dell'Innocenza*. **26 December:** François Couperin appointed *organiste du roi* by King Louis XIV.

1694   Reinhard Keiser's first two operas produced in Brunswick and Hamburg.

1695   Theorist Daniel Merck publishes an early list of standard Italian tempo markings. **April:** Officials in Nuremberg invite Johann Pachelbel to be organist at the Sebalduskirche without trial. **21 November:** Henry Purcell dies in London.

1696   Johann Caspar Kerll publishes *Modulatio Organica* in Munich. Giacomo Antonio Perti begins 60-year tenure as *maestro di cappella* of the basilica of San Petronio, Bologna, Italy. **26 December:** Giovanni Bononcini's *Il Trionfo di Camilla* opens in Rome.

1697 24 October: André Campra's *opéra-ballet L'Europe Galante* premieres in Paris.

1698 28 June: Marc-Antoine Charpentier appointed *maître de musique* at the Sainte-Chapelle, Paris.

1699 Appearance of Nicolas de Grigny's *Premier Livre d'Orgue*. Johann Philipp Krieger makes first settings of Erdmann Neumeister's reform church cantata texts. Georg Muffat publishes *Regulae Concentuum Partiturae*, one of the best treatises on playing continuo.

1700 Johann Kuhnau publishes his Biblical Sonatas for harpsichord. Arcangelo Corelli publishes his Opus 5 violin sonatas, Rome. Neumeister publishes *Geistliche Cantaten statt einer Kirchen-Music*, earliest reform cantata texts. Tomaso Albinoni publishes his Opus 2 concertos, further establishing the fast-slow-fast form as standard for concertos. Bartolomeo Cristofori completes a prototype of the fortepiano in Florence. Printer John Walsh of London introduces faster and cheaper printing technology.

1701 Georg Muffat describes Arcangelo Corelli's "new manner of harmony" in *Auserlesene Instrumental-Musik*. Giuseppe Torelli returns to Bologna as part of the restoration of music at San Petronio. **April:** Johann Kuhnau assumes post of *Thomaskantor* in Leipzig.

1702 Georg Philipp Telemann founds the Collegium Musicum of Leipzig. Telemann appointed music director of Opernhaus auf dem Brühl, Leipzig.

1703 J. S. Bach begins his professional career at age 18 as organist in Arnstadt, Germany. Francesco Gasparini appoints Antonio Vivaldi violin master to the Pio Ospedale della Pietà in Venice. Reinhard Keiser becomes general director of the Theater am Gänsemarkt opera house in Hamburg. Sébastien de Brossard publishes his *Dictionnaire de Musique*. **9 January:** Alessandro Scarlatti appointed assistant *maestro di cappella* at the Congregazione dell' Oratorio, Rome. **23 March:** Antonio Vivaldi ordained to the Roman Catholic priesthood.

1704 24 February: Marc-Antoine Charpentier dies in Paris. **17 August:** Antonio Lotti appointed first organist at San Marco, Venice.

1705 First documented appearance of the horn in an orchestra, Reinhard Keiser's opera *Octavia* in Hamburg. Antonio Vivaldi's trio sonatas Opus 1 published in Venice. **8 January:** George Frideric Handel's first opera, *Almira*, premieres at the Hamburg opera. **April:** Five performances of Jakob Greber's *Gli Amori d'Ergasto* introduce Italian opera to London.

1706   Jean-Philippe Rameau publishes his *Premier Livre de Pièces de Clavecin*. Friedrich Erhard Niedt publishes a thoroughbass manual in his *Musicalische Handleitung*, Hamburg. **February:** Earliest known example of an intermezzo, *Frappolone e Florinetta*, in Venice. **9 March:** Johann Pachelbel buried in Nuremberg. **26 April:** Arcangelo Corelli, Bernardo Pasquini, and Alessandro Scarlatti admitted to the Arcadian Academy of Rome.

1707   Earliest cantatas of J. S. Bach. **Carnival:** Alessandro Scarlatti's opera *Il Mitridate Eupatore* fails in Venice. **May:** Arcangelo Corelli and George Frideric Handel work together in Rome. **9 May:** Dietrich Buxtehude dies in Lübeck. **29 July:** Johann Walther appointed organist at the Stadtkirche in Weimar.

1708   First publication of music for unaccompanied transverse flutes, *Premier Livre de Pièces* of Jacques-Martin Hotteterre. Alessandro Scarlatti reappointed *maestro di cappella* at the Royal Chapel in Naples. J. S. Bach appointed organist to the court of Saxe-Weimar.

1709   Johann Friedrich Fasch founds a second *collegium musicum* in Leipzig. **8 February:** Giuseppe Torelli dies in Bologna. **1 July:** Antonio Caldara appointed *maestro di cappella* to Prince Ruspoli, Rome. **26 December:** George Frideric Handel's first full-length Italian opera, *Agrippina*, opens in Venice.

1710   **Summer:** George Frideric Handel arrives in London.

1711   Estienne Roger of Amsterdam publishes Vivaldi's Opus 3 Concertos. **February 24:** George Frideric Handel's *Rinaldo* opens to acclaim, beginning his long operatic career in London.

1712   Georg Philipp Telemann becomes director of music in Frankfurt and *Kapellmeister* for the Barfüßkirche, initiating a period of intense composition of instrumental music.

1713   François Couperin publishes his first book of *Pièces de Clavecin*. Johann Mattheson publishes his introduction to contemporary music, *Das neu-eröffnete Orchestre*. **8 January:** Arcangelo Corelli dies in Rome. **May:** Antonio Vivaldi's earliest known opera, *Ottone in Villa*, opens in Vicenza. **7 July:** George Frideric Handel's Te Deum celebrates the Peace of Utrecht in London.

1714   Estienne Roger of Amsterdam publishes Arcangelo Corelli's Opus 6 Concertos. The Opéra-Comique of Paris opens. **March:** J. S. Bach promoted to concertmaster at the Weimar court. **22 December:** Death of Tommaso Baj, *maestro di cappella* of the Cappella Giulia in Rome, replaced by Domenico Scarlatti.

1715 Tomaso Albinoni's Opus 7 concertos first in Italy to feature the oboe. **January:** Johann Joseph Fux appointed imperial *Hofkapellmeister* in Vienna. **1 July:** Michel-Richard de Lalande assumes sole directorship of the Chapelle Royale.

1716 J. S. Bach's *Orgelbüchlein* complete. Francesco Gasparini succeeds Caldara as *maestro di cappella* for Prince Ruspoli, Rome. **May:** Governors of Ospedale della Pietà reappoint Antonio Vivaldi as "master of concerts." **Late spring:** Antonio Caldara begins tenure as imperial *vice-Kapellmeister* in Vienna.

1717 George Frideric Handel begins work on the Chandos anthems. Silvius Leopold Weiss begins lifelong residency in Dresden. **Fall:** Antonio Lotti begins two-year residence in Dresden.

1718 George Frideric Handel composes *Esther*, his first biblical English oratorio. Silvius Weiss appointed to the elector's court at Dresden. Apostolo Zeno begins residence at the imperial court, Vienna. **22 June:** Teatro della Pergola in Florence reopens with Antonio Vivaldi's *Scanderbeg*.

1719 Publishing firm of Breitkopf and Härtel founded in Leipzig. **19 April:** Leonardo Vinci's first opera, *Lo Cecato Fauzo*, opens in Naples to broad acclaim. **29 November:** Domenico Scarlatti takes up residence in Lisbon as *mestre de capela* at the royal court.

1720 Famous castrato Farinelli makes his first appearances in Naples. Benedetto Marcello publishes his satire of opera, *Il Teatro alla Moda*. **2 April:** Royal Academy of Music opens in London with Giovanni Porta's *Numitore*. **27 April:** George Frideric Handel's *Radamisto* opens with the Royal Academy in London.

1721 Nicola Porpora and Farinelli score operatic successes in Rome. **March:** J. S. Bach dedicates his Brandenburg Concertos. **10 July:** City of Hamburg invites Georg Philipp Telemann to become cantor. **1 August:** Johann Adolf Hasse's first opera, *Antioco*, opens in Brunswick, Germany. **17 September:** Georg Philipp Telemann installed as cantor in Hamburg.

1722 J. S. Bach compiles Book I of the *Well-Tempered Clavier*. Jean-Philippe Rameau publishes his *Traité de l'Harmonie*, the foundational book for modern harmonic theory. Tomaso Albinoni publishes his Opus 9 concertos. Georg Philipp Telemann appointed director of the Hamburg city opera. Leonardo Vinci composes *Li Zite'ngalera*, a comedy, in Naples. **5 June:** Johann Kuhnau dies in Leipzig. **24 November:** Johann Adam Reincken dies in Hamburg.

1723 May: J. S. Bach begins work as cantor of St. Thomas Church, Leipzig. **13 July:** François Colin de Blamont's *Les Festes Grecques et Romaines*, a *ballet-héroïque*, opens in Paris. **25 December:** Premiere of J. S. Bach's Magnificat.

1724 François Couperin publishes his collection of chamber works, *Les Goûts-réunis*, attempting a synthesis of Italian and French styles. Johann Adolf Hasse settles in Naples for a six-year sojourn. Benedetto Marcello begins attempt to reform sacred music with the first of eight volumes of Psalms of David. **20 February:** George Frideric Handel's opera *Giulio Cesare in Egitto* opens in London. **7 April:** Premiere of St. John Passion of Johann Sebastian Bach in Leipzig.

1725 Estienne Roger of Amsterdam publishes Antonio Vivaldi's *Le Quattro Stagioni* (*The Four Seasons*) as part of a collection of 12 concertos, Opus 8. Johann Joseph Fux publishes *Gradus ad Parnassum*. Antonio Caldara helps to found the Cecilian Society in Vienna. Padre Giovanni Battista Martini appointed *maestro di cappella* at San Francesco in Bologna. **18 March:** Inaugural concert of the Concert Spirituel, Paris. **Carnival:** Leonardo Vinci collaborates with Metastasio in Rome on *Didone Abbandonata*, beginning a long series. **22 October:** Alessandro Scarlatti dies in Naples; Leonardo Vinci appointed his successor at the royal chapel.

1726 Founding of the Academy of Ancient Music, London. J. S. Bach begins to publish Part I of *Clavier-Übung*. François Couperin publishes his collection of trio sonatas, *Les Nations*. Giovanni Porta begins 11-year tenure at the Ospedale della Pietà, Venice. **18 June:** Michel-Richard de Lalande dies at Versailles.

1727 11 April: Premiere of J. S. Bach's St. Matthew Passion, Leipzig. **11 October:** Premiere of George Frideric Handel's Coronation Anthems.

1728 The Royal Academy, George Frideric Handel's opera company in London, closes. Johann David Heinichen publishes "New and Fundamental Treatise on Thoroughbass in Composition" in Dresden. Jean-Marie Leclair plays concerts of his own music at the Paris Concert Spirituel. Georg Philipp Telemann publishes *Der getreue Music-Meister*. **29 January:** John Gay's *The Beggar's Opera* opens in London.

1729 19 January: Princess Maria Barbara of Portugal marries Ferdinando of Spain, bringing Domenico Scarlatti to the Spanish royal court. **December:** revived Royal Academy in London, first performances.

1730 François Couperin publishes his fourth and last volume of *Pièces de Clavecin*, a set of eight suites. Giuseppe Tartini begins publishing his violin works, an advance in violin technique. **Carnival:** Johann Adolf Hasse sets his first Metastasio libretto, *Artaserse*, inaugurating a long association. **Spring:** Hasse appointed *Kapellmeister* to the court of Dresden. **28 May:** Leonardo Vinci dies in Naples. **August:** Metastasio begins residence in Vienna as imperial court poet.

1732 Johann Walther publishes his *Musicalisches Lexicon*, combining biographies with musical terms, in Leipzig. **17 May:** Thomas Arne and the Haymarket Theater, London, produce an unauthorized version of George Frideric Handel's *Acis and Galatea*, possibly reviving Handel's interest in English oratorio.

1733 Kyrie and Gloria of J. S. Bach's Mass in B Minor completed. Pietro Locatelli's violin concertos Opus 3 appears, an advancement in violin technique. Georg Philipp Telemann publishes *Musique de Table*. Antonio Vivaldi begins collaborating with Carlo Goldoni in Venice. **10 July:** Premiere of George Frideric Handel's new English oratorio *Athalia*. **1 September:** François Couperin dies in Paris. **5 September:** Giovanni Pergolesi's controversial comic opera *La Serva Padrona* premieres in Naples. **1 October:** Rameau's first opera, *Hippolyte et Aricie*, opens in Paris. **December:** London's Opera of the Nobility produces Nicola Porpora's *Arianna in Naxo*.

1734 **25 December:** Premiere of J. S. Bach's *Christmas Oratorio*, Leipzig.

1735 J. S. Bach publishes Part II of *Clavier-Übung*. Jacques-Christophe Naudot publishes a rare set of solo flute concertos. Governors of Ospedale della Pietà reappoint Antonio Vivaldi *maestro di cappella*. **23 August:** Rameau's opera *Les Indes Galantes* begins a two-year run of 64 performances in Paris.

1736 **2 April:** Antonio Lotti appointed *maestro di cappella* at San Marco, Venice.

1737 Domenico Scarlatti publishes his first volume of *30 Essercizi*, expanding traditional keyboard technique.

1738 George Frideric Handel, Thomas Arne, Johann Christoph Pepusch, and William Boyce found the Society of Musicians in London. **March:** Antonio Vivaldi dismissed for the last time from Ospedale della Pietà, Venice.

1739 J. S. Bach publishes Part III of *Clavier-Übung*. Johann Mattheson publishes *Der vollkommene Capellmeister*. Georg Philipp Telemann publishes *Essercizii Musici*. **24 July:** Benedetto Marcello dies in Brescia, Italy. **12 September:** Reinhard Keiser dies in Hamburg. **October:** George Frideric Handel completes his Opus 6 Concertos. **1 November:** Handel's *Israel in Egypt* completed.

1740 Niccolò Jommelli composes his first *opera seria* in Rome, *Ricimero Re di Goti*. Mattheson publishes a biographical dictionary of Baroque composers, *Grundlage einer Ehren-Pforte*. **5 January:** Antonio Lotti dies in Venice.

1741 J. S. Bach completes the Goldberg Variations. Jean-Philippe Rameau publishes *Pièces de Clavecin en Trio*, a rare volume of chamber music featuring the transverse flute. Johann Quantz begins lifelong tenure in the service of Frederick, King of Prussia. **13 February:** Johann Joseph Fux dies in Vienna. **27 or 28 July:** Antonio Vivaldi dies in Vienna. **14 September:** George Frideric Handel completes *Messiah*.

1742 J. S. Bach's *Art of Fugue*. C. P. E. Bach publishes his "Prussian" sonatas. J. S. Bach compiles Book II of the *Well-Tempered Clavier*. **13 April:** George Frideric Handel's *Messiah* premieres in Dublin.

1744 C. P. E. Bach publishes his "Württemberg" sonatas. **10 February:** George Frideric Handel's English-language opera *Semele* opens in London.

1745 **4 May:** Jean-Philippe Rameau appointed *compositeur de la musique de la chambre du roy*.

1747 J. S. Bach completes the Canonic Variations on *Vom Himmel Hoch* and composes the Musical Offering. Jean-Baptiste Forqueray publishes his *Pièces de Viole*, one of the last important collections for viols.

1748 Nicola Porpora appointed *Kapellmeister* to the electoral court at Dresden.

1749 J. S. Bach completes the Mass in B Minor. George Frideric Handel composes Music for the Royal Fireworks suite.

1750 Traditional end-year of the Baroque in music history. **4 June:** J. S. Bach dies in Leipzig.

1752 Pergolesi's *La Serva Padrona* plays in Paris, igniting the Querelle des Bouffons. Johann Joachim Quantz publishes *Versuch einer Anweisung die Flöte traversière zu Spielen*. **26 February:** First performance of George Frideric Handel's last major oratorio, *Jephtha*.

1757 **23 July:** Domenico Scarlatti dies in Madrid.

1759 **14 April:** George Frideric Handel dies in London.

1764 **12 September:** Jean-Philippe Rameau dies in Paris.

1767 **25 June:** Georg Philipp Telemann dies in Hamburg.

1784 The Handel Commemoration at Westminster Abbey and the Pantheon, London, assembles massive performing forces to observe (mistakenly) the centennial year of the composer's birth. Music of Arcangelo Corelli is also performed.

1802 Leipziger Singakademie founded, begins to revive a few of Johann Sebastian Bach's choral works.

1829 **11 March:** Felix Mendelssohn revives the St. Matthew Passion of Johann Sebastian Bach in Berlin and begins a widespread Bach revival.

1832 **8 April:** François-Joseph Fétis directs the first of his historical concerts in Paris, an opera retrospective including music of Jacopo Peri and Claudio Monteverdi.

1859 Riedel'scher Verein performs the Mass in B Minor of Johann Sebastian Bach in Leipzig.

1920 **June:** Oskar Hagen produces George Frideric Handel's opera *Rodelinda* at the University of Göttingen, the first revival of an *opera seria* of Handel.

Introduction

In the history of the Western musical tradition, the Baroque period traditionally dates from the turn of the 17th century to 1750. The opening of the
period is marked by Italian experiments in composition that attempted to create a new kind of secular musical art based upon principles of Greek drama,
quickly leading to the invention of opera, and the closing of the period is
marked by the death of Johann Sebastian Bach on 28 July 1750 in Leipzig
and George Frideric Handel's last oratorio, *Jephtha*, completed the following
year in London.

Although the Baroque style early on was brought from Italy into Germany
by the young Heinrich Schütz and into France by Jean-Baptiste Lully (né
Giovanni Battista Lulli), Italians dominated the whole period. It was the
Baroque when composers began to specify dynamics, tempo, and expressive
performance practices for their works, and this language is still with us in
its original Italian: *forte*, *piano*, *crescendo*, *allegro*, *largo*, *cantabile*, and so
on. This is the age of Claudio Monteverdi, Arcangelo Corelli, Alessandro
and Domenico Scarlatti, Antonio Vivaldi, Tomaso Albinoni, and dozens of
lesser-known figures. Throughout the Baroque, many aspiring young musicians from other parts of Europe went to Venice, Florence, Rome, and Naples
to finish their education, including Handel in 1706 and, in a sense, J. S. Bach,
who never visited Italy but spent countless hours copying the scores of Italian
composers. Late in the period, a number of composers of other nationalities,
including Georg Philipp Telemann of Germany and Jean-Philippe Rameau
and the Couperins of France, achieved international fame in their own right.
By the end of the period, there were many important centers of music outside
Italy: Paris, London, Vienna, Hamburg, Dresden, and the lasting historical
irony is that, in the end, despite pervasive Italian influence throughout the
period, the greatest Baroque music came from the minds of two Germans
born in 1685 within one month and a day's journey of one another: Bach and
Handel.

The modern notions of musical "classic" or permanent concert repertory
were unknown during the Baroque so that most of this music had passed out
of fashion by 1750 and remained unknown and unperformed throughout the

19th and early 20th centuries, until the work of the early music revival began to recover it.

Because the history of music in the West is a younger discipline than the history of art, music historians have followed the art historians' lead in the division of that history into time frames and in their names for them. The term *Baroque*, of uncertain etymology, comprises the same time period, c.1600–1750, in the history of art. Although historians will occasionally defend this borrowing of period names by looking for similar characteristics of the two arts, it does not lead to deeper understanding of either when the analogies are pressed too far. Baroque music is founded on a new purpose of specific musical textures, and the history of the period captures slow but significant changes in the harmonic syntax of the musical language. Since these are features of sound—pitch and rhythm—they can translate into features of color and physical shape only by rather vague and metaphorical abstractions. Perhaps it is true that Baroque painting and sculpture may be described as full of "motion" or even an implied "drama," but that would seem to say little about music, an art that always conveys a sense of perceived motion and whose Baroque techniques are actually used in the theater and, therefore, emulate true drama much more closely.

THE ORIGINS OF THE BAROQUE

Most changes in musical style, even fundamental ones, are evolutions, comprised of small events and developments taking place here and there that eventually and unintentionally combine into a new synthesis. The synthesis of the Baroque style, however, was sparked by a deliberate musical reform, an idea. To be sure, evolution of musical language had gone on apace throughout the 16th century, mostly in the secular genres of Italian madrigals and songs, which had taken on clearer harmonic functions of dance music to articulate poetic phrases more clearly and more radical chromaticism for the expression of their thoughts. The widening split between traditions of sacred and secular music was made more or less official by the last promulgation of the Council of Trent in 1563 and their subsequent publications, which essentially froze the traditions of church music composition into a classical language like Latin. This became known as the *stile antico* ("the ancient style") and *la prima pratica* ("the first practice"), as it comprised the techniques first introduced to young composers. The textures and harmonies of the madrigalists, on the other hand, were called *stile moderno* and *la seconda pratica*. Thus, 16th-century music bifurcated, and the history might have continued smoothly with each branch growing slowly further apart had not a group of intellectuals in Florence, known to history as the Florentine Camerata, redi-rected the secular branch in the last quarter of the century with its new idea.

That idea was music drama. The members of the Camerata came to believe that no small part of the great effect of classical Greek drama was that such dramas were sung, and they dreamed of a kind of music where the passions of human drama could be adequately expressed, a *dramma per musica* ("drama through music"). The first product of this thinking was a new musical texture, *lo stile recitativo* ("reciting style"), consisting of a single vocal melody with a harmonic accompaniment that supported the singer's expressions in a natural speech rhythm, without strong meter.[1] This is called a monody. The harmony could occasionally provide adventurously dissonant and chromatic accents of the poetry but never eclipsed the singer, the *dramatis persona*.

Example. Peri and Caccini, *Euridice*, Act I, excerpt. Beautiful mother of Love, from the waves beyond, rise, and with your lovely sparkling light gild the shadowy night.

Eventually these experiments led to the production in 1598 of the first full-length music drama, *La Dafne*, with music of Jacopo Corsi and Jacopo Peri on a libretto of Ottaviano Rinuccini (1562–1621). That opera is lost, but *Euridice* of 1600, based on the Orpheus myth, with words again by Rinuccini and music by Peri and Giulio Caccini, has survived. A more philosophical effort of the same year, *La Rappresentatione di Anima e di Corpo* of Emilio Cavalieri in Rome, who also worked with the Camerata, is often considered the first oratorio. Then Claudio Monteverdi composed *L'Orfeo* for the Duke of Mantua in 1607.

L'Orfeo both sustained and refuted the theories that had given birth to opera: *lo stile recitativo* could be a brilliantly effective technique for *dramma per musica*, but at the same time, recitative alone was insufficient for the evening's play. Synthesizing the two extremes of the cool, contrapuntal intricacy of the *stile antico* of the church tradition and the passionate, volatile simplicity of the *stile moderno*, Monteverdi found a middle way. Many of *L'Orfeo*'s greatest moments are set in recitative, but they are prepared by long passages that have nothing to do with recitative: Renaissance dances, dancing strophic songs, and choruses, even imitative choruses redolent of the *stile antico*.

Thus, *L'Orfeo* is an exemplar of early Baroque style. With the possible exception of recitative (which has precedents in 16th-century instrumental improvisational forms), any given moment of early Baroque music drama sounds very much like songs, madrigals, dances, and even the more extravagant church music of the time. Virtually all the syntactic elements of 16th-century musical language are present in *L'Orfeo* and other contemporary dramatic works. What differs is how those elements are focused and exploited, the purposes for which they are fitted. It is the sum of the parts, the synthesis of the elements that is the novelty: *dramma per musica*. For the first time in the Western musical tradition, music is not put to words for the contemplation of God or human love, nor are the instrumental pieces provided to symbolize liturgical action or for dancing alone. Music becomes a dramatic art, full of narration and reflection. When, in *L'Orfeo*, Euridice laments that Orpheus has looked back at her as he led her out of hell and, thus, has lost her forever "*per troppo amor*" ("through too much love"), her harmonies pathetically recall the Messenger's news of her first death in Act II, about 45 minutes past in real time. No music before this was capable of such an expressive range. When modern descriptions of music refer to "tragic symphonies" or "dramatic modulations" or "seductive melodies," it is this Baroque aesthetic of music drama that provides these metaphors. That is one reason why the invention of opera is one of the most important moments in music history.

Admired today as the first masterpiece of opera, it is hard to prove that Monteverdi's astute synthesis of various musical textures and forms into a single drama singlehandedly vindicated the operatic project in contemporary eyes, but its aesthetic certainly won over the composer. He wrote *Arianna* the following year, 1608. The opera is lost, but its title character's famous lament "Lasciatemi morire" was excerpted, arranged, and circulated all over Italy. He continued to compose various kinds of music drama for the rest of his career.

PUBLIC OPERA

In 1637, six years before Monteverdi died, musicians from Rome performed an opera by Francesco Manelli called *Andromeda* for anyone who paid for admission. Teatro San Cassiano in Venice was so successful that within a decade there were six public opera theaters in the island city. Imitators sprouted abroad, especially in Germany, then in England, Spain, and eastern Europe. In France, the political machinations of the extremely talented Italian-born composer Lully made opera a monopoly of King Louis XIV, and so the *tragédie lyrique* followed a significantly different course of development but, nevertheless, dominated the musical scene for the rest of the century.

Teatro San Cassiano's success profoundly affected the course of music in European culture. For the first time in music history, secular art music became available to people outside the rich and noble classes. To be sure, the entrepreneurs behind these ventures tried to sell expensive boxes to subscribers for an entire season, but in fact, most theaters had less expensive tickets available at short notice for those who could pay. The middle class could begin to enter the world of European art music outside the church.

Public opera theaters changed the careers of composers too. Until then, aspiring composers could only hope for patronage, either by the church, via an appointment at a large cathedral, or by the aristocracy, as a court composer, or perhaps as a combination of the two. Composers composed on demand, for whatever occasions, sacred or secular, that required new music. Public opera offered a new source of livelihood, a liberation from patronage. Composers could begin to choose, in collaboration with librettists, producers, and singers, projects to suit their interests and talents. They might live as self-made men outside the castle walls.

Such changes in musical society percolated, but slowly, through the Baroque. Opera tickets would never be cheap enough for the numerous poor, and virtually no composers of the Baroque lived entirely without patronage. But, however slow, the changes were real and affected European society, to the point that by the turn of the 18th century a visit to the opera house might be compared to going to the movies for mid-20th-century Americans; it was a social event taken for granted, even though in many places outside Italy the opera would be sung in Italian. (Libretto translations were usually available for sale at the theaters.) The best singers, especially the male sopranos or *castrati*, were the rock stars of the age, commanded high fees, and outranked composers and librettists in prestige. The range of possibilities may be seen in the Baroque's two greatest exponents: George Frideric Handel did enjoy occasional patronage but lived independently and made most of his living from opera and other kinds of musical theater in London, while Johann Sebastian

Bach was the last great composer to spend his life, except for a brief period, in the service of the church.

The first operas established a number of patterns that remained more or less unchanged for the entire Baroque. Although many operas had moments of comic relief, genuine Baroque comedies were rare except in the later Venetian opera, before the Metastasian reform. Most of the time stories were taken from Greek and Roman mythology or history, serious in tone, except that almost all ended with the requisite *lieto fine*, or happy ending, often tacked onto a plot headed for tragedy.

The history of operatic music in the Baroque might be summarized as a growing distinction between the two fundamental types of operatic composition: *lo stile recitativo* and arias or songs, pieces with a strict meter and much repetition of text to fill out the time of a formal musical structure. In Monteverdi, recitative flows effortlessly into aria, and his handling of meter is so subtle that it is often impossible to make a firm distinction. By the end of the 17th century, the difference in sound had become unmistakable and so had their respective dramatic functions. The recitative, with its natural speech rhythms, lost intrinsic musical interest and became the operatic music to convey important plot information or to set dialogue, while the arias, with their extended musical structures now accompanied by instrumental ensembles, gave the characters their chance to reflect at length, as a soliloquy, on their situations. Thus, most Italian operas after 1675 follow a fairly predictable pattern of recitative—aria—recitative—aria . . . until the end of the act. This firm division, with a few hybrid moments, such as the *accompagnato* (accompanied recitative), lasted until the end of the Baroque, with aria forms, such as the da capo, becoming ever longer and more elaborate.

INSTRUMENTAL MUSIC

The aesthetic of *dramma per musica* proved so beguiling that, at the beginning of the 17th century, composers could not keep from trying it out in every kind of musical context. In church, the traditional polyphonic masses and motets were utterly transformed, while new operatic genres of sacred concerto, sacred symphony, church cantata, and oratorio were born. The aesthetic also energized an extremely important trend continuing from the 16th century, in parallel with the growing prestige of secular music: the rise of composition for instruments alone and the influence of virtuoso instrumentalists. Here begins the history of the sonata and the concerto.

The 17th century is the first in which almost all the great composers— Monteverdi, Giovanni Gabrieli, Girolamo Frescobaldi, Lully, and finally

Corelli—are organists, harpsichordists, and viol or violin players primarily rather than singers. But this growing prestige would seem to oppose the new aesthetic of *dramma per musica*, since instrumental music has no words on which to found a drama. And yet, the Baroque is a period rich with instrumental music, much more familiar to most modern music lovers than its operas. How was the contradiction of "instrumental drama" resolved?

The first solution occupied the first half of the 17th century. Grafting the opera aesthetic, essentially vocal, onto purely instrumental music in the early 17th century meant abstracting it, making a solo instrument stand in for the solo voice. If the accompaniment were simple, a basso continuo, the result was a solo sonata (It. "played"). Later in the century, if the accompaniment were a larger ensemble, contrasting the sound of the solo against the mass, the result was a concerto.[2]

But what is *lo stile recitativo* when played by an instrument? The earliest solo sonatas of the Baroque by Dario Castello and Biagio Marini (1594–1663) have traditional imitative passages contrasting with others of sudden changes of tempo and tonality, with no sustained pattern, metric, harmonic, or other, lasting very long, very much in the manner of recitative. Such instability is meant to convey the abstracted passions of some anonymous character, just as the music of an actual recitative can turn quickly to match the mood of the words.

To the modern ear, an early Baroque solo sonata can sound like an improvisation, a flight of the fancy with little intrinsic structure, isolated moments of delight with little relation among them. Written-out improvisations on harpsichord and organ already had a long history in 16th-century fantasias and *ricercari*, and they would live on into the Baroque keyboard preludes in the so-called *stylus phantasticus*. But such works never dominated Baroque instrumental music, even though important figures such as Sweelinck, Frescobaldi, Couperin, and J. S. Bach contributed to the repertory throughout the period. The "instrumental recitative" could not succeed on any large scale because it lacks the very element that makes recitative in opera tolerable, its text. The text, in its syntactic patterns on the low levels and then its semantic relations to the larger plot, supplies the structural frames on several levels that listeners need to comprehend long passages of music.

Early attempts at an instrumental idiom that captured the operatic aesthetic brought out the intrinsic contradictions in the two. *Dramma per musica*, at least in the minds of those who imagined it, must be full of contrasts, sudden shifts, and complete flexibility in order to express human passions, the only thing worth expressing. Instrumental music, on the other hand, having no words, requires highly organized and calculated patterns in order for its abstract pitch relations to be processed and enjoyed by the human mind. All its unifying techniques—unity of melodic subject, of tempo, of meter, of tonal center—depended on consistency and continuity and abhorred sudden shifts of sound that could only destroy them. The difference in character might be visualized by comparing a Baroque painting of Paolo Veronese, showing dozens of figures in a great variety of poses and activities, with a nonrepresentative decorative arabesque. The Veronese has a title, usually a story behind the picture, and the entire canvas is full of human figures and other familiar objects, that is, semantic references such as has a text, which the viewer can understand to make sense of the riot of color and action. The arabesque subsists perhaps on a few shapes and line patterns, repeated over and over, beautiful in their predictability. There is no story, so we must have structure to make sense of it.

There was no shortage of structural techniques for music at the turn of the 17th century. The young composer inherited two principal ones from the previous century. One was the technique of imitation characteristic of the *stile antico*, the church music style, the kind of counterpoint whereby the same melody appears in different voices, staggered at various time intervals.

Example. Palestrina, motet *Sicut cervus*, mm. 1–8

The entrances of the subject create the necessary articulations or events of the structure, and their overlap with one another ensures the necessary continuity to keep the music going. Indeed, the 16th century already had a substantial repertory of instrumental genres that exploited this technique. But imitation seemed antithetical to the aesthetic of *dramma per musica* and, in fact, had been explicitly criticized by the Florentine Camerata because it obscured the text so badly through its overlapping texture. Moreover, it reminded one instantly of church music, not the theater, because that was where such techniques had been cultivated for so long.

Dance music offered a second structural technique. Dance forms followed a system of symmetrical phrasing, suited to formal dance patterns, that organized entire sections of music. These sections might be repeated or alternated with others to make large structures. These dance forms, in collections called "suites" or "partitas," would continue to be very important for Baroque instrumental music. The French *clavecinistes* alone have left hundreds of them. But those works date from the middle to later 17th and 18th centuries, whereas at the beginning of the period, around 1600, the staid, predictable forms of dances again seemed opposed to the aesthetic of *dramma per musica*.

How could music isolate a solo violin or flute as an abstract character and yet without words keep the music going with some kind of organization?

The solution arrived at fairly quickly would seem to be the simplest possible: keep the music going with an incessant pulse, a steady beat somewhere in the musical texture that would maintain the perceived motion and extend musical structures forward.

Example. Monteverdi, ritornello from *L'Orfeo*, Act I, showing constant eighth-note pulse

The idea was not new. Imitation, with its constant overlap of melodies, can produce the same effect, and much instrumental music of the 16th century did just that. The difficulty for the Baroque aesthetic was to make this work in a texture for one prominent instrument going forward without help from other overlapping melodies. The listener, confronted with this stream of pulses, requires some means of organizing them to avoid overloading cognitive capacities, in other words, to make some sense of them. This was partly accomplished by a clear meter, the grouping of beats. Renaissance dances, of course, all have clear meter; otherwise, they would not be successful dances. However, the sense of meter that developed in the Baroque was subtly different because it allowed phrasing other than the predictable four or eight bars. Motor rhythm could be tailored to phrases of variable length, at last a source of passionate expression, by exploiting in a new way the most important gift of the dance tradition: harmonic functions.

Harmony in the *stile antico* is traditionally considered a consequence of counterpoint. When the four voices in the Palestrina passage above each sing an independent melody at the same time, chords naturally arise, and it is the composer's business to ensure that no awkward dissonances occur as this happens. That, in a nutshell, is the ancient art of counterpoint. But for technical reasons of melodic construction that developed in the 16th century, certain sequences of chords became preferred and then virtually obligatory. This occurred especially in dances in order to make crystal clear their phrase endings or cadences, so important for the dancers to hear. In other words, harmonies in and of themselves, abstracted from their generating melodies, acquired a grammar or syntax independent of melodic construction. This syntax is called "harmonic function."

Early Baroque composers learned how to control these harmonic functions in order to extend a prominent instrumental melody beyond the predictable phrases of the dance and reach for more flexible and expressive patterns.

Certainly, the techniques of imitation from the *stile antico* and the traditional dance forms did not disappear in the early Baroque. They are heard throughout the period, but they were slowly transformed by the motoric pulse and new feeling for meter, until by the high Baroque (c. 1690–1750) they could be synthesized with the primary technique of motor rhythm. The difference between the imitative ricercar composed early in the period and the imitative fugue composed later on is not merely chronological but that a high Baroque fugue is characterized throughout by the highly integrated techniques of motor rhythm. Dance music found in the high Baroque suites lost its historical relation with actual dancing because of this transformation. The so-called French and English Suites of Bach, his suites for solo violoncello and solo violin, and the first part of his *Clavier-Übung*, as well as the suites of the French *clavecinistes* and the eight "great" suites of Handel, form the peak of the Baroque suite tradition. They observe the external formal markers for allemandes, gavottes, and so on but are so stylized that it is not always easy to hear the standard dance patterns. The dance forms merely provide the frame and a certain character stamp for the mature and relentless Baroque continuity.

INSTRUMENTAL STRUCTURES: COMPOUND MELODY AND HARMONIC EMBEDDING

As the Monteverdi ritornello shows, the instrumental music of the early 17th century could be delightfully inventive and expressive but inevitably short-breathed. Each phrase in Monteverdi's ritornellos, unless imitative, strikes quickly for the harmonic cadence like a drowning man for solid ground. The harmonic functions could be slowed only so much, the cadence delayed only so long. Time is the composer's canvas, and the expressive possibilities of instrumental movements could not aspire to the monumental without some way of extending the structure yet again.

In 1681, Arcangelo Corelli published his trio sonatas Opus 1, the first of six publications that became so famous throughout musical Europe that he became a legend in his own time. (They had probably circulated in manu-script form for years beforehand.) His music exhibits techniques that would greatly affect not only all writing for instruments but also the relation of melody and harmony in the 18th-century musical language. In these measures from Op. 1, No. 3, the second violin part apparently executes a single melodic line (monophony), as a violin normally would, playing one note at a time. But Corelli's melody is not *cantabile*, not "singable." It is full of large and rapid melodic leaps such as no singer of the time would be asked to sing but which are quite idiomatic for the violin and for most other instruments of the time.

Example. Arcangelo Corelli, Op. 1, No. 3, "Allegro"

In the listener's perception, the fast tempo and large leaps cause the melody to split into various pitch ranges, so that the single written melody has the illusion of counterpoint.

This illusion is called a compound melody. It is fundamentally instrumen-tal in character and has two crucial effects. First, it enriches the texture of

Corelli, Op. 1, no. 3, "Allegro," mm. 35-37.

Example. Analysis of compound melody in Corelli, Op. 1, No. 3, "Allegro," mm. 35–37

any "melodic" instrument (those limited to one note at a time) so that even a trio sonata—or, later, in the case of J. S. Bach, a solo violin or cello—can project a variety of unsuspected polyphony. Second, it can decrease the rate of harmonic change, the harmonic rhythm, *without slowing the fundamental pulse* (here, eighth notes). This allows Corelli to extend the range of his harmonic phrases.

But the compound melody is not the only new technique of Opus 1. These pieces are among the first to exploit harmonic function on more than one level of structure. In short, a complete harmonic sentence with its internal functions itself becomes a unit in a series of ordered harmonic events. In natural language, this is called syntactic embedding.

Low-level			subject	verb	object
	She	knew	he	wanted	the car.
High-level	subject	verb	object		

The sentence "He wanted the car," complete with subject, verb, and object, itself functions as the object of a higher-order sentence.

Syntactic embedding in natural language allows the extension of a basic subject-verb-object pattern so that very long sentences may be routinely created and understood. Similarly, embedding in harmonic function creates another level of structure, making it much easier for the human mind to grasp the harmonic information coming in and thus allowing an exponential increase in the range of a harmonic form.

No one can with assurance assign all the credit for the conception and first techniques of harmonic embedding to Corelli alone. The specific techniques are many: pedal point (probably the oldest), sequence, "borrowed" dominant functions, false cadences, chromaticism, to name the most common, and these were part of the current musical language. But documentary evidence makes it clear that, even at the time, music lovers all over Europe who bought Corelli's music realized that there was something special about it. The German composer Georg Muffat referred to a "new type of Harmony," without having the theoretical apparatus to explain it.

But no one doubts the importance of this change in the musical language. Virtually all the later achievements of the high Baroque, including the mightiest compositions of Bach and Handel, would be inconceivable without it. Beethoven's vaunted expansions of musical form depend on it, and indeed, the entire history of harmonic structures right through the 19th century could be written as an exploration of this concept.

One of its first effects was to integrate the ritornello into a larger form, which composers from Vivaldi to Bach would exploit for all kinds of compositions both instrumental and vocal. The ritornello is nothing more than an ear-catching tune, a complete melodic/harmonic structure that ends with a cadence. In early 17th-century operas, ritornellos, such as Monteverdi's above, are very short interludes, complete in themselves, that help to build an operatic scene. By the end of the century, the ritornello became the mainstay of a continuous form. Because of harmonic embedding, the listener understands that this statement, though complete in itself, is only an opening, the first building block of a higher form in which the ritornello will alternate with variations and contrasting ideas played in different tonalities, or keys, finally concluding with a restatement of the original ritornello in its original tonality.

Ritornello Form, one possible scheme:

Melody:	Ritornello	Contrast variation	Ritornello	Contrast variation	Ritornello
Harmony:	Original key		New key I	New key II	Original key

Using one of these forms as a building block on yet a higher level yields the largest Baroque structure, appearing in countless operas, cantatas, oratorios, and to some extent even in concertos: the da capo aria.

Da Capo Aria

A section	B section	A section
Complete ritornello structure	Contrasting material	Complete ritornello structure

Thus, in a historical irony, it was operatic vocal music at the beginning of the 17th century that encouraged new structural techniques in instrumental music, only to be itself reformed by those techniques at the century's end. The great instrumental repertory of the high Baroque, including all the sonatas, concertos, suites, and organ music of Vivaldi, Scarlatti, Albinoni, Torelli,

François Couperin, Rameau, Telemann, Johann Pachelbel, Bach, Handel, and countless other lesser-known figures, plays out as explorations of these fundamental principles of composition inherited from the earlier part of the 17th century. The groundwork of the composition is the steady pulse, which could be slow or fast, in a clear and strong metric framework. Over this lies a much freer network of rhythmic articulations: metric groups, harmonic/melodic phrasing, harmonic rhythm at several levels, points of imitation. These create the articulate small forms, such as the ritornello or fugal exposition, and establish the character of the work: dance-like, imitative, in the manner of a French overture, *cantabile*, and so on. These small forms are organized by tonal centers, which, with modulation, can change in key (pitch center) or mode (type of scale, major or minor) or both at once, and offer a higher level of articulation and structure. In another historical irony, the ancient forms of dance and the ancient techniques of *stile antico* counterpoint, especially imitative counterpoint, once rejected in the early Baroque as inimical to the expression of passions, return, transformed by integration into the new musical language, to new glory in the high Baroque.

SACRED MUSIC

The Baroque has left a treasury of sacred music. The opera aesthetic exercised its influence on Baroque sacred music almost as persuasively as in secular music, and its effect was amplified by an event that preceded its invention, the Council of Trent (1545–1563). The final session of the Council (1563) decreed that "lascivious or impure" aspects of secular music must be kept from the music of the divine liturgy.[3] The long-term effect, enforced less and less as distance from Rome increased, was to enshrine the traditional church polyphony as the *stile antico*. The invention of opera at the beginning of the Baroque confirmed two distinct strains of sacred music: compositions in the increasingly anachronistic *stile antico* and compositions that set sacred words in the operatic *stile moderno*. Traditional sacred texts, most of them liturgical or biblical, appeared in the new genres of sacred concertos, sacred symphonies, and oratorios but in musical textures using solo voices and simple accompaniment as in the opera. It did not take long for church composers to experiment with the new techniques. Ludovico Viadana's *Cento Concerti Ecclesiastici* ("One Hundred Sacred Concertos") with an obbligato figured bass appeared in 1602. The best-known composer of sacred concertos and sacred symphonies today is Heinrich Schütz, a German who composed from 1612 to at least 1666.

Traditional genres, such as the mass and the motet, were similarly transformed. The courts of King Louis XIII and Louis XIV boasted *le grand motet* of vocal soloists, choruses, and fully orchestrated accompaniments by Lully, Marc-Antoine Charpentier, and Michel-Richard de Lalande. The text of the mass was broken up into short segments that could more easily be sung as choruses and solo arias. This is known as the Neapolitan mass, and the greatest exponent is J. S. Bach's Mass in B Minor. The sacred music known as a "church cantata" actually sprang from the secular Italian cantata (It. "sung piece"), which might be likened to a film short, a kind of chamber music drama for one or two singers, a simple instrumental accompaniment of a continuo and perhaps a solo instrument or two. Some dramatic premise, such as Alessandro Stradella's lament of Seneca about to commit suicide, justified a couple of recitative—aria pairs lasting 10 to 20 minutes. In Lutheran Germany, these basic operatic techniques were fitted with biblical texts late in the 17th century along with choruses to create the church cantata. Dietrich Buxtehude, Pachelbel, Johann Kuhnau, Telemann, and of course Bach contributed thousands of sacred pieces to this repertory. In England, the Anglicans enlivened their own anthem tradition with solo voices featured in verse anthems, the most brilliant examples being Handel's Chandos Anthems and Coronation Anthems.

In 1749, Pope Benedict XIV criticized the infection of liturgical music with operatic elements and wished for a return to traditional polyphony in his encyclical *Annus qui*, but it was far too late and had little reforming effect. In Protestant lands, there appears to have been little concern about the new musical style's place in worship, except in the Calvinist reform churches. To be sure, most Baroque composers made some effort to compose sacred music that distinguished itself from pure opera by some musical means or other, to create a difference in sound and not merely words. Most often this meant simply the inclusion of choral movements, which, except in France, were rare in opera. J. S. Bach pioneered the integration of Protestant hymn tunes (chorales) into the Lutheran church cantata so that, in the manner of the ancient cantus firmus, the prominent melodies might have some sacred associations. Imitative techniques in much sacred music, again reminiscent of the *stile antico* even though transformed by the new Baroque sense of rhythm, provided similar semantic cues.

The closest cousin to opera in church was the oratorio. Arising from the musical interludes accompanying devotions in oratories, houses of prayer in late 16th-century Rome, and, later on, from the desire for some kind of musical theatrics during Lent when theaters were closed, the oratorio became a kind of sacred opera by the middle of the 17th century. The plot was not mythological but biblical, the text might be in Latin, there might be an occasional chorus, and there was no staging, but in all other respects, the oratorio was *dramma per musica*. Giacomo Carissimi in Italy and Charpentier in France are important oratorio composers. In Germany, this idea combined with the ancient tradition of singing the Gospels recounting the crucifixion of Jesus just before Easter to produce the musical passion, sung in Palm Sunday or Good Friday liturgies. The two surviving passions of J. S. Bach, the St. John Passion and the St. Matthew Passion, are universally regarded as the climax of this tradition. In England, Handel, under the influence of the great English choral tradition and Jean Racine's biblical tragedies, invented his own peculiar, marvelously successful English oratorio, of which *Messiah* is by far the most famous but least typical example.

There is no better illustration of the stylistic proximity of Baroque operatic and sacred music than the practice of parody. Baroque composers by and large were expected to compose quickly and at times on very short notice, such as for the funeral of an important personage. Often, rather than compose a new piece, it seemed easier to adapt an older one to fit the purpose. Sometimes this meant little more than changing the words, usually from a secular theme to a sacred one, and touching up the orchestrations, as when J. S. Bach recast his secular cantatas BWV 213–215 as the Christmas Oratorio. At other times, the adaptation required more substantial changes in orchestration, the rewriting of vocal parts to suit a particular singer or fitting out what once was an instrumental movement for a chorus, as when Handel converted his *Concerto a Due Chori* into the chorus "Lift Up Ye Heads" from *Messiah*. What is remarkable is how little sense of incongruity the music causes in either its secular or sacred guises.

In the Baroque, parody seems to have caused little of the moral revulsion occasioned by later concepts of inspired art or plagiarism. Bach, except in his early career when he arranged Italian concertos for organ to teach himself Italian compositional techniques, parodied only his own works. Handel too borrowed from himself but also from others, at times quite liberally and rather infamously in his oratorio *Israel in Egypt*. This did raise some eyebrows, but in his own lifetime, he was defended as much as he was criticized for the practice. The German composer, theorist, and critic Johann Mattheson believed that using another's thematic idea in a new work actually complimented the originator.

END OF THE BAROQUE

There is no single, discrete event to mark the end of the Baroque as there is to mark its beginning—although the death of J. S. Bach in 1750 is certainly a historiographical convenience—but rather a number of long-developing and imperceptible changes that begin to coalesce about that time to signal that the age has passed. Certainly, the nurturing aesthetic of music as a dramatic and narrative art did not cease—indeed, it is alive to this day—but the means of articulating and expressing it changed.

The Baroque can be understood as a midway phase between two very long and significant evolutions in musical language, the very sound materials that musicians learn from their cultural environment, with which they attempt to create a style. One is the evolution of tonality, how the sense of key is conveyed, and the other is the decline of melodic syntax, or voice leading, in the face of ascendant harmonic syntax.

Before the Baroque, and well into the period, the concept of tonal center was expressed by its mode, not far from the worldwide concept of mode as a kind of melodic pattern. By 1600, there were 12 modes, all having the same set of pitch-classes, which can be imagined as the "white" notes on a standard keyboard. What made the D mode different from the A mode was how these pitches were used in melodic writing: which notes started and ended the melody, which were emphasized, and so on. The "black" notes were decorative auxiliaries, *chroma* (Gk. "color") or chromatic pitches. After the Baroque, the concept of tonal center was expressed by its key. There are 24 keys, each having a unique set of pitches, and all the black and white notes are structurally equivalent. What makes D major different from A major is the use of G-natural in the first and G-sharp in the second. The difference between the two concepts, mode and key, was expressed in two famous collections of keyboard music that included by design one composition in all possible tonalities: J. S. Bach's *Well-Tempered Clavier* (Books I and II, 1722, c. 1742) and Frederick Chopin's Preludes Opus 28 (1839). Bach follows his first piece in C major with one in C minor because for him, C major and C minor, though quite different in pitch-class set, are different "modes" or "manners" of playing in the same tonal center of C. Chopin follows his C-major prelude with one in A minor because the pitch sets of those keys are nearly identical, although their tonal centers differ.

The practical difference is that in the latter system a composer can signal a change of tonal center from D major to A major quite suddenly simply by sounding a G-sharp. Modulations could be sudden, surprising events. Earlier composers took more time to let the new key of a piece "settle in" by sounding the new starting pitches, ending pitches, and so on.

The taste for sudden, "dramatic," changes within the continuity of a single piece may have also increased the importance of purely harmonic syntax over intricate relations with melodic syntax, or counterpoint. Once again, the Baroque stands midway. Before the Baroque, composers learned the art of voice leading, how to construct melodies that could be gracefully sung. When these careful melodies were combined and sung simultaneously, harmonies arose, but the order (function) of those harmonies was not the chief concern. After the Baroque, drastic disjunctions in melody could be justified by harmony alone, and these could be quite drastic indeed.

Baroque music presents these warring priorities of voice leading (melodic syntax) and harmonic function (harmonic syntax) in constant tension, sometimes showing one in the ascendant, sometimes the other, reconciling them as much as possible, depending upon the genre of composition and the particular disposition of the composer. Sometimes, these priorities change within a single movement. Baroque instrumental music, with its idiomatic compound melodies blurring what were once separate melodies, certainly weakened the voice-leading aesthetic. In one sense, when harmonic construction consistently outweighs the integrity of *all* the melodies in a texture around the middle of the 18th century, the Baroque is over.

These evolutions, like many historical generalizations, are simplified to make the point. The desire for beautiful melody, of course, never disappears, but its priority changes. Similarly, a tonal center after the Baroque is not merely a matter of pitch-class set but how a composer deploys those pitches too. It is the balance that shifts, and in these two fundamental aspects of Western musical language, the Baroque is the tipping point.

These evolutions, taking place so slowly as to be unperceived, like most evolutions in language, may have worked in concert with changes in musical taste that were explicitly recognized at the time. The high Baroque style came under attack by two aesthetic concepts championed by the younger generation of the mid-18th century called *le style galant* and *der empfindsamer Stil* and by a new kind of opera coming out of Italy.

It must seem incredible today, but the intermissions between the acts of *opere serie* performances in the Baroque were often filled with other kinds of musical entertainment. Handel playing the solos for his own organ concertos between the acts of *Saul* would not have been unusual. Beginning about the turn of the 18th century in Naples and Venice, comic *intermezzi* offered satirical vignettes of two to three contemporary (not mythological) characters with simple accompaniment. These little dramas became popular enough to grow into an operatic type on its own, *opera buffa*. A performance of Giovanni Pergolesi's *intermezzo La Serva Padrona* in Paris on 1 August 1752 sparked the Querelle des Bouffons, a pamphlet war between the defenders of the high-art tradition of the *opera seria* and the reformers who believed that music drama had become overgrown with too many musical superfluities standing in the way of the true expression of human passions. The argument is not far from the complaints of the Florentine Camerata, but in this case, the dramatic needs of comedy began to undermine the rhythmic synthesis of the high Baroque.

Mercurial, even explosive emotion within a musical continuity became the priority of the proponents of *der empfindsamer Stil* ("the sensitive style"), most often associated today with the music of Carl Philipp Emanuel Bach, who published an important set of keyboard sonatas in 1742 and 1744. This aesthetic aim amounted to an attack on the most fundamental structural element of Baroque composition, the motor rhythm, which tended to assimilate harmonic changes into its steady, unifying stream. Sudden shifts, stops, and starts could hardly be integrated. Indeed, operatic theory of the time recognized that an aria should be devoted to a single expression, never a bundle of contrasting effects. But by relying on new kinds of coherence of harmonic function and tonality, *der empfindsamer Stil* could free itself from the constraints of motor rhythm.

Le style galant ("the elegant style") appealed to Jean-Jacques Rousseau's ideal of wisdom in simplicity, simplicity of melody without complicated accompaniment. One critic, J. A. Scheibe, even attacked the contrapuntal achievements of J. S. Bach in 1737 as "bombastic [*schwülstig*] and confused." This aesthetic simplified again, although in a different way, the rhythmic synthesis of the high Baroque, slowing the most perceptible kind of harmonic rhythm down to one change per bar or even slower, reducing the bass and inner voices to harmonic filler, and imposing a system of explicit periodic phrasing to organize the melody. The strength of harmonic functions increasingly acquired through the Baroque made this possible.

No one can say whether the success of early *opere buffe* spurred the notions of *der empfindsamer Stil* and *le style galant* or those aesthetic currents prepared the reception of comic opera or one fed back on the others, but all together, they replaced the musical language of the high Baroque with another founded on the rhythm of the phrase rather than the rhythm of the pulse. As with most aesthetic movements, including that of *dramma per musica*, the purist phase was brief. Complex counterpoint returned to find a secure home in the classical style quite rapidly, but just as the return of imitative technique in the high Baroque saw it transformed from what it had been in the *stile antico*, classical counterpoint acquired a novel character.

NOTES

1. There were various names for this texture at the time of its invention, such as *lo stile rappresentativo* (the imitating style), but for the sake of clarity, the more common term is used here.

2. The names "sonata" and "concerto" here are used in the modern sense for the sake of simplicity. Composers at the beginning of the Baroque used them interchangeably with "canzona," "fantasia," "toccata," and other terms. Only after midcentury did they acquire some consistency of usage close to what is stated here.

3. Robert F. Hayburn, *Papal Legislation on Sacred Music* (Collegeville, MN: Liturgical Press, 1979), 28.

ABENDMUSIK (**Ger. "evening music"**). A series of sacred music concerts given at the Marienkirche in Lübeck, Germany. They may have begun under the direction of **Franz Tunder, organist** from 1641 to 1667, as organ recitals, but their repertory expanded to include **sacred concertos** and **oratorios** under the direction of **Dietrich Buxtehude**. Buxtehude instituted the practice of presenting spiritual dramas on five specific Sundays of the liturgical year: the last two Sundays after Trinity and the second, third, and fourth Sundays of Advent. The series at Marienkirche ceased in 1810. Since then, the term has come to mean "concerts in church."

ACADEMY OF ANCIENT MUSIC. Founded in **London** in 1726, it is one of the earliest organizations dedicated to the revival, study, and performance of "ancient music," that is, music that was no longer current, including compositions of **Giovanni da Palestrina**, **William Byrd**, other Renaissance masters, and **Henry Purcell**, already considered ancient although he had just died in 1695. Aristocratic amateur musicians made up the society at the beginning, although **Maurice Greene**, **Giovanni Bononcini**, **Agostino Steffani**, and **Johann Christoph Pepusch** were early members. As it acquired status through its public concerts, the Academy attracted professional musicians and larger audiences, which preferred more recent music, especially the **English oratorios** of **George Frideric Handel**. The Academy met in a long room of a tavern, the Crown and Anchor, in the Strand. It disbanded in 1792. *See also* EARLY MUSIC REVIVAL.

A CAPPELLA (**It. "in the manner of the chapel"**). Choral music sung without instrumental accompaniment.

ACCOMPAGNATO (or *recitativo accompagnato*, **It. "accompanied recitative"**). Type of **recitative** heard in later Baroque **operas** and **oratorios** in which the solo singer is accompanied by the full instrumental ensemble, as distinct from the *secco* **recitative**, harmonized by the basso **continuo** alone. The *accompagnato* sets text full of feeling too variable to be set as an **aria** but too strong to be set as a simple recitative. The sudden onset of the **orchestra** in operatic recitative calls attention to the extreme emotion of the moment without giving up the rhythmic flexibility required by a character in crisis.

ACTUS MUSICUS. See HISTORIA.

AFFEKTENLEHRE (Ger. "theory" or "doctrine of the affections"). A proposition of various musical treatises of the early 18th century, including the *Componimenti Musicali* (1706) of **Reinhard Keiser** and *Das neu-eröffnete Orchestre* (1713) and *Der vollkommene Capellmeister* (1739) of **Johann Mattheson**, which claims that a composer may elicit emotions in the listener by means of discrete technical devices of composition. **Dissonance, chromaticism,** or sudden changes of **key** bring out the darker emotions, for example; faster **tempo** elicits excitement, while slow tempo and major **modes** create calm. More surprising, and perhaps naive, would be Mattheson's claim that a **gavotte dance** rhythm connotes jubilation, a **gigue** burning but fleeting zeal, the **sarabande** ambition, and other similar and very specific semantic associations. Some treatises contain lists of dozens of **passions** with their corresponding musical devices.

It is difficult to know to what extent Baroque composers took such advice seriously. Doubtless, certain associations became commonplaces, such as the appoggiatura "weeping" motive or the use of **flutes** for **laments**, and it is possible that sufficient familiarity with these would produce the semantic association intended for listeners. However, the simple fact that drastically different texts were routinely substituted for the same music in **opera arias**, and that **Johann Sebastian Bach** and many other composers **parodied** much of secular vocal music with new words for church services, suggests that composers could not have believed the semantic necessities of such devices to have been very powerful.

AGAZZARI, AGOSTINO (2 December 1578, Siena, Italy–10? April 1640, Siena). Author of one of the earliest treatises on **thoroughbass**, *Del sonare sopra 'l basso con tutti li stromenti e dell' uso loro nel conserto* ("On playing above a bass with all the instruments and how they are used in an ensemble," Siena, 1607), Agazzari also composed an early *dramma per musica*, the pastoral *Eumelio*, performed during the Carnival season in **Rome** in 1606. The **libretto** concerns a young shepherd boy who foolishly gives himself over to vice, only to be rescued from the underworld by Apollo and Mercury. Despite the moral lesson, Agazzari was apparently excluded from singing at the Sistine Chapel thereafter. He returned to Siena and served as *maestro di cappella* at the cathedral until his death.

AIR DE COUR. The most important genre of vocal composition in the first half of the 17th century in France, especially during the reign of King Louis

XIII. *Airs de cour* were strophic settings of French court poetry, usually translations of Italian pastoral poetry into stanzas of four or eight lines. The composer might set this poetry for four to five singers without accompaniment, the more traditional Renaissance **madrigal texture**, or for a single singer with **lute** accompaniment, the typical early Baroque texture. *See also* BOËSSET, ANTOINE.

ALBINONI, TOMASO GIOVANNI (8 June 1671, Venice–17 January 1750 or 1751, Venice). Today remembered chiefly for his instrumental music, which includes 59 **concertos**, 24 **trio sonatas**, 6 sonatas *da chiesa*, 6 sonatas *da camera*, about 60 **sonatas** for other combinations, 8 *sinfonie*, and 24 *balletti*, in his time Albinoni was also a successful composer of at least 50 **operas**, only 3 of which survive in score, and about 50 **cantatas**.

From the modern perspective, Albinoni's role in the development of the concerto is particularly significant. His concertos Opus 2 (1700) are the first in a consistent pattern of three movements fast-slow-fast, which became the standard form. Opus 5 (1707) introduces the integration of **fugal textures** with brilliant passagework for the soloist, and the concertos Opus 7 (1715) were the first published by an Italian composer to feature the **oboe**.

The eldest son of Antonio Albinoni, a landed businessman, Tomaso studied **violin** and singing while he apprenticed in his father's shops as a stationer.

In 1694, he published his Opus 1, a set of trio sonatas, from which **Johann Sebastian Bach** borrowed four **subjects** for fugues, and saw his first opera *Zenobia, Regina de' Palmireni* open in **Venice**. By the next decade, Albinoni's operas began to appear in other Italian cities including **Naples** (*Rodrigo in Algeri*, 1702) and **Florence** (*Griselda*, 1703). During the 1720s, his operas were performed outside Italy, and he went to Munich to supervise the performance of *I Veri Amici* in 1722 at the court of Maximilian II Emanuel, Elector of Bavaria. At the same time, his instrumental works were in demand all over Europe along with those of **Antonio Vivaldi** and **Arcangelo Corelli**, and in 1722, he published his Opus 9 concertos, often regarded as his finest. One source describes another musical activity, a singing school run by Albinoni in Venice.

In 1705, Albinoni married the soprano singer Margherita Raimondi, and they had six children together. She continued to perform opera after they were married and died in 1721.

Albinoni appears to have retired about 1741. His obituary states that he had been confined to bed for two years before his passing.

ALLEMANDE. Duple-**meter dance** originating in 16th-century Germany, it appeared frequently in early 17th-century *ballets de cour*. After 1650, it was seldom danced but continued to appear at the head of instrumental dance

suites. Such instrumental movements have **binary form**, moderate **tempo**, and fairly sophisticated part writing.

ANERIO, GIOVANNI FRANCESCO (c. 1567, Rome–buried 12 June 1630, Graz, Austria). **Organist** and priest who introduced the Italian-language **oratorio** with his *Teatro Armonico Spirituale* (1619), written for the Oratory of St. Filippo Neri. It contains the earliest surviving obbligato instrumental parts in **Rome**. He also composed several **masses**, 83 **motets**, and the *Selva armonica* (1617), a collection of Latin motets and *madrigali spirituali* in Italian for one to four **voices** representing the latest trends.

ANSWER. The second entrance of the **subject** in an **imitative** passage, which accomplishes the essential overlapping of the subject with itself. In Baroque music, the term is most often applied to **fugues**, in which the answer is usually transposed to the **pitch-class** a perfect fifth higher than the first entrance of the subject. A real answer is **strict**, that is, it preserves the melodic intervals of the original; a tonal answer deforms one or more melodic intervals to fit with the opening **key**.

Example. Johann Sebastian Bach, Fugue in D Major from the *Well-Tempered Clavier*, Book II

Example. Johann Sebastian Bach, Fugue in G Minor from the *Well-Tempered Clavier*, Book I

ANTHEM. A **polyphonic** setting of a Christian text, usually biblical, in English, excluding ordinaries of the **mass** and traditional canticles, such as **Magnificat**. The term dates from the 11th century, an English cognate of *antiphon*. English-language sacred music suddenly rose in status when the first *Booke of Common Praier* (1549) replaced liturgical Latin with English.

Anthems began to acquire **operatic** characteristics in the late 16th century, including explicit use of solo singers in **verse anthems**. By the 17th century, *anthem* commonly referred to sacred vocal music of the Anglican Church. Important composers include **William** and **Henry Lawes**, **John Blow**, and **Henry Purcell**.

After the Restoration, **Matthew Locke** and **Pelham Humphrey** brought from their European travels operatic **textures** and the use of **organ** and various solo instruments to articulate with voices ever more ambitious musical structures, culminating in the **Coronation Anthems** of **George Frideric Handel**. Interest in anthem composition declined along with interest in Anglican liturgy generally from the latter half of the 18th century onward.

ARCHLUTE (It. *arciliuto*). In his 1623 publication *Intavolatura di Liuto* ("Lute **Tablature**"), Alessandro Piccinini claims to have invented the archlute in Padua in 1594 by adding to the traditional **lute** a second pegbox, which holds six to eight courses (*diapasons*) running outside the fingerboard and sounding deep bass register pitches. These courses are about 1.5 times the length of the shorter stopped **strings** contained in the first, traditional pegbox. Its body is smaller than that of the **theorbo**, and its highest two courses are **tuned** to the same pitches as the lute, rather than one octave lower. These differences result in a softer sound, but the expanded pitch range allowed the archlute to gradually displace the theorbo as a **continuo** instrument as the Baroque progressed because its highest courses could play solo melody lines in **arias** and **sonatas**. After 1664, metal-wound gut strings also increased its volume.

Solo music for the archlute was published in tablature in Italy in the first half of the 17th century.

ARIA (It. "air"). Music in a Baroque **opera**, **oratorio**, **cantata**, **Neapolitan mass**, or other genre derived from opera designed for the sustained, singular emotional expression of one character.

The accompaniment for the singer ranges from the basso **continuo** alone to the full ensemble or various subsets of it that might feature solo instruments. The musical structure is entirely self-contained, unified by motor rhythm within a strong **meter** on the low level, and then by melodic forms (e.g., strophic), **ostinato** bass lines, ritornellos, or **key** schemes on higher levels of structure, depending on the specific type of aria composed. All the expressive resources of the musical language appear to amplify the sentiments of the poem. The aria poetry, however, is usually only 4 to 12 lines. Therefore, in order to create a musical expression of sufficient dramatic weight, words in the poem are freely repeated to fill out an aria of sufficient length.

In the early Baroque, arias grew out of **recitative** passages almost seam-lessly, articulated by nothing more than a stronger meter, often a **dance** rhythm, and some periodic phrasing to make up a simple song form. As time passed, more and more, the aria overshadowed the recitative passages, be-coming longer and more sophisticated in its music. Popular virtuoso singers demanded difficult passages to show off their art.

After about 1675, a specific aria form, the **da capo aria**, began to appear frequently in *opere serie*. In the 18th century, the da capo form dominated the *opera seria*, **church cantata**, and oratorio to the exclusion of all other types.

ARIOSO. Music in a Baroque **opera** or one of its generic derivatives po-sitioned midway in character between the **recitative** and the **aria**. There is one singer, but the accompaniment is often richer than the basso **continuo**, including solo instruments having some symbolic connection with the text perhaps, and there is a weak but perceptible **meter**. However, there is no high-level structural articulation provided by repeated melodic phrases or **key** schemes. In fact, the key in force at the end is often not the same as the one at the beginning, leaving significant tension to be resolved by the following number. The text declamation is less free than in recitative in order to coor-dinate with the fuller accompaniment, but no text is repeated.

There are many excellent examples of arioso in the **passions** of **Johann Sebastian Bach**. Each one is followed by a **da capo aria** or other high-level structure.

ARNE, THOMAS AUGUSTINE (12 March 1710, London–5 March 1778, London). An important figure in the 18th-century musical theater of **London**, Arne contributed **overtures**, songs, **dances**, and other incidental music to over 100 stage productions between 1733 and 1777. Much of this music is lost and the rest little known, except for **symphonies**, overtures, and instrumental works drawn from the stage productions. He also composed 7 **trio sonatas**, 8 **harpsichord sonatas**, 28 **odes** and **cantatas**, 2 **masses**, 2 **oratorios**, and 2 **motets**.

Thomas Arne was born into a family of furniture dealers and upholsterers but began studying music at the Eton School. He was apprenticed to a lawyer from 1726 to 1729 but abandoned that profession for music, and his father probably helped finance his first theatrical venture, the Little Theatre at the Haymarket in London in 1732. On 17 May that year, the Haymarket mounted an unauthorized version of **George Frideric Handel**'s *Acis and Galatea*, which caused Handel to revise the work and perhaps to take a second look at English-language music drama. Arne produced his own first **opera**, *Rosa-mund*, on 7 March 1733.

On 15 March 1737, Arne married the soprano Cecilia Young, and through her and her sister, an established tragedienne, Arne made valuable contacts in the London theater. In 1738, along with Handel, **William Boyce**, and **Johann Christoph Pepusch**, he founded the Society of Musicians, later the Royal Society. In 1740, he supplied music, including the song "Rule Britannia," for a **masque** of James Thomson called *Alfred* and later converted the piece into an oratorio (1745) and then a fully staged opera (1753).

In the 1750s, Arne's career ran into difficulties. He lost the support of key players in the theater, and his marriage broke up. He took on Charlotte Brent, a former pupil, as his mistress, and thereafter, his fortunes revived somewhat.

ART OF FUGUE (Original title: *Die Kunst der Fuge*). A collection of **fugues** and **canons** all based on the same **subject** or close variant thereof, composed by **Johann Sebastian Bach**, BWV 1080, dating about 1742 and first published in 1751. Although most of the fugues are playable on a **keyboard**, the publication presents the music not in keyboard format but as a score with each **contrapuntal voice** on a separate staff. This practice follows other similar publications by Bach's predecessors **Girolamo Frescobaldi** and **Johann Jacob Froberger** and has encouraged numerous arrangements for other instruments (e.g., **string** quartet).

The same subject is recognizable in all the fugues and canons in the Art of Fugue, but its treatment varies: **inversion, diminution**, rhythmic variation, **augmentation**, and combination with other subjects in **invertible counterpoint** are some of the techniques on display.

The order of the fugues, and indeed whether Bach thought of the work as an object of performance, is not clear. He left the final fugue unfinished in his autograph manuscript.

ARTUSI, GIOVANNI MARIA (c. 1540–18 August 1613). *See* MADRIGAL; MONTEVERDI, CLAUDIO.

AUGMENTATION. Transformation of a melody by lengthening all the durations of its notes by a fixed ratio, for example, twice as slow, four times as slow, and so forth. *See also* DIMINUTION.

Example. Subject from D-sharp Minor Fugue, *Well-Tempered Clavier* I, mm. 1–3, by Johann Sebastian Bach

Example. Original subject speed in bass voice, augmentation at half speed in soprano, intermediary speed in alto

B

BACH, CARL PHILIPP EMANUEL (8 March 1714, Weimar–14 December 1788, Hamburg). The second surviving son of **Johann Sebastian Bach** and his first wife Maria Barbara Bach (1684–1720), C. P. E. Bach, although trained by his father, left a body of music composed of **textures** and experiments in harmony and rhythm, often called the *empfindsamer Stil* ("sensitive style"), that would influence the classical style of the later 18th century: about 150 **keyboard sonatas**, 20 **symphonies**, 52 **concertos**, 600 songs, 20 **passions**, and a few other sacred works. He also wrote *Versuch über die wahre Art das Clavier zu spielen* ("Treatise on the True Manner of Keyboard Playing," Berlin, 1753–1762, two volumes), today considered an important source of information about mid-18th-century music and performance traditions.

C. P. E. Bach entered the university at Frankfurt an der Oder in 1734 but, by 1738, was already in Berlin and then appointed court **harpsichordist** by King Frederick the Great in 1740. During the next decade, he published two of his most influential volumes of keyboard sonatas, the so-called Prussian sonatas of 1742 and the Württemberg sonatas of 1744. In 1747, a visit from his father occasioned the composition of the **Musical Offering**.

In 1768, C. P. E. Bach succeeded **Georg Philipp Telemann** as director of music in **Hamburg**. In the course of his duties as director of public concerts, he revived *Messiah* of **George Frideric Handel** and the Credo of his father's **Mass in B Minor**.

BACH, JOHANN SEBASTIAN (21 March 1685, Eisenach, Thuringia, Germany–28 July 1750, Leipzig). In his own day, J. S. Bach was recognized within German-speaking principalities as a brilliant performing musician, particularly when **improvising** on **keyboard** instruments, and by connoisseurs as one of the great composers of the time. Today, his work continues to influence Western sacred music more than that of any other single composer, and in the secular repertories, Bach's voice is so predominant in the Western tradition that the year of his death has been traditionally observed as the end of the Baroque period. No serious musician would dispute that his work remains unequalled in the fields of **organ** music, sacred music of the Lutheran tradition, unaccompanied writing for **violin** and **cello**, and especially **fugue** writing, for which his name is nearly synonymous. In fact, he composed masterworks in every genre of the early 18th century except **opera**. His musical style intensified the source of high Baroque continuity, the motor rhythmic pulse, to an unprecedented degree, but within this incessant stream of sound, through an unflagging control of harmonic articulation, phrase rhythm, and harmonic rhythm at all levels, Bach could create effects of acceleration, tension, and resolution that are uniquely his own. Even beginning listeners learn to identify the Bach sound quickly. Yet, through his mastery of all the large-scale forms of the Baroque, his music owns an astonishing variety of sound and impression.

His works are traditionally divided into periods matching the positions he held (e.g., "Weimar **cantata**") because, as with virtually all Baroque composers, the kinds of music composed depended directly on what was demanded by the job. The first period comprises two postings in Lutheran churches at Arnstadt (1703–1707) and Mühlhausen (1707–1708) and produced a small number of early **church cantatas** and organ works. The second covers his work at the chapel of the Duke of Saxe-Weimar (1708–1717) as court organist and chamber musician and includes many of his large compositions and collections for organ. Next, Bach went to serve as *Kapellmeister* for Prince Leopold of Anhalt-Cöthen (1717–1723), an appointment that produced many of his works for various ensembles, including the **Brandenburg Concertos**. Finally, he was hired as cantor for Thomaskirche in **Leipzig** (1723–1750), where he stayed for the rest of his life and wrote an astounding number of works for the Lutheran liturgy. Modern research has blurred this neat correlation—for example, by discovering that a good many Lutheran cantatas were composed at Weimar, that instrumental composition figured significantly in the later Leipzig years—but it remains a useful first approach to the more than one thousand compositions of J. S. Bach.

Johann Sebastian himself traced his Bach family of professional musicians to the mid-16th century. His father, Johann Ambrosius Bach, was an organist and professional musician of Eisenach. He died when Johann Sebastian was 10 years old (1695), and his mother the previous year, so the boy moved to Ohrdruf to live with his elder brother Johann Christoph to continue his musical education. He studied organ, **harpsichord**, and composition, mostly by copying works of recognized masters. He attended the Lyceum in Ohrdruf where he received a classical education. In 1700, he entered the Michaelisschule without paying tuition in return for singing in the choir of the Michaelkirche in Lüneberg and probably studied organ and composition with Georg Böhm (1661–1733).

At the age of only 18, he won the appointment as organist to the New Church at Arnstadt, Thuringia, remaining there from 1703 to 1707. In the first of several such episodes throughout his life, he disputed with his employers, this time about overstaying his leave granted in October 1705 to travel to Lübeck in order to hear the celebrated **Dietrich Buxtehude**. After this, Bach was appointed organist at the Blasiuskirche in Mühlhausen, Thuringia, where the musical resources were better. During this period, Bach composed the famous *Toccata and Fugue in D Minor* BWV 565 (before 1708?) and other early organ works and his first church cantatas: *Aus der Tiefe* BWV 131 (1707), *Gott ist mein König* BWV 71 (1708), and *Christ Lag in Todesbanden* BWV 4 (1708). He married one of the singers at the Blasiuskirche, his cousin Maria Barbara Bach, on 17 October 1707.

There is some evidence of popular opposition to the sophistication of his musical program at the church. In the middle of 1708, Wilhelm Ernst, Duke of Saxe-Weimar, heard him play and offered him the post of court organist with a large increase in salary. Here, the refined musical taste of the prince and an excellent musical establishment elicited a major portion of Bach's unsurpassed oeuvre for the pipe organ, including the *Toccata, Adagio, and Fugue in C Major* (BWV 564, c. 1712), the *Passacaglia in C Minor* (BWV 582, before 1712), and his first major pedagogical collection, the set of **chorale preludes** known as the *Orgelbüchlein* ("Little Organ Book" BWV 599–644, c. 1713–1715). In March 1714, Bach was promoted to the court's second-highest post, concertmaster, which required the composition once per month of a church cantata for small instrumental and vocal ensemble in order to fit into the confined space of the chapel at the Weimar castle (e.g., *Weinen, Klagen, Sorgen, Zagen* BWV 12 [1714]). At least 18 church cantatas date from this period, as well as the important secular "Hunt" Cantata, BWV 208 (1713).

Bach's autodidactic practice of collecting and copying the scores of other musicians continued unabated through all these years, and at some point during the Weimar period, he commenced an intensive study of new compositions of all kinds coming out of Italy, especially those of **Arcangelo Corelli**, **Giovanni Legrenzi**, and **Antonio Vivaldi**, of which he often made his own arrangements for organ. Many Bach critics believe that it was this acquaintance with Italian techniques of high-level organization, such as the **da capo aria**, combined with Bach's native German training in **counterpoint** that produced the synthesis known as the mature musical style of J. S. Bach.

Bach seems to have discovered late in 1716 that the duke was trying to engage **Georg Philipp Telemann** (1781–1767) for his court's top musical post of *Kapellmeister*. In turn, Bach secured an offer from Prince Leopold of Anhalt-Cöthen, but his request to Duke Wilhelm for release was so rude that he was imprisoned from 6 November to 2 December 1717. Then he moved to Cöthen (Thuringia) to be *Kapellmeister* to Prince Leopold, where he directed an ensemble of professional court musicians. At Cöthen, Bach composed or collected many of his harpsichord **suites**, works for solo violin and cello, **sonatas**, and other ensemble works, such as the Brandenburg Concertos (BWV 1046–1051, dedicated 1721). During this time, Bach also seems to have collected recently composed **preludes** and fugues for harpsichord into his second great pedagogical collection, the first book of the *Well-Tempered Clavier* (BWV 846–869, 1722).

Bach now traveled with some frequency, although not far, at least in comparison to opera composers. His fame as an improviser and performer on the organ had become so great that he was often sought to be the official examiner of newly constructed organs in Saxony and Thuringia and to play the inaugural recitals on them once he had approved their construction. In May 1720, Bach along with five other court musicians accompanied the prince to Carlsbad. He returned after 7 July only to find that his wife Barbara had succumbed to a sudden illness and had already been interred. Barbara had born Johann Sebastian seven children, including **Carl Philipp Emanuel Bach** and **Wilhelm Friedemann Bach**, who became major European composers in their own right. After a customary mourning period, Johann Sebastian married Anna Magdalena Wülcken on 3 December 1721, who would bear him 13 more children, including the great composer Johann Christian Bach (1735–1782). Anna Magdalena, a good musician herself, became one of Johann Sebastian's principal assistants.

In the same year, Bach's employer Prince Leopold married Friderica, Princess of Anhalt-Bernburg, who was not a music lover as was the prince, and it is probable that this less-enthusiastic court regime encouraged Bach to think again of new employment. In 1723, the post of cantor at St. Thomas Church in Leipzig became vacant upon the death of **Johann Kuhnau**. The city officials who were to make the appointment first offered the post to Telemann and then to Christoph Graupner (1683–1760), both declining because they secured higher pay elsewhere. On 7 February 1723, Cantatas BWV 22 and 23 were auditioned as test pieces, and J. S. Bach assumed the post in May.

The position of *Thomaskantor* of Leipzig was one of the more prestigious in 18th-century Germany. Leipzig was a thriving city, and Bach had charge of all the liturgical music in the city, supervised the choirs and organists of the principal churches of the Thomaskirche, Nikolaikirche, the "New Church" dedicated to St. Matthew, and the Petruskirche. He held the third rank in the school for boys and was required to teach them Latin, a duty the *Thomaskantor* managed to hire out.

The Thomaskirche possessed a substantial library of music composed by preceding cantors for liturgical use, but nevertheless, Bach determined from the moment of his arrival to embark upon one of the most prolific efforts in the Western music history: the composition of five liturgical cycles of church cantatas (according to his obituary written c. 1751, but only something less than three cycles survive), each cycle containing about 60 works, one work for each Sunday or major feast during the Lutheran liturgical year. This project required Bach to compose, **orchestrate**, and rehearse a composition averaging 20 minutes in length for a large ensemble almost every week for the period from 1723 to c. 1729. Occasionally, Bach drew upon the library or rearranged one of his Weimar cantatas, but even in an age when dashing off new works was considered one of a composer's necessary skills, the sustained quality and obvious attention to detail in these works, not to mention the additional composition of the **St. John Passion** (1724), the **Magnificat** in D (1724), the **St. Matthew Passion** (1727), and numerous cantatas for secular occasions, make this explosion of creativity barely credible today.

Toward 1730, Bach became increasingly unhappy with the lack of support for his program from the town authorities. He described the minimum requirements for "an adequate church music" in a detailed memorandum, dated 23 August 1730, but to no avail. His disappointment was not entirely musical; his personal library of theological works and a Bible with many annotations in his own hand confirm his deep spirituality and belief in orthodox Lutheranism. His music is shot through with religious symbols and learned expressions of sacred text. Very likely, he saw his position as *Thomaskantor* as a vocation, a kind of mission, and wished to carry it out with all due excellence.

In July 1733, he submitted to the Elector Friedrich August II of Saxony the score of a *Missa brevis* composed on a grand scale, the Kyrie and Gloria that would later be incorporated into the **Mass in B Minor**, in what is thought to be an attempt to win an appointment there at the chapel in **Dresden**. In November 1736, he received an honorary title of *Hofkomponist* ("court composer") but no salaried appointment.

He continued to fulfill his duties as *Thomaskantor*, but with his disenchantment, Bach's prodigious compositional production of more than one new cantata per week at the beginning of his Leipzig tenure fell off. In the 1730s, he often **parodied** his older compositions to meet liturgical demands (e.g., **Christmas Oratorio**, 1734, BWV 248). He turned to musical outlets outside the church. He became director of the Leipzig **Collegium Musicum** in April 1729, where he could perform his **concertos**, often newly arranged for the good players that the Collegium provided. He devoted more attention to compiling pedagogical works for keyboard. Part I of the ***Clavier-Übung*** had been published in 1731 (Opus 1, BWV 825–830), and the following decade saw the publication of the other three parts. About the year 1740, Bach once again collected preludes and fugues for keyboard of all types and for all the possible **keys** in what is now known as Book II of the *Well-Tempered Clavier* (BWV 870–893).

The last decade of Bach's life is marked by encyclopedic works of abstract, almost mathematical character: the last word on **variation** technique and **canon** in the **Goldberg Variations** (c. 1741), immediately followed by the **Art of Fugue** (c. 1742). A visit to his son Carl Philipp Emanuel in May 1747, court harpsichord player to Frederick of Prussia, elicited the study in **chromatic** counterpoint known as the **Musical Offering**. When Bach applied for membership in June 1747 to the Correspondirende Societät der Musicalischen Wissenschaften (Corresponding Society for Musical Science), he submitted the *Canonic Variations on "Vom Himmel Hoch"* (BWV 769) as proof of his qualifications. Finally, in 1749, he completed the Mass in B Minor, Roman Catholic liturgical music of the highest sophistication for which there was no known commission and no occasion for performance during Bach's lifetime. Thus, Bach's last two decades adumbrate the modern composer who creates after his own inspiration rather than for a particular event or liturgy but, moreover, represent a kind of spiritual retreat in the contemplation of pure music.

From the latter half of 1749, Bach's health declined, and he suffered from blindness. He endured two operations in March and April 1750 by an English eye doctor, John Taylor, who would also operate on **George Frideric Handel**. Neither was successful. Bach suffered a stroke in late July and died on the evening of 28 July 1750.

For the rest of the 18th century, Bach's music went into almost total eclipse. One reason is that Bach's learned counterpoint had been out of fashion in Europe, replaced by the competing aesthetics of *le style galant* on the one hand and *der empfindsamer Stil* on the other. Second, even had that not been the case, the notion of constantly recycling the best music as "classics" was not yet born of the Enlightenment. Indeed, that is why Bach once felt compelled to compose a new cantata every week. Third, Bach published very little of his music: two early cantatas and the *Clavier-Übung*. The rest remained in manuscript, and although Bach carefully retained copies of virtually everything he composed, these were sold off to various collectors immediately after his death in order to provide something for his now impoverished widow. This unfortunate circumstance partly accounts for the loss of a significant part of his oeuvre.

The few exceptions that remained in circulation were the *Well-Tempered Clavier*, the *Clavier-Übung*, and the **chorales**, abstracted from the cantatas, which were all used by teachers of harpsichord, organ, piano, and composition. For over a half-century, this was the only portion of Bach's music known even to the likes of Wolfgang Amadeus Mozart (1756–1791) and Ludwig van Beethoven (1770–1827).

In the 19th century, small islands of appreciation such as the Berliner Gewandhaus appeared. Then, Felix Mendelssohn's partial revival of the St. Matthew Passion in 1829 in Berlin created a sensation among the historically minded romantic musicians, and by 1850, the Bachgesellschaft (Bach Society) was founded to publish a complete edition, finished in 1897. Performers and editors of those days routinely interpreted "historical" music according to romantic tastes so that the sizes of **choruses** and **orchestras** would be far beyond anything Bach had in mind, to say nothing of added dynamics, changed orchestrations, and other "improvements."

About the same time, however, a more "scientific" historicism in certain musicians began to question such liberal adaptations. Interest in manuscripts, contemporary theorists, original instruments, and other sources grew ever more intense until the mid-20th century saw the creation of ensembles that tried to recreate "authentic" performances such as Bach himself might have known. While the most egregious of 19th-century abuses certainly required remedy, Bach's own common practice of transcribing and adapting his own works for other musical media suggests that his art accommodates a wide variety of interpretations.

In 1950, Wolfgang Schmieder published his *Bach-Werke-Verzeichnis*, a catalog of Bach's works (rev. ed. 1990). His BWV numeration, now running to over 1120 works (including doubtful and spurious works), is the most common way of precisely identifying a Bach composition today. The catalog, however, is not chronological but categorical; BWV numbers cannot be trusted to indicate priority of composition even within a category.

It would be difficult to overstate the influence of Johann Sebastian Bach on the world of music in the 21st century. The listening public may be less aware of this, but hardly any professional musician of the Western tradition remains untouched by his music.

Three general kinds of influence might be suggested. The first is in musicianship, which is entirely appropriate since, in his time, Bach was renowned as a sympathetic and effective music teacher and had pupils from his days at Mühlhausen until May 1750. Bach composed all manner of keyboard studies for the beginner on upward to the virtuoso so that every student of piano, harpsichord, or organ learns them from childhood. Moreover, these "studies," drawn from the easier Anna Magdalena's Notebook to the **inventions** to the most challenging *Clavier-Übung*, are so beautiful that they may be enjoyed by everyone as pure music. Violinists, cellists, and **flutists** have the same kind of heritage in Bach's unaccompanied suites and sonatas. For this reason, envious players of other instruments have transcribed this music for virtually every instrument, ancient and modern. Again, this is entirely justified by Bach's own practice. Transcription seems to inflict little harm on the musical integrity. The universal and enduring qualities that have made Bach's music the most studied the world over seem to arise from the complex relations and coordinations, often very abstract, that he has built into the notes themselves.

The second influence is in compositional technique. The 385 "Bach Chorales," the settings of **hymns** that Bach made for his cantatas, are tiny, magnificent exemplars of the central harmonic language of the Western tradition and, as such, have been studied by composers in training from their earliest publication in 1765 and 1769 by Carl Philipp Emanuel Bach through the present day. Anyone wishing to learn how to compose fugues or to use other **contrapuntal** techniques in conjunction with this harmonic system turns to the works of Bach: the *Well-Tempered Clavier*, the Goldberg Variations, the Art of Fugue.

The third influence, of course, would be in the concert repertory. Schools of music everywhere routinely require Bach's music for degree recitals, particularly for keyboard instruments. His domination of the organ repertory is probably unequalled by any other single composer for any other repertory. It is true that large **symphony** orchestras and choruses may perform his music less often that they did 50 years ago, owing to a self-consciousness about performance authenticity brought on by the **early music revival**, but in compensation, there have grown up numerous ensembles dedicated to historically conscious performances of Bach.

BACH, WILHELM FRIEDEMANN (22 November 1710, Weimar, Germany–1 July 1784, Berlin). Oldest son of **Johann Sebastian Bach** and his first wife, Maria Barbara Bach (1684–1720), Wilhelm Friedemann Bach was a brilliant **keyboard** virtuoso whose career appears to have failed its potential. His public performances were mostly **improvisations**, and he was reluctant to commit notes to paper. He left about four dozen solo keyboard works, mostly for **harpsichord**, 8 **concertos**, 6 *sinfonie*, 5 **trio sonatas**, and about 25 **church cantatas**.

After training with his father and the **violinist** Johann Gottlieb Graun (c. 1702–1771), Bach became **organist** at the Sophienkirche in **Dresden** in 1733. In 1746, he became organist at St. Mary's Church in Halle but left that position in 1764. Eventually, he settled in Berlin in 1774 as a private teacher and freelance keyboard recitalist.

BALLET DE COUR **(Fr. "court ballet").** Costumed ensemble **dances** of the French royal court of the first half of the 17th century, usually performed in ballrooms with scenery. By the 1650s, the *ballet de cour* had developed into two types: the abstract *ballet à entrées* and the *ballet mélodramatique*, which acted out a narrative, articulated in **printed** programs or in music sung between the acts. The individual dances either mimed actions of the narrative or presented abstract patterns. In either case, the music was composed to a particular dance rhythm: **allemande**, **bourrée**, **chaconne**, **courante**, **galliard**, **gavotte**, **gigue**, **loure**, marche, **minuet**, **passacaille**, **passepied**, rigaudon, **sarabande**, and others. In the 1660s, **Jean-Baptiste Lully** composed *comédie-ballets* and *tragédie-ballets* before turning to full-fledged **opera** in the ***tragédie lyrique***. *See also* MASQUE.

BAROQUE PITCH. Pitch standards varied by time, place, and performance circumstance in the Baroque and were not the same as the modern standard of $A^4 = 440$ Hz. This is why recent recordings of Baroque music played on "historical instruments" sound lower in pitch than the stated **key** on a modern piano.

In the 17th century, when most instruments were manufactured in a few urban centers, there was substantial agreement that A^4 be actually higher than the modern, about 465 Hz. **Michael Praetorius** called this *Cornettenthon* ("cornet tone"), which became the standard expression for instrumental pitch. Late in the century, however, French advances in instrument manufacture brought a new standard, the *ton de chambre* or *Cammerton* ("chamber tone") of $A^4 = 415$. On the other hand, church **organs** built in the 17th century could not adapt to the new standard so retained the older, now called *Chorton* ("choir tone"), and accommodated the *Cammerton* by transposing their parts when playing music with other instruments. Music for choirs was usually written in *Chorton*. Instrumental parts intended to accompany them would be written at a pitch higher than actually desired, since their **tuning** would result in the part sounding lower.

BASSO CONTINUO. *See* CONTINUO.

BASSOON (Fr. *basson*, Ger. *Fagott*, It. *fagotto*). A double-reed wind instrument made of several lengths of wood with a conical bore, linked and bound together so as to make a single long tube. The image of sticks bound together, a *fagot* in 17th-century French, gave rise to the modern German and Italian words for bassoon. The English and French words describe its low pitch range. In Baroque music, the bassoon provided bass lines with characteristic color, and it could act as a melody instrument for a **continuo**.

The first jointed bassoons were made in 17th-century France. They quickly displaced their ancestor, the dulcian, owing to their lighter weight, greater pitch range, and greater flexibility. Bassoons quickly spread to England and Germany by the 1680s.

By the late Baroque, the bassoon began to be recognized as a solo instrument. **Georg Philipp Telemann** composed a **solo sonata** for bassoon in 1728 and **Antonio Vivaldi** has several **solo concertos**.

Baroque bassoon.

BASSO OSTINATO. *See* OSTINATO.

BEGGAR'S OPERA, THE. A so-called ballad **opera** composed of spoken dialogue punctuated with comic **song** texts set to well-known melodies. The **libretto** is by John Gay, and the musical arrangement is attributed to **Johann Christoph Pepusch**. There are 69 songs, mostly strophic forms in simple arrangements, 23 of which have been traced to various folk song sources and 18 to named composers, including **Henry Purcell** and **George Frideric Handel**.

The drama concerns a secret love match between a notorious highwayman, Captain Macheath, and Polly Peachum, daughter of a swindler and his common-law wife. Among the targets of its satire are Sir Robert Walpole, prime minister of England, Italian *opera seria*, the opera company known as the Royal Academy, conventional social structures and morality, and the conventions of tragedy.

The Beggar's Opera opened at the Lincoln's Inn Fields theater on 29 January 1728. It was an instant and overwhelming success and remains one of the most frequently mounted musical productions in the English language.

BERGAMASCA. A tune appearing as the basis for Italian and French instrumental **variation** sets in the late 16th and 17th centuries. The tune was often accompanied by the cadential progression I-IV-V-I, which could be repeated as an **ostinato**.

BERNHARD, CHRISTOPH (1 January 1628, Kohlberg, Pomerania [today, Poland]–14 November 1692, Dresden, Germany). Best known today as a music theorist, his account of music and **rhetoric** in composition in his *Tractatus Compositionis Augmentatus* (c. 1657) figures prominently in modern understanding of Baroque musical aesthetics. During a long career in **Dresden** and **Hamburg**, he left 3 **masses**, 12 Latin **motets**, 25 **sacred concertos**, 5 sets of funeral music, and 14 songs. A significant body of his music is lost, including the funeral music commissioned by **Heinrich Schütz**.

Documents record his singing under Schütz at the court of the elector of Saxony in Dresden in 1648. On 1 August 1655, he was promoted to *vice-Kapellmeister*, and he was sent to Italy on two occasions after 1656 to study by the Elector Johann Georg II, who preferred Italian- style music. In 1663, Bernhard moved to Hamburg, succeeding **Thomas Selle** as cantor of the Johanneum and director of all civic church music for the city. He joined with his friend and former colleague **Matthias Weckmann** to promote the activities of the Hamburg **Collegium Musicum** until Weckmann's death on 24 February 1664. At this point, Johann Georg II summoned Bernhard back to Dresden to educate his grandchildren, and on 24 August 1681, he was made sole *Kapellmeister*.

BIBER, HEINRICH IGNAZ FRANZ von (baptized 12 August 1644, Wartenberg, Bohemia–3 May 1704, Salzburg, Austria). One of the most brilliant **violinists** of his time, Biber's reputation rests chiefly on his violin **sonatas**, especially the 16 **Rosary Sonatas** that require variant **tunings** of the violin known as *scordatura*. He also composed 2 **operas**, 3 secular **cantatas**, and, after taking charge of the choir school in Salzburg in 1684, 15 musical dramas for the school. Late in life, he turned to sacred music: eight **masses**, two requiems, nine **motets**, and two vespers services. Documents list over 100 works for instrumental ensemble, of which 19 survive.

Biber's violin sonatas demand the most advanced technical facility of any 17th-century violin sonatas, far greater than his more famous Italian contemporaries. The player must negotiate shifting to the seventh position, and double and triple stops make possible **ostinato** movements even in unaccompanied works.

Few details of his musical education survive, but sometime before 1668, he was in the service of Prince Johann Seyfried Eggenberg of Graz. In 1668, he joined the service of the bishop of Olmütz and then, while on a trip to buy violins, joined the service of the archbishop of Salzburg in summer 1670, rising through the ranks to *Kapellmeister* in 1684. The Emperor Leopold I made him a knight in 1690.

BIBLICAL SONATAS (Johann Kuhnau, published 1700, Leipzig). Set of six **sonatas** for **keyboard** by **Johann Kuhnau** famous as an example of Baroque musical referentialism, or instrumental program music. Each of these *Musicalische Vorstellung einiger biblischer Historien* ("Musical Portrayal of Some Bible Stories") is accompanied by a title (original in German) as follows:

The Fight between David and Goliath
Saul Cured by David through Music
Jacob's Wedding
Hezekiah, Sick unto Death and Restored to Health
Gideon, Savior of Israel
Jacob's Death and Burial

An Italian note accompanies the several movements of each sonata, describing for the player its representational content, conveyed through semantic associations of rhythmic patterns, **consonances**, **dissonances**, **mode**, and **tempo**.

BINARY FORM. A musical structure consisting of two sections often called "strains," usually referred to as A and B in formal analysis. Each strain

Example. Johann Jacob Froberger, Courante from E Minor Partita in binary form

concludes with a strong **cadence** and each is enclosed in the written score by repeat signs. Thus, the composer writes only the two strains, A and B, but the performer(s) executes A A B B.

A strain may be as brief as a single melodic-harmonic phrase, perhaps six measures as in the figure, although the B strain is often longer when it contains more harmonic development, such as **modulation**. The traditional formal designations A and B are not intended to signify differences in character: usually the two strains are based upon the same motivic material and sound very much alike.

In the 16th century, binary form is associated with **dance** music, where its predictable phrasing and repetitions aided the choreography. Baroque dance movements, such as **allemandes**, **courantes**, **sarabandes**, **gigues**, and others of the **suite** repertory, are frequently cast in binary form. The longer dance movements typically modulate to the dominant **key** at the end of the first (A) strain and return to the (home) tonic key in the second (B) strain, often passing through other keys en route. In the courante of **Johann Jacob Froberger** in the figure, the A strain begins in E minor and concludes in B minor, while the B strain begins in B minor, passes through G major, and concludes in E minor, the home tonic.

Occasionally, a longer dance will be made of two binary forms organized into a higher-level ternary form. In the first "English" Suite for **keyboard** of **Johann Sebastian Bach** (BWV 806), for example, **Bourrée** I in A Major composed in binary form is followed immediately by Bourrée II, also in binary form in A minor (parallel **mode**), after which a note in the score "Bourrée I da capo" directs the player to repeat the first Bourrée:

Bourrée I	Bourrée II	Bourrée I
A A B B	C C D D	A A B B

Some performance traditions prescribe that the reprise of the first binary be performed without observing the repeat signs, thus: A A B B C C D D A B.

Binary forms may be found in both instrumental and vocal music of the 16th century. In England, many dances have three strains, and the **pavan** continued to be composed this way through the 18th century. Movements of Baroque **sonatas**, **trio sonatas**, and **concerti grossi** that feature dance movements are also composed in binary form. Most of the keyboard sonatas of **Domenico Scarlatti** are in binary form, and the double repeats of the classical sonatas descending from his work are a vestige. A **variation** set composed upon a tune in binary form will usually present all the variations in binary form as well.

BLOW, JOHN (baptized 23 February 1649, Newark, Nottinghamshire, England–1 October 1708, London). The most important composer of the Restoration period before his pupil **Henry Purcell**, he composed mostly vocal works, including about 115 **anthems**, 9 Latin **motets**, 37 **odes**, 17 devotional songs, 110 secular songs, 16 **catches**, 8 **services**, and a **masque**, *Venus and Adonis* of 1683. Three small chamber works, at least 8 **organ voluntaries**, and about 75 short movements for **harpsichord**, including **dance suites**, also survive.

John Blow, the second child of Henry and Katherine Blow, may have attended the Magnus Song School in Newark, and was probably recruited to sing in the choir of the **Chapel Royal** by **Henry Cooke** in winter 1660–1661. He won his first appointment, as organist at Westminster Abbey, on 3 December 1668 and composed one of his earliest anthems, "Oh Lord, I Have Sinned," for the funeral of the Duke of Albemarle. He became attached to the court as musician for the **virginals** in January 1669 and as gentleman of the Chapel Royal on 16 March 1673 or 1674, moving up in October 1676 to be one of the three official organists. He resigned from this post three years later to create an opening for the brilliant Purcell, and Blow took up the post again after Purcell died in 1695.

In July 1674, he succeeded **Pelham Humfrey** as master of the Children of the Chapel and supervised the training of young musicians. Among his charges were important figures of the next generation, including **William Croft** and **Jeremiah Clarke**.

In September 1674, Blow married Elizabeth Braddock, daughter of Edward, another gentleman of the Chapel Royal. They had two boys and three girls, but only the girls survived their father. Elizabeth died in childbirth in 1683.

Blow accumulated a number of honors during his career. He received the first Lambeth degree of doctor of music conferred by the dean of Canterbury, when he was not yet 30 years old. He provided three anthems for the coronation of King James II in 1685 and three more for that of William and Mary in 1689. He was commissioned to set the annual odes for St. Cecilia's Day celebrations in 1691, 1695, and 1700. In that year, a new post, the composer of the Chapel Royal, was created for him.

Blow is buried in Westminster Abbey.

BOËSSET, ANTOINE (1586, Blois–8 December 1643). The most important composer of *airs de cour*, Boësset was appointed *Maître des Enfants de la Musique de la Chambre du Roy* ("Master of the Children for the King's Chamber Music") in 1613 and continually added appointments at the royal court through 1634. He published nine volumes of *airs de cour*, beginning in 1608, and over 200 of these songs were also published in **lute tablature**, creating a substantial repertory for that instrument. The seventh book of 1630 contains a "*basse continue pour les instruments*," the first reference in **print** to a basso **continuo** by a French composer.

BOISMORTIER, JOSEPH BODIN DE (23 December 1689, Thionville, France–28 October 1755, Roissy-en-Brie). Composer of a few popular ballets, some **motets**, and songbooks, Boismortier enlarged the French instrumental repertory, particularly that of the **transverse flute**, by over 600 pieces published in over 100 volumes. His music is aimed at the amateur player, does not demand advanced technical skills, and was so popular that he was able to live handsomely without holding an official post from about 1724, when he began publishing, until his death.

He lived in Metz from 1700 to 1713, then Perpignan to 1723, then **Paris**. He was *chef d'orchestre* at the theaters of Foire St. Laurent from 1743 to 1745 and at the Foire St. Germain in 1745, affording him contact with the *opéra comique*.

BONONCINI, GIOVANNI (18 July 1670, Modena, Italy–9 July 1747, Vienna). One of the most successful **opera** composers of the Baroque, he and his works appeared in **Naples, Rome, Venice, Vienna, London, Paris,** Madrid, Lisbon, and countless smaller venues. He composed 31 *opere serie,* 21 **serenatas,** 7 Italian **oratorios,** 8 concerted Latin **motets,** an **anthem,** and a significant body of instrumental music, including 12 *concerti da camera,* 12 *trattenimenti da camera,* 48 *sinfonie* for various combinations of instruments, 12 **trio sonatas,** 8 *divertimenti da camera,* and 6 duos for violoncello, Bononcini's principal instrument. Among his roughly 300 extant **cantatas** is *Impara a non dar fede,* cited by **Benedetto Marcello** as a standard audition piece for singers in the late Baroque.

Son of composer Giovanni Maria Bononcini, he was orphaned at age eight and moved to Bologna, where he studied at San Petronio with Giovanni Paolo Colonna (1637–1695). Owing to three instrumental publications by age 15, he was admitted into the Accademia Filarmonica on 30 May 1686. In 1687, he became *maestro di cappella* at the church of San Giovanni in Monte. In 1691, Bononcini went to Rome, entered the service of the Colonna family and the Spanish ambassador, and began working with the **librettist** Silvio Stampiglia. Bononcini's opera *Il Trionfo di Camilla* ("Camilla's Triumph," 1696) was immediately brought to Naples and produced in 18 other Italian cities by 1710; in London, it was given 63 times between 1706 and 1710 in the very first years of Italian opera there.

After Lorenzo Colonna died in August 1697, Bononcini joined the court of Emperor Leopold I in Vienna and remained until 1712. Then, he entered the service of Emperor Charles VI's ambassador to Rome, Count Gallas. In the summer of 1719, the Earl of Burlington engaged Bononcini for the newly established Royal Academy of Music in London, and his works dominated the inaugural season 1720–1721. Despite this success, his ties to various Jacobite patrons who supported Stuart claims to the English throne and his Catholic religion apparently prevented him from being engaged for the following season. He mounted his opera *Ermine* in Paris in 1723, was reengaged by the Royal Academy for the season of 1723–1724, went to France again in summer 1724, and entered the service of the Duchess of Marlborough, for whom he directed private concerts consisting mostly of his own music.

He was caught out in an embarrassing case of unacknowledged borrowing from **Antonio Lotti,** a practice quite common at the time, at a meeting of the **Academy of Ancient Music.** The episode also besmirched the reputation of his friend, the composer **Maurice Greene.** Shortly after that, Bononcini left England and spent time in Paris (spring 1733), Madrid (December 1733), and Lisbon (until 1736) before returning to Vienna. The Empress Maria Theresa granted him a small pension, which allowed a modest retirement.

BOURRÉE (also bourée). A duple-**meter dance** in fast **tempo**, usually begun with a half-beat upbeat, composed in four-measure phrases that build a **binary form**. It frequently appears in 17th-century *ballets de cour* and in instrumental **suites** through the end of the Baroque.

BOUZIGNAC, GUILLAUME (c. 1587 near Narbonne?, France–after 1642). Details of his life are obscure, with a great gap between 1609 and 1624 when he does not appear anywhere in France. He seems to have made an itinerant living as *maître de musique* at schools and churches in Angoulême, Grenoble, Bourges, Rodez, and Clermont-Ferrand. Nevertheless, his influence on sacred music in France in the early 17th century was considerable: 9 liturgical **motets**, 3 **masses**, 4 vespers services, and about 115 paraliturgical motets in Latin.

BOYCE, WILLIAM (baptized 11 September 1711, London–7 February 1779, London). Although his list of works includes over 75 **anthems** and 4 other settings of the **Te Deum**, Boyce was known in his own lifetime mostly for his stage music, including six **masques** and contributions of incidental music and songs to many other productions, for his **odes** (mostly composed after 1755 when he succeeded **Maurice Greene** as Master of the King's Musick), and a famous publication in 1747 of 12 **sonatas** for two **violins** and **continuo**. He also composed 3 later sonatas for two violins, 10 **voluntaries**, 12 **overtures**, and 6 **concertos**. Today, the most frequently heard music of Boyce is his set of eight **symphonies** of 1760.

Boyce was enrolled at the school of St. Paul's Cathedral in 1719, where he studied with **Johann Christoph Pepusch** and Greene, with whom he remained a close associate well into the 1730s. He was appointed a member of the **Chapel Royal** in May 1736, by which time several of his anthems were already in repertory. In 1738, along with **George Frideric Handel**, **Thomas Arne**, and Pepusch, he founded the Society of Musicians, later the Royal Society. His ode *See Famed Apollo* received rapturous acclaim in Dublin in December 1740, to be exceeded only by his **serenata** *Solomon* of 1742.

Boyce married Hannah Nixon on 9 June 1759, and his son William was born in March 1764. He suffered from slowly increasing deafness, which appears to have made it difficult for Boyce to perform his church duties by the 1760s. His reputation survived, however, and after a grand service that included his own anthem *If We Believe That Jesus Died*, Boyce was interred in the crypt of St. Paul's.

BRANDENBURG CONCERTOS (Johann Sebastian Bach, BWV 1046–1051). A set of six instrumental compositions dedicated to the Margrave

Christian Ludwig of Brandenburg in March 1721. Much of the music is thought to antedate the dedication, and **Johann Sebastian Bach parodied** some movements in later works.

The term "**concerto**" in Bach's title is intended to be understood not only in the narrow 18th-century Italian connotation of a composition for one or more soloists and **orchestra** in three movements (fast-slow-fast) but also in the broader 17th-century connotation of "instrumental music." Only the second, fourth, and fifth concertos of the Brandenburg set bear comparison to the Italian **concerto grosso** because there is a clear demarcation of a *ripieno* group (orchestra) and a *soli* group, but even these remain exceptional because of the unusual choices of instruments for soloists and in the omission of the orchestra in the slow movements of the second and fifth, resulting in chamber **sonatas** *a quattro*.

The first concerto is remarkable in its use of hunting **horns** with difficult parts, and the inclusion of a fourth movement, in which a **minuet** alternates with other kinds of **dances**. In the third concerto, all the instruments are at times soloists, and all combine at other times to create a kind of orchestral accompaniment, thus blurring the line between *soli* and *ripieni*. The sixth is really a piece of chamber music for seven instruments (including the **continuo**), unusually scored for low-pitched **strings**. Its first movement is highly **canonic**.

The Six Brandenburg Concertos

No.	BWV	Key	Scoring	Movements / performance time
1	1046	F major	Solo violino piccolo, three oboes, two hunting horns, bassoon, strings, continuo	[Allegro] Adagio Allegro Menuetto / 22 min.
2	1047	F major	Solo violin, recorder, oboe, trumpet, strings, continuo	[Allegro] Andante Allegro assai / 12 min.
3	1048	G major	Three solo violins, three solo violas, three solo cellos, continuo	[Allegro] Adagio Allegro / 11 min.
4	1049	G major	Solo violin, two solo recorders, strings, continuo	Allegro Andante Presto / 16 min.
5	1050	D major	Solo violin, flute, harpsichord, strings, continuo	Allegro Affettuoso Allegro / 21 min.
6	1051	B-flat major	Two solo violas, two solo violas da gamba, solo cello, continuo	[Allegro] Adagio, ma non tanto Allegro / 18 min.

BUXTEHUDE, DIETRICH (c. 1637, Helsingborg?, [modern] Sweden–9 May 1707, Lübeck, Germany). Regarded since the 18th century chiefly as the most influential **organist** in the generation before **Johann Sebastian Bach**, recently the recovery and recording of Buxtehude's vocal and ensemble music have broadened his reputation. The young Bach's famous pilgrimage from Arnstadt to Lübeck in1705 to visit Buxtehude is well known, but Buxtehude also entertained **George Frideric Handel** and **Johann Mattheson** in 1703 and was the dedicatee of **Johann Pachelbel**'s 1699 publication *Hexachordum Apollinis*. For organ, he composed 3 self-standing **fugues**, 3 well-known **ostinatos** (1 **passacaglia**, 2 **chaconnes**), 8 **canzonas**, 5 **toccatas**, and 22 "**preludia**," which almost always contain extended fugues along with **improvisatory** music. He also left 47 **chorale preludes** and **chorale fantasias** for organ and at least 113 sacred vocal works on Latin and German texts, most in the form of **chorale** settings and **sacred concertos**. Three **librettos** for **oratorios** survive, but the music is lost. His secular music includes 17 **keyboard suites** (including, perhaps, the 7 suites composed on the character of the planets, mentioned by Mattheson), 5 **variation** sets, and at least 23 **sonatas**, most requiring **violin** and viola da gamba.

Buxtehude's place of birth and even nationality is obscure. His father, Johannes Buxtehude, was appointed organist at the Olaikirche in Elsinore, Denmark, in 1641, where Dietrich attended the Latin school and probably began his musical education with his father. In 1660, he became organist at the Marienkirche in Elsinore. On 5 November 1667, **Franz Tunder**, organist at the Marienkirche in Lübeck, one of the most important musical posts in north Germany, died, and on 11 April 1668, Buxtehude was chosen out of a field of several applicants to replace him. With this appointment, Buxtehude became, in effect, the director of all musical activities in the city save the **opera**.

He became a citizen of Lübeck on 23 July 1668 and on 3 August married Tunder's daughter Anna Margarethe. It is possible that the marriage was a condition of employment, a customary practice that would apply to Buxtehude's own successor. They had seven daughters together.

At the Marienkirche, Buxtehude played a large organ of 52 stops, and he composed into his own organ works a range of divisional contrasts, including demanding parts for the pedal division, which alone had 15 stops, more than any of the three manual divisions. The preludes for which he is best known alternate improvisatory passages (the *stylus phantasticus*) with strict **imitative** passages very often developed into full-blown fugues.

The keyboard suites follow the "classic" French pattern of **allemande-courante-sarabande-gigue**, with an occasional **double**, the opening three **dances** often based on the same thematic material.

For his sacred vocal works, Buxtehude draws prose texts from either the Lutheran German Bible or the Latin Vulgate, setting them as sacred concertos, or spiritual poetry. If the poetry is associated with a chorale melody, that melody may be set in a variety of ways ranging from a traditional **cantus firmus** to a contemporary **aria** form.

In 1678, Buxtehude expanded the tradition of *Abendmusik* organ recitals at the Marienkirche to include sacred concertos and oratorios on spiritual themes presented on five specific Sundays of the liturgical year. These concerts featured vocal soloists and extensive instrumental accompaniment.

On 16 May 1707, Buxtehude was buried in the Marienkirche.

BYRD, WILLIAM (1543, Lincoln?, England–4 July 1623, Stondon Massey, Essex). Dying too soon to respond to the earliest Italian currents of Baroque style, Byrd nevertheless influenced composition in 17th-century England through his consummate mastery of the *stile antico*. His sacred music exhibits a personal and complex **contrapuntal** technique that makes no use of **cantus firmus**, paraphrase, or **parody** technique, unusual for the time. Among his students were **Thomas Tomkins**, and possibly **Thomas Weelkes** and **John Bull**.

Although a Roman Catholic, he composed over 65 English **anthems**, but in later years, he composed mostly for the Catholic rites, an act which demanded discretion. His most famous works today, the Latin **masses** for three **voices** (c. 1592–1593), four voices (c. 1593–1594), and five voices (c. 1595), he **printed** in limited editions without title pages. After 1590, he undertook the immense project of setting an entire liturgical cycle of mass propers for feast days, the *Gradualia* (two volumes, published 1605 and 1607), in addition to about 70 other Latin **motets**. Byrd also composed 5 **preludes** and other liturgical pieces for **keyboard**, 11 **fantasias** for **viol consort**, at least 2 **canons**, 7 **In Nomines**, all for viol consort, 8 fantasias, 14 sets of **variations**, 19 **pavan** and **galliard** pairs, and over 20 other **dance** movements, all for keyboard.

C

CABANILLES, JUAN BAUTISTA JOSÉ (baptized 6 September 1644, Algemesí near Valencia, Spain–29 April 1712, Valencia). The most important composer of Spanish **organ** music in the mid-Baroque. The accounts of Cabanilles's surviving *tientos*, **versets**, **toccatas**, **variations**, **dances**, and other organ works vary, but some run over one thousand.

On 15 May 1665, he was appointed second organist at the Valencia Cathedral and, as required by the cathedral chapter, ordained to the priesthood on 22 September 1668. By April 1666, he had become first organist and retained that post until his death.

CACCINI, GIULIO (8 October 1551, Tivoli?, Italy–buried 10 December, 1618, Florence). An outstanding singer and singing teacher, he allied himself at an early age with the Medici court in **Florence**, and thereby came into contact with **Jacopo Peri**, Ottavio Rinuccini (1562–1621), and other members of the **Camerata**. He contributed music to early versions of *Dafne*, the first **opera**, and composed a small portion of *Euridice*. He claimed to have invented the **monodic** style of singing and published his methods of expressive vocal **ornamentation** in *Le Nuove Musiche*.

CADENCE. An articulation that signals the conclusion of a melodic-harmonic phrase, analogous to the conclusion of a complete sentence, either declarative or interrogative, in speech. Cadences organize the musical information of the Baroque musical language at the middle levels of structure. They define one musical phrase and articulate it from the next. Because their occurrence identifies the tonic **pitch-class**, cadences also make perceptible the **key** of the moment and are therefore essential for articulating **modulations** (changes of key).

In Baroque music, there are five common types: authentic or full, half, Phrygian, deceptive, and plagal. By far, the most common is the authentic cadence. The harmony progresses from weak-beat dominant **function** (V or its derivatives) to strong-beat tonic function (I or i) while the principal melody completes the scale either by descending 2-1 or ascending 7-8. Thus the authentic cadence produces the perception of movement to conclusion and stability, a resolution of harmonic and melodic tension. Its origin is most likely the Renaissance suspension cadence *subsemitonum modi* ("semitone under the mode"), which produces the penultimate major triad occurring just before the final of the **mode**, with the melodic 7-8 resolution by half-step that adumbrates the syntax of the Baroque major and minor scales.

If the dominant function is displaced to the strong beat of the **meter** while the melody pauses on scale degree 2, 4, 5, or 7, the phrase is complete without resolution of harmonic tension on that level, a musical question, metaphorically speaking. This is the half cadence.

If such a half cadence occurs not with the dominant function of the prevailing major key, but with the dominant function of its relative minor (e.g., in C major, cadencing on an E-major triad rather than a G-major triad), this kind of half cadence is called Phrygian. The name derives from the half-step movement of the bass (e.g., in C major, from F to E) typical of the conclusion of a melody in the medieval Phrygian mode.

A deceptive cadence substitutes another chord for the I (or i) triad in an authentic cadence that can accommodate the tonic pitch-class in the melody but has much weaker or absent tonic function. The formulas V-vi (in major mode) or V-VI (in minor mode) are the most common. There is a resolution of melodic tension but not harmonic, thus the deceptive effect.

The plagal cadence is the oldest and derives from the *stile antico* practice of concluding a **contrapuntal** composition by allowing one of the **voices**, usually the soprano or tenor, to reach its last note, the tonic pitch-class, and hold it, while the other voices continue to move among notes consonant with the tonic, gradually coming to rest in the last tonic triad. The conclusion is therefore not of the instant, but drawn out. In Baroque music, the most common harmonic formula for the plagal cadence is IV-I (in major mode) or iv-i (in minor) because both those triads contain the tonic pitch-class. A famous example occurs at the end of the "Hallelujah" **chorus** of **George Frideric Handel**'s *Messiah*.

Composers can control the strength, or conclusive power, of any cadence by a variety of means, a primary source of the great richness of Baroque articulation. When the constituent harmonies are relatively short in duration, the cadence is weaker than when they are long. When the constituent harmonies are **inverted**, the cadence is weaker than one with harmonies in root position. The presence of the tonic pitch-class in the highest sounding voice strengthens the cadence, and its absence weakens it. Finally, the effect of any cadence depends greatly on the strength of the perceived meter and the disposition of the chords with respect to it. If the weak-beat to strong-beat association of the cadence is weakened or reversed, cadential effect may decrease considerably or even disappear.

Therefore, the mere presence of a harmonic formula such as V-I in no way guarantees cadential effect. It is a necessary but not sufficient condition. *See also* CADENZA.

CADENZA (It. "cadence"). An **improvisational** passage associated with an important **cadence** executed by the soloist in a Baroque **aria** or **concerto** movement. The improvisatory character is produced by a temporary suspension of the **meter** or by the domination of formulaic passagework idiomatic to the instrument or both.

Cadenzas appear to have originated as early as the 16th century, growing from conventional **ornamentations** of cadential formulas, but came to prominence mostly through **opera** arias in the early 18th century, and cadenzas of **da capo arias** remained the most common type through the end of the Baroque. They most commonly occur in conjunction with the last important cadence of the singer, immediately before the onset of the final ritornello in the (A) section of the da capo aria or at the very end of the (B) section. The cue is a pause in the accompaniment on dominant **function** harmony or, less frequently, an **inverted** tonic harmony, in any case without completing the harmonic phrase. In this sense, the cadenza is an expansion from within of a simple cadential formula. The singer signals the conclusion of the cadenza by returning to that harmony, usually with a trill, and then the accompaniment resolves into tonic harmony and a resumption of the motor rhythm and meter.

Stories of long-winded abuses by soloists are not hard to find in Baroque criticism. There was little to be done to control the flights of opera singers showing off, but composers of concertos sometimes wrote cadenza material into the fabric of the movement in order to ensure some conformity of musical thought and reasonable proportion with the concerto. Famous examples include the cadenza for **violin** in the last movement of the "Spring" concerto of **Antonio Vivaldi**'s *Four Seasons* and the brilliant cadenza for **harpsichord** just before the final ritornello of the opening movement of the Fifth **Brandenburg Concerto** of **Johann Sebastian Bach**.

The material of such composed cadenzas may consist of little but virtuoso passagework organized into **sequences**, as in the Bach example or in the famous *Capricci* for the violin concertos of **Pietro Locatelli**. Others, such as the Vivaldi, may share motivic relationships with the material of the ritornello, a strategy recommended by **Johann Joachim Quantz** because then the cadenza must "confirm the prevailing passion of the piece."

CALDARA, ANTONIO (1671, Venice–28 December 1736, Vienna). An immensely prolific composer of remarkable range, Caldara figured prominently in the musical life of both **Rome** and **Vienna** during the high Baroque.

He composed at least 78 **operas**, 44 Italian **oratorios**, 12 other dramatic works, 13 **madrigals**, 250 Italian **cantatas**, 110 **masses** and mass fragments, 12 **motets**, many other assorted sacred works, 12 **trio sonatas** *da camera*, 12 trio sonatas *da chiesa*, 55 other **sonatas** for various instruments and combinations, 12 *sinfonie*, 500 **canons**, and 44 *lezioni* ("lessons") for **cello**, his own principal instrument. Most of his vocal music is lost, and so despite prominence in his own time, he remains an obscure figure today. Sometimes criticized for formulaic writing, Caldara was nevertheless exceptional among his colleagues because he neither borrowed material from other composers nor **parodied** his own works.

He was the son of **violinist** Giuseppe Caldara and probably learned music from him and then from **Giovanni Legrenzi**, *maestro di cappella* at San Marco in **Venice**. He received a permanent appointment to San Marco as cellist and alto singer in 1695. By that time, he had already seen his opera *L'Argene* produced in 1689 and his trio sonatas *da chiesa* published as Opus 1 in 1693. Two mass movements date from 1696, and at least two oratorios were performed between 1697 and 1699, the year of publication for 12 cantatas for solo voice.

In that year also, Duke Ferdinando Carlo Gonzaga of Mantua made Caldara his *maestro di cappella da chiesa e del teatro*. The composer traveled with his patron to Casale, Genoa, and Venice while composing operas for him during the disruptions caused by the War of the Spanish Succession. Caldara left Mantua in 1707, sojourned in Rome, where he met **Arcangelo Corelli**, the **Scarlattis**, and **George Frideric Handel**, among other luminaries, and then spent time performing operas in Barcelona before returning to Rome in March 1709. On 1 July, he was appointed *maestro di cappella* to Prince Ruspoli, whose spectacular tastes allowed Caldara's fluency in composition to flourish: by 1715, he had composed about 180 cantatas, the 12 motets Opus 4, and many oratorios for the Lenten season.

Caldara married Caterina Petrolli, a contralto attached to the Ruspoli household, on 7 May 1711.

After much waiting and politicking, Caldara won the position of *vice-Kapellmeister* at the imperial court in Vienna, over the opposition of *Kapellmeister* **Johann Joseph Fux**, and began work probably in May or June 1716. His duties included the composition of at least one opera per year for occasional celebrations, at least one oratorio for Lent, working with **librettist Apostolo Zeno** for 11 of them, and a great variety of sacred music. In addition, he supplied music for patrons outside Vienna. Caldara, who as a composer of sacred music was as comfortable with the *stile antico* as with operatic styles, became a founding member of the Cecilian Society, an organization founded in Vienna in 1725 for the revival of the Roman Catholic traditions of sacred music, which spawned influential chapters all over Europe during the 18th and 19th centuries.

In the last six months of his life, Caldara completed two operas and a complete polyphonic vespers service. The recorded cause of death, *Gelbsucht und inner Brand* ("jaundice and fever"), may not be unrelated to sheer exhaustion.

CAMERATA. A group of intellectuals led by the **Florentine** courtier Giovanni Bardi (1534–1612) meeting from about 1574 through 1589. Among the participants were the humanist Girolamo Mei (1519–1594) and the Florentine musicians **Giulio Caccini** and Vincenzo Galilei (c. 1520–1591), father of the astronomer, and among their interests was ancient Greek music and its power to move the passions. Their researches led them to believe that ancient Greek music consisted of a single melodic line, always sung in a narrow, consistent register that connoted a particular expression, using rhythms derived from the accent patterns of the words being sung. All Greek tragedies were sung this way. Therefore, the **polyphony** of their own time could never hope to achieve the expressive power of Greek music, because the current music's simultaneous melodies presented several registers, many rhythms, and various melodic contours at once, thus obscuring any expression. Galilei claims to show how music should be dramatic in two compositions, which do not survive, a set of **lamentations** for Holy Week and a setting of Count Ugolino's lament from the *Divine Comedy*.

The ideas of the Camerata clearly resonate with the inventions of **recitative** and *dramma per musica*, and Caccini was personally involved with them, but the musical techniques for these precede the Camerata, and because the Camerata itself produced no **operas**, their influence on its invention is disputed.

CAMPRA, ANDRÉ (baptized 4 December 1660, Aix-en-Provence–29 June 1744, Versailles). The dominant composer for the French musical theater in the first two decades of the 18th century, Campra composed the first *opéra-ballet* in 1697, inaugurating a tradition of unabashed comedy in France after the death of the tragedian **Jean-Baptiste Lully**. His two dozen works for the musical theater also comprise **ballets**, *divertissements*, and *tragédies lyriques*. He also left 22 French **cantatas**, at least 60 **motets** and psalms, a requiem **mass**, and a plainsong mass.

Campra's first teacher was most likely his father, Jean-François, a **violinist** and surgeon. He sang in the choir of St. Sauveur at Aix-en-Provence and began clerical studies in 1678 but showed his dramatic inclinations early when he was nearly dismissed in early 1681 for participating in local theatrical productions without permission. Later that same year, however, he was appointed chaplain.

From August 1681 to May 1683, he was *maître de chapelle* at Saint Trophime in Arles. He then assumed the same title at Saint Étienne in Toulouse beginning in June 1683. He improved the musical resources of what was already considered the best choir in the city, and the authorities sent him to **Paris** in January 1694 for four months study. He did not return to Toulouse but instead succeeded Jean Mignon as *maître de musique* at Notre Dame

Campra's Music Dramas

Work	First performance[1]	Genre, librettist
L'Europe Galante	24 October 1697	Opéra-ballet, A. H. de Lamotte
Vénus, Feste Galante	27 January 1698	Divertissement, A. Danchet
Le Carnaval de Venise	20 January 1699	Comédie lyrique, J.-F. Regnard
Hésione	14 July 1701	Tragédie en musique, A. Danchet
Aréthuse	14 July 1701	Ballet, A. Danchet
Tancrède	7 November 1702	Tragédie en musique, A. Danchet after Tasso
Les Muses	28 October 1703	Opéra-ballet, A. Danchet
Iphigénie en Tauride	6 May 1704	Tragédie en musique, J.-F. Duché de Vancy and A. Danchet
Télémaque	11 November 1704	Tragédie en musique, A. Danchet
Alcine	15 January 1705	Tragédie en musique, A. Danchet after Ariosto
Le Triomphe de l'Amour	11 September 1705	Opéra-ballet, Danchet after Quinault
Hippodamie	6 March 1708	Tragédie en musique, P.-C. Roy
Les Fêtes Vénitiennes	17 June 1710	Opéra-ballet, A. Danchet
Idoménée	12 January 1712	Tragédie en musique, A. Danchet after P. J. Crébillon
Les Amours de Vénus et de Mars	6 September 1712	A. Danchet
Télèphe	28 November 1713	Tragédie en musique, A. Danchet
Enée et Didon	29 October 1714, Marseilles	Divertissement
Camille, Reine des Voisques	9 November 1717	Tragédie en musique, A. Danchet
Untitled	17 May 1718, Lyons (music lost)	Ballet, F. Gacon
Les Âges	9 October 1718	Opéra-ballet, L. Fuzelier
La Feste de l'Isle-Adam	1722 (music lost)	divertissement
Les Muses Rassemblées par l'Amour	February 1724 (music lost)	Divertissement, A. Danchet
Les Sauvages	14 September 1729 (music lost)	Divertissement
Achille de Déidamie	24 February 1735	Tragédie en musique, A. Danchet

[1]All premieres in Paris unless otherwise noted

Cathedral. In May 1696, he was made canon at Saint Jean-le-Rond and appears as a composer of Latin tragedies on the programs of the Jesuit College Louis-le-Grand from 1698. In these years, Campra attracted the notice of the Duchess de la Ferté, the future regent of France Philippe d'Orléans, and the Duke de Sully.

On 24 October 1697, Campra's *opéra-ballet L'Europe Galante* premiered. Campra, worried about how traditional views about the nature of French drama prevailing at Versailles might affect his career, published this **opera** and the following year's *Vénus, Feste Galante* anonymously. But *L'Europe Galante* was a great success that allowed Campra to leave Notre Dame on 13 October 1700 and concentrate on the theater. His next success was a more traditional *tragédie en musique, Tancrède* (1702).

The first two decades of the 18th century saw Campra at the peak of his popularity. He published his first two books of *cantates françoises* and four books of motets. King Louis XV awarded him an annual pension of 500 livres on 15 December 1718. In 1722, he entered the service of the Prince de Conti. He also composed intermittently for the **Chapelle Royale** until poor health made him give up this work in 1742. He spent his last years in a small apartment in Versailles, sustained by his pensions.

CANON. A passage or composition made entirely of **strict imitation** in at least two **voices**. The canon is classified by the interval between the first notes of the leading and following voices (e.g., "canon at the fifth"). In a self-standing canonic composition, traditionally only one melody is written out along with a Latin rule (canon), which specifies the **pitch-class** interval and the time interval needed for the following voices. Canons were considered part of the *stile antico* during the Baroque and are therefore not common, with the significant exception of some late instrumental works of **Johann Sebastian Bach** that contain exemplary demonstrations of various canonic techniques. *See also* ART OF FUGUE; *CLAVIER-ÜBUNG*; GOLDBERG VARIATIONS; MASS IN B MINOR; MUSICAL OFFERING; CHORALE PRELUDE; *ORGELBÜCHLEIN*.

CANTATA (It. "sung"). Developing directly from the experiments in *dramma per musica* at the close of the 16th century, especially the **continuo madrigal** and **continuo aria**, the cantata grew quickly into the most important secular genre of vocal chamber music in the Baroque. In its mature form, the cantata presented a single scene of music drama for one or two singers, no staging, and minimal instrumental accompaniment, often the **continuo** alone. As a kind of dramatic chamber music, cantatas were perfectly suited to an evening's entertainment for an aristocratic salon, or any similar gathering in limited space, and patrons constantly demanded new ones through the end of the Baroque. Dramatically inclined composers obliged: **Giacomo Carissimi** composed about 150 cantatas, **Nicola Porpora** about 132, **Antonio Caldara** over 250, **Giovanni Bononcini** over 300. The young **George Frideric Handel** composed over 100 in just two years (1707–1709) while learning his art in Italy, and the most prolific of all, **Alessandro Scarlatti**, is believed to have composed over 600 cantatas. All of these composers spent at least a portion of their careers in **Rome**, the center of cantata composition through the 17th and first part of the 18th century.

Like its complementary term *sonata*, that is, "played," in the first half of the 17th century *cantata* simply meant music composed for singers, usually one or two, with simple harmonic accompaniment, and so was musically indistinguishable from works called *arie, lamenti, scherzi, musiche*, and even **madrigals**, all of which exhibit the **monodic texture** that founded the early Baroque style. The earliest occurrence in a musical context is the 1620 reprint of *Cantade et Arie* of **Alessandro Grandi**.

In these early cantatas, musical form is unpredictable. **Recitative** passages could pass easily into music with various strong **meters**—in other words, short **arias**—which could then dissolve back into recitative. Such fluidity often set even strophic texts, composers preferring to express through music individual lines and words rather than the periodic text structure.

The texts themselves treat amorous, mythological, historical, satirical, even devotional subjects. Most commonly they are dramatic monologues. The context might be rather abstract, such as an unrequited or abandoned lover or perhaps a shepherd's lament, or it might be well known to the educated listener, such as Scarlatti's dialogue of Marc Anthony and Cleopatra.

The formal development of the cantata resembled more and more closely the development of **opera** as the 17th century progressed. The distinction between aria and recitative grew ever more well defined. By the century's end, perhaps spurred by the great influence and prestige of Alessandro Scarlatti, cantata arias were most commonly **da capo arias** and in the early 18th century almost invariably so. Typically, a later Baroque cantata begins with a recitative and ends with the second of two da capo arias. Instrumentation also grew richer: **obbligato** solo instruments, such as **violin** or **oboe**, became common, and some cantatas might be adorned with a small **orchestra**.

Italian-language cantatas were composed throughout 17th and 18th century Europe, as were Italian-language operas, but other lands also developed the cantata genre in their home languages after 1700, although they achieved neither the numbers nor the prestige of the Italian genre. In France, there are about 800 in all, a comparatively small number from the pens of **Marc-**

Antoine Charpentier, Jean-Philippe Rameau, Louis-Nicolas Clérambault, and **André Campra** but none from **Michel-Richard de Lalande**. About 320 English-language cantatas survive, all dating after the advent of Italian opera about 1705, but the genre seems not to have attracted the most important English composers, not even Handel, who continued to compose Italian cantatas into the 1740s. Spanish cantatas were of two kinds: a secular *cantada humana* and a liturgical type classified according to its liturgical function (e.g., *cantada di Navidad*). In Germany, the cantata became a very important kind of liturgical music, the **church cantata**.

CANTUS FIRMUS (Lat. "fixed chant"). Compositional technique whereby the composer takes a preexisting melody, usually from the traditional repertories of Gregorian or medieval chant, Lutheran **chorales**, and so forth and sets it in long durations (determined by him) while composing original **counterpoint** to accompany it. The technique originated in southern France in the 12th century. In the Baroque, the frequency of its use declined slowly but persisted through the period in **masses**, **organ masses**, and **motets** in the Roman Catholic tradition, **church cantatas** and **passions** of the Lutheran tradition, **anthems** of the Anglican tradition, and **organ preludes** of all Christian traditions.

The virtues of the technique are its repetition, its sustained tones, and its origin in tradition.

Its repetition allows a **texture** of unflagging rhythm typical of the Baroque to be extended for far longer duration than it could have otherwise sustained. Repetition also unifies the composition while allowing creativity and change in the added **contrapuntal voices**.

The sustained quality of the cantus firmus produces a subtle musical tension based on the disparate speeds in the texture. The composition cannot end until the voices match up. For this reason, the cantus firmus often drops out of the texture before the final **cadences**. When the cantus firmus changes speeds during a movement, it always becomes faster in order to facilitate the matching (e.g., **Johann Sebastian Bach, Cantata** BWV 4, first **chorus**).

The use of a traditional melody instantly assures a semantic reference for all those who know it. Baroque **chorale cantatas** and **chorale preludes** from the Lutheran tradition take advantage of the same principle.

CANZONA. Derived from the 16th-century **polyphonic Parisian** *chanson*, by the turn of the 17th century, canzona connoted a composition for **keyboard** or instrumental ensemble. The principal Baroque composers are **Giovanni Gabrieli** (*Sacrae Symphoniae*, 1597; *Canzoni et Sonate*, 1615) and **Girolamo Frescobaldi** (*Recercari et Canzoni*, 1615).

The canzona usually begins with an **imitative** passage marked by the long-short-short rhythm in the **subject** that was so typical of the Parisian *chanson*. Like a **motet**, after an authentic **cadence**, the canzona might present a new subject to be imitated or contrast the imitative **texture** with a **homophonic** passage. Gabrieli often returns to the opening passage to round off the work.

Christian liturgies in Italy and German-speaking countries often employed the canzona as a **prelude** or **verset**.

CAPRICCIO. A term of wide-ranging usage, in the early Baroque, it is most often associated with **harpsichord** pieces, which, while often exhibiting sophisticated **imitation**, depart from strict rules of **voice** leading and exhaustive treatment of the **subject**. The **keyboard** publications of **Girolamo Frescobaldi** are a major source of this type. Later, the term appears to conform to the immediate context of its usage: in **suites** it may connote a **dance** form; in **Pietro Locatelli's** **violin sonatas**, it refers to **improvisatory** passages.

CARISSIMI, GIACOMO (baptized 18 April 1605, Marino near Rome–12 January 1674, Rome). The dominant composer of mid-17th century **Rome**, Carissimi is best known today for his 11 influential **oratorios**, especially ***Jephte***. He also composed a **mass** for five **voices**, at least 110 Latin **motets**, and 148 Italian **cantatas**. There may be other stage and sacred works by him, as there are many unauthenticated attributions.

The youngest of six children born to Amico and Livia Carissimi, nothing is known of Giacomo's early training. He sang in the choir at Tivoli Cathedral from 1623 and played the **organ** there from 1624. In 1628, he was appointed *maestro di cappella* at San Ruffino in Assisi. Before his 24th birthday, he joined the Collegio Germanico e Hungarico, an important Jesuit seminary with a reputation for excellent music in Rome, and upon the departure of the *maestro di cappella*, Lorenzo Ratti, about 1 December, Carissimi was appointed in his place two weeks later. This was an excellent post, especially for a musician so young, and Carissimi remained there for the rest of his life. As his reputation spread, he attracted private pupils, including **Marc-Antoine Charpentier** about 1654, **Johann Caspar Kerll** before 1656, **Christoph Bernhard** in 1657, and possibly **Agostino Steffani** in the early 1670s.

His reputation also attracted offers from other cities. Authorities in **Venice** asked Carissimi to stand to replace **Claudio Monteverdi** as *maestro di cappella* at San Marco in 1643, and numerous potentates tried to recruit him for the service of Archduke Leopold William in Brussels, son of the Holy Roman Emperor. Carissimi ultimately refused all such offers, preferring to remain in his native city where his excellent post allowed him to augment his income from various sources nearby. In 1656, Queen Christina of Sweden, living in Rome, appointed him *maestro di cappella del concerto di camera*.

When Carissimi died, the Jesuit authorities at the Collegio Germanico obtained an order from Pope Clement X prohibiting anyone, under pain of excommunication, from removing any of Carissimi's autograph scores from the college.

CASTELLO, DARIO (active in first half of the 17th century, Venice). Although little is known of his life, Castello, a virtuoso player of wind instruments at St. Mark's in **Venice**, published two important volumes of early **sonatas** in 1621 and 1629 that were reprinted many times in the first half of the century. These sonatas are typical of the attempt to translate the aesthetics of *dramma per musica* into abstract instrumental idioms. Composed for various instruments, each sonata has three or four sections or movements of contrasting **tempo** and affect. Movements having strong **dance** rhythms follow others having hardly any **meter** at all, thus mimicking the contrast in the **aria** and **recitative textures** of **opera** and **cantata**.

CASTRATO. A male singer who has undergone surgical castration before puberty in order to maintain his soprano or alto vocal range into adulthood. Employed by the papal chapel since the 16th century, *castrati* found new and much more illustrious careers in the Italian **opera**, where they were cast in youthful leading male roles, such as Julius Caesar. This is why many male leads in Baroque operas are composed in the soprano or alto range. The particular timbre of their voices and their long adult musical experience and lung capacity earned stardom and riches for a few *castrati*, such as Francesco Bernardi (d. 1759), who worked with **George Frideric Handel** and was known on stage as "Senesino," and Carlo Broschi, the famous **"Farinelli."**

CAVALIERI, EMILIO DE' (c. 1550, Rome–11 March 1602, Rome). Remembered today as the composer of the first **oratorio**, the *Rappresentatione di Anima e di Corpo*, and for his contributions to the famous **Florentine intermedi** of 1589, Cavalieri also composed at least four other dramatic works, now lost, a set of **lamentations** of Jeremiah in the *stile moderno* (published 1599), and a few other surviving vocal works.

Cavalieri was active in the oratorio movement and at the same time worked as a political agent for the Medici family in **Rome**. He was brought to Florence, appointed to take charge of artists and musicians on 3 September 1588, and began preparations for the wedding of Grand Duke Ferdinand to Christine of Lorraine the following year. He was often sent to Rome on diplomatic missions and, on one of these, composed his famous oratorio for Carnival seasons of 1600.

CAVALLI, FRANCESCO (family name also known as Caletto, Bruni, Caletti-Bruni) (14 February 1602, Crema, Italy–14 January 1676, Venice). Composer, **organist**, and singer, his more than 30 **operas** dominated the **Venetian** musical theater from 1639 to 1669 and defined more than anyone what is meant by "**Venetian opera**." He also published two collections of sacred music: the first in 1656 containing a **mass**, a **Magnificat**, and 21 **sacred concertos** for two to 12 **voices**; and the *Vesperi* of 1675 containing three complete vespers services for eight voices, including three Magnificats, five sacred concertos, a six-voice Magnificat, and an eight-voice requiem mass.

Born to Italian composer and organist Giovanni Battista Caletti, Francesco attracted the attention of the Venetian governor of Crema, Federico Cavalli, who brought this remarkable boy soprano to Venice and placed him in the chapel choir at San Marco on 18 December 1616. Francesco adopted his patron's surname. On 18 May 1620, he was appointed organist at the Church of San Giovanni e Paolo. He resigned on 4 November 1630. Apparently, he no longer needed the position because he had married Maria Sozomeno on 7 January 1630, the widow of a wealthy Venetian, Alvise Schiavina. In 1647, they rented a *palazzo* on the Grand Canal. She died in 1652, leaving no children but most of her property to him, and Cavalli remained in the house until his death.

Her landholdings and dowry of 1,200 ducats allowed the composer to invest early in the nascent public operas of Venice, beginning on 14 April 1638, when he signed an agreement to produce operas at the first public opera house, Teatro San Cassiano. The first Cavalli opera, *Le Nozze di Teti e di Peleo*, opened on 24 January 1639.

At San Marco, **Claudio Monteverdi** had been Cavalli's *maestro di cappella* since the boy's arrival in 1616. Whether Cavalli studied formally with the master is unknown, but it seems clear that Cavalli assisted with the composition of some details of Monteverdi's final opera *L'Incoronazione di Poppea* (1642). Earlier, Cavalli had competed for the post of second organist at the basilica and was appointed on 23 January 1639. Although his salary rose from 140 ducats to the maximum of 200 by 1653, higher than the first organist, Massimiliano Neri, and in practice, he played the role of first organist, he was not officially appointed first organist until 11 January 1665, after Neri's departure.

By that point, Cavalli's fame as an opera composer had been spread across Europe by traveling opera companies performing his works. *Egisto* provided **Paris** with one of its first experiences of music drama in 1646, and it may have also reached **Vienna**. From 1652, he attracted commissions from opera houses in other cities: **Naples**, Milan, and **Florence**. His 1648 opera *Giasone* became so popular that it remained in the traveling repertory until the end of

Cavalli's Operas

Opera	First performance	Librettists and sources
Le Nozze di Teti e di Peleo	24 January 1639, Venice	O. Persiani
Gli Amori d'Apollo e di Dafne	1640, Venice	G. F. Busenello
Didone	1641, Venice	Busenello
Amore Innamorato	1 January 1642, Venice, music lost	G. F. Loredan and P. Michiel
La Virtù de' Strali d'Amore	1642, Venice	G. Faustini
Egisto	1643, Venice	Faustini
Ormindo	1644, Venice	Faustini
Doriclea	1645, Venice	Faustini
Titone	1645, Venice, music lost	Faustini
Giasone	5 January 1648, Venice	G. A. Cicognini
Euripo	1649, Venice	Faustini
Orimonte	20 February 1650, Venice	Faustini
Oristeo	1651, Venice	Faustini
Rosinda	1651, Venice	Faustini
Calisto	28 November 1651, Venice	Faustini after Ovid Metamorphoses
Eritrea	17 January 1652, Venice	Faustini
Veremonda, l'Amazzone di Aragona	21 December 1652, Naples	Cicognini, rev. L. Zorzisto
Orione	June 1653, Milan	F. Melosio
Xerse	17 January 1654, Venice	N. Minato
Statira Principessa di Persia	18 January 1855, Venice	Busenello
Erismena	30 December 1655, Venice	A. Aurelli
Artemisia	10 January 1656, Venice	Minato
Hipermestra	12 June 1658, Florence	G. A. Moniglia
Antioco	25 January 1658, Venice	Minato
Elena	26 December 1659, Venice	Faustini and Minato
Ercole Amante	7 February 1662, Paris	F. Buti after Ovid Metamorphoses
Scipione Africano	9 February 1664, Venice	Minato
Mutio Scevola	26 January 1665, Venice	Minato
Pompeo Magno	20 February 1666, Venice	Minato
Eliogabalo	None	Anonymous
Coriolano	27 May 1669, Piacenza, music lost	C. Ivanovich
Massenzio	None, music lost	G. F. Bussani

the 17th century. *Xerse* and *Erismena* were also staples of Venetian opera, all characterized by faster, more complex, and more comic plots than were typical of the court and academic operas earlier in the century.

In April or May 1660, Cavalli, who generally traveled little, went to Paris at the invitation of Cardinal Mazarin to compose *Ercole Amante*. Preparations for the spectacle delayed production, and in the interim, Cavalli's 1654 opera *Xerse* was given in the Louvre with the title role changed from soprano to baritone, the original three acts redistributed to five, and with new *entrées de ballet* composed by **Jean-Baptiste Lully**. Cavalli returned to Venice in summer 1662.

On 28 November 1668, he succeeded Giovanni Rovetta as *maestro di cappella* at San Marco and spent his last years concentrating on sacred music, publishing his *Vesperi* in 1675. He was buried in the church of San Lorenzo in Venice.

CAZZATI, MAURIZIO (1616, Luzzara near Reggio nell' Emilia, Italy–1678, Mantua). Composer who reformed the *cappella musicale* at the church of San Petronio in Bologna and established its reputation as a center of excellent music in general and as the origin of the **sonata** for **trumpet** and **strings** in particular with his Opus 35 (1665). He published 10 volumes of instrumental music, including the first **violin** sonatas published by a San Petronio composer, his Opus 55 (1670). There are also 10 volumes of secular vocal music, 4 lost **operas**, 11 lost **oratorios**, and 46 volumes of sacred music.

An ordained priest, Cazzati was appointed *maestro di cappella* at Sant' Andrea in Mantua in 1641 and then to the same post at the Accademia della Morte in Ferrara in 1648 and again at the church of Santa Maria Maggiore in Bergamo in 1653. He returned to his old job in Ferrara in April 1657 and then was elected to the post where he would make his reputation, *maestro di cappella* at San Petronio in late 1657.

Cazzati instituted a regular choir of 35 singers and a group of well-paid instrumentalists for the liturgy at San Petronio, but despite the audible improvements he made and the reputation he built, his tenure there was marked by politically motivated controversies over the syntax in his sacred compositions. The vestry supported him, but he was finally forced out in June 1671. He went to Mantua to serve the Gonzaga family as *maestro di cappella di camera* and the cathedral as *maestro di cappella*. He continued his prolific pace of composition and publishing.

CELLO. The bowed **string instrument** played between the legs and the most common bass melody instrument in the Baroque, especially in **continuo** ensembles. The original name *violoncello*, of which "cello" is an English abbreviation, first appears in the Opus 4 **sonatas** of Giulio Cesare Arresti (1625–1704) in **Venice** in 1665. A volume of sonatas almost certainly destined for the cello but designated on the publication for *violoncino* dates from 1641, also Venice.

Although variant **tunings** (*scordatura*) occur, the modern cello tuning of its four strings to the pitches C^2 G^2 D^3 A^3—one octave below the **viola**—was fairly standard already by the beginning of the Baroque. Occasionally, a cello might have a fifth string, usually E^4. **Johann Sebastian Bach** composed his sixth **suite** for unaccompanied cello for such an instrument.

The earliest significant makers were the same men who perfected the **violin**: Gaspari da Salò of Brescia and the Amati family of Cremona and their disciples. The instrument in the late 16th and early 17th century was larger than the modern cello, but the replacement of gut strings by gut wound with metal, beginning about 1660, permitted the body of the instrument to be shortened somewhat, allowing greater left-hand facility without sacrificing acoustic quality.

The history of bow construction mirrors that of the violin bow. Cello players, unlike **viol** players, almost always used an overhand bow grip.

The solo repertory for the cello began to flower toward the end of the 17th century when instrumentalists attached to San Petronio in Bologna, such as Giovanni Battista degli Antoni (1660–c. 1696) and Domenico Gabrieli (1651–1690), began to publish volumes of *ricercari* for the instrument. While at the *Ospedale della Pietà* in Venice, **Antonio Vivaldi** composed 27 **solo concertos** and at least one **concerto** for two cellos for his young students to play. He, along with his contemporaries **Benedetto Marcello, Nicola Porpora, Joseph Bodin de Boismortier, Michel Corrette**, and many others, published volumes of cello sonatas. Baroque **continuo arias** in **operas** and **oratorios**, of course, have important solo parts for cello. Today, however, the most famous Baroque music for solo cello, practiced and performed by all serious players, is J. S. Bach's set of unaccompanied suites.

***CENTO CONCERTI ECCLESIASTICI* (It. "One Hundred Sacred Concertos").** The title of Ludovico Viadana's Opus 12 (1602), the first published collection of sacred music to include a **figured basso continuo**. The **concertos** are pragmatically designed so that with the continuo they may be sung by one, two, three, or four voices without distortion of the text. For this reason, the **meter** is strong; these are not sacred **recitatives** in **operatic** style. *See also* SACRED CONCERTO; SACRED SYMPHONY.

CESTI, ANTONIO (baptized "Pietro" 5 August 1623, Arezzo, Tuscany–14 October 1669, Florence). Cesti began his musical career as a provincial church musician, but his immense gifts as a singer and then composer produced a triumphant, if brief, career in **opera**. For a while, he was more popular in **Venice** than her native son **Francesco Cavalli**, and accounts of the first performance of Cesti's opera *Il Pomo D'Oro* ("The Golden Apple") in **Vienna** on 12 and 14 July 1668, with its 23 sets and spectacular machinery, appeared throughout the continent and made it the most famous opera of the century. An earlier opera, *Orontea* (1656), was revived 17 times over three decades, very unusual for the time. Cesti also left about 65 **cantatas**, 4 **motets**, and a *sepolcro*.

Cesti was a chorister in Arezzo and joined the Franciscan order in 1637, when he took the name "Antonio," and, on 10 July, entered the monastery of San Francesco in Arezzo. On 8 March 1644, he became **organist** at the cathedral at Volterra and then, on 27 February 1645, *magister musices* of the Franciscan seminary there. He is recorded as *maestro di cappella* at the cathedral until 1649.

From 1647, however, Cesti began to appear as a singer in opera, and he may have sung in a revival of Cavalli's *Giasone* in **Florence** in May 1650. He definitely sang in that opera in Lucca in September, as well as in two others. His reputation and contacts increased, and his own first opera, *Alessandro Vincitor di Se Stesso*, opened at the theater of San Giovanni e Paolo in Venice in January 1651.

In December 1652, Cesti was appointed director of the Kammermusiker at the court of Archduke Ferdinand Karl in Innsbruck. The Kammermusiker were a select group of Italian singers dedicated to the performance of operas and cantatas for regular entertainment of the court.

In 1659, Cesti journeyed to **Rome** to seek permission to leave the Franciscans. This he was granted on 1 March. He impressed many with his singing,

Cesti's Music Dramas

Opera	First performance	Librettists and sources
Alessandro Vincitor di Se Stesso	20 January 1651, Venice	F. Sbarra
Il Cesare Amante	1651, Venice	A. Rivarota after M. Bisaccioni
La Cleopatra	4 January 1654, Innsbruck	Revival of Il Cesare Amante
L'Argia	4 November 1655, Innsbruck	G. F. Apolloni
Orontea	19 February, 1656	G. A. Cicognini
La Dori	1657, Innsbruck	G. F. Apolloni
La Magnanimità d'Alessandro	4 June 1662, Innsbruck	F. Sbarra
Il Tito	13 February 1666, Venice	N. Beregan
Nettunno e Flora Festeggianti	12 July 1666, Vienna	Faustini
Le Disgrazie d'Amore	19 February 1667, Vienna	F. Sbarra
Le Semirami	9 July 1667, Vienna	G. A. Moniglia
La Germania Esultante	13 July 1667	F. Sbarra
Il Pomo D'Oro	12, 14 July 1668	F. Sbarra

and Pope Alexander VII appointed him to the papal choir in December 1659. This landed Cesti in difficulty at the end of 1661, when he returned without permission to Innsbruck with the archduke, who in concert with Emperor Leopold I and the grand duke of Tuscany barely managed to save Cesti from excommunication. Leopold brought Cesti to Vienna in April 1666 with the appointment "Honorary Chaplain and Director of Theatrical Music."

Court records in Florence document his presence there in 1669 as *maestro di cappella*. Rumors of poisoning "by rivals" circulated after his death in October of that year but have not been confirmed.

CHACONNE (also It. *ciaccona* or *ciacona*). Triple-**meter dance** originating in late 16th-century Spain, commonly associated with **ostinato** bass patterns in instrumental **variations** and 17th-century **arias**. In France, these bass pitch patterns (in scale degrees) were: a) 8-7-6-5, b) 8-5-6-5, c) 1-5-2-5, or d) 1-2-3-4-5. These bass melodies, always in major **mode**, would be phrased in 2, 4, 8, or 16 measures, with an elided **cadence** that allowed infinite repetitions.

Although originally a fast dance, as an instrumental form of the later Baroque, the chaconne often had moderate **tempo**. Ostinato basses lengthened, along with the harmonic formulae and mode. Some Baroque theorists equate the chaconne with the **passacaglia**.

Perhaps the most famous Baroque chaconne is the final movement of the D Minor **Partita** for Solo **Violin** of **Johann Sebastian Bach** BWV 1004, a brilliant set of variations demanding exceptional technique and lasting about 15 minutes.

CHALUMEAU (also *scialumò*, *schalamaux*, *salmoè*). Woodwind instrument made of an enclosed tube of air set into vibration by the player blowing through a single reed, thus closely related to the **clarinet**. The chalumeau appears at the end of the 17th century as an attempt to amplify the **recorder**. It does not have an important Baroque repertory, but the chalumeau was employed by composers working in **Vienna** and Germany for a few decades in the 18th century, and **Georg Philipp Telemann**, who played the instrument, composed a **concerto** in D minor for two chalumeaux, and occasionally called for it in scores even after he began using the clarinet in 1721.

CHANDOS ANTHEMS. Set of 11 **verse anthems** and one **Te Deum** composed for James Brydges, later Duke of Chandos, by **George Frideric Handel** in 1717–1718 while he was in residence at Brydges's Cannons estate in Edgeware, England. The scoring is for woodwinds, **strings**, three or four-**voiced** choir, and soloists. The texts are psalms, psalm paraphrases, or other devotional verse.

CHAPELLE ROYALE. The private chapel of the French court. King Louis XIV divided the musical direction of the Chapelle Royale among four *sous-maîtres*, each of whom directed for one-quarter of the year. The *sous-maître* composed **masses** for the king, trained the choir, and supervised its performances. By 1708, the choir was large for its time: 11 soprano voices, 18 *hautes-contres*, 23 tenors, 24 baritones, and 14 basses.

In 1683, by a coincidence of two deaths and two retirements, all four *sous-maître* positions were vacant, and the king ordered a competition to select their replacements. He personally intervened to ensure that **Michel-Richard de Lalande** received one of the posts. By 1714, Lalande had taken over all four supervisory quarters of the year.

Because it was private, the sacred music of the Chapelle Royale did not have to conform to the severe restrictions imposed upon the regular churches, and so the *grands motets* of **Jean-Baptiste Lully**, Lalande, and others could exploit the **textures** of the *stile moderno* and rich Baroque **orchestration**.

CHAPEL ROYAL. Private chapel attached to the English court and home of one of the foremost vocal ensembles of Europe until the 18th century. The Chapel Royal choir originated as a group of administrator clerks temporarily assigned to sing at English royal liturgies. It maintained very high standards under royal patronage during the Elizabethan period, while music in outlying parishes languished under Puritan influence. Its membership consisted of 32 gentlemen and 12 children, who received a general education as well as musical training under the master of the children.

Abolished during the Commonwealth (1649–1660), it recovered much of its stature under Charles II (after 1660), who augmented its vocal and instrumental resources with the King's **Violins**, a band of 24 **string** players in imitation of the court of France. He retained **Henry Cooke** to restore its high standards; Cooke obliged by recruiting and training **John Blow**, **Pelham Humfrey**, and **Henry Purcell**, among others.

Under the Hanoverians and the general secularization of English society, the Chapel Royal declined as a musical institution, although it survives to the present.

CHARPENTIER, MARC-ANTOINE (1643, Paris–24 February 1704, Paris). Eclipsed in fame during his own lifetime by **Jean-Baptiste Lully**, who monopolized the production of French **opera** until 1687, Charpentier became the most important composer of French sacred music of the 17th century. His works, virtually all in the *stile moderno* but remarkably diverse in character, include 11 **masses**, 37 **antiphon** settings, 19 Latin **hymns** (mostly for solo voice and **continuo**), 10 **Magnificats**, 9 litanies, 54 **responsories** for the **Tenebrae** services of Holy Week, 4 settings of the **Te Deum**, 84 psalms, and about 207 **motets**. He has left a small body of secular music: 29 songs (*airs sérieux et à boire*), 12 French **cantatas**, 15 works of various types for the musical stage (5 more are lost), and 14 sets of incidental music for the productions of Molière's *Troupe du Roy* in the 1670s. There are also 32 purely instrumental pieces meant for sacred services and 9 other instrumental works.

Charpentier never received an official court appointment but, nevertheless, was kept busy composing sacred music for the dauphin of France, the Sainte-Chapelle, and various notables, in part because he reliably matched the music to suit the occasion. His masses could be intimate, with small forces, when necessary, but also achieve the grandeur of his mass for 20 soloists and 4 choirs, each with reinforced accompaniment and its own organ and continuo. The 207 motets, in addition to the psalms, which might be counted motets, are always tailored to the occasion. Forty-eight of them are "elevation" motets, quiet pieces to be sung during the consecration of the Catholic mass. The French court tradition decreed that every mass should end with verse 9 of Psalm 20, "O Lord, save the king, and hear us in the hour when we call upon thee," and so Charpentier made 25 settings of these "*Domine salvum fac regem*" motets. Another 35 motets are sometimes called **oratorios** because of their dramatic character.

Charpentier's father was a master scribe in **Paris**, but little is known about his early education. As a young man, he went to **Rome**, arriving between May 1666 and December 1667 and remaining until spring 1670, where he possibly studied with **Giacomo Carissimi**. Returning to Paris, he was hired into the largest private musical establishment in France, that of Marie de Lorraine, where he served as composer in residence and singer until just before she died in 1688. Here, Charpentier composed psalm settings, dramatic motets, and some other stage works.

By the late 1670s, he had supplied sacred music for convents and abbeys about Paris that began to attract crowds. In 1679–1680 and then in 1682 and after, he was commissioned by the dauphin of France to compose music for his own chapel. In 1683, Charpentier entered a competition for a posting in the **Chapelle Royale**, but illness caused him to withdraw. (A competitor was **Michel-Richard de Lalande**, who won one of the four positions available.) Nevertheless, the king bestowed a pension on him two months later. Sometime in the 1680s, he became *maître de chapelle* at the Jesuit *Collège de Clermont* and then of the Jesuit church of St. Louis in Paris, through which he connected to other Jesuit institutions. For all these, he composed sacred music.

After the death of Lully, Charpentier tried composing a *tragédie lyrique*, *Médée*, which opened on 4 December 1693, but it was not a success. About this time, he became music teacher to Philippe d'Orléans, Duke of Chartres, and future regent of France.

Finally, the prestigious post of *maître de musique* at the Sainte-Chapelle of Paris fell vacant in May 1698, and on 28 June, Charpentier was named to his first permanent appointment and composed some of his finest sacred music while holding it until his death. One source claims that he is buried there, but the location of the grave is unknown. Charpentier's renown faded quickly, but fortunately, he carefully preserved copies of his music, which have survived to rehabilitate his reputation.

CHITARRONE (It. "large guitar"). Seventeenth-century sources indicate that the term *chitarrone* is an alternative to **theorbo**.

CHOIR. *See* CHORUS; *CORI SPEZZATI.*

CHORALE. Borrowed from the German, where it connotes sacred song, in English "chorale" refers more precisely to Lutheran congregational vernacular **hymns** and their four-**voice** harmonizations.

Martin Luther enthusiastically promoted the chorale from the first collections appearing in 1524 as a central element in Lutheran liturgy in the belief that worshippers should participate in the proclamation of the Word of God. By the late 16th century, the repertory was sufficiently large and inculturated so as to supply an inexhaustible resource of material for Baroque compositional forms: **chorale motet, chorale mass, chorale cantata**, and much of the great repertory of **organ preludes** stemmed from this popular sacred music. In such guises, the chorale melody might be sung or played out in long durations with surrounding free melody, as was the ancient **cantus firmus**, or it might serve as the **subject** of **imitative counterpoint**, with each chorale phrase initiating a new section.

Lutheran authorities clearly believed that the playing of chorale melodies in various guises as a prelude to liturgy could prepare the congregation to sing them. Otherwise, the impetus for composers to use them was semantic association: chorale melodies long associated with particular feasts could amplify or specify the intended meaning of a composition, as when **Johann Sebastian Bach** implants *O Lamm Gottes unschuldig* ("O Innocent Lamb of God") as a cantus firmus in the midst of the opening **chorus** from the **St. Matthew Passion**.

From the technical standpoint, sounding the chorale melody in long notes in the ancient manner of a cantus firmus provides a framework that can sustain a massive composition. Again, the opening St. Matthew Passion chorus is exemplary. In addition, the slow chorale melody resisting the relentless

Baroque motor rhythm produces a musical tension arising directly from the **texture**. *See also* CHORALE CONCERTO; CHORALE FANTASIA; CHORALE PARTITA; CHORALE PRELUDE.

CHORALE CANTATA. German **church cantata** based on a Lutheran **chorale** melody and text, in several self-contained movements. In its strict sense, no text foreign to the original chorale text is used, and a chorale cantata *per omnes versus* sets all its strophes, with the same melody in varying musical **textures** as the melodic foundation for each movement. The most famous example of this type is Cantata BWV 4 (1708), *Christ Lag in Todesbanden*, of **Johann Sebastian Bach**.

More loosely, the term includes those **cantatas** that make explicit use of a chorale melody in at least one movement. Seventeenth-century figures include **Franz Tunder, Matthias Weckmann, Dietrich Buxtehude**, and many others. **Friedrich Zachow** and **Johann Kuhnau** expanded the form by inserting **arias** between the chorale movements at the turn of the 18th century. The best-known works of this type today are the Bach cantatas from his second cantata cycle at **Leipzig**, 1724–1725.

CHORALE CONCERTO. A setting of Lutheran **chorale** melodies in the musical language of the *stile moderno* to create a specifically Lutheran form of **sacred concerto** early in the 17th century. One important collection is the *Opella Nova* (1618) of **Johann Hermann Schein**, in which the composer either sets the chorale as a **cantus firmus** in the tenor, while other **voices** sing motivic embellishments of it, or he treats the chorale freely in all **voices**. Another is the *Newe geistliche Concerten* (1631–1640) of **Samuel Scheidt**, in which the composer sets 80 chorales, usually in several strophes in the manner of **chorale partitas** for **organ**.

CHORALE FANTASIA. A **fantasia** based upon a **chorale** melody, typical of the north German **organists** in the 17th century. Important early examples appear in **Samuel Scheidt's** *Tabulatura Nova* of 1624; other important composers include **Heinrich Scheidemann, Franz Tunder**, and **Dietrich Buxtehude**. Generally, the chorale fantasia dissects the chorale melody, setting each phrase as a point of **imitation** or as a **cantus firmus**.

CHORALE MASS. Setting of the Kyrie and Gloria texts (Greek and Latin) for Lutheran **masses** using Lutheran **chorale** melodies in **counterpoint**, flourishing in the second half of the17th century until the early 18th century in central Germany.

CHORALE MOTET. Vocal **polyphonic** composition based exclusively on the text and melody of a Lutheran **chorale**, in one through-composed movement or several short ones, dating from the end of the 16th century. Typically, each phrase of the melody serves as a point of **imitation**. (The analogous **organ** genre is the **chorale prelude**.) Instruments may double the vocal parts. Most chorale motets were composed during the first two decades of the 17th century—an important source is the series of *Musae Sioniae* of **Michael Praetorius**—after which the genre merged with the **sacred concerto** and **chorale cantata**. *See also* MOTET.

CHORALE PARTITA. A set of **variations** on a **chorale** melody for **organ**, originating in the latter half of the 17th century in northern Germany. Often, the number of variations corresponds to the number of verses in a chorale text.

    Dietrich Buxtehude and **Johann Pachelbel** rank as important composers of chorale partitas, and the **Canonic** Variations on *Von Himmel Hoch* BWV 769 (1747) of **Johann Sebastian Bach** is, as usual, a crowning contribution from late in the period.

CHORALE PRELUDE. An **organ** composition that prepared the congregation to sing a Lutheran **chorale** by using it as the principal thematic material. Such pieces were commonly **improvised** from the late 16th century onward, but composers, such as **Johann Pachelbel**, also made and collected formal compositions based on well-known chorales for use throughout the liturgical year. The greatest of these collections is the ***Orgelbüchlein*** of **Johann Sebastian Bach**.

    The most common ways of using the chorale melody in Baroque music are: as a **cantus firmus**, in durations much longer than the surrounding **texture**, most often in the soprano **voice** (e.g., *Der Tag, der ist so freudenreich*, BWV 605); as an **ornamented** version that blends the melody into the texture by adopting the same rhythmic motives (e.g., *Nun komm, der Heiden Heiland*, BWV 599); by using each melodic phrase to construct a fughetta (e.g., *Komm, Heiliger Geist*, BV 652); as a **canon** (e.g., *Gottes Sohn ist kommen*, BWV 600). Many of J. S. Bach's works combine these methods.

CHORALE VARIATIONS. *See* CHORALE PARTITA.

CHORUS. A **polyphonic** ensemble of singers. The term connotes at least two singers per vocal melody (part), although, in the performance of Baroque music, there can be many more singers per part, approaching one hundred in all for festival occasions. (The composition that ends an ***opera seria*** with all the characters singing one voice per part is called a *coro*.) In the Baroque, the chorus was essential in many kinds of sacred music and in some kinds of **opera**, **oratorio**, and other forms of music drama.

Choral singing for religious services, Protestant and Catholic, is a direct continuation of performance practices in the Renaissance, whereby plain-chant, polyphonic **masses** and **motets**, and other liturgical works would be sung during the liturgies by an all-male choir. The most ancient tradition provides that this music, particularly in Roman Catholic liturgies, be sung without instrumental accompaniment (*a cappella*), but in fact, the pipe **organ** and other instruments were used at certain times and places to support the singers by doubling their melodies. Any Baroque composer writing a sacred piece in *stile antico* would use the chorus according to this tradition.

In the *stile moderno*, such as for a 17th-century **Neapolitan mass**, much music would be given over to solo singers in operatic style, but the poly-phonic chorus would still retain a significant role in the work, a vestige of a sacred semantic that could be reinforced by liberal use of **imitative textures** and **cantus firmus** redolent of the *stile antico*. Protestant **sacred sympho-nies** and **church cantatas** in Germany, as well as Anglican **anthems**, used the chorus in a similar manner, although a few scholars believe that **Johann Sebastian Bach** intended his church cantatas to be sung with one voice per part. Virtually all choral movements in *stile moderno* employ instrumental accompaniment.

In secular music, choruses of mixed male and female voices make an appearance with the very first operas. In **Claudio Monteverdi**'s *L'Orfeo* (1607), the chorus at times provides Greek-style dramatic commentary and at other times appears as a kind of "crowd" character—shepherds and nymphs, infernal spirits—that would survive through modern times. Monteverdi's conception of operatic chorus was adopted *in toto* by the French for the *tragédie lyrique*, while in the Italian *opera seria* of the late 17th century the chorus disappeared. The chorus is important in German *Singspiele* and in the English **masques** and operas before the importation of Italian opera into **London** beginning around 1705.

The Baroque oratorio and **passion**, positioned midway between the sacred and secular worlds, employed choruses regardless of country. Again, at times the chorus is a character in the oratorio's plot, at other times a commentator on it. The most famous exponents of such choruses are J. S. Bach in his pas-sions (1724, 1727) and **George Frideric Handel** in his **English oratorios** (from 1718).

CHRISTMAS CONCERTO. A **concerto** intended to accompany Eucha-ristic adoration on Christmas Eve, originating in late 17th-century Italy.

To make the Italian "**concerto grosso**" appropriate for a Christmas liturgy, composers included a "pastorale" movement, with 6/8 or 12/8 time signature that included drone effects in the bass and melodies in rocking parallel thirds and sixths in the high instruments. This **texture** recalled a peasant custom of providing bagpipe and woodwind music for reenactments of the shepherds adoring the Christ child at the manger (Luke, chapter 2). The *pastorale ad libitum* in **Arcangelo Corelli**'s famous **Op. 6**, No. 8 (about 1690, published 1714) is the last movement so that it may be omitted when the concerto is performed apart from Christmas. Other Christmas concertos include **Giuseppe Torelli**'s Op. 8, No. 6; **Francesco Manfredini**'s (1680–1748) Op. 3, No. 12; and **Pietro Antonio Locatelli**'s (1695–1764) Op. 1, No. 8. *See also* KUHNAU, JOHANN.

CHRISTMAS ORATORIO, JOHANN SEBASTIAN BACH, BWV 248. The most famous of **Johann Sebastian Bach**'s three **oratorios**, it is actually a set of six self-contained **church cantatas** linked by the birth narratives from the St. Luke and St. Matthew Gospels running through them all. Bach performed them during the six festival days of the Christmas season of 1734–1735: Christmas Day; St. Stephen's Day and Holy Innocents (26 and 27 December); Feast of the Circumcision (1 January); Sunday (2 January); and Epiphany (6 January).

The text is set much as in Bach's **passions**. The Gospel text is sung to tenor **recitative**, with speeches by the shepherds or another group given to through-composed "**madrigal**" **choruses**. Solo **ariosos** and **arias** comment upon the events. Each **cantata** begins with a substantial chorus introducing the day's theme, except the second, in which a sublime pastoral *sinfonia* sets the scene instead, and concludes with an often highly elaborated summary **chorale**.

Most of the concerted movements in the Christmas Oratorio are **parodies** of secular cantatas composed for the Elector of Saxony in 1733 and 1734. Each cantata has a different scoring, reflecting the theme of the day, so that for example the second day, setting the shepherd narrative, eschews the festival brass and requires only the "pastoral" colors of **flutes**, **oboes d'amore**, **oboes da caccia**, **strings**, and **continuo**. Performing the entire set requires in addition three **trumpets**, two **horns**, and **timpani** and about two hours' time. The choral parts, as in much Bach, are challenging.

CHRISTMAS ORATORIO, HEINRICH SCHÜTZ (*Historia der freuden- und gnadenreichen Geburth Gottes und Marien Sohnes, Jesu Christi***, SWV 435).** The most frequently performed of the *historia* of **Heinrich Schütz**, first heard on Christmas Day at the Elector of Saxony's court chapel in **Dresden** in 1660. The German **libretto** is a compilation of the birth narratives from the Gospels of St. Luke (2:1–20) and St. Matthew (2). The narration is sung to

recitative in the tenor range. Schütz composed the speaking roles of the angel (soprano), Herod (bass), the shepherds (soprano, mezzo, alto), the magi (three basses), and Herod's counselors (two tenors, two basses) as seven concerted pieces, mostly in strict **meter**, called "**intermedi**." All of them, along with an introductory and a concluding **chorus** and most of the recitative, are in F major. The instrumentation of each intermedium varies to reflect the character singing. The work calls for two **violins**, two "violettas," one **viola**, one **cello** or viola da gamba, two **recorders**, two **trumpets**, two **trombones**, **bassoon**, and **continuo** and requires about 40 minutes to perform. The most recent modern critical editions are edited by Günther Graulich for the Stuttgarter Schütz-Ausgabe (1998) and Neil Jenkins for Novello (2000).

CHROMATICISM. The use of pitches not contained within the **key**, **mode**, or scale in force at a given moment in a composition. The most common chromaticism in Baroque music is **functional** chromaticism, which has two techniques. In one technique, the chromatic pitches create temporary functions in a key subsidiary to the main key; in the other, harmonies that normally function within a key are chromatically altered while retaining the same function (e.g., by lowering the root one half-step, the ii^6 in minor mode becomes the "Neapolitan sixth"; by raising the root one half-step, the iv^6 in minor mode becomes an augmented sixth).

The other type of chromaticism is melodic, whereby the chromatic pitches decorate a diatonic structural pitch, or fill in a melodic gap between two diatonic structural pitches. Because of its variability in the sixth and seventh scale degrees, the minor mode is a frequent source of melodic chromaticism, even though, strictly speaking, these pitches are within one of the scale variants.

CHROMATIC SEQUENCE. *See* SEQUENCE.

CHURCH CANTATA. Hybrid of the secular Italian **cantata** and the German **sacred concerto** tradition of the 17th century, the church cantata became the principal form of newly composed Lutheran liturgical music in Germany around the turn of the 18th century. The term "church cantata" is retrospective, first applied to the works of **Johann Sebastian Bach** and his predecessors by 19th-century editors of his music. In German sources, the term is not found before 1700.

During the 17th century, the intersection of the various types of **chorale** settings, the Italian secular cantata, and the German sacred concerto resulted in a great variety of liturgical works that can claim some relation with what is commonly accepted as the 18th-century Lutheran church cantata. Texts might be purely biblical, drawn from traditional chorales, or a mixture of both. The heavy dependence of the sacred concerto on textual structure, with short sections linked by **recitative** or succeeding one another immediately, continued through the century. In one typical procedure, called the "concerto-aria cantata" by some historians, the work began with a sacred concerto **texture** on a biblical text, frequently including a **chorus**, then a **strophic aria** for solo voice setting the verses of a chorale, ending with a second **concerto** section. Some of the leading composers of such church cantatas include **Franz Tunder, Matthias Weckmann, Dietrich Buxtehude, Johann Kuhnau, Johann Philipp Krieger, Friedrich Zachow**, and **Johann Pachelbel**. Collections were published by composers G. C. Wecker in 1695, Krieger in 1697, and Nicolaus Niedt (died 1700) in 1698.

In 1700, **Erdmann Neumeister** published *Geistliche Cantaten statt einer Kirchen-Music* ("Sacred Cantatas in Place of Liturgical Music"), which offered verses in recitative and **da capo aria**, Neumeister's preferred form of **aria**, in the Italian manner. Such texts were known as "**madrigal**" texts but intended for devotional use. He followed up with cycles in 1711 and 1714, incorporating biblical and traditional chorale texts into such **operatic** verses to make the "reform" cantata texts for which he became famous, although this synthesis was anticipated by Duke Ernst Ludwig of Meiningen by 1704. Five of Neumeister's texts were set by J. S. Bach. Unless based on explicit chorale melodies, the arias and recitatives from such cantatas are musically indistinguishable from opera movements.

The Bach corpus of about 200 extant church cantatas (of supposedly 300 composed) is by far the best-known repertory of the genre today, composed largely in two furious periods of activity from 1713 to 1716 in Weimar and from 1723 to 1729 in **Leipzig**. He composed most of them for particular liturgies. The writing for the chorus and vocal soloists is the most technically demanding in church music before the 19th century.

Bach's promotion to concertmaster of the Weimar court in 1714 required of him a monthly cantata. He composed these to **librettos** written mostly by Salomo Franck according to the Neumeister pattern. The scoring and the pattern of movements vary widely.

His Leipzig cantatas commonly call for a four-**voice** choir and four-part **string** ensemble, **continuo** and a variety of obbligato instruments and vocal soloists. Bach's obituary states that he composed "five annual cycles of church pieces for all the Sundays and holy days, running from the first Sunday after Trinity to Trinity Sunday." These should amount to 300 works, but only the first two cycles (1723–1725) are fairly complete. A typical pattern of movements for a Leipzig cantata would be:

Chorus (biblical text)–Recitative–Aria–Recitative–Aria–Chorale

Insertions of additional movements were made if the text demanded them. For the second annual cycle, Bach composed **chorale cantatas** almost exclusively. These make explicit use of a chorale melody, chosen for the particular feast, as a **cantus firmus** in the opening chorus, in the concluding movement as a simple **hymn**-like setting, and, occasionally, in the inner movements. The texts for the inner movements could be paraphrases of the traditional chorale text. The chorale cantata seems to be a peculiarity of Bach's cantata composition; use of chorale melodies in cantatas by his contemporaries was exceptional.

Bach's output of cantatas (a new one every week in his early Leipzig years), however, was exceptional only in the quality of its music. **Georg Philipp Telemann**, for example, is thought to have composed about 1,700 church cantatas in 12 liturgical cycles, and lesser-known names with comparable productivity could be cited.

CHURCH SONATA. An instrumental composition in several movements or sections, dating from the 17th or early 18th century, that might be used to substitute for **organ versets** in a Roman Catholic **mass**. The traditional term *sonata da chiesa* appears only infrequently in contemporary sources; any ensemble **sonata** using **imitation** and other suitable sacred idioms might be so used. Although the movement pattern of slow-fast-slow-fast was once thought to be the defining feature, the sources show a wide variety of orders.

CLARINET. Woodwind instrument made of an enclosed tube of air set into vibration by the player blowing through a single reed. Clarinets come in a great variety of sizes, although most common are the instruments of treble range in B-flat and A. Tradition ascribes the invention of the clarinet to Johann Christoph Denner of Nuremberg at the beginning of the 18th century. Closely related in its construction to the **chalumeau**, the clarinet was designed to play higher notes more easily, the defining feature appears to be the "speaker key," which opens a small hole for that purpose.

The Baroque repertory for the clarinet is small, and there is often confusion with the chalumeau and the **clarino**. **Antonio Vivaldi** may have called for the clarinet in his 1716 **oratorio** *Juditha Triumphans* and definitely used it later on in some of his **concertos**.

CLARINO. German term indicating a high **trumpet** part.

CLARKE, JEREMIAH (c. 1674–1 December 1707, London). Composer of the famous "Prince of Denmark's March," the earliest evidence of Clarke is as a chorister at the **Chapel Royal** when James II was crowned in 1685.

By 1692, he had been appointed **organist** at Winchester College, and on 6 June 1699, he was appointed vicar-choral at St. Paul's Cathedral. He moved up to organist in January 1704. On 15 May 1704, Francis Pigott, organist at the Chapel Royal, died, and Clarke and **William Croft** were sworn in as joint organists to replace him. It appears that Clarke ended his own life, perhaps owing to an unhappy love affair, by shooting himself on 1 December 1707. He composed 22 **anthems**, 10 **odes**, 2 settings of the **Te Deum**, 2 **suites** for wind band, 2 suites for **harpsichord**, over 40 other short works for harpsichord, and the incidental music for 8 plays.

CLAVICHORD. Small **keyboard** instrument widespread in the Renaissance but surviving into the Baroque mostly in Germany, Spain, Portugal, and Scandinavia as a practice and composing instrument. The keyboard causes brass blades, or *tangents*, to rise and strike **tuned** strings, whose vibrations are communicated to a soundboard that amplifies them. Because the tangents remain in contact with the strings after being struck, they affect the pitch and may modify the sound in expressive ways if the player manipulates the keys. However, the volume of the clavichord is very small, and so it was not suitable for public performance.

CLAVIER-ÜBUNG **(Ger. "Keyboard Practice").** Set of four publications of **keyboard** music composed by **Johann Sebastian Bach**. The general title, *Clavier-Übung*, is Bach's, following the preceding cantor of St. Thomas Church, **Leipzig**, **Johann Kuhnau**, who published two volumes under this title in 1689 and 1692.

Clavier-Übung, Part I contains six **partitas (suites)** BWV 825–830, published from 1726 to 1731.

Clavier-Übung, Part II, 1735, contains the Italian **Concerto**, BWV 971, for solo keyboard and the Ouverture in the French Style, BWV 831, which contains a **French overture** followed by movements of a **dance** suite.

Clavier-Übung, Part III, 1739, contains mostly **organ** music for Lutheran liturgy, sometimes called the Lutheran **Organ Mass**. That part is bounded by the great **Preludium** in E-flat Major at the beginning and the so-called St. Anne **Fugue**, also in E-flat, at the end. Four unrelated duets for solo organ follow.

Clavier-Übung, Part IV, about 1741, is the **Goldberg Variations**.

CLÉRAMBAULT, LOUIS-NICOLAS (19 December 1676, Paris–26 October 1749, Paris). Regarded as one of France's finest **organists** in the first half of the 18th century, Clérambault was organist at the Maison Royale de Saint-Cyr from 1714, St. Sulpice in **Paris** from about the same time, and at the Jacobins of Rue St. Jacques in Paris from 1719. He published one volume of **harpsichord** music in 1704 and one of **organ** music, slightly later, that contains two **suites**. He also composed, probably before 1710, an unpublished volume of solo **violin sonatas** and **trio sonatas** for two violins and **continuo**. As a composer, however, he was most renowned for his 25 French **cantatas**, published in five volumes from 1710 to 1726. Mostly setting scenes from Greek mythology, such as the **lament** and revenge of Medea (*Medée*, 1710), some are richly scored for **flutes** and strings in addition to continuo.

COLEMAN, CHARLES (buried 8 July 1664, London). An important musician in the **London** musical theater, he sang the part of Hymen in Robert White's **masque** *Cupid's Banishment* in 1617, sang the music of **William Lawes** in *The Triumph of Peace* in 1634, but is remembered today as the composer of instrumental music for the first English **opera**, *The Siege of Rhodes*, in 1656.

COLLEGIUM MUSICUM. A German tradition, usually centered on major universities, of amateur and semiprofessional musicians, often students, gathering periodically to play together the fashionable music of the day. Although *collegia* might offer concerts, the atmosphere was generally informal. One important *collegium musicum* was founded by **Georg Philipp Telemann** in **Leipzig** in 1702; its direction was assumed in 1729 by **Johann Sebastian Bach**.

COMÉDIE-BALLET. See BALLET DE COUR.

CONCERTINO. The ensemble of soloists in a concerto grosso. *See also* RIPIENO.

CONCERTO. The common modern understanding of the term is a composition for **orchestra** and one or more outstanding solo instrumentalists usually arranged in three movements, fast-slow-fast. A concerto for one such player is a **solo concerto**; a concerto for more than one is a **concerto grosso**, an appellation made famous by the **Opus 6** concerti grossi of **Arcangelo Corelli**. The concerto exploits the contrasts of the massed ensemble against the one or the few, as well as the virtuosity of the solo parts.

The term dates from the beginning of the Baroque, but such a comparatively precise understanding came only after the turn of the 18th century, when important publications of **Tomaso Albinoni, Giuseppe Torelli**, and above all the **Opus 3** (1711) of **Antonio Vivaldi** appeared to establish the presence of soloists and the three-movement format as central to the concerto genre. But exceptions abound well into the 18th century. Vivaldi composed "concertos" for orchestra without any soloists, the third of **Johann Sebastian Bach**'s **Brandenburg Concertos** has a solo role for every player save the **continuo**, and none of the **Opus 6** concertos of **George Frideric Handel** has three movements.

Bach even titled some of his **church cantatas** "concertos," playing on an older understanding derived from the Italian root *concertare*, meaning "to agree" or "to work together," a 17th-century usage that could be applied to most any composition in the *stile moderno*. More confusion arises from early Baroque writers, such as **Michael Praetorius (*Syntagma Musicum*, 1618)**, who cite the Latin *concertare*, meaning "to contend with," which appears to adumbrate the opposition of the soloists to the larger ensemble. Indeed, in the early 17th century, when so much experimentation produced new generic terms to describe new developments, "concerto" had little consistent usage and was associated with vocal music perhaps more than instrumental music. The earliest known occurrences, the collection of church music and **madrigals** called *Concerti di Andrea, et di Gio. Gabrieli*, published in **Venice** in 1587, as well as the important *Cento Concerti Ecclesiastici* of 1602 (Venice) and the many **sacred concertos** by **Claudio Monteverdi**, **Heinrich Schütz**, and many other Italian and German composers, are essentially vocal art with instrumental accompaniment.

One theory of the origin of the instrumental concerto—and the concomitant narrowing of the generic concept—points to a practice of performing **sonatas** in musical centers of Bologna and **Rome** after 1660, whereby, in certain passages, extra players would double up on parts normally played by one, thus creating the essential contrast between soloist and ensemble. A distinction in status between permanent, salaried players of an establishment and lesser players hired to amplify the music on a specific occasion may also have encouraged the concerto. If a **trio sonata** is performed this way, one arrives immediately at the typical concerto grosso of Corelli, where the solo group consists of two **violins** and **cello**.

The German composer and theorist **Johann Joachim Quantz** wrote in 1752 that the first concertos had been published by Torelli as six *concerti a quattro* in Opus 5 in 1692. Albinoni seems to have established the three-movement fast-slow-fast format as a norm in his Opus 2 of 1700, and in his Opus 5 of 1707, these slow movements have more substantial lyrical solo melodies. But in his Opus 3 of 1711, Vivaldi synthesizes the various treatments of the solo instruments and provides a model of high-level organization based on the ritornello that became the predominant prototype of the genre.

This prototype was adaptable to a variety of Baroque performance contexts, including churches, musical societies, and court entertainments, and so was imitated widely throughout Europe. In Germany, **Georg Philipp Telemann** composed over 100 of them for a remarkable variety of solo instruments. In England, Corelli's student **Francesco Geminiani** carried on his teacher's tradition. In France, Jacques-Christophe Naudot (1690–1762) published a set of solo **flute** concertos in 1735, and **Jean-Marie Leclair** published two important collections of violin concertos, Opus 7 of 1737 and Opus 10 of 1745. The last important Baroque composers of concertos in Italy were **Giuseppe Tartini** and **Pietro Locatelli**. Locatelli expanded the ritornello by using more than one theme, and all his concertos include a **capriccio** or **cadenza** at the end, making what had been anticipated in a few violin concertos of Vivaldi an expected feature of the later concerto.

CONCERTO GROSSO (It. "big concerto"). Although the term's usage in the Baroque was far from consistent, the common understanding today follows that of the theorist **Johann Joachim Quantz**, who defined it in 1752 as a composition for more than one solo instrument and **orchestra**. The fame of **Arcangelo Corelli**'s concerti grossi **Opus 6**, which calls for two **violin** and **cello** soloists, certainly contributed to the modern concept. But even in modern parlance, "concerto grosso" is not always used when the soloists are more than one (e.g., "Concerto for Two Violins" of **Antonio Vivaldi**). In other respects of composition, the concerto grosso does not differ from the norms of **concerto**.

The most famous collections of concerti grossi heard today, besides Corelli's Opus 6, would be the six **Brandenburg Concertos** of **Johann Sebastian Bach** and **George Frideric Handel**'s Opus 6. *See also* SOLO CONCERTO.

CONCERT SPIRITUEL. One of the earliest important concert series in the modern sense, the Concert Spirituel was founded by Anne Danican Philidor (1681–1728) for the performance of instrumental music and sacred music with Latin texts on religious feast days when theaters were closed, according to the terms of a privilege granted by the **Paris** Opéra. The inaugural concert was given on 18 March 1725. The proscription against **operatic** works and the French language was relaxed beginning in 1728.

The Concert Spirituel quickly became a prime venue for the presentation of new works and virtuoso singers and players. The performances, until 1784 given at the Salle des Suisses at the Tuileries, could be sumptuous, as when **Georg Philip Telemann** saw his setting of Psalm 72 performed there with forces numbering over 100 musicians. The series ended during the French Revolution in 1790 but, by then, had spawned many imitators in Europe.

CONSONANCE. A harmonic interval with relatively little intrinsic tension. In Baroque music, consonant intervals include the so-called perfect consonances of the unison, octave, and fifth and the imperfect consonances of the minor third, major third, minor sixth, and major sixth. Baroque theorists believed, with Pythagoras, that consonances are produced by frequency ratios of relatively small whole numbers (e.g., octave 2:1, fifth 3:2), thus are acoustic consonances, but then had difficulty accounting for what might be termed "syntactic consonances," such as the minor seventh (16:9), an acoustic **dissonance** that is often treated as a consonance in Baroque **counterpoint**, and the perfect fourth (4:3), an acoustic consonance often treated as a dissonance when made with the bass **voice**.

CONSORT. In modern usage, a consort is an ensemble of like instruments of varied pitch ranges gathered to play music of the 16th and 17th centuries, especially English music. Thus, we have "consort of **viols**" or "viol consort," "**recorder** consort," and occasionally a "consort of voices." In the Baroque, the term instead usually referred to an instrumental ensemble of mixed types, or sometimes to the music itself. (The oft-heard "broken consort," indicating a group of **string** and wind instruments, appears nowhere in 17th-century sources and seems to be an anachronistic invention.) The 1591 anonymous source *The Honourable Entertainment* describes "an exquisite consort, wherein was the **lute**, Bandora, Bass-Violl, Citterne, Treble-violl, and **Flute**," a combination indicated for a number of consort publications thereafter. However, imprecision or flexibility in the desired performing instruments is the rule in 17th-century sources of consort music.

Consort music, while in style having little connection with the Italian Baroque, was the most important genre of music for ensemble in England through the early Restoration period. Important composers include **William Lawes**, especially in his collection *The Royal Consort*, **Matthew Locke**, and **Henry Purcell**.

CONTINUO. Ensemble of at least one melodic bass instrument and one chord-playing instrument (most frequently **harpsichord**, **lute**, **theorbo**, or **guitar** for secular music, **organ** for sacred music) that provides the harmonic progressions and structure in Baroque compositions. Beginning as an efficient and simple frame for **operatic monody** around 1600, the continuo became so customary that Baroque scores include a **figured bass** for continuos even when a large ensemble provided all the necessary harmonic information. In **solo sonatas** and **trio sonatas**, the bass melody was as important to the **contrapuntal texture** as the featured solo instruments, often engaging in **imitation** and full of motivic references in the best examples. Continuo practice fell out of use in the late 18th century when slower harmonic rhythms in periodic phrases made its power of harmonic articulation unnecessary. *See also* THOROUGHBASS.

CONTINUO ARIA. An **aria** for vocal soloist accompanied only by the **continuo**.

CONTINUO MADRIGAL. A **madrigal** for one or two vocal parts, accompanied by **continuo**. Appearing in Italy early in the 17th century as one of many experiments with **monodic texture**, it eventually replaced the traditional madrigal of four or more vocal parts that required no instruments because the pitches sung by the singers supplied all necessary harmonic content. By assuming this harmonic role, the continuo allowed more dramatic vocal composition for soloists.

The continuo madrigal had evolved smoothly into the chamber **cantata** by the mid-17th century.

CONTRAPUNTAL. Adjective form of **counterpoint**.

COOKE, HENRY (c. 1615, Litchfield, England–13 July 1672, Hampton Court). Composer who influenced considerably the generation of English composers coming of age during the Restoration through his teaching and the boys' choir called the Children of the **Chapel Royal**, which he started from nothing and built to a high standard of performance. Cooke trained the boys, including **Pelham Humfrey** and **John Blow**, not only in singing but also in **lute**, **organ**, and **violin**. Cooke wrote two acts for England's first **opera**, *The Siege of Rhodes*, in 1656 and sang the part of Solyman. This music is lost. He also composed 32 **anthems**, 10 **odes** and songs, 3 devotional songs, 2 Latin **motets**, a setting of the Nicene Creed, and a set of funeral sentences.

Cooke was trained in the chapel of King Charles I and fought for the royalists during the civil war. He was made master of the Children of the Chapel Royal on 29 September 1660 and retired from that post, owing to illness, on 24 June 1772.

CORELLI, ARCANGELO (17 February 1653, Fusignano, Italy–8 January 1713, Rome). Composer who became a legend throughout Europe in his own lifetime through his **violin** playing and pedagogy and his six publications of instrumental music for **strings**. The set of violin **sonatas** Opus 5 and **concerti grossi Opus 6**, which contains the famous **Christmas Concerto**, have been studied and played more or less continuously since their first appearance, thus ranking as two of the earliest classics in the Western tradition.

Corelli, the last of five children, was named for his father, a prosperous landowner, who had died one month before he was born, and was raised by his mother Santa Raffini Corelli. He is reported to have studied with a priest in Faenza but received his principal training in Bologna, beginning in 1666.

There, he could learn from a number of established players and composers associated with the great church of San Petronio. In 1670, he entered the Accademia Filarmonica.

The next documented appearance of Corelli comes from **Rome** in 1675, when he is listed as a member of an **orchestra** playing **oratorios** for Lent. Similar engagements follow through 1679, when Corelli himself mentions in a letter that he has entered the service of Queen Christina of Sweden, who had taken up residence in Rome following her conversion to Catholicism. She is the dedicatee of his first publication, the **trio sonatas** Opus 1 of 1681. Its success was unparalleled at the time and would see 39 reprints before the end of the 18th century.

By this point, Corelli was one of the leading musicians in Rome. In February 1687, he is documented leading a tremendous ensemble of 150 string players and 100 singers for an *accademia di musica* of **Bernardo Pasquini** at Queen Christina's Palazzo Riario. On 9 July of that year, he was hired by Cardinal Pamphili as *maestro di musica* and went to live in his palace. In 1690, he transferred to the household of Cardinal Ottoboni, where *accademie di musica* were regularly held on Monday evenings. Corelli dedicated his Opus 4 to Ottoboni.

He acquired wealth and honors. In 1684, he was admitted to the *Congregazione di Santa Cecilia*, along with **Alessandro Scarlatti**, and on 26 April 1706, along with Scarlatti and Pasquini, to the Arcadian Academy of Rome. In May 1707 and April 1708, he worked with the young **George Frideric Handel**, performing two of his early oratorios.

By 1708, Corelli's health was no longer good, and he retired later that year, possibly to devote himself to composition. In 1712, he concluded an agreement with Estienne Roger of Amsterdam for the publication of his **concertos** Opus 6. But he died before the publication appeared, and he was buried in the church of Santa Maria della Rotonda (Pantheon) in Rome.

Aside from a few other instrumental compositions, Corelli's legacy comes down in his six publications, containing 48 trio sonatas, 12 sonatas for solo violin, and 12 concerti grossi. Indeed, he is one of the first composers who owe their international fame to the medium of publication rather than manuscript.

Arcangelo Corelli's Publications

Opus 1	*Sonate a tre* (two violins, continuo)	Rome, 1681
Opus 2	*Sonate da camera a tre* (two violins, continuo)	Rome, 1685
Opus 3	*Sonate a tre* (two violins, continuo)	Rome, 1689
Opus 4	*Sonate a tre* (two violins, continuo)	Rome, 1694
Opus 5	*Sonate* (violin and bass)	Rome, 1700
Opus 6	*Concerti grossi* (concertino: two violins, cello; ripieno: two violins, viola, basso continuo)	Amsterdam, 1714

In modern times, Corelli has not been considered the innovator in composition that his contemporaries heard, quite possibly because his techniques have become so fundamental to composition since 1700 that we have lost sight of how original they were for his time. His contemporary **Georg Muffat**, composer and theorist, remarked in his *Auserlesene Instrumental-Musik* of 1701 that Corelli had invented "a new manner of Harmony, never before heard in these parts," perhaps referring to basic techniques of harmonic embedding on which composers elaborated for the next two centuries. *See* the introduction for an explanation of the technique.

CORI SPEZZATI (It. "split choirs"). **Texture** in which independent melodies of a single **polyphonic** composition are distributed among two or more distinct choirs, which often sing at considerable distance from each other in a church. Such polychoral music frequently overlaps one choir with another and, at climactic moments, calls for all choirs to sing together. Evidence from northern Italian churches in the late 16th century indicates that one or more of the choirs may have been instrumental, affording an even greater contrast of timbre.

Tradition associates the practice with the Basilica San Marco in **Venice** because of its widely separated choral galleries, each with its own **organ**, and especially because of the spectacular works of Andrea (c. 1510–1586) and **Giovanni Gabrieli**, Claudio Merulo (1533–1604), Giovanni Croce (1557–1609), and others composing there in the last quarter of the 16th century. However, firm evidence of polychoral music in other northern Italian cities is earlier: from Treviso in 1521, from Ferrara in 1529, from Bergamo in 1536.

In the early Baroque, **Michael Praetorius**, **Johann Hermann Schein**, **Samuel Scheidt**, and **Heinrich Schütz** continued the tradition into the 17th century as it faded elsewhere, using German as well as Latin texts. Vestiges of the technique appear in certain choral works of **Johann Sebastian Bach**, especially the **motets**, and in certain **English oratorios** of **George Frideric Handel**.

CORNETT (It. *cornetto*, Ger. *Zink*, Fr. *cornaboux*). A wind instrument made first of animal horn and then of wood with a conical bore and fingerholes, widely used in the 16th and 17th centuries. The air in the column is set into vibration by the player's lips, and the fingering resembles **recorder** fingering.

The cornett is prominent in ceremonial works of the early Baroque, in sacred music of the **Venetian** school, in **Claudio Monteverdi**'s first **opera** *L'Orfeo* and his **Vespers of 1610**, and in conjunction with **organs** and brass instruments to support **choral** singing into the 18th century.

Cornetto. Modern copy by John McCann. Photo by Miles Dudgeon.

CORO (It. "chorus"). Composition ending an *opera seria* by uniting all the principal characters in a single number. Each singer has his or her own melody, but all sing the same words, which nearly always express the sentiments of the *lieta fine* (It. "happy ending") that was conventional for Baroque **opera**. Because only the main characters sing, and because there is only one voice to each vocal line, the *coro* is dramatically and sonically distinct from the operatic **chorus**, and that is why the Italian word is retained in English-language discussions of *opera seria*.

CORONATION ANTHEMS. Set of four **anthems** composed by **George Frideric Handel** and performed on 11 October 1727 for the coronation of King George II. Scored for a large five- to seven-**voice chorus**, woodwinds, **trumpets**, **timpani**, and **strings**, they introduced to the English public the weight of choral sound associated with Handel's later **English oratorios**.

CORRENTE. Triple-**meter dance**, closely related to the French **courante** but thought to be livelier in **tempo** and simpler in its **counterpoint**.

CORRETTE, MICHEL (10 April 1707, Rouen–21 January 1795, Paris). **Organist** and teacher with a predilection for the lighter genres of composition, Corrette was musical director from 1732 to 1739 of the theater at Foire St. Germain and St. Laurent where he composed vaudevilles and *divertissements* for the *opéra comique*. He was organist at Sainte Marie from 1737 until 1790. From the late 1730s, he wrote method books containing detailed information about 18th-century performance practice.

COUNCIL OF TRENT. The 19th Ecumenical Council of the Roman Catholic Church (Trent, northern Italy, 13 December 1545–4 December 1563). Decrees specific to liturgical music were issued from sessions 22 to 24 (September 1562–November 1563) and provided that liturgical music should make words easy to understand and that no "lascivious or impure" elements of secular music should intrude. Abolishing **polyphony** in favor of chant may have been discussed but was not legislated. A number of composers, including **Giovanni da Palestrina**, used **inventive homorhythmic textures** in polyphony to clarify diction to follow the Council's wishes, although this effort weakened with distance from **Rome**. Nevertheless, the coincident invention of radically new **operatic** textures at the close of the 16th century helped to define consciously the church style, the *stile antico*, by rejecting traditional **counterpoint**.

COUNTERPOINT. **Polyphonic** musical **texture** featuring more or less equally salient melodies, or **voices**. In Baroque music theory, the term is nearly synonymous with composition, and early in the period, an important distinction was drawn between traditional and contemporary practices. The stricter syntax derived from high-Renaissance church music might be termed *contrapunto osservato*, *musica antica*, *lo stile antico*, *la prima pratica*, or *contrapunctus gravis*, while the later freer counterpoint might be termed *contrapunto commune*, *musica moderna*, *lo stile moderno*, *la seconda pratica*, or *contrapunctus luxurians*. Specific techniques of counterpoint important to the Baroque include free counterpoint, **invertible counterpoint**, **cantus firmus**, **ostinato**, and various kinds of **imitation**. *See also* COUNCIL OF TRENT; *GRADUS AD PARNASSUM*; HOMOPHONY; HOMORHYTHMIC; MONOPHONY.

COUNTERSUBJECT. A melody heard in **counterpoint** against a **subject**. In a **fugue**, the opening **voice** presents the countersubject while the second entering voice presents the subject.

COUPERIN, FRANÇOIS (*"le grand,"* **10 November 1668, Paris–11 September 1733, Paris**). Recognized in his own day as *le grand*, "the great" one of perhaps the most famous musical family in France, Couperin's compositions for **harpsichord** capped the French "classical" *claveciniste* tradition and include 27 **suites** or *ordres*, as he entitled them, 8 **preludes**, and an independent **allemande**. He also made a distinct contribution to Baroque chamber music with his 12 *concerts* appearing in his third volume of harpsichord music (see chart), 6 **trio sonatas**, and 2 suites for **viols** with **figured bass**. A church musician for his whole career, his innumerable **organ improvisations** are lost, of course, but he left evidence of what they might have sounded like in his 2 **organ masses** and 18 other **versets**. He also composed about 40 **motets** (12 of these are lost), and 3 **Tenebrae** services (music for Holy Week), with perhaps 6 more lost. Other vocal music includes 11 *airs* (songs) and at least 5 vocal **canons**.

His **keyboard** suites or *ordres*, published in four books between 1713 and 1730, moved quickly to the center of French harpsichord repertory. They often depart from the standardized grouping of allemande, **courante**, **sarabande**, and **gigue**. He composed many of the **dances** as *espèces de portraits* with descriptive and fanciful titles accompanying or replacing the standard generic dance classification: *La Majestueuse* ("the majestic woman"), *La Ténébreuse* ("the mysterious woman"), *Le Petit-Rien* ("the little nothing"). Like the "classical" suite, the movements of Couperin's *ordres* are unified by **key** but varied in **tempo** and **meter**.

In his publications of 1724–1726 (see chart), Couperin recognizes two principal sources of his compositional inspiration and technique: the music of **Arcangelo Corelli** and **Jean-Baptiste Lully**. He makes it his business to demonstrate the deep commonality of musical language beneath the superficial differences of tone and **ornamentation**, especially in *Les Goûts-réunis*.

Couperin's father, Charles, had been organist at St. Gervais, taking over for **Louis Couperin**, since 1661. François probably began his musical studies with his father, but Charles died in 1679, and 10-year-old François was most fortunate to be befriended and tutored by Jacques-Denis Thomelin, the king's own organist (*organiste du roi*). He began to substitute for **Michel-Richard de Lalande**, the new organist, and on 1 November 1685, the church council awarded him a salary of 300 livres, and he became permanent organist at St. Gervais the following year.

François Couperin's Major Publications

Title	Date (all in Paris)	Contents
Pièces de Clavecin . . . Premier Livre	1713	Five *ordres* for harpsichord
L'Art de Toucher le Clavecin	1716	Treatise on harpsichord playing; one allemande and eight preludes
Second Livre de Pièces de Clavecin	1716	Seven *ordres* for harpsichord
Troisiéme Livre de Pièces de Clavecin	1722	Seven *ordres* for harpsichord; four *Concerts Royaux*, chamber works for violin, flute, oboe, viol, bassoon, and harpsichord
Les Goûts-réunis, ou Nouveaux Concerts	1724	Ten *concerts*, chamber works, mostly for one treble instrument and continuo; trio sonata for two violins and continuo, *L'Apothéose de Corelli*
Apothéose Composé à la Mémoire Immortelle de l'Incomparable Monsieur de Lully	1725	Chamber work for two violins, two flutes, and other unspecified instruments
Les Nations, Sonades et Suites de Simphonies en Trio	1726	Trio sonatas, each paired with a dance suite
Pièces de Violes avec la Basse Chifrée	1728	Two suites for viols with continuo
Quatrième Livre de Pièces de Clavecin	1730	Eight *ordres* for harpsichord

On 26 April 1689, he married Marie-Anne Ansault, who had good connections in the government. The couple had at least four and probably five children, two of whom died in infancy and one of whom, the talented harpsichordist Marguerite-Antoinette, eventually succeeded her father as court harpsichordist.

On 26 December 1693, King Louis XIV chose Couperin to succeed his teacher Thomelin as *organiste du roi*, in which position he earned 600 livres for three months duty per year. This great leap in status opened to Couperin the highest levels of society, and he soon became the teacher of the Duke of Burgundy, the Count of Toulouse, the dowager Princess of Conti, and two daughters of the Duke of Bourbon. He also had ties to the English Stuart court in exile outside **Paris** in Saint Germain-en-Laye, and documentary evidence shows that he played in concerts at Versailles. About 1702, he was made *Chevalier de l'Ordre de Latran*.

When Couperin published his second volume of harpsichord music in 1717, the title page could identify him as *Monsieur Couperin*, "organist of the king's chapel, director of his majesty's chamber music, and professor of composition and accompaniment for my Lord the Dauphin, Duke of Burgundy." He was one of the three or four most famous musicians in France by this point.

In the years following the death of King Louis XIV (1715), it appears that Couperin occupied himself less with teaching and music at court and more with publishing his own music. In 1723, to lighten his workload, he managed to have his cousin Nicolas Couperin appointed as his assistant at St. Gervais. In 1730, declining health forced him to give up his court appointments.

COUPERIN, LOUIS (c. 1626, Chaumes-en-Brie, France–29 August 1661, Paris). Considered as the second-most important composer of one of the great musical families of France, after his nephew **François Couperin** (*"le grand"*), Louis's **harpsichord** music includes 12 **preludes**, 12 **chaconnes**, 17 **allemandes**, 32 courantes, 31 **sarabandes**, and about 20 other **dance** movements of various types. His **organ** music includes 2 preludes, 33 **fugues** (some entitled *"fantasie"*), 27 plainchant **versets**, and 8 other works. There are also two fantasies for **viol** duet, one **solo sonata** and two **trio sonatas** (called *"simphonie"*), and two fantasies for wind band.

Almost nothing is known of his life before 12 August 1651, when his organ manuscript first gives **Paris** as the place of composition, indicating a move from his home area. Sometime in 1651 or 1652, **Johann Jacob Froberger** visited Paris and evidently exercised considerable influence on Couperin. Couperin was appointed organist at the church of St. Gervais on 9 April 1653 and lived in the organist's lodging in Paris with his two brothers. He may also have been employed by the diplomat Abel Servien of Meudon in 1656 and

1658. In the mid-1650s, he entered the service of King Louis XIV as a treble viol player and is recorded as playing in at least four **ballets**.

COURANTE. Triple-**meter dance** in stately **tempo**, often appearing as the second of the obligatory dances of the "classical" **suite**, after the **allemande**. The earliest examples appear in the late 16th century, closely associated with the Italian **corrente**.

COURT ODE. *See* ODE.

CROFT, WILLIAM (baptized 30 December 1678, Nether Ettington, Warwicks–14 August 1727, Bath). Perhaps best known today as the composer of **hymn** tunes, especially "St. Anne" ("O God, Our Help in Ages Past"), Croft was the source of 85 **anthems** and at least 8 **odes** often used in civic celebrations, such as the signing of the Treaty of Utrecht. He also composed 5 Anglican **services**, 18 **sonatas**, and various **organ voluntaries** and songs.

Croft seems to have been a protégé of **John Blow**. By 1700, he was organist at St. Anne's Church in Soho. When **Jeremiah Clarke** died in 1707, Croft succeeded him as organist of the **Chapel Royal**, and when Blow died in 1708, Croft succeeded him as composer and master of children. In July 1713, he took a doctorate of music from Oxford University along with **Johann Christoph Pepusch**. His two-volume collection, *Musica Sacra* (1724), was the first set of anthems to be engraved in score rather than parts.

D

DA CAPO ARIA. Baroque **aria** form in ternary structure (ABA). Arising in the last quarter of the 17th century, the da capo aria dominated *opera seria*, **cantata**, and **oratorio** composition in the 18th century almost to the exclusion of all other aria types.

The first large section (A) of the aria ends in the **key** of its beginning with a melodic-harmonic **cadence** sufficiently strong to conclude the whole work. But the second section (B) follows immediately, usually much shorter than (A) with reduced **orchestration**, almost always in a contrasting key, often in a different **tempo** or **meter**, often modulating away from the key of its opening, all these effects creating significant tension to resolve. At the end of the (B) section in the score, the composer writes the message *da capo* (It. "from the top"), indicating that the first section (A) should be literally repeated. Thus, although only two sections of music are composed, a ternary form (ABA) results in performance.

In practice, the return of the (A) section is not always literal. The singer often adds melodic embellishments to the composer's original lines. Sometimes the composer skips over the aria's instrumental introduction (ritornello) by writing *dal segno* (It. "from the sign") instead of *da capo*, indicating that the (A) section should repeat not from the first measure but from some point further on.

The degree of contrast between the (A) and (B) sections may correspond to the semantic content of the poem. The (A) section will set from two to six lines of verse, usually four; the (B) section usually two. The **librettist** writes the poem with the da capo aria in mind, and a sharp contrast of sentiment in the (B) verses will elicit a corresponding musical contrast from the composer.

Because the (A) section of the da capo aria usually sets more text, it must be longer and its expression dominates the plot at the point it is heard. This section depends upon ritornello technique for its mid-level organization. The **ritornello** introduces the aria's melodic, harmonic, and rhythmic ideas as an instrumental introduction. The vocal passages derive directly from the ritornello, and the singing is interrupted by shorter ritornellos to articulate the form in the manner of an instrumental **concerto**.

The following is a diagram of Cleopatra's aria "Tu la mia stella sei," from Act I of **George Frideric Handel**'s *Giulio Cesare in Egitto* (1724). In the (A) quatrain, Cleopatra, who has set her sights on Julius Caesar, sings that her star of hope gives her pleasure; in the (B) quatrain, that shortly will be seen how constant and loving her heart is. The (B) section is, therefore, a subtle variation on the theme of hope, so Handel retains the tempo, meter, and **violin** and bass accompaniment of the (A) section but uses minor **modes** rather than the major modes, perhaps to suggest some doubt on her part.

It is quite typical that Cleopatra's aria could be sung by any character in any **opera** who is hoping for something. The poem remains abstract, never referring by name to a single character, thing, or event that would identify these words as those of Cleopatra in the opera *Giulio Cesare in Egitto*. This abstraction allowed arias to be substituted and transferred from one production to another, often to meet the demands of a particular singer or meet some other contingency. On the other hand, the da capo arias in oratorios and **passions**, perhaps owing to their biblical texts and subjects, generally cannot transfer so easily.

(A)		Ritornello (9 m.)	B-flat major
	Tu la mia stella sei,	Vocal solo (24 m.)	B-flat major (14 m.)
	Amabile speranza,		
	E porgi ai desir miei,	Ritornello fragment (3 m.)	F major (10 m.)
	Un grato bel piacer.	Vocal solo (32 m.)	B-flat major
	Tu la mia stella sei,		B-flat major (2 m.)
	Amabile speranza,	Ritornello (7 m.)	C minor (11 m.)
	E porgi ai desir miei,		B-flat major (19 m.)
	Un grato bel piacer.		B-flat major
(B)	Qual sia di questo core	Vocal solo	D minor (2 m.)
	La stabile costanza		C minor (6 m.)
	E quanto possa amore,		D minor (10 m.)
	S'ha in breve da veder		
(A)			
	Tu la mia stella sei,		
	etc.		

DANCE. A principal form of instrumental music in the Renaissance whose **metric** patterns, phrase structures, and forms were integrated into experiments in "operatic" **sonatas** and **concertos** in the early 17th century to ground the musical syntax of instrumental music in the high Baroque. In order to coordinate their complicated steps, Renaissance dancers required strong rhythmic cues from the dance music: strong beats as distinct from weak, phrase endings, **cadences**. In such an environment, the essential syntax of **functional harmony** arose during the 16th century as the primary means of articulation.

In contrast with the vocal genres, the continuity of dance traditions from the 16th into the 17th century was unbroken. All the innumerable local traditions persisted, with new popular dances, such as the **courante**, replacing older ones, such as the *branle*, and through household **keyboard** and **string** instrumental arrangements, they expanded their appeal beyond the practice of actual dancing. As the Baroque wore on, many dance types ceased to be danced but lived on in stylized instrumental versions containing some vestige of their original rhythmic characters. **Suites** of such dances were among the most widely practiced and popular genres of keyboard music through the end of the period.

Ballets were an essential component of the earliest French **opera** tradition, the *tragédie lyrique*.

So fundamental was the influence of dance on compositional techniques and the musical language of the Baroque that typical dance rhythms and meters, even their characteristic **binary forms**, found their way into genres that otherwise had no connection with dance: **trio sonatas** *da camera*, **solo sonatas**, **solo concertos**, **concerti grossi**, **French overtures**, even **church cantatas** and **organ** works. Operas began fashioning short **arias** as dance forms in the mid-17th century, and arias with the strong metric stamp of **sicilianas**, **minuets**, or other dances are heard through the end of the period. *See also* ALLEMANDE; BOURRÉE; CHACONNE; CORRENTE; GALLIARD; GIGUE; HORNPIPE; LOURE; PASSEPIED; PAVAN; SARABANDE.

D'ANGLEBERT, JEAN HENRY (baptized 1 April 1629, Bar-le-Duc, France–23 April 1691, Paris). His *Pièces de Clavecin avec la Manière de Jouer* of 1689, containing richly engraved **dance suites**, **organ fugues**, and arrangements of music by **Jean-Baptiste Lully** for his pupil the Princesse de Conti, is one of the most important publications of the French *clavecinistes*. Its table of **ornaments** was copied by **Johann Sebastian Bach** and became his standard. Other D'Anglebert manuscripts contain arrangements of **orchestral** and **opera** music by Jean-Baptiste Lully and of **lute** music by **Denis Gaultier** and his contemporaries.

Virtually nothing is known of his early life and musical training. The earliest documentation of his residence in **Paris** is his marriage to Madelaine Champagne on 11 October 1659. He entered the service of King Louis XIV on 23 October 1662 as *ordinaire de la musique de la chambre du roi pour le clavecin* ("in charge of chamber music for **harpsichord**").

***DER VOLLKOMMENE CAPELLMEISTER* (Johann Mattheson, 1739).** An encyclopedic introduction to the art of professional musicianship at the end of the Baroque, the treatise is the most ambitious of **Johann Mattheson**'s many writings. Its most original aspects include a summary of the relationship of musical composition to **rhetoric** and language in general, a comprehensive *Affektenlehre* (theory of emotional expression in music), and a theory of good melody, which he believed to be the soul of a good composition.

Mattheson's theory of melody includes what the Baroque knew as "**invention**," working with small musical ideas or motives. Thereafter, he identifies five qualities necessary for the composition of a good melody: *facility*, or accessibility to listeners; *clarity*, the expression of a single passion; *flow*, a melody without interruption, alluding perhaps to the fundamental Baroque continuity of the motor rhythm; *charm*, the construction of melodies largely from stepwise motion, avoiding large leaps; and *variety*, avoiding too many similar gestures in succession.

***DIDO AND AENEAS* (Henry Purcell, 1689).** Although in his own lifetime it was the least known of his stage works, today *Dido and Aeneas* is the best-known and most critically esteemed music drama of **Henry Purcell**. Purcell's autograph score is lost, and the oldest copy of the **opera** is the so-called Tenbury manuscript of the last quarter of the 18th century. Thus, certain details of the first performance, such as the vocal ranges of the **chorus**, remain in question.

It appears that the opera was commissioned by Josias Priest to be performed by his Chelsea boarding school for girls, and the first known performance took place on an unknown date in 1689. Nahum Tate, poet laureate of England, wrote the **libretto**.

The plot is a free adaptation of Book IV of Virgil's *Aeneid*, in which Prince Aeneas of Troy sues Queen Dido of Carthage for love, only to abandon her and set out for Italy in order to found the city of **Rome**. The queen, in despair and disgrace, kills herself in the final scene. *Dido and Aeneas* is one of the very few Baroque operas to end tragically.

Tate adapted the story to safeguard the young girls from too much sensuality and to provide more solo roles. He invents the queen's confidant, Belinda, as well as a troop of delightful witches, who, disguised as divinities, persuade Aeneas to set sail for "Italian ground." Purcell sets their mischief with comic music, and thus, the opera winsomely combines the comic with the tragic. The witches, the prince's Trojan sailors, and the queen's courtiers provide Purcell with opportunities for many fine choral numbers. There are also **dance** movements in the tradition of French opera: "The Triumphing Dance," "Echo Dance," "Sailors' Dance," and "Witches' Dance."

Because the **da capo aria** had not yet arrived in England, the pace of *Dido and Aeneas* is faster than that of most any *opera seria*, and the "songs" showcase the typical 17th-century structural devices of refrain, repetition between soloist and chorus, and especially the **ostinato**, the most famous example of which is Dido's last **aria**, "When I am laid in earth," composed over a descending **chromatic** bass ostinato traditionally associated with mourning.

Dido and Aeneas calls for as many as four solo sopranos (Dido, courtiers, possibly the Sorceress), one baritone (Aeneas), and one tenor (sailor). The role of the Sorceress is variously sung by a soprano, contralto, or baritone. A **string orchestra** of **violins**, **violas**, **cellos**, and string basses plus **continuo** is required. The opera takes about 45 minutes to perform.

DIMINUTION. Transformation of a melody by shortening all the durations of its notes by a fixed ratio (e.g., twice as fast, four times as fast, etc). *See also* AUGMENTATION.

Example. Johann Sebastian Bach, Fugue in C-sharp Minor from the *Well-Tempered Clavier*, Book I, mm. 35–36. Diminution of top melody in m. 35 occurs in m. 36.

DISSONANCE. A harmonic interval with significant intrinsic tension, requiring movement to a **consonance** (resolution). In Baroque music, dissonant intervals include the minor second, major second, minor seventh, major seventh, and all **augmented** or diminished intervals. When the bass **voice** of a **polyphonic texture** produces a perfect fourth, it is also treated as a dissonance.

DIVERTISSEMENT. A distinct scene composed of songs, **choruses**, and **dances** performed within a 17th-century or early 18th-century French theater piece, such as a *comédie-ballet* or *tragédie-ballet*. Conceived most often as entertainments apart from the main drama, in the work of **Jean-Baptiste Lully**, they may be integrated into the action. In the early 18th century, composers, such as **André Campra**, often composed *divertissements* as independent theater pieces.

DOUBLE COUNTERPOINT. *See* INVERTIBLE COUNTERPOINT.

DOUBLE DOTTING. Also called "overdotting," it is the practice of playing a typical dotted rhythmic pattern—a dotted quarter followed by an eighth note, for example—as if there were a second dot next to the quarter and as if the eighth note were a sixteenth, thus increasing the ratio of inequality from 3:1 to 7:1.

Example. George Frideric Handel, *Messiah*, opening Sinfony, mm. 1–4, original notation

Example. George Frideric Handel, *Messiah*, opening Sinfony, mm. 1–4, as performed with double dotting

This performance practice is associated particularly with the **French overture**, the opening section of which presents a long passage of dotted rhythms in slow **tempo**. Most musicologists believe that the 17th-century performance tradition provides that these passages be performed in double-dotted fashion, despite the notation, and such an interpretation is what is normally heard in performances and recordings of French overtures and their related genres since about 1970, including the example above. However, the scholar Frederick Neumann claimed that the routine practice of double-dotting was fictitious, and the matter is still controversial.

DOUBLE FUGUE. A **fugue** that presents two **subjects** in **invertible counterpoint**. In one type, the time interval between the first entrance of the subject and another subject in a different **voice** is very short, creating the effect of hearing two different subjects at once, which then may be combined in invertible counterpoint with each other and with new **countersubjects** as the fugue proceeds. In another type, the fugue opens with a substantial section in **imitation** on a single subject, **cadences**, and follows with another section using a different subject, concluding with a third section that combines the two subjects.

DRAGHI, ANTONIO (1634?, Rimini, Italy–16 January 1700, Vienna).
The principal influence on the music at the imperial court in **Vienna** during the last third of the 17th century, Draghi composed about 120 works of various types for the musical stage, including introductions to ballets, small comedies, and many *opere serie*, some of them to his own **librettos**, as well as about 50 chamber **cantatas**, 16 **oratorios**, 29 *sepolcri*, and 2 **masses**.

His musical career began at age 11 when he was engaged as a soprano singer at the basilica of San Antonio in Padua in November 1645. Singing engagements in Ferrara and **Venice** followed in the 1650s. In 1658, he was appointed as a bass singer for the imperial court in Vienna and came to notice with his first libretto for the **opera** *L'Almonte*, with music by Giuseppe Tricarico (1623–1697), performed in Vienna on 9 June 1661. He wrote other librettos and then his own music for *La Mascherata* in 1666. By 1669, he was *Kapellmeister* for the dowager empress, chosen over **Giovanni Legrenzi**, and then *Kapellmeister* to the imperial court in 1682, a position he held until his death.

***DRAMMA PER MUSICA* (It. "drama through music" or "drama for music").** Term applied to the aesthetic principle that founded the earliest **operas** (c. 1600–1640) as well as to the operas themselves composed at that time. The principle, revolutionary in the history of Western music, is that music should be a dramatic agent, expressing the states of characters and capable of narration beyond the text in a staged drama. Genres descending from this concept just in the Baroque period include all forms of opera and their subgenres (**aria**, **recitative**, *sinfonia*, etc.), as well as **oratorio**, **cantata**, **sacred concerto**, **sacred symphony**, and possibly the **solo sonata** and **solo concerto**.

DRESDEN. The capital city of Saxony developed quickly into one of the most important centers for Baroque music from the very beginning of the period, when **Michael Praetorius** and **Heinrich Schütz** were first appointed to the Hofkapelle. After the Thirty Years War broke up the brilliant chapel music from about 1531 to 1554, the revival of music in Dresden brought in numbers of Italian musicians well acquainted with the latest developments, particularly in **opera**. By the 18th century, the Dresden opera was internationally famous and counted **Antonio Lotti** and **Johann Adolf Hasse** among its principal composers.

Dresden began to build a reputation in music after 1547, when Duke Moritz achieved the rank of elector. On 22 September 1548, Elector Moritz revived the Hofkapelle. Praetorius became *de facto* director in 1613, and Schütz was "**organist** and director of musicians" by fall of 1615, *Kapellmeister* in 1621. The school of the Kreuzkirche supplied boys for the principal choir. Support also came from the five town musicians, the *Stadtpfeifer* ("city pipers"), who could provide accompaniment to sacred music and also secular works played on crumhorns, pipes, **cornetts**, dulcians, and **trumpets**.

Under Elector Johann Georg II (ruled 1656–1680), the Hofkapelle recovered from the catastrophic Thirty Years War and, in 1666, numbered 53 musicians. The principal composers of the period were all Italians trained in **Rome**, possibly with **Giacomo Carissimi**: Giovanni Andrea Bontempi (c. 1624–1705), Vincenzo Albrici (1631–1696), and Marco Giuseppe Peranda (1625–1675). Bontempi's *Il Paride* brought recent operatic style to Dresden in 1662, and a new theater, the *Comödienhaus*, opened in 1667 with Pietro Andrea Ziani's (c. 1616–1684) *Il Teseo*.

The reign of Elector Friedrich August I, "the Strong," from 1694 to 1733, increased the musical reputation of the city further. His instrumental ensembles employed players who, departing from traditional practice, specialized in a single instrument, and their precision and quality of performance was renowned. Among these players was the virtuoso **violinist** Johann Georg Pisendel (1687–1755), who studied with both **Giuseppe Torelli** and **Antonio Vivaldi** and then tirelessly promoted the Italian solo violin **concerto** in Dresden, which in turn influenced the new generation of young German composers early in the 18th century: **Johann Sebastian Bach**, **Johann Friedrich Fasch**, **Johann Joachim Quantz**, and others. Indeed, these players may have inspired some of the virtuoso instrumental writing in the Kyrie and Gloria of Bach's **Mass in B Minor**, which were composed for the Dresden court **orchestra**.

Antonio Lotti was persuaded to take a leave from his post at San Marco in **Venice** to direct the opera in Dresden from 1717 to 1719, and three of his operas opened the new Hoftheater and celebrated the wedding of the Crown Prince Friedrich August to Princess Maria Josepha of Austria. The theater could seat 2,000 people, making it one of the largest in Europe.

Sometime after Carnival but before Ascension in 1730, **Hasse** was granted the title of *Kapellmeister* by Elector August I, and Hasse and his wife, the brilliant soprano Faustina Bordoni, arrived there about 6 or 7 July 1731. Thereafter, Hasse composed at least 15 operas for the theaters at Dresden and at Hubertusburg, the elector's summer residence. Many of these were the original settings for **librettos** of **Metastasio**. Hasse remained in Dresden until 1763.

DU MONT, HENRY (born Henry de Thier, c. 1610, Looz near Hasselt, modern Belgium–8 May 1684, Paris). The dominant figure in sacred music in mid-17th-century **Paris**, Du Mont published 114 *petits motets* between 1652 and 1681 and also composed 26 *grands motets*, as well as 37 French psalm settings. His most remarkable and often performed sacred music is the collection of five original plainchant **masses**, an early effort at restoring what was considered a corrupt tradition. His secular music includes 21 songs, 5 **symphonies**, and a few **dance** movements for ensemble. As a professional **organist**, he must have composed or **improvised** a significant body of organ music, but very little survives.

On 14 June 1621, Henry Du Mont and his brother Lambert entered the choir school of Onze-Lieve-Vrouwekerk in Maastricht and continued through the Jesuit college. Henry became organist of the church there in 1629. In Paris, on 4 April 1643, he signed a contract to be organist at the church of St. Paul. He took French nationality in 1647.

In 1652, he published his first volume of motets and became the **harpsichordist** to the Duke of Anjou, brother of King Louis XIV. In July 1660, he was appointed organist to the queen, then as *sous-maître* of the **Chapelle Royale** in July 1664, for one quarter of the year under the court system, then for half the year in 1668. Thereafter, he continued to acquire appointments and benefices, all the while continuing at St. Paul and making frequent trips to Maastricht. He retired in Paris in 1683.

DURANTE, FRANCESCO (31 March 1684, Frattamaggiore, Aversa, Italy–30 September 1755, Naples). Unlike most leading composers working in **Naples** in the early 18th century, Durante made his reputation not in **opera** but in church music, composing more than 25 **masses** in all liturgical styles, 8 **Magnificats**, 3 requiems, 3 sets of **lamentations** for Holy Saturday, 6 litanies, over 30 psalm settings, 13 other **motets**, 6 "spiritual" **cantatas**, and 3 "sacred dramas." His secular music is limited: 12 vocal duets, 11 **concertos**, 4 **sonatas**, 9 **keyboard toccatas**, and at least 6 keyboard sonatas, one of which is entitled "The Four Seasons of the Year." His reputation as a teacher spread through the continent; **Giovanni Pergolesi** and several important post-Baroque composers were his students.

His father, Gaetano, was a woolcomber, and Francesco was his seventh of eleven children. He studied under his uncle at the Conservatorio di San Onofrio a Capuana in Naples until 1705, and on 3 June of that year, his first compositions were heard in Naples. After that, he may have studied in **Rome** with **Bernardo Pasquini**. In 1728, Durante was appointed *primo maestro* of the Conservatorio dei Poveri di Gesù Cristo. He left that post for reasons unknown in 1739 and, on 25 April 1742, was elected *primo maestro* at the oldest conservatory in Naples, Santa Maria di Loreto, which prospered under his leadership. He added the same post at his own school, San Onofrio, on 1 January 1745.

E

EARLY MUSIC REVIVAL. The summation of efforts by musicians and scholars to bring into current performance repertory forgotten musical works of the past. These efforts were largely uncoordinated, made in many different places in Europe and North America with a variety of goals in mind, but all spurred by the conviction that "ancient" music had intrinsic value that should not be lost. The movement is prefigured in certain 18th-century institutions, such as **London**'s **Academy of Ancient Music**, founded in 1726, and **Vienna**'s founding, with the help of **Antonio Caldara**, of the Cecilian Society in 1725, but by far, the lion's share of the early music revival occurred long after the Baroque period was over. Nevertheless, its importance for the place of Baroque music in today's world can hardly be overestimated since, without the efforts of these musicians and scholars, there would be virtually no Baroque music available to hear.

The early music revival was one of the byproducts of a fundamental shift in European attitudes toward the art of music. During the Baroque, the composition of music was considered a kind of craft or trade and composers little better than servants, although extraordinarily talented ones to be sure. Music itself was their handiwork, something to be created for an occasion, such as a church service or wedding, used for a short time, often only once, and put aside. The idea of rehearing a composition because of its intrinsic qualities as music, the idea of a musical "classic" analogous to works of literature, had to wait until romanticism promoted the image of a composer as inspired artist. When that happened in the 19th century, a great body of forgotten music lay in libraries and archives awaiting rediscovery, a musical Pompeii.

The early music revival consisted of a great number of studies, researches, experiments, concerts, and seminars slowly growing in number during the 19th century into a torrent throughout the 20th century. A few of these might be cited as particularly influential on the revival of Baroque repertory and typical of the thinking behind these efforts.

First would be the renowned performance in Berlin, conducted by the great romantic composer Felix Mendelssohn (1809–1847) at the age of 20, of the **St. Matthew Passion** of **Johann Sebastian Bach** on 11 March 1829, thought, mistakenly, to be the centennial anniversary of the premiere. This ignited an explosion of interest in Bach's music, culminating in the first complete edition of his works, published in 46 volumes from 1851 to 1899, and the birth of professional musicology in Germany.

Second might be the series of "historical concerts" inaugurated at the **Paris** Conservatoire on 8 April 1832, organized by a Belgian scholar, François-Joseph Fétis (1784–1871). The first program surveyed the history of **opera**, presenting music of **Jacopo Peri**, **Giulio Caccini**, and **Claudio Monteverdi** through Fétis's contemporaries. He carried out his popular series in Paris and Brussels for 20 years and spawned many imitators in other European cities.

A third is the tireless campaign of Arnold Dolmetsch (1858–1940), a Frenchman living permanently in England, to build, play, and market the instruments appropriate for playing early music, beginning in the late 1890s with **viols**, and then moving on to **harpsichords** and **virginals** and his famous series of **recorders**. In 1917, he moved to Haslemere, outside London, where he expanded his workshop, entertained inquisitive visitors, and began an annual festival of concerts in 1925. An early offshoot of his beliefs, though without his direct participation, would be the German *Orgelbewegung*, the effort to research and build pipe **organs** as they functioned and sounded in the Baroque.

Fourth is the spectacular career of Wanda Landowska (1879–1959), the first performing star of the early music revival, a piano virtuoso who converted to play the harpsichord in 1905. By 1913, she had been invited to offer a course in harpsichord by the Hochschule für Musik in Berlin, and her brilliant playing of Bach, **François Couperin**, **Jean-Philippe Rameau**, and **Domenico Scarlatti** all over Europe and America established the harpsichord as the essential Baroque **keyboard** instrument.

Another landmark performance is the production of **George Frideric Handel**'s opera *Rodelinda* in June 1920 at the University of Göttingen, under the direction of art historian Oskar Hagen (1888–1957). As Mendelssohn's revival of the St. Matthew Passion had spurred interest in Bach, so did this modest academic production, reported in 40 German newspapers, touch off an explosion of interest in Handel, his operas in particular. One formidable obstacle to this revival, the many *castrato* solo parts in these operas, began to be overcome in the 1940s and 1950s by the countertenor Alfred Deller, whose singing in the high register was so persuasive that it inspired a generation of countertenors to follow.

Finally, after World War II, came certain small recording companies—Musicraft (since 1937), Vox, Westminster, among the best known—to spread and popularize this music that could but rarely be heard as the standard concert fare of Europe and America. Contracting young and as yet little-known musicians to play unusual music permitted these companies to record a large body of music at low cost. Occasionally, they would strike gold and create a warhorse of early music, such as *The Four Seasons* **concertos** of **Antonio Vivaldi**, a perennial best-seller after 1950.

Virtually all the protagonists of the movement believed that "ancient music" should be revived because of its aesthetic qualities, but how the revival should be carried out in order to best bring out such qualities has been controversial since the beginning and has evolved continuously.

One of the oldest views holds that early music requires adaptation to suit contemporary tastes and listening habits, almost in the manner of translating and adapting a piece of Greek theater for the modern stage, or else listeners will not understand its great qualities. Mendelssohn left most of the **arias** out of his St. Matthew Passion; Fétis routinely rescored and reharmonized the music for his Baroque concerts; Hagen reordered Handel's arias, cut the **da capos**, and transposed the *castrato* roles. Generally, this view has lost favor, especially in the latter half of the 20th century; its opponents claim that, in the adaptations, essential qualities of the music are no longer true.

Opposite to the adaptation view is the view that a performance of Bach or Handel must recreate exactly what happened in the 18th century: historical instruments, playing technique, singing technique, **ornamentation**, performance venue, all these and more are to be replicated in order to be authentic and realize the aesthetic qualities of the music. In the extreme, this position holds that the performers should not interpret the music, merely execute it. But recent and meticulous historical research, far from defining what should be done in every case, has revealed that the sound of a work in the 18th century would have changed every time it was performed, sometimes radically, to meet the circumstances of the moment. The exchange or reordering of arias in an opera, the substitution of instruments in a **sonata** or concerto, even the excerpting or elimination of movements was routine. The cold performance, without interpretation, has been criticized as impossible and absurd: no score, certainly not a Baroque score, contains all the information that informs the musical execution of a composition. Performance without interpretation does not exist.

Many performers in recent times take a middle position. They argue that presenting Baroque music in a modern concert cannot possibly reproduce all the circumstances of the original. Indeed, the idea of a public concert of the St. Matthew Passion is already anachronistic. Therefore, compromises with historical authenticity must be made. Landowska played Bach on a Pleyel harpsichord built on an iron frame with a 16-foot stop, unheard of in Bach's time, because she needed to fill the concert hall with sound. Interestingly, this approach aligns with another, quite distinct view that performers must always respect "the composer's true intention," a romantic vestige. It seems reasonable that no composer, in the interest of historical replication, would want his music to be rendered inaudible if another means were available. At the same time, knowledge of historical practices is indispensable because many of them result in superior music.

And so, in recent practice, performers of Baroque music synthesize many of these views but condition them all to purely aesthetic concerns. They decide that playing Bach on instruments that he knew is preferable, not just because that is what he wished, not because of historical authenticity, but because his music sounds best that way. And if certain listening skills must be acquired—to appreciate the da capos of Handel's arias, for example—that is no more than what learning any fine music requires.

ENGLISH ORATORIO. Particular form of **oratorio** developed and, in the opinion of most critics, perfected by **George Frideric Handel**. It derives from the older Italian oratorio the tradition of biblical characters dramatizing a biblical plot in **operatic recitative** and **aria**, but it departs from the tradition in three essential ways. First, there is no hint of its liturgical origins. The **libretto** is entirely operatic in form, eliminating any text that is not dialogue and thus any need for a narrator. Handel performed these works in public theaters and sold tickets. Second, his English oratorios are not always biblical dramas. Some are mythological, *Theodora* is Christian but not biblical, and *Messiah*, the most famous English oratorio of all, has no characters and is cast in the manner of a scriptural reflection. Third, the characteristic that most marks Handel's English oratorios for listeners is the addition of the **chorus** as a commentator or actor (e.g., the people of Israel), a tradition taken from **Jean-Baptiste Lully** (and the *tragédie lyrique*), who imitated Pierre Corneille (1606–1684) and Jean Racine (1639–1699), who took the idea from classical Greek dramas.

It was the regular and continuing performance of *Messiah* and a very few of Handel's other oratorios, a practice very unusual for the time, into the late 18th century, that made the English oratorio by far the most influential of all oratorio types on future composition.

EQUAL TEMPERAMENT. *See* TUNING.

EURIDICE **(Jacopo Peri, music; Ottavio Rinuccini [1562–1621], libretto; 1600).** The earliest known **opera** for which the complete music survives, composed about three years after **Jacopo Peri**'s first opera, *Dafne*, and seven ahead of **Claudio Monteverdi**'s *L'Orfeo*. *Euridice* was composed for the wedding festivities of King Henry IV of France and Maria de' Medici. The first performance took place in the Pitti Palace in **Florence** on 6 October

1600, under the direction of **Emilio de' Cavalieri**. Peri sang the part of Orfeo, and his rival **Giulio Caccini** also participated and recomposed some of the music. Peri and Rinuccini mounted a revival in Bologna in 1616.

The opera begins with the personification of Tragedy singing a prologue of seven stanzas. In Act I, shepherds and nymphs celebrate the nuptials of Orfeo and Euridice. Happiness continues in Act II, until the messenger Dafne tells Orfeo that Euridice has been killed by a snake bite. Orfeo vows to join her in Hades. In Act III, Arcetro reveals that Venus herself has conducted him there. In Act IV, Venus exhorts Orfeo to persuade Pluto, by the power of his singing, to release Euridice once more to the living world. Pluto agrees to this, without condition. Act V presents a conclusion of pastoral rejoicing.

Each act ends with a strophic song for mixed **chorus** and solos that reflects on the action. Except for two other strophic songs, the rest of the action is set in what would later be called *stile recitativo*, which Peri himself described as a music halfway between speech and song.

EXIT ARIA. An **aria** from an *opera seria*, often virtuoso in character, that tries to assure the singer applause by having his or her character exit the stage while singing the last **cadences**. *Opera seria* **librettos** often contrived their dramaturgy to have as many exit arias as possible.

F

FANTASIA (FANTASY). Free composition for **lute**, **keyboard**, or instrumental ensemble, originating in the mid-16th century.

In Italy, the fantasia could be characterized by **improvisatory** as well as highly organized **imitative** passages and is therefore indistinguishable from the **ricercar**. The principal exponent in the early Baroque is **Girolamo Frescobaldi**, especially in his *Fantasie a Quattro* (1608) and his *Fiori musicali* of 1635.

In England, the fantasy was a sophisticated imitative piece usually composed for **viol consort** that could have one **subject**, several subjects, two contrasting sections, or a succession of several sections. The principal 17th-century composers of this English fantasia include **William Byrd**, **Orlando Gibbons**, **Thomas Tomkins**, and John Jenkins.

In northern Europe, the fantasy based on a single subject was preferred by **Jan Pieterszoon Sweelinck**, who taught this tradition to the north German school of **organists**. When the subject is a **chorale** melody, the work becomes a **chorale fantasia**, an important repertory in the German Baroque. Some historians also trace the development of the late Baroque **fugue** along this line. **Johann Jacob Froberger** also brought his teacher Frescobaldi's imitative practice north into German-speaking lands.

In 1656, the French keyboard composer **Louis Couperin** suddenly substituted the title "fugue" for "*fantasie*" in his manuscripts, an early hint of a semantic shift. In the 18th-century, fantasia begins to be associated more exclusively with the free, improvisatory playing of the modern connotation, close to the **capriccio** and late **toccata**. The most famous example of this kind would be the *Chromatic Fantasy and Fugue* of **Johann Sebastian Bach** (BWV 903), which contains startling rhythmic discontinuities and **modulations** and even a passage like **recitative**.

FARINELLI (born Carlo Broschi, 24 January 1705, Andria, Apulia, Italy–16 or 17 September 1782, Bologna). The most famous singer of the Italian *castrato* tradition, his spectacular career saw him collaborating with and competing against the leading **opera** composers of the late Baroque, serenading the depressed King Philip V of Spain, and retiring, very rich, to his own country estate outside Bologna in 1761.

Farinelli (his stage name) first appeared in public at the age of 15 in **Naples** singing the soprano role of the shepherd boy in **Nicola Porpora**'s *Angelica e Medoro*, which also marked the beginning of a lifelong friendship with the opera's **librettist**, the young **Metastasio**. By the mid-1720s, he was singing the prima donna roles in **Rome** as well as Naples in operas by Porpora, Carlo Pollaroli, and **Leonardo Vinci**. After 1724, he began to appear in **Venice**, Milan, **Florence**, Parma, and other northern Italian cities, always to rapturous receptions. **George Frideric Handel** failed to lure him to **London** in 1729, but Farinelli accepted a contract in 1734 to compete against him by singing operas of Porpora and **Johann Adolf Hasse** with the Opera of the Nobility. Despite public acclaim, he broke his contract in 1737 and went to join the royal court at Madrid. His principal duty was to sing **arias** for the king each evening. After Philip V's death in 1746, he collaborated with Metastasio in the production of operas in Madrid and Aranjuez until the death of King Ferdinand VI in 1759.

FASCH, JOHANN FRIEDRICH (15 April 1688, Buttelstädt, near Weimar, Germany–5 December 1758, Zerbst, Saxony-Anhalt, Germany). After **Georg Philipp Telemann**, probably the most famous German composer toward the end of the Baroque. For 36 years, he held a relatively provincial position in Zerbst, but his works were performed in **Hamburg, Leipzig, Vienna**, and Prague. Most of his vocal compositions—13 **masses**, 66 **church cantatas**, 9 church cantata cycles, 14 **serenatas**, and 4 **operas**—are lost, but his instrumental works survive in manuscript and represent an important preclassical oeuvre: 87 **overtures**, 18 **solo concertos**, 46 ensemble **concertos**, 18 **trio sonatas**, 12 **sonatas** *a quattro*, and 19 **symphonies**.

Coming from a family of musicians, Fasch was recruited at age 13 by **Johann Kuhnau** for the St. Thomas School in Leipzig. He founded a *collegium musicum* at the university there in 1708 through which Fasch became familiar with the Italian concertos of **Antonio Vivaldi** and others. Despite having little formal training in composition, he was invited to compose operas by Duke Moritz Wilhelm of Saxe-Zeit in 1711 and 1712, and, thereafter, he held positions as **violinist** in Bayreuth in 1714, as **organist** in Greiz until 1721, and then as *Kapellmeister* in Prague, before reluctantly accepting the same post in Zerbst in 1722. He was not altogether happy with the strict Lutheran regime there, but although he visited elsewhere, particularly **Dresden**, he remained in Zerbst for the rest of his life.

FEBIARMONICI. Generic name for itinerant **opera** companies traveling about Italy during the 17th century from the 1630s on. These companies did much to ignite interest in opera in its first century. One such, under the direction of Francesco Manelli (1594–1667), staged the first known opera open to the public, his *Andromeda*, at Teatro San Cassiano in **Venice** in 1637.

FIGURED BASS. A musical shorthand for the basso **continuo** part of a composition consisting of a bass melody written in conventional musical notation, under which are written Arabic numerals and accidental signs indicating precise intervals over each written bass pitch. These intervals in turn denote **pitch-classes** to combine with the written bass pitch to produce the chord desired.

Example. Figured bass from George Frideric Handel, "Water Music" Suite in G Major, minuet

Because pitch-classes, not precise pitches, are indicated by the figures, it is up to the continuo player to realize how many notes are to be played, their spacing, and so forth, at the moment of performance. In theory, infinitely many realizations of a single figured bass are possible.

Example. One possible realization of the figured bass given above

FIORI MUSICALI (It. **"Musical Flowers"**). A celebrated set of three **organ masses** of **Girolamo Frescobaldi** (**Venice**, 1635). The three cycles of **organ versets** for Sunday **mass**, for Mass of the Apostles, and for Mass of the Virgin offer all the typical organ genres and idioms of the time—**toccatas, fantasias, canzonas, ricercars**, and so forth—except works explicitly based on popular tunes (saving the two concluding **capriccios**).

FLORENCE. Long a center of arts and culture under the patronage of the Medici, Florence is important to Baroque music because it is the birthplace of **opera**. The main players in this experiment so pivotal to the history of

Western music—**Jacopo Peri, Giulio Caccini**, and **Emilio de' Cavalieri**—all worked at the Medici court. Florence is also the home of the **Camerata**, the group of intellectuals under the direction of the Count Giovanni Bardi (1534–1612) who appear to have invented the idea of *dramma per musica* and its successors.

The last decade of the 16th century saw a series of experiments in music drama at the Medici court succeeding the famous **intermedi** of the 1589 wedding of King Henry IV of France and Catherine de' Medici. There were at least three pastorales by Laura Guidiccioni completely set to music by Cavalieri: *Satiro* and *La Disperazione di Fileno* of 1590 and *Il Guioco della Cieca* ("The Blind Game") of 1595. Caccini, rival of Cavalieri, wrote in 1614 that these works had no **recitative**, but no music survives to corroborate his report. Then came the first full-length opera, Peri's *Dafne*, with a **libretto** by Ottavio Rinuccini (1562–1621), in 1598, followed by **Euridice** in 1600, the earliest surviving opera. Two years later, Caccini's own *Euridice* was published. Visiting dignitaries from Mantua, Ferrara, and other cities soon spread the news about opera.

Florence continued to witness operas, almost entirely of local composition, some at court and some in theaters operated by academies, through the 17th century. Florence also had well-supported churches and religious confraternities to supply sacred music, but for the most part, it was not renowned beyond Tuscany.

In the last decade of the century, Florence began to make efforts to hear operas from elsewhere. Prince Ferdinando de' Medici became a supporter of **Alessandro Scarlatti** and carried on correspondence with him and other foreign composers. He supported Bartolomeo Cristofori's (1655–1732) new **keyboard** invention, the **fortepiano**. He may have entertained **George Frideric Handel** in 1708 and 1709. Then, on 22 June 1718, the Teatro della Pergola reopened with a performance of **Antonio Vivaldi**'s *Scanderbeg*. After that, the city saw foreign operas more frequently.

FLUTE. This familiar woodwind instrument that produces sound when the player blows across a column of air contained within a wooden tube, setting it to vibrate, had two principal forms during the Baroque. Before the 18th century, the terms "flute," "*flauto*," "*Flöte*," or any equivalents referred to the wooden instrument played straight out from the mouth, today called "**recorder**." The wooden instrument played as a modern flute, to the side, was called "**transverse**," "*traverso*," or "*traversière*." *See also* BACH, JOHANN SEBASTIAN; BOISMORTIER, JOSEPH BODIN DE; HOTTETERRE; QUANTZ, JOHANN JOACHIM.

FOLIA. An **ostinato** pattern popular in the 17th century and standardized by the 18th century: in slow **tempo**, triple **meter** with the second (weak) beat lengthened and dotted in the manner of a **sarabande**, and usually in D minor or G minor. Many Baroque composers exploited the folia, the most famous example perhaps being the final movement of **Arcangelo Corelli**'s **Sonata for Violin**, Op. 5, No. 12 (1700).

Example. Melodic-harmonic pattern for La Folia.

FORQUERAY, ANTOINE (1672, Paris–28 June 1745, Mantes, France). Famous virtuoso of the viola da gamba, who was reputed to have accomplished on his instrument everything that was possible on the more agile **violin**. While still a youth, he was often commanded to provide music during the mealtimes of King Louis XIV, and in 1689, he was appointed *ordinare de la chambre du roi*. When he was 20, a contemporary wrote that he was the greatest **viol** player of his age. His pupils included the Duke of Orleans, his son Louis, the Duke of Burgundy, and the Duke of Bavaria, all of whom enriched Forqueray considerably.

In 1697, he married a **harpsichordist**, Henriette-Angelique Houssu, and they gave concerts together but did not get on well. They separated five times but managed to have a daughter and a son, **Jean-Baptiste Forqueray**.

Very few of Forqueray's 300 compositions for viol survive. They are pieces that show off his virtuosity, particularly in the high register, over a simple harmonic accompaniment. *See also* GAULTIER, DENIS; MARAIS, MARIN.

FORQUERAY, JEAN-BAPTISTE (3 April 1699, Paris–19 July 1782, Paris). Like his father, **Antoine Forqueray**, Jean-Baptiste was a virtuoso viola da gambist, who, even as a child of six, astonished audiences and King Louis XIV with his technical facility. The father, however, became jealous of the son, had Jean-Baptiste imprisoned in 1715 and exiled in 1725. Jean-Baptiste's influential friends provided for his return to France in February 1726.

He married an amateur **harpsichordist**, Jeanne Nolson, on 29 July 1732, and, through her connections in French intellectual society, was able to meet and play for **Georg Philipp Telemann** and **Jean-Philippe Rameau**. Jeanne Nolson died on 22 December 1740. Then Forqueray married a more famous harpsichordist, Marie-Rose DuBois, on 13 March 1741, and succeeded his father as *ordinaire de la chambre du roi*, a position he held until 7 July 1779. Long before then, in 1760, he seems to have retired from active playing.

In 1747, Forqueray published a volume of *Pièces de Viole* but attributed their composition to his father. Their adventurous harmonic content and advanced viola da gamba technique have convinced historians instead that the compositions are Jean-Baptiste's. In any case, they represent the zenith of viola da gamba technique as well as an invaluable source of information about late-Baroque performance practice on **string instruments**.

FORTEPIANO (also PIANOFORTE). Term used to refer to the earliest pianos. In 1698, Bartolomeo Cristofori (1655–1732), curator of instruments at the Medici court in **Florence**, was working on a new kind of **keyboard** instrument that could play loudly and softly (It. *forte*, *piano*) and had completed a prototype by 1700. His solutions to the technical problems to be overcome in such an instrument continued to be employed in various guises for the first century of the instrument's history. The German pipe-**organ** builder Gottfried Silbermann (1683–1753) began work on fortepianos in the 1730s and, in 1747, showed a model to **Johann Sebastian Bach**, who approved of it and agreed to become a sales agent. Such development, however, was too late for the Baroque, for while the flexible nature of much Baroque keyboard music, especially J. S. Bach's, allows performance on a variety of instruments, there is virtually no Baroque music specifically designed for the fortepiano.

FOUR SEASONS, THE (It. *Le Quattro Stagioni*, Antonio Vivaldi). The most famous example of Baroque program music, *The Four Seasons* comprise the first four **concertos** from **Antonio Vivaldi**'s Opus 8 published in 1725. They are almost entirely solo **violin** concertos, although there are occasionally brief solos for other **string instruments**. Each concerto bears the name of one of the seasons of the year—Spring, Summer, Autumn, Winter—and imposes a musical picture of its character upon the normal attributes of a Baroque **solo concerto**.

Details of the pictures—"singing of birds," "murmuring of branches," "shivering cold," "thunder and lightning"—are drawn from a set of four anonymous pastoral sonnets associated with the concertos. In most cases, the succession of musical subjects follows the images of the sonnets quite closely. Some scholars believe that Vivaldi himself wrote the sonnets.

The Spring, Autumn, and Winter concertos follow the form of the Italian concerto that had become fairly standard by 1725: a fast movement, a slow movement in a contrasting but related **key**, and concluding fast movement in the original key. In Spring and Autumn, the finale is a **dance**. The Summer concerto, however, presents an unpredictable alteration of slow and fast passages based on simple scales or brief motives rather than fully developed ritornellos. The **tonality** of G minor throughout provides coherence.

All four concertos were performed at the **Concert Spirituel** of **Paris** in 1728, and the Spring concerto especially remained popular through the middle of the 18th century, before disappearing from the repertory. Early recordings of *The Four Seasons* became a driving force in the **early music revival** of the 1940s and 1950s.

Each concerto is scored for solo violin, string **orchestra**, and **continuo** and requires from 9 to 11 minutes to perform. The solo violin part is quite difficult even by modern standards.

FREE IMITATION. Type of **imitation** by which the melodic intervals of the **subject**'s entrances subsequent to the first entrance are altered in their numerical components. Traditionally, only the numerical part of the interval is judged: the melodic interval from the tonic to the third degree in a minor **key** counts as identical to the interval from the tonic to the third degree in a major key, even though the first interval is a minor third and the second a major third.

FRENCH HORN. *See* HORN.

FRENCH OVERTURE. Instrumental introduction to a *ballet de cour*, *tragédie lyrique*, *grand motet* of the mid-17th century, and to many English dramatic works and Italian *opere serie* later on, including most of **George Frideric Handel**'s. The earliest unequivocal French overture was composed in 1658 by **Jean-Baptiste Lully** for his *Ballet d'Acidiane*.

The French overture begins with a slow, **homophonic** passage characterized by iambic dotted figures, in some traditions **double dotted**:

Example. George Frideric Handel, *Messiah*, opening Sinfony, mm. 1–4

This rhythm was commonly understood to symbolize the majesty and glory of King Louis XIV. After a half **cadence**, a faster **fugal** passage would follow. Sometimes the full cadence of this section would lead back to a shorter recapitulation of the dotted-rhythm passage.

In the 18th century, the French overture was associated with **suites**, or even occurred as an isolated movement, sometimes as a **keyboard** work. **Georg Philipp Telemann** and **Johann Sebastian Bach** composed sets of **dances** for instrumental ensemble called *ouvertures* headed by a French overture.

FRESCOBALDI, GIROLAMO ALESSANDRO (baptized 9 September 1583, Ferrara–1 March 1643, Rome). Along with **Jan Pierterszoon Sweelinck** in the Netherlands, Frescobaldi was one of the first great composers of **keyboard** music in the Western tradition. His approximately 60 **toccatas**, 13 **fantasias**, 11 **partitas**, 20 **capriccios**, 21 **ricercars**, 58 **canzoni**, 30 other **dance** movements including **ostinatos**, 25 **versets** (mostly *Kyrie eleison* and *Christe eleison* movements), 4 **hymn** arrangements, and 3 **Magnificat** versets exemplify every important keyboard genre of the early Baroque, and reveal Frescobaldi's ability to build significant structures from small motives. His musical language draws from virtually all contemporary sources, from the strictest *stile antico* church music to the **chromaticisms** of the **madrigalists** to the free rhythm of **monody**. His music had been disseminated to all important musical centers of Europe by the century's end, quoted in the most famous treatise on composition, *Gradus ad Parnassum* of **Johann Joseph Fux**, and copied by **Johann Sebastian Bach** and his disciples. No keyboard composer of the time equaled Frescobaldi in influence.

He also composed about 50 **canzonas** for small ensembles of varied combinations of instruments, 19 madrigals, 3 madrigals in *stile moderno* with **continuo**, more than 40 **arias**, 37 **motets**, and 2 **masses** for 8 **voices** each.

Girolamo was born to Filippo Frescobaldi, a landowner in Ferrara, who may have been something of an **organist**. Very little is known about Girolamo's early life or musical training, although some documents hint at a prodigious talent for keyboard instruments. In his own *Capricci* of 1624, Frescobaldi claims that he studied with Luzzasco Luzzaschi of the Ferrarese court, one of the most renowned organists of the late 16th century. A 1683 document lists Girolamo Frescobaldi as the new organist of the Accademia della Morte in Ferrara in 1597 when he was 14 years old.

At some point, he attracted the patronage of the Bentivoglio family, one of the most powerful in Ferrara. For a few months, January to May 1607, a document indicates Frescobaldi as the organist of Santa Maria in Trastevere in **Rome**, but then, through the influence of Enzo Bentivoglio, Frescobaldi was elected to the post of organist for the Cappella Giulia at St. Peter's, the resident body of musicians at the papal basilica. He assumed his position on 29 October 1608, after a summer tour with Bentivoglio to Brussels, the composer's only trip outside Italy. The Cappella Giulia paid Frescobaldi only 72 scudi a year, but he was able to increase his annual income, sometimes to 500 scudi and more, by playing occasional services at other churches and by teaching wealthy patrons.

In 1609, the composer was charged with seducing a singer in Enzo Bentivoglio's service, one Angiola Zanibelli, with the promise of marriage. He denied the charge, but the controversy may have caused a break in relations with the Bentivoglio family. In February 1613, Frescobaldi married Orsola Travaglini of Milan. They had already registered their child Francesco the previous June, and in July 1613, a daughter, Maddalena, was born. They had two more children, Stefano in 1616 or 1617, and Caterina in 1619.

Sometime between the middle of 1610 and the end of 1611, Frescobaldi entered the service of Cardinal Pietro Aldobrandini, where he remained until 1628, except for a brief period in Mantua from February to May 1615. In November of that year, the Grand Duke of Tuscany, Ferdinando II de' Medici, appointed Frescobaldi court organist. He was the most highly paid musician at the Medici court.

In April 1634, he returned to Rome under the patronage of the Barberini family, whose patriarch was Pope Urban VIII. Frescobaldi once again assumed his post as organist at the Cappella Giulia, but at a salary increased to 96 scudi.

Frescobaldi's Keyboard Publications

Title	Publication	Contents
Il Primo Libro delle Fantasie	1608, Milan	12 fantasias
Toccate e Partite d'Intavolature di Cimbalo . . . Libro Primo	1615, Rome	12 toccatas; partitas, capriccios, dance movements, and ostinatos
Recercari et Canzoni Franzese fatte sopra Diverse Oblighi in Partitura . . . Libro Primo	1615, Rome	Ricercars on solfege subjects and canzonas
Il Primo Libro di Capricci fatti sopra Diversi Soggetti et Arie in Partitura	1624, Rome	12 capriccios
Il Secondo Libro di Toccate, Canzone, Versi d'Hinni, Magnificat, Gagliarde, Correnti et Altre Partite d'Intavolatura di Cembalo et Organo	1627, Rome	11 toccatas, 6 canzonas, 7 versets, 11 dances, 4 partitas
Fiori Musicali di Diverse Compositioni, Toccate, Kyrie, Canzoni, Capricci, e Recercari, in Partitura	1635, Venice	3 organ masses
Canzoni alla Francese in Partitura	1645, Venice	11 canzonas with names (e.g., "La Crivelli")

Of his many pupils, the most famous to music history is **Johann Jacob Froberger**, who was sent from the imperial court in **Vienna** to study in Rome from 1637 to 1641. From January 1643, Frescobaldi taught the sons of another Barberini, Don Taddeo, Prince of Palestrina.

In these last years of his life, Frescobaldi played in the famous Lenten performances of **oratorios** at the Oratorio del Crocifisso. Witnesses attest to a towering ability to **improvise** at the **harpsichord**. Frescobaldi was buried at the Church of the Holy Apostles in Rome, but his tomb was lost during an 18th-century reconstruction.

FROBERGER, JOHANN JACOB (baptized 19 May 1616, Stuttgart, Germany–6 or 7 May 1667, Héricourt, France). A student of **Girolamo Frescobaldi**, Froberger brought his teacher's **contrapuntal** methods to **Vienna**, where he was court **organist**, and then to the Netherlands, France, England, and Germany. The influence of his 30 **suites** is credited with making the suite one of the foremost of **keyboard** genres. He also composed 20 **toccatas**, 14 **ricercars**, 17 **capriccios**, 7 **fantasias**, and 6 **canzonas**, a few other movements for keyboard, and 2 **motets**.

Three of Froberger's earlier suites from a 1649 manuscript have three movements: **allemande, courante, sarabande**. All six suites in a 1656 manuscript have four: allemande, **gigue**, courante, and sarabande. Thus, in neither source is found the "classic" order of allemande, courante, sarabande, and gigue, and in fact, the manuscripts do not label these sets "suites," even though these **dances** are clearly bound together in sets by common **keys** and often common melodies.

Johann Jacob Froberger's father, Basilius, had been a member of the Württemberg ducal chapel choir from 1599, eventually becoming *Kapellmeister* by 1621, and so his son was born into an international musical establishment in Stuttgart. Johann Jacob may have studied with his father; certainly, he heard a great variety of music from Italy, France, and England.

It is not known why, in the midst of the Thirty Years War, Froberger went to an opposing capital, Vienna, about 1634. Nevertheless, he held the post of imperial organist there from 1 January to 30 October 1637. In June of that year, he was granted a scholarship to study in **Rome** with Frescobaldi, possibly contingent upon his conversion to Catholicism, which did occur, possibly in Rome. Froberger returned to his post in April 1641 and remained until October 1645, whereupon he went back to Rome to study with **Athanasius Kircher** and possibly **Giacomo Carissimi**. During this study, Froberger learned to compose with Kircher's device, the *arca musurgica*, which he demonstrated to the emperor upon his return to Vienna in September 1649.

Froberger next visited **Dresden**, late 1649 or early 1650, and there he met **Matthias Weckmann**, who became a lifelong friend, and possibly **Heinrich**

Schütz and **Christoph Bernhard**. By March 1650, he was at the Brussels court of Archduke Leopold Wilhelm von Hapsburg, having already passed through Cologne and Düsseldorf, according to one of Froberger's students. His tour, thereafter, took him to Zeeland, Brabant, Flanders, Antwerp, and **Paris**, performing there in September 1652. From there, he went to **London** but, not finding much musical life during the Commonwealth period, returned to France. By April 1653, he had stopped in Heidelberg and Nuremberg and finally rejoined the imperial court at Regensburg. He remained with the imperial chapel until June 1657, when his emperor, Ferdinand III, died.

Froberger was not retained by Leopold I, the next emperor, probably for political or religious reasons. Froberger appears to have done more traveling, certainly performing in Mainz in September 1665. Thereafter, he seems to have retired to Héricourt at the dower house of the Duchess Sibylla.

FUGA. See FUGUE.

FUGUE. A composition, or a significant, self-contained portion of a larger composition, based entirely on **imitation**. The **subject** is announced unaccompanied:

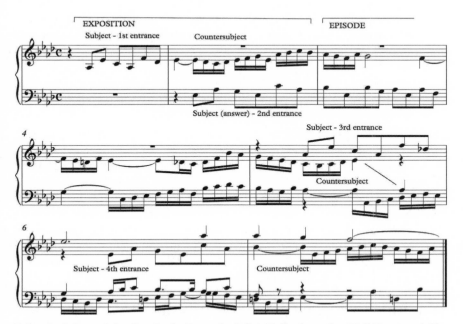

Example. Johann Sebastian Bach, Fugue in A-flat Major from the *Well-Tempered Clavier*, Book I, mm. 1–7

Most commonly, a single subject and its **countersubject** provide all the motivic material for the entire fugue; occasionally, fugues may have multiple subjects (**double fugue**, etc.). A two-**voice texture**, the minimum, is rare; three and four voices are most common; five and six occasionally occur, especially in vocal music. Baroque fugues occur most frequently in sacred music as a means of constructing choral numbers in **masses, oratorios, cantatas, motets,** and so forth and as **organ** repertory, which may have a peripheral function, as **prelude** or postlude music, in Christian liturgy.

The Latin word *fuga* ("flee") has been associated since the early 15th century with imitative composition in various genres: popular song, round, catch, **canon,** motet, **fantasia, ricercar, canzona.** But while some of those terms could include other textures, *fuga* came to be associated exclusively with imitative texture by the 17th century.

There is no traditional form for fugues, but there are many conventional terms (see example). An *exposition* of the fugue presents a complete subject, or *entrance*, in any voice, whereas an *episode* works with material derived from the exposition. A *stretto* (It. "tightened") is an exposition in which the entries are overlapped more quickly than originally.

The acknowledged master of the **keyboard** fugue is **Johann Sebastian Bach**. His cantatas, **passions,** masses, and motets also contain many choral fugal movements, but in this application of fugal technique, he is joined in mastery, although of a more dramatic kind, by his contemporary **George Frideric Handel**, whose fugues in **English oratorios** inspired later composers of oratorios.

FUNCTIONAL HARMONY. This harmonic syntax developed in the 16th century and coming of age by 1700 remains today the most common harmonic system, and is essential to the Baroque musical language. Triads and other chord structures created from the pitches of a given **key** acquired particular syntactic roles in the musical phrase more or less independent of the simultaneous melodies sounding at the same time. Modern theory describes three principal functions: the tonic function (I), which represents stability or resolution of tension; the dominant (V), which creates tension to be resolved; and the subdominant (IV), which mediates between them. The Roman numerals used to describe such functions represent the most common scale degrees that provide the roots of the chords for those functions. Thus, the archetypical harmonic form of a phrase is I-IV-V-I, although, as in any grammar, the schema may be elaborated, varied, extended, and so forth.

FUX, JOHANN JOSEPH (5 January? 1660, Hirtenfeld, Styria [modern Austria]–13 February 1741, Vienna). The most important figure in the

Austrian Baroque, his attachment to the Hapsburg court and perhaps his own personal taste led him to specialize in church music: over 90 **masses**, most of them in **operatic** style, 9 requiem masses, 33 litanies, 24 complete vespers and many other individual prayer settings for the Divine Office, over 120 **motets**, and 13 **oratorios**, among which 6 are *sepolcri* on themes of Christ's **passion**. He also composed 22 Italian operas and a significant body of instrumental music: 53 **trio sonatas**, 20 small works for **keyboard**, 12 **partitas** and various other **overtures** and *sinfonie* for instrumental ensemble. His most abiding influence on the history of music, however, is as a pedagogue: his *Gradus ad Parnassum* (1725) is the most influential manual of composition ever written and is still in use today.

Johann Joseph was the son of a peasant, Andreas, who had a connection with the local church in Hirtenfeld and may have introduced him to musicians there. In 1680, Johann was able to enroll at the university at Graz and, in the following year, commenced his Jesuit education, first at the Ferdinandeum at Graz and then at Ingolstadt, where he studied music, languages, logic, and law until 1687.

In 1685, he began his professional career in music as **organist** at the church of St. Moritz. He left this post in 1689 and, according to one dubious account, may have entered the service of Leopold Karl von Kollonitsch, Archbishop of Hungary, during which he may have traveled to **Rome** and met composers **Arcangelo Corelli**, **Bernardo Pasquini**, and Ottavio Pitoni (1657–1743). Pitoni was a champion of the music of **Giovanni da Palestrina**, who would figure highly in Fux's *Gradus ad Parnassum*.

In June 1696, Fux married Clara Juliana Schnitzenbaum, the daughter of a member of the imperial household in **Vienna**. In 1699, they adopted the daughter of Fux's stepbrother Peter, Eva Maria, and after Peter died in 1724, they adopted his son, Matthew. Clara Fux died on 8 June 1731.

When Fux was married in 1696, he was already organist at the Schottenkirche in Vienna. He quit this post in 1702 in order to devote more time to his composition activities at the imperial court. He took on the post of *vice-Kapellmeister* at St. Stephen's Cathedral in 1705 and *Kapellmeister* from 1712 to 1715. He had been officially appointed as a court composer in April 1698, and he survived several changes of regime, finally winning the appointment as *Hofkapellmeister* by Emperor Charles VI in January 1715, which he held until his death. The chief duty was the composition of church music, but occasionally, he was called upon for other things, such as the opera *Costanza e Fortezza* (28 August 1723) to commemorate the coronation of Charles VI as King of Hungary.

At the end of *Gradus ad Parnassum*, Fux complains of illness, and thereafter, his output declines rapidly. He appears to have died of "a raging fever."

G

GABRIELI, GIOVANNI (c. 1554–1557, Venice?–August, 1612, Venice). Composer most associated with the spectacular **Venetian** school of composition, owing to his brilliant deployment of both instrumental and vocal forces in sacred music for *cori spezzati*. Techniques of combining contrasting groups of voices and instruments of various sizes, clearly differentiated especially in his later works, demonstrated at the opening of the Baroque powers of articulation soon to become intrinsic to the new genres of **concerto**, **sacred symphony**, and **sonata**. The Venetian polychoral tradition remained vital not only in the music of his successors at San Marco—**Claudio Monteverdi**, **Francesco Cavalli**, and **Antonio Lotti**, among the most important—but also in the music of his foreign students, such as **Heinrich Schütz** and in choral music all over Europe. The *grands motets* of **Marc-Antoine Chapentier**, **passions** of **Johann Sebastian Bach**, and the occasional **chorus** in **George Frideric Handel**'s **English oratorios** can, in some sense, trace their origins to Gabrieli.

Giovanni Gabrieli studied with his uncle Andrea Gabrieli (c. 1510–1586) and then with the great Orlandus Lassus (c. 1530–1594) in Munich from 1575 to (probably) 1579. He substituted for Claudio Merulo (1533–1604) as **organist** at San Marco in Venice and won a permanent post there on 1 January 1585. After Andrea's death, Giovanni supervised the collection and publication of his uncle's works and assumed the role of principal composer at St. Mark's. His own major publications are the *Sacrae Symphoniae* (1597) and *Canzoni et Sonate* (1615). His more than 100 **motets** and **mass** movements are almost all for *cori spezzati* of two or three choirs. He also composed **canzonas**, sonatas, **ricercars**, **fantasias**, and **toccatas** for instruments, as well as a significant repertory of early organ music. He is buried in the Church of Santo Stefano, Venice.

GALLIARD. A lively triple-**meter dance**, probably of northern Italian origin, popular in the 16th and 17th centuries. It often follows a duple-meter **pavan** based on the same melody.

GASPARINI, FRANCESCO (19 March 1661, Camaiore, near Lucca, Italy–22 March 1727, Rome). Gasparini collaborated with many of the brightest lights of Italian music during his productive career. During his prime in **Venice**, he may have composed three or four **operas** per year, possibly as many as 50 in all, and apparently many **cantatas**, but most of his music has not yet been recovered.

Gasparini's career began in **Rome** in 1682 as **organist** of the *Madonna dei Monti*. He may have studied with **Arcangelo Corelli** and **Bernardo Pasquini**. His first operas were produced in Livorno in 1686, and in 1689, he was elected to the *Congregazione di Santa Cecilia* and met **Alessandro Scarlatti**, who, in 1705, sent his son **Domenico** to Venice to study with him. Gasparini himself had gone to Venice in 1701, appointed *maestro di coro* for the *Ospedale della Pietà*, where he hired **Antonio Vivaldi** in 1703.

In 1713, Gasparini returned to Rome and, in 1716, succeeded **Antonio Caldara** as *maestro di cappella* for Prince Ruspoli. His daughter was temporarily engaged to **Metastasio**. He continued to compose operas for Rome until 1724. His last appointment was as *maestro di cappella* at St. John Lateran, June 1726.

GAULTIER, DENIS (1597 or 1603?, Marseilles?–late January 1672, Paris). "Gaultier le jeune" never had an official appointment but, along with his cousin **Ennemond Gaultier**, was reputed to be the finest **lutenist** of his time. Before 1631, the activities and musical sources of the two are often confused.

His oeuvre, found in the manuscript *La Rhétorique des Dieux* (c. 1652) and the **prints** *Pièces de Luth* (c. 1669) and *Livre de **Tablature*** (c. 1672), consists mostly of **dances**. Many of these were transcribed for **harpsichord**. *See also* FORQUERAY, ANTOINE; MARAIS, MARIN.

GAULTIER, ENNEMOND (1575, Villette, Dauphiné, France–11 December 1651, Nèves). "Le vieux Gaultier" served as *valet de chambre* to Maria de' Medici from 1600 to 1631 and became famous as one of the best players and teachers of the **lute**. He retired in 1631, and none of his music was published during his lifetime. The manuscript attributions are often confused with music of his cousin **Denis Gaultier**. His compositions are almost entirely **dances**.

GAVOTTE. French court **dance** popular from the late 16th century to the end of the Baroque. In duple **meter**, it begins with a subdivided upbeat (e.g., two quarter notes) and is in moderate to fast **tempo**. Melodic phrases are in four-measure units, and **binary form** is typical. Gavottes appear frequently in

17th-century French *ballets de cour* and then in instrumental **suites** throughout the Baroque.

GAY, JOHN. *See BEGGAR'S OPERA, THE.*

GEMINIANI, FRANCESCO (baptized 5 December 1687, Lucca, Italy–17 September 1762, Dublin). One of the outstanding **violinists** of his time, Geminiani, beginning in 1748, also left six treatises valuable for their discussion of **continuo** playing and **ornamentation** practices at the end of the Baroque. His compositions are impossible to count because so many of them are reworkings of earlier works or arrangements of music of other composers, especially that of **Arcangelo Corelli**. He published 48 violin **sonatas**, and of 47 published **concerti grossi**, 23 are original, and 24 are arrangements of Corelli **trio** and violin **sonatas**. He also published an ornamented version of Corelli's Violin Sonata Op. 5, No. 9.

Geminani's father was a violinist at the *Cappella Palatina* in Lucca and probably taught his son. Francesco played professional violin in **Naples** by December 1706 and then, on 27 August 1707, returned to Lucca to take his father's position. During this period, he may have studied with Corelli and **Alessandro Scarlatti**. He left Lucca in September 1709. He appears in **London** in 1714, where he began a career for himself as a violin teacher and, with occasional public performances, won considerable notice.

Geminiani left London for **Paris** in 1732 and then, on 6 December 1733, arrived in Dublin to enter the service of Charles Moore, Baron of Tullamore. Apart from occasional trips to Paris to publish his works, and to London, he remained in this service until his death. His last public performance took place on 3 March 1760.

GIBBONS, ORLANDO (baptized 25 December 1583, Oxford–5 June 1625, Canterbury). Composer, member of the **Chapel Royal**, probably from 1605. An **organist** by profession, he made significant and very popular contributions to the Anglican repertory: 40 **anthems**, a short **service**, a second service, 3 psalms, and 2 **Te Deums**. His secular music includes about 20 **madrigals**, including the famous "The Silver Swan," about 25 **fantasias** and 10 other **dance** movements for **viol consort**, 10 fantasias, and 14 other works for **keyboard**.

GIGA. *See* GIGUE.

GIGUE (also It. *giga*, Eng. "jig"). Lively **dance** in compound duple or triple **meter** (e.g., 6/8 or 9/8), originating in the British Isles and imported to France by the great **lutenist Denis Gaultier** and then made popular after 1657 by **Johann Jacob Froberger** in his **keyboard suites**. Thereafter, the gigue became the dance that often concluded an instrumental suite of the later Baroque. *See also* HORNPIPE.

GLORIA IN D (Antonio Vivaldi, RV 589; 1708). Well-known setting of the Gloria, an ordinary prayer of the Roman Catholic **mass**. The scoring calls for two soprano soloists and one alto, a four-**voiced choir**, and an **orchestra** of two **flutes, oboe, oboe d'amore, bassoon**, three **trumpets, timpani, organ**, and **continuo**. **Antonio Vivaldi** composed the Gloria in the manner of a "**Neapolitan**" or **cantata** mass, with the text segmented into 12 self-contained movements, all together requiring about a half hour to perform. The solo **arias** are in the **operatic** style of the high Baroque; the choral **textures** range from solemn **homophony** to a concluding **double fugue**.

GOLDBERG VARIATIONS (Johann Sebastian Bach, BWV 988). By common consent one of the greatest sets of **keyboard variations** ever composed in the Western tradition, **Johann Sebastian Bach** published the Goldberg Variations as the fourth and last volume of his *Clavier-Übung* about 1741. The title, "Goldberg Variations," derives from Bach's student Johann Gottlieb Goldberg (1727–1756), who, according to Bach's first biographer, Johann Nikolaus Forkel (1749–1818), asked Bach for some variations to play for his employer, Count Keyserlinck of Russia, during his bouts of insomnia. Bach's own title page says *Aria mit 30 Veränderungen* ("Aria with 30 Variations").

Like many variation sets, and especially **ostinato** variations of the Baroque, but unlike most variations composed later, the Goldberg Variations are variations on a bass melody. Therefore, the harmonic structures of the opening and closing "aria" and 30 variations in between have a very similar **binary form**: **modulation** from G major to D major in the first strain and then from D to E minor through C major and returning to G major in the second. The only harmonic license allowed is use of the parallel minor, G minor, for variations 15, 21, and 25.

Over this recurring, varying bass melody is imposed an encyclopedia of Baroque instrumental styles and forms: fughetta, **French overture**, two-part **invention**, virtuoso **fantasia** for two keyboards of a **harpsichord**, quodlibet, and **dance** forms, among others. Then there are the nine **canons**.

The canons of the Goldberg Variations are composed for the upper **voices** and occur in every variation that is a multiple of three: Variation 3, Variation 6, and so forth, until Variation 27. Furthermore, the canonic interval of **imitation** equals the number of the variation divided by three; canon at the unison for Variation 3, canon at the third for Variation 9, and so forth. There is no better example in all his works of Bach's passion for order and musical logic.

The Goldberg Variations include some of the most technically challenging keyboard music of the entire Baroque. Although almost certainly intended for the two-manual harpsichord, today, many pianists play them in concert, and there are also instrumental arrangements. A performance requires from about 45 to 90 minutes, depending on whether the repeats are observed.

GRADUS AD PARNASSUM **(Johann Joseph Fux, 1725).** The most famous and influential manual of composition ever published, used by Franz Joseph Haydn (1732–1809), Wolfgang Amadeus Mozart (1756–1791), Ludwig van Beethoven (1770–1827), and countless other composers down to today. Unlike its contemporary *Traité de l'Harmonie* of **Jean-Philippe Rameau** (1722), *Gradus ad Parnassum* presents no new or startling theories about **counterpoint**, harmony, or other fundamental musical relations. Its genius is in its synthesis of various accounts of **contrapuntal** syntax into a graduated program of study, known as species counterpoint.

In species counterpoint, students begin their study with the simplest possible combination of melodies, the first species, in which every note of a given melody, the **cantus firmus**, is matched with a note of a new melody, the counterpoint, to create a two-**voiced** composition. In second species, the student is allowed two notes of counterpoint for each note of the cantus firmus. In third species, four notes are allowed, including syntactic **dissonances**. In fourth species, the dissonant suspension is introduced, and in fifth species, all the previous four are combined against the cantus firmus. After this, three- and four-voiced **textures** are introduced, **imitation** and **fugue** writing, and finally various styles of music, **modes**, and other contexts of application.

Gradus ad Parnassum is composed in Latin in classical dialogue format. The author, **Johann Joseph Fux**, writes himself into the text as the student Josephus who is patiently instructed by the master Aloysius, the personification of **Giovanni da Palestrina**, by this point in the Baroque, the representative *par excellence* of all that was good and traditional in counterpoint. Numerous musical examples appear, some with technical mistakes made by Josephus to be corrected by Aloysius in the manner of an individual lesson in composition that the reader is privileged to observe.

GRANDE ÉCURIE. An instrumental ensemble charged with the performance of ceremonial music, usually outdoors, for the court of King Louis XIV of France. Musique de la Grande Écurie consisted of five groups: one group of 12 all playing **trumpets**; another of 12 playing **violins, oboes,**

cornetts, and sackbuts; a fife and drum corps of eight; six players of crum-horns and **trumpets marine**; and a group of six playing oboes and **musettes**.

GRANDI, ALESSANDRO (1586?–second half of 1630, Bergamo). One of the most prolific composers of the early Baroque, his 177 **motets**, 5 **masses**, 16 **sacred concertos**, 35 psalm settings, 40 **madrigals**, and about 50 **cantatas** did much to establish in northern Italy the *stile moderno* with dramatic vocal writing and **continuo**.

His origins are obscure. His first documented appointment is as *maestro di cappella* of the confraternity of the Accademia della Morte in Ferrara. In 1604, he joined the establishment at San Marco in **Venice** under **Giovanni Gabrieli**. In 1610, he returned to Ferrara as *maestro di cappella* at the Accademia dello Spirito Santo and then took the same post at the cathedral sometime between 1615 and 1617. During this second Ferrara period, he began to publish motets.

Grandi was lured back to San Marco with a good salary, beginning on 31 August 1617, and became assistant to *maestro* **Claudio Monteverdi** in November 1620. From this point, his publications of sacred music in the new style increased dramatically.

In 1627, his reputation was sufficient that he was unanimously elected as *maestro di cappella* at the church of Santa Maria Maggiore in Bergamo. He died during the plague of 1630.

GRAND MOTET. Type of **motet** associated with the courts of Kings Louis XIII and XIV. Nicolas Formé (1567–1638), *sous-maitre* of Louis XIII, directed an ensemble of two five-**voiced choirs**, one chiefly of soloists and the other, larger, weighted to the lower registers. This tradition was continued by **Henry Du Mont** with 20 *grands motets* composed from c. 1663–1683, followed by 12 works of **Jean Baptiste Lully**, 24 of Pierre Robert (c. 1618–1699), 77 by **Michel-Richard de Lalande**, and over 85 by **Marc-Antoine Charpentier**. After 1725, many of these were heard publicly at the **Concert Spirituel** in **Paris**.

The *grand motet* usually sets a Latin psalm text, dividing the verses into vocal solos, small **choruses**, and large choruses. In the works composed after 1660, **orchestral symphonies** articulate the musical structure, and the vocal distributions vary more. *See also* VERSE ANTHEM.

GREENE, MAURICE (12 August 1696, London–1 December, 1755). Before he was 40 years old, Greene held all the major musical appointments around **London** as a consequence of his church music: 6 settings of the **Te Deum**, 3 **oratorios**, and over 95 **anthems** (including 14 full anthems, 44 verse anthems, 21 solo anthems, and 24 orchestral anthems composed for the annual Festival of the Sons of the Clergy at St. Paul's Cathedral). He also composed 2 pastorals, a masque, many songs and other assorted vocal pieces, 6 overtures, 12 voluntaries for harpsichord, and a number of suites for harpsichord.

Son of the Reverend Thomas Greene, chaplain of the Chapel Royal, Maurice was probably educated at St. Paul's by Jeremiah Clarke. In 1718, Greene became organist at St. Paul's. He began building his repertory of sacred music in response to his new duties. He taught the future composers William Boyce and John Stanley. He also became friendly with George Frideric Handel at this time, but later they became enemies as Greene was promoted by the parliamentary parties and Handel by the royal.

About the time of his appointment to St. Paul's, Greene married Mary Dillingham (1699–1767) and had five children with her, only one of whom, Katharine, survived him.

Greene was a founding member of the Academy of Ancient Music, which often performed his works. On the death of William Croft, in August 1727, Greene was appointed to succeed him as organist and composer of the Chapel Royal. On 6 July 1730, his setting of Alexander Pope's *Ode on St. Cecilia's Day* was performed at Cambridge University, which awarded him a doctorate of music on 7 July. He was made Master of the King's Musick in 1735.

GRIGNY, NICOLAS DE (baptized 8 September 1672, Rheims, France– 30 November 1703, Rheims). Grigny composed a single volume of organ music, the influential collection of organ masses known as the *Premier Livre d'Orgue* of 1699, which challenged the technique of turn-of-the-18th-century organists with its five-voiced fugues and demanding pedal parts.

Growing up within a family of musicians, Grigny apparently studied also with Nicolas Lebègue while Grigny was organist at the abbey church of St. Denis in Paris from 1693 to 1695. About 1697, he was appointed organist at the cathedral at Rheims and held that position until his death.

GROUND. English term for an ostinato bass. "Ground," dating from the late 16th century, may refer to a bass melody that repeats to unify a set of variations in the upper voices, a harmonic progression tied to such a bass melody, a progression independent of the bass, or an entire composition using these techniques. Before 1670, grounds were composed for solo instruments. With the influence of Jean-Baptiste Lully's music in England during the Restoration, grounds were composed for other media, including English opera. There are three in Henry Purcell's *Dido and Aeneas*.

GUITAR (It. *chitarra spagnuola*, Sp. *guitarra*). The Baroque guitar differed from the modern in several ways. The instrument was often highly decorated with a rounded back rather than flat, and the **strings** were secured at the bottom of the body rather than on the table. Baroque guitars had five courses of strings rather than six and, when used to realize a **figured bass**, usually could not play the notated bass melody at pitch. **Tunings** of the strings were not standard and instead adapted to the particular task at hand. Often, these tunings were reentrant, by which strings were not tuned to a series of ascending pitches but an alternating pattern of intervals that rose and fell in order to accommodate the particular melodic patterns desired.

In the early Baroque, the typical guitar idiom was considered to be strumming simple chord accompaniments for singing, but with the advent of the new **monodic textures** deriving from **opera** in Italy, subtler harmonic accompaniments appropriate for **continuo** playing became widespread. As early as 1589, the famous **intermedi** for the Medici wedding celebrations in **Florence** called for guitars as continuo instruments.

Music for guitar typically appears as a **tablature** specific for the instrument, and the earliest such tablature for the five-string instrument dates from the second half of the 16th century. The Italian system known as *alfabeto*, which used alphabetic letters to denote the frets of the guitar to be played, dominated the 17th century.

H

HAMBURG. Because Holy Roman Emperor Frederick I granted Hamburg the status of an Imperial Free City in 1189, Hamburg never had an aristocratic court to patronize music on a grand scale. Yet, as a founding member of the Hanseatic League of trading cities in the 13th century, Hamburg prospered, and after the acceptance of Lutheranism in 1539, its serious religious atmosphere made sacred music to be held in high esteem. Then, in the late 17th century, it rose rapidly to prominence as a center of German **opera**.

The most important musical post in Hamburg during the early Baroque was that of *Stadtkantor* ("city cantor"). As in **Leipzig**, the cantor ranked third in the Johanneum Lateinschule and was responsible for all the music in four to five parish churches of the city. Important occupants include **Thomas Selle, Christoph Bernhard, Georg Philipp Telemann,** and **Carl Philipp Emanuel Bach**.

Hamburg was particularly important for the development of the **passion**. The first passion sung in **polyphony** dates from 1609, and Selle's St. John Passion of 1643 was the first to include the instrumental interludes that would become so important to the mature genre. Hamburg also became famous as the home of great **organs** and organists. One of the most important builders of the Baroque, Arp Schnitger (1648–1719), lived in nearby Neuenfelde and built more than 20 organs for Hamburg alone. One of the outstanding organists of the mid-17th century, **Matthias Weckmann**, founded a *collegium musicum* in 1660.

The success of the Hamburg Collegium was a sign of the increasing interest in secular music and the concomitant decline of sacred music, which crept over northern Europe after the Thirty Years War (1618–1648). The next unmistakable sign was the founding of a public German opera company by a group of town officials and musicians in the early 1670s. To calm the outraged church authorities, the so-called Gänsemarkt Opera opened on 2 January 1678 with *Der erschaffene, gefallene und auffgerichtete Mensch* ("Created, Fallen, and Saved Mankind") of Johann Theile (1646–1724), and for a period, all the subjects of the German operas were biblical. Texts and song forms were all German until Johann Sigismund Kusser (1660–1727) began to introduce Italian techniques about 1693. The Gänsemarkt Opera's fame peaked under the administration of the most important composer of German Baroque opera, **Reinhard Keiser**, so much so that the likes of **Johann Mattheson** and **George Frideric Handel** were drawn there to learn about musical theater. Handel composed his first opera, *Almira*, for Hamburg, opening in January 1705. Keiser, despite frequent periods of financial mismanagement, composed at least 60 operas for his theater.

The slow decline of the Hamburg opera in the face of competition from Italian touring companies was temporarily halted by Georg Philipp Telemann, who took control in 1722 and composed 20 operas for the Gänsemarkt Opera. Indeed, the city authorities increased his salary substantially to prevent him from accepting the post of *Thomaskantor* in Leipzig in 1723. (The Leipzig council had to settle for **Johann Sebastian Bach**.) Telemann, however, had lost interest by the late 1730s, ending the first period of German language opera.

HANDEL, GEORGE FRIDERIC (23 February 1685, Halle, Saxony, Germany–14 April 1759, London). Although for many music lovers the name of Handel is inextricably linked with what is taken to be a religious piece, the **oratorio** *Messiah*, the lion's share of Handel's career and compositional oeuvre is devoted to the profane passions and histrionic conventions of the musical theater. While Handel enjoyed the occasional patronage of the great families of **Florence** and **Rome** during his sojourn in Italy (1706–1710) and of English nobility and royalty (along with pensions) after his permanent move to **London** in 1712, he made his living chiefly by composing **operas** for a paying public and thus was one of the first major composers to liberate himself from both court and church. Between 1705 and 1741, he composed over 40 operas, mostly Italian *opere serie* based on historical and mythological plots for small companies of professional singers, usually Italian.

It is simplistic to say that Handel invented the **English oratorio** as a way to save his theatrical career after the foreign *opera seria* would no longer sell to the London public, since there is an overlap of over 20 years between his first oratorio (1718) and last opera (1741), and yet, there is some truth to this traditional view. He did suffer both competition with a rival opera company and the public's growing indifference to any Italian opera production through the mid-1730s, and although he persisted until 1741 with *Imeneo* and *Deidemia*, both of which failed, he attempted no more operas after *Messiah* premiered in 1742. The success of his new English-language genre provided him with his new livelihood.

His life in composition, therefore, may be considered in three phases: his education in music and theater in Germany and Italy (to 1710), his opera career in London (1711–1741), and his oratorio career (1718–1751).

Handel's musical style, whether in *opera seria*, English oratorio, the 70-odd Italian **cantatas**, the 32 **anthems**, 9 **motets**, the Brockes **Passion**, or significant repertory of **sonatas** and **concertos**, is always founded on the aesthetic of music drama. Like all his colleagues of the high Baroque, he unifies his music in a continuity of motor rhythmic pulse, but within that consistency, through his own brand of **counterpoint** and handling of large-scale forms and musical **textures**, Handel creates the *coup de théâtre*, the musical climax that turns even the most learned passages into dramas. One need only think of the "Amen" to *Messiah*.

Handel's father, Georg Händel (1622–1697), wanted his son to study law, not music, but Herr Händel was also the barber-surgeon to the Duke of Saxe-Weissenfels, who once happened to hear the boy play. The duke changed Georg Händel's mind. George Frideric then studied **harpsichord**, **organ**, and composition with **Friedrich Zachow**, organist at the Liebfrauenkirche in Halle. Handel's future career may have been stimulated by a visit to Berlin in 1702, where he met opera composer **Giovanni Bononcini** and heard his *Cefalo* and *Polifemo*. In summer 1703, he left Halle for **Hamburg** and joined the opera **orchestra** there as second **violinist** and **continuo** harpsichordist. During the fortuitous absence of **Reinhard Keiser**, the Hamburg Theater's principal composer, Handel composed his first operas in 1705, *Almira* and *Nero* (see opera chart).

In the latter half of 1706, Handel traveled to Italy, probably visiting Florence but certainly Rome by early 1707, where he quickly earned the patronage of Carlo Cardinal Colonna and Benedetto Cardinal Pamphili. Handel composed a number of motets, two Italian-style oratorios, *Il Trionfo del Tempo e del Disinganno* (1707) and *La Resurrezione* (April 1708). For **Naples**, he wrote a dramatic cantata on a story that he would set again in England: *Aci, Galatea, e Polifemo* (June 1708). Working in these genres, derived from opera, honed Handel's musical-dramatic skills. Finally, in **Venice**, his full-length opera *Agrippina* opened the Carnival season on 26 December 1709, to great acclaim. In 1710, Handel returned to Germany. The elector of Hanover, future King George I of England, began his family's long association with Handel by appointing him court *Kapellmeister*. But Handel, allowed to travel by the terms of his appointment, went on to London ahead of the elector in the autumn of 1710.

Though later than most cities on the continent, London was falling under the spell of imported Italian opera. Arrangements and excerpts had been heard since 1705, but Handel's *Rinaldo* of 1711 was the first original full-length Italian opera for London with an Italian cast. Based on Tasso's tale of the heroic knight bewitched by an enchantress, the opera was full of spectacular scenery, magical effects, and Handel's music and was a sensation. The more lyrical *Il Pastor Fido* was not so popular, so Handel followed with three more heroic operas by 1715.

In May 1719, Handel was commissioned by the lord chamberlain to go to the continent and engage opera singers to establish the Royal Academy of Music, a joint stock company supported by King George I and financed by subscribers who hoped to profit. The Royal Academy, with operatic contributions from **Giovanni Porta**, Bononcini, and Attilio Ariosti (1666–1729), provided all Handel's operatic activity until it closed in 1728. His first effort there, on 27 April 1720, *Radamisto*, "was by far the finest opera seria hitherto heard in London; it employed the largest orchestra, including **horns** (their operatic debut in England) as well as **trumpets**; and it shows Handel's absolute mastery of the form for the first time" (Winton Dean, *Opera Seria*, 1969). The series also includes perhaps Handel's most famous *opera seria*: *Giulio Cesare in Egitto* (1724).

On 29 January 1728, John Gay's ***The Beggar's Opera*** opened at the Lincoln's Inn Fields Theater. Its popular success, with its simple English songs and satire of the Royal Academy, is sometimes regarded as the beginning of the end of Handel's opera career in England. But Handel went back to Europe from February until July in 1729 and engaged new singers to sing in a reconstituted Royal Academy. Over the next 12 years, he persevered under various auspices and venues with 17 more Italian operas despite political opposition, operatic competition fueled by a feud between King George II and Frederick Prince of Wales, and a debilitating illness in April 1737, when a paralysis of the right hand caused him to take vapor baths at Aix-la-Chapelle (Aachen). Many of these operas were not successful and had to close after a few performances, despite the excellence of the music.

Handel's Operas

Opera	First performance	Librettists and sources
Almira	8 January 1705	F. C. Feustking after G. Pancieri
Nero	12 February 1705	F. C. Feustking
Roderigo (lost)	January 1708	After F. Silvani *Il Duello d'Amore e di Vendetta*
Die verwandelte Daphne (lost)	January 1708	H. Hinsch
Agrippina	26 December 1709	V. Grimani
Rinaldo	24 February 1711	Giacomo Rossi after Tasso *Gerusalemme Liberata*
Il Pastor Fido	22 November 1712	Rossi after Guarini
Teseo	10 January 1713	Nicola Haym after Quinault *Thésée*
Silla	2 June 1713	G. Rossi
Amadigi di Gaula	25 May 1715	After A. H. de Lamotte *Amadis de Grèce*

Opera	First performance	Librettists and sources
Radamisto	27 April 1720	After D. Lalli, G. de Scudéry L'Amour Tyrannique
Muzio Scevola (act III only)	15 April 1721	P. A. Rolli after Livy
Floridante	9 December 1721	Rolli after Silvani La Costanza in Trionfo
Ottone, re di Germania	12 January 1723	Haym after Pallavicino Teofane
Flavio, re di Longobardi	14 May 1723	Haym after Noris, Flavio Cuniberto
Giulio Cesare in Egitto	20 February 1724	Haym after Bussani
Tamerlano	31 October 1724	Haym after A. Piovene Il Bajazete and J. Pradon Tamerlan
Rodelinda, regina de' Longobardi	13 February 1725	Haym after Corneille Pertharite, Roi des Lombards
Scipione	12 March 1726	Rolli after Salvi Publio Cornelio Scipione
Allessandro	5 May 1726	Rolli after O. Mauro La Superbia d'Alessandro
Admeto, Re di Tessaglia	31 January 1727	After A. Aureli Antigona Delusa da Alceste
Riccardo Primo, Re d'Inghilterra	11 November 1727	Rolli after F. Briani Isacio Tiranno
Siroe, Re di Persia	17 February 1728	Haym after Metastasio
Tolomeo, Re di Egitto	30 April 1728	Haym after C. S. Capace Tolomeo e Alessandro
Lotario	2 December 1729	After Salvi Adelaide
Partenope	24 February 1730	After Stampiglia
Poro, Re dell' Indie	2 February 1731	Metastasio
Ezio	15 January 1732	Metastasio
Sosarme, Re di Media	15 February 1732	After Salvi Dioniso Rè di Portogallo
Orlando	27 January 1733	Capace after Ariosto Orlando Furioso
Arianna in Creta	26 January 1734	After P. Pariati Teseo in Creta
Ariodante	8 January 1735	After Salvi Ginevra after Ariosto Orlando Furioso
Alcina	16 April 1735	After Ariosto Orlando Furioso
Atalanta	12 May 1736	B. Valeriano La Caccia in Etolia
Armino	12 January 1737	After Salvi
Giustino	16 February 1737	After Beregan
Berenice	18 May 1737	After Salvi Berenice, Regina d'Egitto
Faramondo	3 January 1738	A. Zeno
Serse	15 April 1738	After N. Minato after Stampiglia
Imeneo	22 November 1739	After Stampiglia
Deidamia	10 January 1741	Rolli
Semele	10 February 1744	William Congreve after Ovid
Hercules	5 January 1745	Thomas Broughton after Ovid, Metamorphoses 9 and Sophocles Trachiniae

At first glance, Handel's Italian operas appear to adhere closely to the continental conventions of *opera seria*. The plots portray mythical characters, such as Roland, or extraordinary historical personages, such as Julius Caesar, in political and moral difficulties. Casts are small, about a half-dozen major roles, and there is no Greek-style **chorus**, although, at the opera's conclusion, all the characters remaining alive will combine in a *coro* of spiritual unanimity for the requisite *lieto fine* ("happy ending"). And the music is dominated by solo **arias**, the great majority of them **da capo arias**.

But Handel also departs from European practice significantly. He preferred **librettos** to have a minimum of **recitative**, which forced his arias to function in ways beyond the expressive reaction, often to convey information or character that advanced the plot. To this end, his arias, compared to those of his colleagues, are filled with counterpoint in faster harmonic rhythm, which allows a more flexible phrase structure essential for Handel's climactic moments. He continued to exploit forms such as the **siciliana**, **minuet**, and **French overture**, which, by the 1730s, had gone out of fashion in Europe. Critics have remarked that Handel's dramaturgy looked backward as much as it looked forward.

What Handel sought in such techniques was great control over the music drama. He almost never worked with finished librettos but adapted old ones or used works in progress so as to shape the plot to his musical requirements. And because he continually had to change casts, locations, and fashions, he did not conceive his operas as finished works in the romantic sense, even though the dramatic aims are clear, but rather as dramatic studies capable of continual shaping.

Handel's dramatic compositions also include about 60 Italian chamber cantatas composed during his sojourn in Italy from 1706 to 1709, two duet cantatas dating about 1722, and then another group of seven from 1741 to 1746. In this last set, Handel tried out motives and themes that would show up in his oratorios *Messiah* and *Belshazzar*.

On 7 July 1713, the nation celebrated the Peace of Utrecht, ending the War of the Spanish Succession, with Handel's **Te Deum** and *Jubilate*, and from then on, hardly a noteworthy public ceremony passed without an anthem of Handel. From 1717 to 1718, he composed 12 **Chandos Anthems** for the private chapel of James Brydges, later duke of Chandos. For the coronation of King George II and Queen Caroline at Westminster Abbey, on 11 October 1727, he composed four more anthems brilliantly scored, including *Zadok the Priest*, which made such an impression that the work has been required at every royal coronation in England since then. The death of Queen Caroline in December 1737 was commemorated in the little-known but superb funeral anthem "The Ways of Zion Do Mourn," later adapted to become Part I of his oratorio *Israel in Egypt*. On 27 November 1743, a new Handel Te Deum again commemorated a British national triumph, this time the victory of King George II and Lord Stair over the French in the Battle of Dettingen.

The opera period saw Handel create a substantial repertory of instrumental music. Most famous is the set of three great **suites** for orchestra known as the **Water Music** (probably 1715 or 1717). In November 1720, he published *Suites de Pièces pour le Clavecin . . . Premier Volume*, containing eight suites for harpsichord. In the latter half of 1723, he was appointed music teacher to the royal princesses Caroline and Anne, and it is possible that some of his **solo sonatas** Opus 1 and **trio sonatas** Opus 2 originated for private concerts for the royal household at this time. Another set of seven trio sonatas Opus 5 appeared in 1739. That same year, Handel began a series of concerts featuring reworked English-language vocal music at the theater of Lincoln's Inn Fields, for which he also composed a set of 12 **concerti grossi** over a four-week period in September–October 1739. Certainly among the greatest of all Italian-style concertos, he titled them "Grand Concertos Opus 6," which very likely refers pointedly to the most famous set of the time, the **Opus 6** of **Arcangelo Corelli**, whose music was so popular in England that it shared the stage with Handel's at the Handel Commemoration of 1784. During the intermissions of his oratorio concerts, Handel himself played the solo part of his organ concertos (Opus 4 and Opus 7), which he continued to compose into 1751, his last year of active composition.

It is these 20 or so English oratorios, and in particular, *Messiah* (1741), that carried Handel's reputation into posterity and that weigh most heavily on his reputation today. The first signs of the new genre show up in 1718 while he was in the service of James Brydges and composed the first versions of *Esther* and *Acis and Galatea*. He was forced to revise these works in 1732 when unauthorized productions of the 1718 originals were mounted in London that year. In 1733, Handel composed *Athalia*, which attains the dramatic dimension of a three-act opera, sustained by sumptuous scoring and Handelian choruses. But his principal period of oratorio composition began in the late 1730s with the composition of *Alexander's Feast* and *Saul*, the latter graced with a libretto of Charles Jennens, who would later compile the librettos for *Messiah* and *Belshazzar*. In *Saul*, the elements of Handel's typical pattern for English oratorio are brought together in a masterwork: the drama of envy drawn from the Old Testament, arias sung by named characters, the chorus as both the people of Israel and commentator in the Greek fashion, all cast in musical forms adapted to dramatic need. *Messiah* is essential as an intrinsic work of art and as a historical marker for the end of Handel's career as a composer of Italian *opera seria*, but it is not characteristic of the works composed year after year in the 1740s.

English oratorio	First performance	Librettists and sources
Acis and Galatea	May 1718	John Gay et alia after Ovid
Esther	1718?	Alexander Pope and John Arbuthnot after Racine after the Book of Esther
Deborah	17 March 1733	Samuel Humphreys after Judges 5
Athalia	10 July 1733	Humphreys after Racine after 2 Kings and 2 Chronicles
Alexander's Feast	19 February 1736	Newburgh Hamilton after John Dryden
Saul	16 January 1739	Charles Jennens after 1 Samuel and 2 Samuel
Israel in Egypt	4 April 1739	Exodus
Messiah	13 April 1742	Compiled by Jennens from Old and New Testament
Samson	18 February 1743	Newburgh Hamilton after Milton after Judges 14–16
Joseph and his Brethren	2 March 1744	James Miller after Genesis 41–44
Belshazzar	27 March 1745	Jennens after Daniel 5, Jeremiah, Isaiah, Herodotus, and Xenophon
Occasional Oratorio	14 February 1746	Hamilton after Milton and Spenser
Judas Maccabaeus	1 April 1747	Thomas Morell after 1 Maccabees and Josephus
Joshua	9 March 1748	Morell?
Alexander Balus	23 March 1748	Morell after 1 Maccabees
Susanna	10 February 1749	Anonymous after Apocrypha
Solomon	17 March 1749	Anonymous after 2 Chronicles, 1 Kings 5, and Josephus
Theodora	16 March 1750	Morell after Robert Boyle: The Martyrdom of Theodora and Didymus
The Choice of Hercules	1 March 1751	Robert Lowth: The Judgment of Hercules (adapted)
Jephtha	26 February 1752	Morell after Judges 11 and George Buchanan: Jephtes sive Votum
The Triumph of Time and Truth	11 March 1757	Morell after Pamphili Il trionfo del Tempo

Never ceasing to experiment nor to recognize a commercial opportunity, in this period, Handel also composed *Semele* and *Hercules*, two English-language works whose simplified choruses combine with Greek plots to produce a curiously successful hybrid of oratorio and opera. The defeat of the internal rebellion by Prince William in 1746 brought on the *Occasional Oratorio* and *Judas Maccabaeus*, both unabashed political celebrations yet composed of typical oratorio elements.

On 21 January 1751, Handel began to compose an oratorio on the same story as the **Giacomo Carissimi** work that he knew well, *Jephtha*. But the work was interrupted by rapidly deteriorating eyesight, and he did not complete the score until 30 August. He composed no large new pieces after that, although, through the aid of his assistant, John Christopher Smith, he managed to effect revisions and contribute some new songs and arias to revivals. William Blomfield, royal surgeon, operated unsuccessfully on Handel's eye in November 1752, as did John Taylor (who had operated on **Johann Sebastian Bach**) in August 1758.

Handel continued to participate in performances and to revise and revive his work throughout the 1750s, finishing in 1759 with a revision of his 1749 oratorio *Solomon*. On 6 April, he attended a last performance of *Messiah* and died on 14 April. At his own request, he was buried in Westminster Abbey, and it is reported that 3,000 people attended the burial service.

Such a number would be astronomical for any other composer of the Baroque because composers, no matter how great, were not idolized as great artists as they would be in the 19th century. But for Handel, it was yet another sign of the singular esteem of the English public and how much he had affected English society. As early as 25 February 1723, when he had been in the country a little more than a decade, he was made composer of music of His Majesty's **Chapel Royal**, a title that earned him nothing because, as an alien, he could not earn a stipend paid by the Crown. That matter was resolved in 1727 when an act of Parliament made him a British subject. Oxford University offered him an honorary doctorate of music in 1733, which he did not accept, but he did premiere *Athalia* in the city. The sculptor Louis Roubiliac created a commissioned marble statue of Handel for the Vauxhall Gardens in 1738 and then another for his tomb, showing the composer with an open score to *Messiah*, unveiled on 10 July 1762. Already John Mainwaring's biography had appeared in 1760, the first biographical monograph of any composer in the Western tradition.

Even such adulation might have faded had it not been for *Messiah*. As it opened in Dublin in April 1742, one newspaper gushed that the work "was allowed by the greatest Judges to be the finest Composition of Musick that ever was heard." Its 1749 revival inaugurated a series of annual charity performances for the Foundling Hospital, and since then, it very likely has been performed every year somewhere in the world, thus making it the oldest large-scale classic in the Western canon. Most of the rest of Handel's music lay shelved in the cultural attic along with virtually all other Baroque music composed to that time. Thus, Handel survived into the 19th and 20th centuries primarily as the composer of a single work, misunderstood as purely religious, glorified by the story of its inspired composition in 23 days.

This image of a musical saint was tainted late in the 19th century by admirers' growing awareness of Handel's **parody** practices, which include not only the reworking of music composed by himself but also substantial use of music by contemporaries, occasionally without much reworking at all. (That is why it is impossible to count Handel's works precisely; what is to count as a "new" work?) This "borrowing" violated the romantic concept of music as inspired and utterly personal, original art. Deeper understanding of all composers' parody practices in the Baroque has removed most of the opprobrium from Handel, but it does appear that he borrowed more from others than most, and the reasons for it remain unexplained.

A renewed appreciation of the wider corpus of Handel's repertory counts as one of the finest achievements of the **early music revival**. The 1920s in particular saw efforts in Germany to perform some of the operas and in England the more neglected oratorios. Ignorance of Baroque performance practices and the latent romantic tendency to "improve" the scores with modern orchestrations and transpositions hobbled these performances a great deal, but as the century progressed, historical research slowly removed such detritus. Since the 1970s, a more sensitive fidelity to Handel's performance practices, the explosion in the number of musicians and singers prepared to execute them, and even the advent of the compact-disc recording format, much more practical for Handelian forms, have restored the grandeur to music long forgotten.

HARMONIC FUNCTION. *See* FUNCTIONAL HARMONY.

HARP. Claudio Monteverdi's first **opera**, *L'Orfeo*, calls for two small Renaissance harps in Orfeo's serenade to Charon.

George Frideric Handel composed a single **concerto** for harp, Op. 4, No. 6 in B-flat major, and several solos for harp in several of his **English oratorios** and operas: *Esther* (1718), *Giulio Cesare in Egitto* (1724), and *Saul* (1739), where it has particular symbolic value as the instrument of David. In all of these, the harp required is most likely the triple harp, with three ranks of **strings**. Two outer ranks are **tuned** identically to diatonic pitches, and the third inner rank has the remaining **chromatic** pitches.

HARPSICHORD (Fr. *clavecin*; **Ger.** *Cembalo, Flügel*; **It.** *cembalo, clavicembalo*; **Sp.** *clavicordio*). Apparently invented at the end of the 15th century, the harpsichord became the most important **keyboard** instrument for Baroque secular music, and virtually every major composer after 1650, if not a virtuoso **violinist**, was a virtuoso harpsichordist (many were both).

In sacred music, it had to compete with the pipe **organ** but was often used in preference to the organ even in church owing to its clarity of articulation and much smaller, portable size. Owing to the development of a musical language that increasingly favored abstract instrumental compositions, the harpsichord repertory peaked in the Baroque, as did its technical development. After 1750, the **fortepiano**, owing to its power to play all gradations of loud and soft tones, gradually supplanted the harpsichord, which was virtually forgotten after the turn of the 19th century.

The harpsichord differs fundamentally from the fortepiano and organ in that it produces tones by the plucking of strings under tension. It shares this essential technique with the **spinet** and **virginal** but differs from them in that the stringing of a harpsichord runs in a plane extending longitudinally directly away from the player seated at the keyboard, parallel to the keys, with the long bass strings to the left and the shorter treble strings to the right, resulting in a wing shape, while the spinet's stringing is oblique to the keyboard and the virginal's is at right angles (transverse).

The wing-shaped wooden harpsichord case has at least eight components. The long straight piece on the left (bass) side is the *spine*. This attaches at the far end to the *tail* at an acute angle. A curved piece, the *bentside*, follows the shortening length of strings back toward the keyboard to the right of the player, where it is anchored by a short *cheekpiece*. The *wrest plank* ties the cheekpiece to the spine above the keyboard and completes the frame, and the entire wing is held together by the *bottom*, a broad and flat piece of wood that encloses the sounding cavity along with another similar piece, the *soundboard*, which is attached within the wing by wooden liners. Braces of various kinds, often tying the bentside to the spine by running under the soundboard, prevent the collapse or twisting of the frame under the tension of the many **tuned** strings. Finally, a *lid* may cover the entire case. Often, the visible part of the soundboard and the underside of the lid are decorated with painted images and laudatory mottoes in Latin.

Each key on the harpsichord, as well as virginal and spinet, is actually a long piece of wood, most of which is out of sight, acting as a lever. When the harpsichordist depresses a key, the lever pushes up one or more thin pieces of wood called *jacks*. Each jack has a slot cut into its top, and the slot is fitted with a quill or leather *plectrum* mounted onto a movable *tongue*. The rising plectrum plucks the string, producing the tone. When the player releases the key, the jack falls back down to its resting position while a bit of soft cloth contacts the vibrating string, dampening the sound abruptly, and a tiny spring behind the tongue pushes it back to its original position, ready to rise again at the next touch of the player. The rapid and forceful plucking of the string

Single-manual harpsichord constructed by Thomas Klenck, Hamilton, New York.

produces the sharp attack that could articulate the rapid harmonic rhythm of Baroque music so well.

The mechanism is simple enough that most harpsichordists tune and maintain their own instruments. However, because there is no way to vary the displacement of the plucked string, the volume of the sound cannot be varied by the touch of the player. Most Baroque harpsichords have multiple sets of strings and jacks, so that a player could choose to pluck one, two, or three strings tuned to a single **pitch-class** at once by depressing a single key. The third set is usually tuned to sound one octave higher than the standard (4′ or "four-foot" as opposed to 8′ or "eight-foot" strings, terms derived from organ pipe lengths). These auxiliary sets of strings may be engaged or disengaged by *jackslides* located under or at the side of the keyboard and, in this way, can make the instrument louder or softer but only by discrete, not gradual, changes of volume, sometimes called "terraced dynamics." Because the jacks for auxiliary strings had to pluck the strings at different points for the same string, their engagement could produce different timbres, and so, such harpsichords were capable of registrations analogous to organ registrations, albeit with much subtler differences. Of course, the player can only effect dynamic and timbral contrasts when the composition allows moving the jackslide.

Late in the 16th century, apparently, the double-manual harpsichord was invented by an unknown Flemish maker, possibly related to the famous Ruckers workshop, whose models began to dominate all of northern Europe by 1700. Two keyboards (manuals) are situated one above the other. Each one has an independent set of jackslides, which by the mid-17th century could also be coupled, allowing each keyboard to produce a different volume and timbre of sound, depending on the instrument. The double-manual harpsichord also facilitates the playing of **contrapuntal** music when the hands must frequently cross. Some of the **Goldberg Variations** of **Johann Sebastian Bach** expressly demand a second manual "*a 2 Clav.*"

In Baroque music, the harpsichord is most frequently heard as an accompanimental instrument, chiefly as the chord-playing instrument required of a basso **continuo**, especially in secular contexts where no pipe organ was available. The simple harmonic **textures** played by the continuo were essential to the aesthetic aims of the earliest Baroque experiments in **monody** and **opera** at the turn of the 17th century, and the continuo's success in providing efficient and expressive harmonic accompaniment quickly carried over into the new genres that spun off from opera: **sonata**, **concerto**, **sacred concerto**, *sinfonia*. Even when more complex contrapuntal textures supplied all the pitch information needed for harmonic structure, the continuo is included as a matter of course and contributes to the stereotypical Baroque sonority featuring a harpsichord in the background.

Harpsichordists, therefore, had to be able to realize a **figured bass** and generally had solid training in **thoroughbass improvisation**.

After the earliest experiments in Baroque instrumental composition, the left-hand bass part of the continuo developed into an equally important part of the contrapuntal texture in chamber music. Thus, the third **voice** of the trio in a "**trio sonata** for two violins and continuo" is this bass melody, which, in the best examples, is full of **imitations** and motivic interplays with the featured solo parts. The so-called **solo sonatas** of Johann Sebastian Bach for violin or **flute** are, in effect, trio sonatas because he composed both the left and right hands with such melodies in **counterpoint** with the featured soloist.

The Baroque repertory featuring the harpsichord as a solo instrument is rich indeed. Carrying over from the Renaissance into the 17th century are

toccatas, ricercars, fantasias, canzonas, dances, suites, preludes, ostinatos, and sets of **variations**. The principal composers of harpsichord music in 17th-century Italy are **Girolamo Frescobaldi** and Claudio Merulo (1533–1604); in the Netherlands, **Jan Pieterszoon Sweelinck**; in Austria, **Johann Jacob Froberger**; in France, **Nicolas Lebègue, Jean Henry D'Anglebert**, and, toward the end of the century, the **Couperins** and **Elisabeth Jacquet de La Guerre**; and in England, **John Blow** and **Henry Purcell**.

The premier composers of harpsichord music in the 18th century are **Jean-Philippe Rameau, George Frideric Handel, Georg Philipp Telemann, Johann Kuhnau, Domenico Scarlatti** (who pioneered the solo sonata for harpsichord), and, in a class by himself, Johann Sebastian Bach. Except for Scarlatti's music and some of Kuhnau's, most of these harpsichord publications are dance suites. Bach nearly always presents his harpsichord music in the form of didactic collections for harpsichord students and student composers: the two volumes of the *Well-Tempered Clavier*, the so-called French Suites and English Suites, volumes one and two of the *Clavier-Übung*, the Goldberg Variations, and the **Art of Fugue** are all designed to elucidate central problems of composition as well as to tax the harpsichord player.

The harpsichord as the featured soloist in a concerto arrives only well into the 18th century. The best-known Baroque concertos today are the concertos of J. S. Bach: seven for solo harpsichord, three for two harpsichords, two for three harpsichords, and one for four, a **parody** of **Antonio Vivaldi**'s Concerto for Four Violins, Op. 3, No. 10. Many, perhaps most, of these concertos are arrangements of Bach's own concertos for other instruments.

After a long period from 1810, when virtually no harpsichords were played or built, interest revived as a major component of the **early music revival** in the middle of the 19th century. Key events in this history include the recitals of piano virtuoso Louis Diémer (1843–1919) of music on an instrument from 1769 of Pascal Taskin; the campaigns of Arnold Dolmetsch (1858–1940) in England and America to revive the harpsichord; the career of the first modern harpsichord virtuoso, Wanda Landowska (1879–1959), who performed and taught regularly on an instrument designed by the Pleyel firm, incorporating much piano technology and framing; and the opening of the Boston workshop of Frank Hubbard (1920–1976) and William Dowd (1922–2008) in 1949, the first to attempt harpsichord construction according to historical evidence of Renaissance and Baroque manuals and treatises.

HASSE, JOHANN ADOLF (baptized 25 March 1699, Bergedorf, Germany–16 December 1783, Venice). Although most of his work was quickly forgotten after he died, while active, Hasse was the most renowned composer of Italian *opera seria* in Italy and German-speaking lands. He composed at least 58 **operas**, mostly *seria*, but also a few comedies, which were produced in many important opera centers: **Naples**, **Venice**, Milan, **Dresden**, and **Vienna**, and he was the favorite composer of the age's most eminent opera **librettist**, **Metastasio**. Hasse composed fluently, with a particular gift for vocal melody, which he generally displayed to full advantage without distraction from **contrapuntal textures**. Besides the operas, he composed about 11 **intermezzi**, 11 Italian **oratorios**, 60 Italian chamber **cantatas**, and 33 more cantatas for voice and **orchestra**. His instrumental music includes 54 **concertos**, mostly for **transverse flute** and **strings**, and 24 **trio sonatas**. He also composed sacred music, most of it for four-**voiced** choir and orchestra: 15 **masses**, 2 requiems, 36 single mass ordinary settings, 10 mass offertories, 21 psalms, 18 **antiphons**, six **hymns**, and 38 **motets** for solo voice and orchestra.

Hasse was born the second of five children to Peter Hasse and Christine Klessing, who was daughter of Bergedorf's mayor. In 1718, he joined the **Hamburg** opera company and quickly established himself as a tenor of reputation, but his career changed when his opera *Antioco* opened at Brunswick on 1 August 1721. Soon, he left Germany for a long tour of Venice, Bologna, **Florence**, and **Rome**, finally settling in the major opera center of Naples for six years, until 1730. He converted to Roman Catholicism. He studied with **Alessandro Scarlatti** and possibly **Nicolo Porpora**, worked with the superstar *castrato* Carlo Broschi (**Farinelli**), and his rise in Neapolitan opera was spectacular. He composed seven serious operas for six seasons, not to mention many smaller musical dramas.

Hasse appeared in Venice for the 1730 Carnival season, a milestone of his career. In his opera *Artaserse*, he set a libretto of Metastasio, later to become his most important collaborator, for the first time. Farinelli liked the **arias** of *Artaserse* so well that he sang them in a related *pasticcio* in **London** in 1734, and then for Philip V, King of Spain, he sang "Per questo dolce amplesso" and "Pallido il sole" every evening during his service of 1737–1746. Hasse also met in Venice another famous singer, the mezzo-soprano Faustina Bordoni (c. 1700–1781), whom he married in June 1730 and who created many of the female protagonists in his later operas.

Sometime after Carnival but before Ascension in 1730, Hasse was granted the title of *Kapellmeister* to the court of the Elector August I of Saxony at Dresden, but he and Faustina Bordoni did not arrive there until 6 or 7 July 1731. Although this appointment lasted until 1763, the couple took frequent and substantial leaves of absence to various cities of Italy and Vienna to produce operas that had been commissioned by the nobility of Europe. He first worked in Vienna in 1731 and was active there and in Venice in 1733. In these years, his acquaintance with Metastasio grew. Eventually, Hasse would set all the poet's opera librettos except *Temistocle*.

Hasse's operas to 1750

Work	First performance	Librettist
Antioco	11 August 1721, Brunswick	B. Feind after A. Zeno
Il Sesostrate	13 May 1726, Naples	A. Carasale
L'Astarto	December 1726, Naples	A. Zeno and P. Pariati
Gerone Tiranno	19 November 1727, Naples	After A. Aureli
Attalo, Re di Bitinia	May 1728, Naples	F. Silvani
L'Ulderica	29 January 1729, Naples	
La Sorella Amante	Spring 1729, Naples	B. Saddumene
Tigrane	4 November 1729, Naples	F. Silvani
Artaserse	February 1730, Venice	Metastasio, rev. G. Boldini
Dalisa	May 1730, Venice	Lalli after N. Minato
Arminio	28 August 1730, Milan	A. Salvi
Ezio	Fall 1730, Naples	Metastasio
Cleofide	13 September 1731, Dresden	M. Boccardi after Metastasio
Catone in Utica	26 December 1731, Turin	Metastasio
Cajo Fabricio	12 January 1732, Rome	After A. Zeno
Demetrio	January 1732, Venice	Metastasio
Euristeo	May 1732, Venice	Lalli after A. Zeno
Issipile	1 October 1732, Naples	Metastasio
Sireo Re di Persia	2 May 1733, Bologna	Metastasio
Tito Vespasiano	24 September 1735, Pesaro	Metastasio
Senocrita	27 February 1737, Dresden	S. Pallavicino
Atalanta	26 July 1737, Dresden	S. Pallavicino
Asteria	3August 1737, Dresden	S. Pallavicino
Irene	8 February 1738, Dresden	S. Pallavicino
Alfonso	11 May 1738, Dresden	S. Pallavicino
Viriate	Carnival 1739, Venice	Lalli after Metastasio
Numa Pompilio	7 October 1741, Hubertusburg	S. Pallavicino
Lucio Papirio	18 January 1742, Dresden	A. Zeno
Didone Abbandonata	7 October 1742, Hubertusburg	Metastasio
Endimione	July 1743, Naples?	Metastasio
L'Asilio d'Amore	7 October 1743, Hubertusburg	Metastasio
Antigono	10 October 1743, Hubertusburg	Metastasio
Ipermestra	8 January 1744, Vienna	Metastasio
Semiramide Riconosciuta	4 November 1744, Naples	Metastasio
Arminio	7 October 1745, Dresden	G. Pasquini
Lo Starnuto d'Ercole	Carnival 1745, Venice	
Eurimedonte e Timocleone	Carnival 1746, Venice	Zanetti
La Spartana Generosa	14 June 1747, Dresden	G. Pasquini
Leucippo	7 October 1747, Hubertusburg	G. Pasquini
Demofoonte	9 February 1748, Dresden	Metastasio
Attilio Regolo	12 January 1750, Dresden	Metastasio

In 1745, King Frederick the Great of Prussia visited and heard Hasse's **Te Deum** and *opera seria Arminio*. The king, a fine musician, thereafter often invited the composer and his wife to Potsdam. The Prussian bombardment of Hasse's Dresden house in 1760, causing the loss of many manuscripts, may have soured this relationship. Porpora, possibly Hasse's teacher in Naples, was brought to Dresden in 1748 to teach the Princess Maria Antonia of Saxony and was given the title *Kapellmeister*, but Hasse was promoted to *Oberkapellmeister* in 1750.

In 1763, Hasse joined the imperial court in Vienna where he worked closely with Metastasio. In 1775, he and Faustina Bordoni retired to Venice. She died on 4 November 1781. Hasse is buried in the Church of San Marcuola.

HEINICHEN, JOHANN DAVID (17 April 1683, Krössuln near Weissenfels, Germany–16 July 1729, Dresden). Author of the one of the most important treatises of the late Baroque, *Der General-Bass in der Composition, oder Neue und gründliche Anweisung* ("New and Fundamental Treatise on the **Thoroughbass** in Composition," **Dresden**, 1728), which prompted the contemporary historian Charles Burney to call him "the **Rameau** of Germany," Heinichen was, from 1717 until his death, the *Kapellmeister* at the court of the elector of Saxony in Dresden and composer of 8 **operas**, 5 **serenatas**, 63 **cantatas**, 24 **concertos**, 5 *sinfonie*, 7 solo **violin sonatas**, 9 **trio sonatas**, 4 ensemble sonatas, 12 **masses**, 2 requiems, 3 **Te Deums**, 15 **church cantatas**, and 35 Latin **hymns** and **motets**.

He trained with **Johann Kuhnau** at the St. Thomas School in **Leipzig** from 30 March 1695 and, beginning in 1702, studied law at Leipzig University. While practicing law, he composed occasional court music and led the **Collegium Musicum**. In 1710, he abandoned his law career and went to **Venice**, where he composed two successful operas and met **Antonio Vivaldi**, **Francesco Gasparini**, and **Antonio Lotti**, among others. In 1712, he was in **Rome**, teaching Prince Leopold of Anhalt-Cöthen, future employer of **Johann Sebastian Bach**.

HIDALGO, JUAN (28 September 1614, Madrid–31 March 1685). The most influential Spanish composer of the 17th century, Hidalgo collaborated with the eminent dramatist Pedro Calderón de la Barca (1600–1681) to create the first Spanish musical dramas. They produced a **semi-opera** *Fortunas de Andrómeda y Perseo* ("The Fates of Andromeda and Perseus"), which contains the earliest surviving Spanish **recitative** (*recitado*), in 1653, and a full **opera**, now lost, called *La Púrpura de la Rosa* ("The Crimson of the Rose"), in 1660. Another opera from about the same time, *Celos aun del Aire Matan* ("Jealousy, Even of the Air, Kills"), does survive, the earliest complete Spanish opera extant.

Hidalgo appears to have begun his professional career as a **harpist** in the Spanish royal chapel about 1630. By 1645, he was acting as the chapel's principal composer. He composed about 15 works for the stage in addition to numerous *villancicos*. Three **masses** and three **motets** also survive.

HISTORIA. German-language musical setting of a Bible story, most commonly the birth, **passion**, resurrection, or ascension of Christ, used in a Lutheran liturgy. In the 16th and first half of the 17th century, the sung text was strictly scriptural: a Gospel sung to a recitation tone for narration and for individual speaking roles, to **polyphony** for group responses. Later techniques from Italian **opera** appeared—**recitative**, **aria**, **continuo** accompaniment—and also nonbiblical commentary, particularly in passions. In Saxony and Thuringia, composers might call such liturgical dramas *actus musicus*; such works distinguished themselves from the *historia* only by greater emphasis on dramatic presentation. When nonbiblical commentary began to be added in the later 17th century, the *historia* became the **oratorio passion**. *See also* BACH, JOHANN SEBASTIAN; CARISSIMI, GIACOMO; CHARPENTIER, MARC-ANTOINE; ORATORIO; SCHÜTZ, HEINRICH.

HOMOPHONY (HOMOPHONIC). A musical **texture** of one perceptually salient melody, or **voice**, and one or more accompanying voices (e.g., most songs for solo voice). The effect is analogous to the figure and ground relationship in painting.

HOMORHYTHMIC. A **polyphonic texture** in which all the simultaneous **voices** move precisely together, that is, all with the same pattern of note durations.

HORN (Fr. *cor*, It. *corno*). The horn makes its first appearance in art music of the West (as opposed to its older, widespread use in hunting animals) in the theater. There is evidence that **Francesco Cavalli**'s *Le Nozze di Teti e di Peleo* (**Venice**, 1639) and **Jean-Baptiste Lully**'s *La Princesse d'Elide* (1664) called for horn. The first documented **orchestral** use dates from 1705 in **Reinhard Keiser**'s opera *Octavia* (**Hamburg**).

Up to this point, a horn was constructed as a single coiled tube, without valve mechanisms, which meant that different pitches had to be culled by the player's lips and force of breath from the partial frequencies (overtones or harmonics) of the instrument's fundamental pitch derived from the length of tubing. Thus, each instrument could play more or less in one **key** only. About 1700, however, the Leichnamschneider brothers of **Vienna** began to replace the fixed mouthpiece of the horn with a removable socket, into which fitted *crooks*, tubing couplers of varying length. This invention allowed players to change the size of their instruments, in effect, by substituting one size crook for another, and thereby to play in different keys.

It is remarkable how quickly composers took advantage of such developments and the growing virtuosity of horn players. As early as 1715, **George Frideric Handel**'s **Water Music**, a number of **Johann Sebastian Bach**'s **church cantatas**, his First **Brandenburg Concerto** (before 1721), and the fearsome "Quoniam" from the **Mass in B Minor** (1733) all have horn parts that try the techniques of professional players today.

HORNPIPE. British **dance** similar to the **gigue** in character and usually danced by a single person. In the 17th century, the great majority are in triple **meter**, characterized by the following rhythm:

$\frac{3}{2}$ ♩ ♩ ♩ ♩ | Example. Typical rhythmic pattern for the hornpipe.

In the 18th century, hornpipes were more often in duple meter but showing similar syncopations. Stylized instrumental hornpipes in collections were composed by **Henry Purcell**, **Thomas Arne**, and **George Frideric Handel** in his **Water Music** (Nos. 9 and 12).

HOTTETERRE. Celebrated family of French musicians, composers, and makers of woodwinds whose advances in the construction of **transverse flute**, **oboe**, and **bassoon** allowed these instruments to compete with agile **string instruments** in the execution of Baroque figuration in the second half of the period. The earliest ancestor appears to be Loys de Haulteterre (died c. 1628) of Normandy. One of his three sons, Jean Hotteterre (1610–1692), moved to **Paris** where he and his sons Jean (c. 1630–1668) and Martin (1635–1712) established a reputation for fine instruments and fine playing at the royal court. Martin's son Jacques-Martin (1673–1763), not a maker, became the most celebrated composer for transverse flute in the French school, publishing the first duets for unaccompanied transverses in his *Premier Livre de Pièces* of 1708 and an important treatise, *Principes de la Flûte Traversière* in 1719.

HUMFREY, PELHAM (1647 or 1648–14 July 1674, Windsor, England). One of the bright lights of the first generation of Restoration composers, his European travels acquainted him with the latest Italian and French **operatic** trends to import to England. He composed 20 **anthems**, 1 **service**, 5 devotional songs, 24 secular songs, 3 court **odes**, and 2 short **masques**, for a production of *The Tempest* in 1674.

Of his origins, little is known. By 1660, he was a chorister at the **Chapel Royal** under the direction of **Henry Cooke**. He embarked on a European tour in 1664 after his voice broke. **William Boyce** believed that he studied with **Jean-Baptiste Lully**, but his travels are undocumented. He returned to England by March 1666 and, on 26 October 1667, was sworn in as a Gentleman of the Chapel Royal. On 14 July 1674, he succeeded his teacher, Cooke, as master of the Children of the Chapel Royal, and later that year, he married Cooke's daughter Katherine. They had one daughter who died in infancy.

Humfrey is buried in the south cloister of Westminster Abbey.

HYMN. A devotional song. The term, of obscure Greek origin, refers to repertories in every major religion that have the following characteristics: the texts are sacred but nonscriptural strophic poetry; the melodies, through elements of repetition, periodic phrasing, and **meter**, have strongly patterned structures that make them easy to learn and remember; the songs have popular roots, often arise outside of authorized liturgies, and then grow into some liturgical role.

These features are not present in all repertories translated as "hymns," but taken together, they form a cluster concept that can set this sacred music apart from other types. In the Baroque, there are three major types and many local or national hymn genres.

The Roman Catholic hymns heard during the Baroque are traditional Latin texts mostly composed during the late Middle Ages: **Te Deum** is perhaps the most famous. Traditionally, they are not heard during **mass** but only at liturgies of the divine office (hours). Although coming from the plainchant tradition of unison singing without harmony or meter, in the Baroque, composers such as **Marc-Antoine Charpentier** set the texts, with or without the traditional melodies, in *stile moderno* with a **continuo** accompaniment at the very least.

The Lutheran hymn is called "**chorale**." Chorales were sung by congregations at Sunday liturgies.

The Anglican hymn is very much like the Lutheran chorale in musical **texture** and character, but its texts are English.

![I]

IL RITORNO D'ULISSE IN PATRIA. **("The Return of Ulysses to His Homeland," Claudio Monteverdi).** The penultimate of **Claudio Monteverdi**'s surviving stage works, the **opera** premiered during the 1639–1640 Carnival season at the Teatro San Giovanni e Paolo in **Venice**. The **libretto** is by Giacomo Badoaro (1602–1654).

Monteverdi's autograph does not survive. The principal source sits in the National Library in **Vienna**, a score that preserves the vocal melodies and an unfigured bass, with few other elaborations. Therefore, modern performances of *Ulisse* are reconstructions in some sense and will vary considerably one from another.

The opera adapts Books XIII–XXIII of Homer's *Odyssey* into a prologue and three acts. The plot is greatly simplified but includes scenes of Penelope's despair, the suitors' pressuring her, the emotional reunions of Ulysses with his faithful servant Eumete and his son Telemaco, the bow contest, and the great reunification scene of Ulysses and Penelope. The principal roles are Ulysses (baritone), Penelope (soprano), and Telemaco (tenor). Other roles include gods and goddesses, servants, and Penelope's suitors, requiring a cast of at least 14, depending upon doubling, and a **chorus**. The opera takes about three hours to perform.

IMITATION. A **contrapuntal texture** featuring a single motive (**subject**), that is, a melody overlapping with itself. The first entrance of the subject is called the *dux* (leading **voice**), and the copying voice is called the *comes* (following voice), also the **answer**.

Example. Johann Sebastian Bach, Fugue in D Major from the *Well-Tempered Clavier*, Book II, mm. 1–4

Baroque music has many specific techniques of imitation, which describe how precisely the *comes* copies the *dux* (**strict imitation, free imitation**), whether the answer changes the tonal orientation of the music (real answer, tonal answer), and how the subject may change in the course of the imitative passage (**inversion**, retrograde, **diminution, augmentation**). *See also* FUGUE.

IMPROVISATION. The extemporaneous composition of music was a skill essential to the Baroque musician. Indeed, the line between improvised composition and written-out composition is blurred in that many scores of Baroque **toccatas, preludes**, and other genres derived from improvisational habits may be polished versions of creations on the spot.

Traditions of liturgical improvisation carried over directly from the 16th century. In Roman Catholic **masses**, the **organist** could replace required plainchants with improvisations based on their melodies. In Lutheran liturgies, the organist would improvise an organ prelude based on a **chorale** about to be sung, as well as the harmonic progressions that supported the singing.

Typical situations new to the Baroque included: the realization of a **figured bass**, required in virtually all Baroque ensemble music, instrumental and vocal; the singing or playing of **cadenzas** in **arias** and **concertos**; and the supplying of **ornamentation** to music written out.

IN NOMINE. Peculiar English genre of **contrapuntal** instrumental music arising in the early 16th century. The name refers to the text *in nomine Domini* that occurs in the Sanctus of a Latin **mass**, but its accompanying melody was taken as a **cantus firmus** by John Taverner (c. 1490–1545) from a plainchant **antiphon**, *Gloria tibi Trinintas*. Generations of English composers tested their contrapuntal mettle with this cantus firmus until the end of the 17th century.

INTERMEDIUM (pl. INTERMEDI). (1) Short vocal compositions, usually for solo voice with **lute** or **keyboard** accompaniment, inserted between the acts of a spoken drama, originating in the Medici court in **Florence** in 1539. The texts were commentaries on mythological themes or stories. The intermedi for the play *La Pellegrina* ("The Pilgrim Woman") for the wedding of Grand Duke Ferdinand I and Cristina of Lorraine, in 1589, combined the talents of **Emilio de' Cavalieri, Jacopo Peri**, and **Giulio Caccini** and is, therefore, considered to be a forerunner of the first **operas**.

(2) A concerted vocal work, in the manner of an operatic **aria**, that breaks up the **recitative** presentation of the biblical text in a German *historia*. The speeches of the angel, the shepherds, and King Herod, in the **Christmas Oratorio** of **Heinrich Schütz** are the intermedi.

INTERMEZZO. An Italian comic music drama usually composed in two scenes or short acts with only two or three characters performed during the intermissions of a three-act *opera seria*. The earliest known example is *Frappolone e Florinetta*, performed in **Venice** in February 1706 between the acts of **Francesco Gasparini**'s *Statira*. It is probable that Gasparini composed the intermezzo as well. In the following decades, the intermezzo became popular and developed into the full-length **operatic** genre, the *opera buffa*. **Giovanni Pergolesi**'s *La Serva Padrona* (1733) is a particularly influential example.

INTONAZIONE. Brief, **improvisatory** composition for pipe **organ** that sets the pitch for a choral work to follow. Andrea and **Giovanni Gabrieli**'s *Intonati d'organo* (1593) is the first appearance of the term. *See also* TOCCATA.

INVENTION. Generally, invention in the Baroque refers to skilful fashioning of musical motives, ritornellos, and other melodic-rhythmic materials with which a composer builds a piece. It appears explicitly in the title of **Antonio Vivaldi**'s Opus 8 **concertos**, *Il Cimento dell' Armonia e dell' Inventione* ("The Test of Harmony and Invention"), and in **Johann Mattheson**'s theory of melody in *Der vollkommene Capellmeister*.

Modern listeners are more familiar with the term through the 15 two-**voice** inventions of **Johann Sebastian Bach** (1723), a collection of didactic **imitative keyboard** works that, like the *Well-Tempered Clavier*, albeit on a much smaller scale, presents various kinds of imitative invention in 15 different **keys**. Bach evidently took his title from Francesco Antonio Bonporti's (1672–1749) *Inventioni da Camera*, Opus 10. Bach's similar collection of three-voice works is commonly called "three-part inventions" even though Bach titled them *Sinfonie* in his autograph.

INVERSION. (1) Transformation of a **subject** by inverting each of its melodic intervals about a central **pitch-class**, usually the first one of the subject, which acts as an axis of symmetry.

Example. Johann Sebastian Bach, Fugue in D Minor from the *Well-Tempered Clavier*, Book I, mm. 13–15. Subject occurs in the soprano voice beginning m. 13. Its inversion occurs in the alto voice beginning m. 14.

(2) Any form of a chord that does not sound its root in the bass **voice**.

INVERTIBLE COUNTERPOINT. Type of **counterpoint** that produces a syntactically sound harmonic progression regardless of which of the combined melodies is heard above the others. In a two-**voice** invertible counterpoint, or double counterpoint, melody A may sound above melody B in pitch range, or B above A, both arrangements producing well-formed harmonic progressions. In triple counterpoint, any of melodies A, B, or C may sound highest or lowest or in the middle range.

ISRAEL IN EGYPT. An **English oratorio** composed by **George Frideric Handel** between 1 October and 1 November 1739. The **libretto**, probably by Charles Jennens (1700–1773), Handel's *Messiah* librettist, sets the Exodus story.

The work exists in two versions. The first version has three parts:

Part I: Elegy on the Death of Joseph (sources: Job, Lamentations, Psalms)
Part II: Liberation of the Israelites from Egypt (Exodus)
Part III: The Canticle of Moses (Exodus)

Handel had composed Part I for another occasion, the funeral of his pupil and friend Queen Caroline in December 1737. Handel liked the music so well that he was loath to let it go with a single performance. Generally, a composition tailored for such a specific occasion could not easily find a place in the growing concert repertory, but Handel, mainly by changing the feminine pronouns to masculine, transformed the entire work into the original first part of his 1739 **oratorio** *Israel in Egypt.*

When Friedrich Chrysander (1826–1901) compiled his monumental edition of Handel's complete works late in the 19th century, he saw no reason to include this music in his edition of *Israel in Egypt* because, except for a few words, it was identical to the *Funeral **Ode*** and because Handel himself had cut the "Elegy" section from subsequent performances of the oratorio. Almost all later editions of *Israel in Egypt* followed Chrysander's, and so the oratorio traditionally is performed in two parts rather than Handel's original three.

The original Part I is somberly scored for four-**voice chorus** (split sopranos in No. 6), **strings**, **oboes**, **organ**, and **continuo**. It requires about 40 minutes to perform. Parts II and III are scored for strings, oboes, **bassoons**, **trumpets**, **trombones**, **timpani**, six vocal soloists, and double four-voiced chorus and requires about one and one-half hours to perform.

The work is remarkable among Handel's oratorios for its close adherence to the biblical text, its contemplative as opposed to narrative libretto, its frequent borrowings from 17th-century sacred works, and its preponderance of choral numbers.

J

JACQUET DE LA GUERRE, ELISABETH (baptized 17 March 1665, Paris–27 June 1729, Paris). Her *Céphale et Procris*, produced 15 March 1694 at the Académie Royale de Musique, was the first **opera** composed by a woman in France, but de La Guerre was much better known as a virtuoso **harpsichordist** and teacher in **Paris**. Her first volume of harpsichord pieces appeared in 1687. She also composed six **violin sonatas**, six **trio sonatas**, three volumes of French **cantatas**, a **Te Deum** (lost), and a volume of 14 pieces playable on either harpsichord or violin.

Coming from a family of musicians, Elisabeth Jacquet was already playing the harpsichord at the court of King Louis XIV by age five and appeared there until 23 September 1684, when she married an **organist**, Marin de La Guerre.

JEPHTE **(Giacomo Carissimi, before 1650).** One of the most celebrated of the early Latin **oratorios**, *Jephte* tells the story of the Israelite general Jephthah who promises the Lord that, if he is granted victory over the Ammonites, he will sacrifice the person who meets him first (Book of Judges 11:29–40). The Israelites are indeed victorious, but when returning to his people, the first person Jephthah meets is his only daughter. He allows her two months to wander the mountains in lament of her virginity before he fulfills the vow.

Giacomo Carissimi composed the work for the confraternity of the Santissimo Crocifisso. The oratorio has two named roles for solo singers: Jephte and Filia (daughter). Other soloists sing the narration (*historicus*) in **recitative**. A **chorus** also provides some narration and sings the part of the people of Israel. The climax of the work comes at the end, the **lament** "Plorates colles" sung by the daughter and her companions, which became one of the most popular excerpts of the 17th century.

A performance of *Jephte* requires four soprano soloists (including Filia), one alto, one tenor (Jephte), and two basses, if no roles are doubled, in addition to two **violins**, a viola da gamba, and basso **continuo**. It takes about 25 minutes to perform. A critical score edited by Adelchi Amisano was published by Ricordi in 1977.

JOMMELLI, NICCOLÒ (10 September 1714, Aversa, Italy–25 August 1774, Naples). Jommelli's experiments in *dramma per musica*, particularly the so-called obbligato **recitative** in which instruments other than **continuo** played, constitute a key transition from the Baroque to classical style. The English historian Charles Burney witnessed the encore of one of these passages in a 1754 performance of *Attilo Regolo* in **London**, the only time he had ever seen a recitative received so warmly. In addition to his 80 **operas** and 12 other pieces for musical theater, Jommelli composed a significant body of sacred music: 30 psalm settings, 14 **oratorios**, 2 **masses**, a requiem, and 12 mass **motets**, among other works. His instrumental oeuvre is small but looks forward to the classical quartet **texture**: 13 **sonatas** *a quattro*, at least 2 **trio sonatas**, and 2 **concertos** for **harpsichord**.

Jommelli trained at the Conservatorio San Onofrio and the Conservatorio Pietà dei Turchini in **Naples** in the late 1720s. He began his professional career with two comedies, *L'Errore Amorosa* ("The Amorous Mistake") in 1737 and *Odoardo* in 1738, but his first *opera seria*, *Ricimero Re di Goti* of 1740, **Rome**, won him the patronage and lifelong esteem of Cardinal Henry Benedict, Duke of York.

In the early 1740s, Jommelli composed operas for Bologna, Turin, Padua, Ferrara, and **Venice**, and in the island city, he received his first permanent appointment at the Ospedale degli Incurabili, probably in 1745, for which he composed sacred music. He was in Rome again by 1747 and wrote more operas for that city, Parma, and Naples. In 1750, he was appointed *maestro coadiutore* of St. Peter's in Rome, eliciting another period of sacred music.

In August 1753, Jommelli entered the service of Duke Carl Eugen of Stuttgart and the following year was officially made *Oberkapellmeister*. Disagreements with the duke caused Jommelli's departure in 1769, and he spent his last years writing operas in Naples. When he died, he was considered one of the greatest composers of his time.

KAPELLMEISTER. See *MAESTRO DI CAPPELLA*.

KAPSPERGER, GIOVANNI GIROLAMO (a.k.a. Johann Hieronymus; c. 1580, Venice?–January 1651, Rome). Son of an Austrian military official and known as *il Tedesco della tiorba* ("the German of the **theorbo**"), Kapsperger today is remembered as the outstanding composer for theorbo, **lute**, and **guitar** working in Italy during the early Baroque. He published four volumes of pieces for *chitarrone* beginning in 1604 and two for lute, another book of **dances**, and a volume of 18 *sinfonie*. He also composed at least 20 **motets**, 21 **sacred concertos**, 2 **oratorios**, and 3 **masses**. His secular music includes a book of five-**voiced madrigals**, a few **cantatas**, and, remarkably, eight books of *villanelle*, secular songs of poetry less serious than madrigals.

Kapsperger was already well received in noble houses of **Rome** by 1605 as a virtuoso. In 1612, his *Maggio Cantata* was performed in **Florence** for the Grand Duchess Maria Maddalena. In 1622, his oratorio on Saints Ignatius and Francis Xavier was heard at the Collegio Romano in Rome, and by 1624, he had entered the service of Cardinal Francesco Barberini and began to collaborate with **Girolamo Frescobaldi**, Luigi Rossi, and other musical luminaries. He remained there until 1646.

KEISER, REINHARD (baptized 12 January 1674, Teuchern near Weissenfels, Germany–12 September 1739, Hamburg). The most important Baroque composer of **opera** in the German language. Besides his five **oratorios**, eight **motets**, six **church cantatas**, about a dozen secular **cantatas**, and a small repertory of instrumental music (two **concertos**, one **suite** for **keyboard**, four suites for chamber ensemble, and four ensemble **sonatas**), Keiser composed about 70 operas, of which about 20 survive, although rarely performed. At the beginning of his career, his operas showed a flexibility of musical form in the **arias** and entirely German **librettos** (*Singspiele*). After the turn of the 18th century, when the influence of Italian opera companies began to be felt even as far north as **Hamburg**, Keiser mixed in Italian poetry for some of the arias, which after 1710 he composed consistently in **da capo** form.

Reinhard Keiser was born to the **organist** Gottfried Keiser and Agnesa Dorothea Etzdorff. In July 1685, Reinhard enrolled at the St. Thomas School in **Leipzig**, where he may have studied music with **Johann Kuhnau**. The contemporary biographer **Johann Mattheson** claimed, however, that his composition skill derived entirely from natural gifts and the independent study of Italian music.

In 1694, he was appointed chamber composer at the court opera of Brunswick, collaborating with court poet F. C. Bressand to produce his first opera, *Procris und Cephalus*. Remarkably, another Keiser opera, *Basilius*, was produced that year at the important Theater am Gänsemarkt in Hamburg. By 1698, Keiser had composed five more operas for the Brunswick court, but in 1696 or 1697, he had already moved to Hamburg to succeed Johann Kusser (1660–1727) as the musical director of the Gänsemarkt. In 1703, he became general director. When he had to close in 1704 because of financial difficulties, Keiser took his new opera *Almira*, intended for Hamburg, to Weissenfels instead. Somehow, the libretto found its way into the hands of the 20-year-old **George Frideric Handel**, whose own setting led to difficulties with Keiser because of its success in Hamburg in 1705.

Keiser's administration of the Hamburg opera came to an end in 1707, and he appears to have left Hamburg and visited wealthy friends. But he returned, working under a new director, J. H. Sauerbrey, and, between 1709 and 1718, composed about 40 operas for the Gänsemarkt.

In 1718, the administration changed again, and Keiser was not retained as music director. He sought court positions in Gotha, Eisenach, and Stuttgart but was unsuccessful. In 1721, he joined an opera troupe of Hamburg musicians in Copenhagen and composed seven operas but was never appointed at the Danish court. He returned to the Hamburg opera under the direction of **Georg Philipp Telemann** and composed five new operas and two revised operas between 1722 and 1726. In 1727, another change of opera administration pushed him out, and although he was able to succeed Mattheson as the cantor of the Hamburg cathedral, the post paid him but little. He retired in 1735.

KERLL, JOHANN CASPAR (9 April 1627, Adorf, Saxony, Germany–13 February 1693, Munich). A student of **Giacomo Carissimi** and acquaintance of **Johann Jacob Froberger** in **Rome**, Kerll transmitted the Italian styles of the mid-17th century to Brussels (1647–1656), Munich (1656–1673), and **Vienna** (1673–1683), where he held posts. *Oronte*, the first of his 11 **operas** (all lost), opened the public opera house in Munich. His sacred music consists of 17 **masses** and a requiem, 3 *Missae breves* (Kyrie and Gloria only), and at least 16 **sacred concertos**. He is particularly noted for his **keyboard** music: eight **toccatas**, at least six **canzonas**, and the *Modulatio Organica* (1696,

Munich), a collection of eight **versets**, one for each of the traditional church **modes**, to be played in alternation with verses of the **Magnificat**, composed in response to the plague of 1679.

KEY. Depending upon context, key may denote: (1) the first **pitch-class** of a diatonic scale that is a collection of seven pitch-classes plus the duplication at the octave, (2) a tonal center (tonic) identified by a unique collection of pitch-classes, (3) a tonal center (tonic) established as the most stable pitch-class of a musical structure, to which all melodic and harmonic motion tends.

Baroque composers may establish or define the tonic pitch-class or key for a passage of music using various techniques, alone or in subtle combinations. One is to sound all the pitch-classes of a scale or enough of them to exclude all other scale possibilities. Another is to create a melodic or harmonic **cadence**; a cadence always finishes, or implies a finish, on the tonic pitch, thus identifying it. Or, a composer may simply emphasize the tonic pitch in some explicit fashion, such as by sounding a **pedal point**. In Baroque music, the identity of the key in force is not often in question; tonal ambiguity is rare and reserved for special effects or expressions.

Some writers consider major and minor scales on the same tonic to denote two different keys (e.g., "the key of C major" and "the key of C minor"). Others consider them two "**modes**" of the same key of C because of the identical tonic.

Baroque compositions are usually classified by key and mode (e.g., "**sonata** in D minor" or "**concerto** in A major"). *See also* INTRODUCTION; TONALITY.

KEYBOARD. Because they are capable of supplying a complete harmonic accompaniment to singers or solo instruments as part of the basso **continuo**, keyboard instruments have been essential participants in Baroque music since its beginning, and their importance only increased throughout the period. For sacred music, the most important by far was the pipe **organ** because of its association with churches since the 10th century, although in elaborate concerted works the **harpsichord** might also be used. In secular music—**suites**, **solo sonatas**, and as continuo for **sonatas** and **concertos** primarily—the harpsichord reigned supreme. Other keyboard instruments, used mostly for domestic activities of practice and composition, include the **clavichord**, **virginal**, and **spinet**. The **regals** is a small organ used mostly for secular music. The **fortepiano**, ancestor of the modern piano, was developed just as the Baroque closed.

KIRCHER, ATHANASIUS (2 May 1601, Gelsa, near Fulda, Germany–27 November 1680, Rome). One of the most brilliant thinkers of the Baroque, Kircher wrote 30 books, including the *Musurgia Universalis* of 1650, a work that continued to influence music theory all over Europe but, particularly through its 1662 German translation, for the entire Baroque. In this work, Kircher accounts for the phenomenon of music as a rational expression of God's order in the universe but, at the same time, synthesizes a German interest in the affective and **rhetorical** aspects of music with the composer's concern for the **contrapuntal** syntax of Gioseffo Zarlino (1517–1590), the standard author on *stile antico*. A wise and accurate critic, he gives musical examples from the works of **Agostino Agazzari, Giacomo Carissimi, Girolamo Frescobaldi**, and **Giovanni Girolamo Kapsperger**, among others.

Kircher received a thorough Jesuit training at Fulda (1612–1618), Paderborn (1618–1622), and Mainz (1624–1628), where he was ordained. He held professorships of mathematics, oriental languages, physics, and philosophy at Würzburg (1629), Avignon (1631), **Vienna** (1633), and finally **Rome** (1633–1680), where he settled at the Collegio Romano. *See also AFFEKTENLEHRE.*

KRIEGER, JOHANN PHILIPP (baptized 27 February 1649, Nuremberg, Germany–6 February 1725, Weissenfels). A key figure in the German middle Baroque, Krieger spent 45 years as *Kapellmeister* at the court of Weissenfels, where he composed 12 **trio sonatas**, 12 **solo violin sonatas**, 6 **suites** for wind instruments, 8 ensemble **sonatas**, and 18 German **operas** (*Singspiele*, Italian operas being forbidden there). More than anything, however, Krieger influenced the development of the German **church cantata**. According to his own catalog, he composed over 2,000 of them, of which 76 survive. Moreover, beginning in 1699, he was the first to set the reform **cantata** texts of **Erdmann Neumeister**, future deacon at Weissenfels, and likely encouraged Neumeister's work.

Details of Krieger's life appear in **Johann Mattheson**'s *Grundlage einer Ehren-Pforte*. A prodigious talent, Krieger studied **organ** and composition in Copenhagen from about 1665 to 1670 before becoming *Kapellmeister* in Bayreuth in 1672. The following year, he was given leave to study in **Venice** and **Rome**. In 1677, he was appointed organist at the court of Halle, which in 1680 moved to Weissenfels. Krieger became *Kapellmeister* that year.

KUHNAU, JOHANN (6 April 1660, Geising, Erzgebirge, Germany–5 June 1722, Leipzig). A major figure in German music at the turn of the 18th century, he was the immediate predecessor of **Johann Sebastian Bach** as cantor of Thomaskirche in **Leipzig**. Although Kuhnau composed at least 62 **church cantatas**, 14 Latin **motets**, a **Magnificat**, a **passion** according to St. Mark, and 2 **masses**, this considerable body of sacred music remained unpublished, and his single **opera** and a few other early stage pieces are lost, so he influenced his contemporaries principally through his published **keyboard** music: 14 **suites**, 2 **preludes**, 2 **fugues**, a **toccata**, and 14 **sonatas**, including the famous **Biblical Sonatas** for **harpsichord** (1700, Leipzig). Unlike J. S. Bach, Kuhnau exhibited all the various talents and interests that the Leipzig city council evidently desired in the *Thomaskantor*: Kuhnau was not only an esteemed composer and **organist** but also had built a distinguished law career, translated scholarly works from French and Italian into German, learned mathematics, Greek, and Hebrew, and had written a satirical novel, *Der musicalische Quack-Salber* ("The Musical Quack Doctor"). These self-motivated studies allowed him to carry out the multifarious teaching, administrative, and musical duties of his post with distinction.

Much information about Kuhnau's life comes from his autobiography published in **Johann Mattheson**'s collection, *Grundlage einer Ehren-Pforte* (1740). His intelligence and musical talent were evident early on, so he was sent to study in **Dresden** in 1670. By 1671, he was a chorister at the Kreuzkirche, where he attracted the attention of the *Kapellmeister* Vincenzo Albrici (1631–1696). Another member of the Kreuzkirche staff, Erhard Titius, who had become cantor at Zittau, invited Kuhnau to continue his education at the prestigious Johanneum school there. After Titius died in 1682, Kuhnau filled in as cantor. He then moved to Leipzig, matriculated in law at the university, and after an unsuccessful application in 1682, won the post of organist at Thomaskirche in 1684. He published his law thesis in 1688 and began to practice.

In 1689, Kuhnau married and eventually had eight children. Before the turn of the century, he published all his keyboard music, built up his renown as an organist, and engaged in literary and linguistic scholarship. When the *Thomaskantor* Johann Schelle died on 10 March 1701, the authorities quickly elected Kuhnau as his successor, and he took up his new and prestigious post in April 1701.

His career as cantor was not without difficulties. The growing Leipzig opera drew promising young singers away from enrolling at St. Thomas School. Then, in 1701, **Georg Philipp Telemann** arrived in Leipzig to study law and immediately founded his **Collegium Musicum**, which also attracted some of Kuhnau's students, and Telemann even inveigled the mayor, going over Kuhnau's head, to allow himself to compose for St. Thomas Church. Frequent illness troubled Kuhnau during this period, and in 1703, he learned that the city council had inquired of Telemann whether he might wish to succeed Kuhnau should he die.

In the end, such intrigues counted as mere annoyances, and Kuhnau's career at St. Thomas was generally characterized by the esteem of Germany's best musicians.

L

LALANDE, MICHEL-RICHARD DE (15 December 1657, Paris–18 June 1726, Versailles). Lalande succeeded in replacing the towering figure of **Jean-Baptiste Lully** in the favor of King Louis XIV of France, not on the strength of his theater music but rather through the great impression made by his *grands motets*, about 15 of which he had already composed before Lully's death in 1687. Exhibiting a considerable range of musical language, these sacred works could present a Gregorian **cantus firmus** alongside the most brilliantly **orchestrated textures** of **opera**. About 77 of them in all survive, and they became the staple of the French sacred music repertory for the royal court until the French Revolution a century later. They achieved a wide fame after the **Concert Sprituel** began in 1725. By 1770, 41 different *grands motets* of Lalande were given at least 590 performances before large crowds at these famous concerts.

In addition, Lalande composed 16 *petits motets*, 9 **Tenebrae** services, 9 so-called Elevation motets sung during the consecration of the **mass**, and 9 motets for the text *Domine fac salvum regem* required at the royal chapel. His compositions for the stage include six **ballets** or *opéra-ballets*, two pastorales, four comedies, and three *divertissements*. There are also 18 **suites** composed of **airs**, 3 compositions for **trumpet**, and 9 other **symphonic** movements.

Michel-Richard de Lalande was born the 15th child of a **Paris** tailor, Michel, and his wife, Claude Dumoutiers. Little is known of his musical training. He was admitted to the choir of the royal chapel of St. Germain-l'Auxerrois in Paris on the same day as **Marin Marais**, 15 April 1667. When the director, François Chaperon, left for the Sainte Chapelle, he asked Lalande for some of his earliest Tenebrae services to be sung during Holy Week. According to a posthumous "Discours" engraved in an edition of some of Lalande's *grands motets* dated 1730–1734, the composer played the **organ** for King Louis XIV in 1678, but, because of his youth, did not win any appointment then.

He was good enough an organist, however, to be appointed at the Jesuit church of St. Louis, the Petit St. Antoine, St. Jean-en-Grève, and St. Gervais, where he replaced Charles Couperin until the heir apparent to the organist post, **François Couperin**, should reach 18 years of age in 1686. In the meantime, Lalande won one of four positions, for the October–December quarter of the year, at the royal court as *sous-maître du roy*. (**Marc-Antoine Charpentier** also entered the competition but withdrew.) The "Discours" claims that the king himself made sure that Lalande would take one of the four quarters. In January 1685, the king appointed him one of three *compositeurs de la musique de la chambre* and, in January 1689, to the most desirable post of *surintendant de la musique de la chambre*, to which he added the singular honor of having a complete manuscript of Lalande's *grands motets* composed to that date made by the court copyists.

In July 1684, Lalande married Anne Rebel, a singer, daughter of a court musician, and half-sister of the conductor of the Paris Opéra. They had two daughters, Marie-Anne born in 1686 and Jeanne born in 1687, who became excellent singers but who both died of smallpox in a plague of May 1711. Anne Rebel died on 5 May 1722. He then married Marie-Louise de Cury, daughter of a court surgeon. They had one daughter, Marie-Michelle.

In the remaining 15 years before Louis's death, Lalande consolidated his position at the royal court. In September 1693, he added the January–March quarter to his *sous-maître* responsibilities, the April–June quarter in March 1704, and finally, two months before the king's death, the last July–September quarter. In the meantime, in 1709, Lalande entirely took over the post of *compositeur de la musique de la chambre*. On 1 July 1715, one man, Lalande, controlled all the music of the royal chapel for the first time.

No sooner had he built this empire for himself than Lalande began slowly to relieve himself of all his responsibilities, beginning in 1718, usually making sure that his students were appointed to the vacancies he created. In 1723, he asked King Louis XV to have the *sous-maître* position shared among four composers again. One of those succeeding to the three vacancies was **André Campra**.

Lalande died of pneumonia and is buried in the church of Notre Dame de Versailles.

LAMENT (It. *lamento*). Vocal composition setting an extended text expressing intense grief or mourning, the lament came to prominence at the beginning of the Baroque as one of the genres arising from experiments in *dramma per musica*. Enormously influential early on was the lament of Ariadne, the princess abandoned by Theseus on the isle of Naxos, from **Claudio Monteverdi**'s 1608 **opera** *Arianna*. The opera is lost, but Monteverdi's own publication of Ariadne's excerpted lament, first as a **madrigal**, "Lasciatemi morire," in 1614 and then as an extended **monody** in 1623, confirms the powerful effect of this moment in the original opera.

The monody is an admixture of **aria** and **recitative**. In its early development, the lament was not a type of aria. In his Eighth Book of Madrigals,

Monteverdi published *Lamento della Ninfa* ("Lament of the Nymph"), a similarly constructed mournful scene but containing a central aria composed as an **ostinato** over a descending tetrachord in the bass, that is, a repeating bass melody descending the scale steps 8-7-6-5. His pupil **Francesco Cavalli** used the same ostinato for Apollo's lament in his 1640 opera *Gli Amori di Apollo e di Dafne*, and thereafter, the association of the descending tetrachord ostinato and the lament grew ever stronger. Soon the lament became a type of aria based on this tetrachord ostinato. Even instrumental movements could use "lament" in their titles when they employed it.

In the 1650s and 1660s, laments were so popular that an opera might have three or even four of them spaced throughout the evening. They could be heard with similar frequency in **cantatas** and **oratorios**. After the advent of the **da capo aria**, composers still used the tetrachord as a symbol of grief, even when they did not exploit the structural properties of the ostinato.

LANDI, STEFANO (baptized 26 February 1587, Rome–28 October 1639, Rome). Today, Landi is remember chiefly for composing the musical drama *Il Sant' Alessio*, first performed at the palace of Cardinal Francesco Barberini in **Rome** on 18 February 1632. This "sacred **opera**" tells the story of Alessio who gives up a wealthy lifestyle in Rome to do charitable works and so, despite being fully staged at the Barberini palace, is regarded as a landmark in the history of the **oratorio**.

Landi, trained as a philosopher, ordained a priest in 1607, and beneficed at St. Peter's in Rome in 1624, carried out a parallel career as a musician. He began as **organist** of Santa Maria in Trastevere in 1610 and, even after his appointment at St. Peter's, served as *maestro di cappella* at Santa Maria dei Monti from late 1624. He published one opera, *La Morte d'Orfeo* ("The Death of Orpheus"), 3 volumes of **motets**, a volume of psalm settings, 2 **masses**, 18 **madrigals**, and 8 volumes of "**arias**," 4 of which are lost.

LA SERVA PADRONA ("The Servant Become Mistress," Giovanni Battista Pergolesi, 1733). The most famous of the early **intermezzi** leading to the full-length *opera buffa* that challenged the dominance of the *opera seria* in the second half of the 18th century. Its two brief acts for two singers and simple **orchestration** were first performed between the acts of **Giovanni Battista Pergolesi**'s *opera seria Il Prigionier Superbo* on 5 September 1733 at the Teatro San Bartolomeo in **Naples**. The little piece made a sufficient impression to be taken to other Italian cities, **London**, and **Paris**, where it played at the Théâtre des Italiens in 1746 and then more controversially, in 1752, at the Académie de Musique, where it exploded into prominence as the flashpoint for the Querelle des Bouffons, a pamphlet war about **opera** on the comparative merits of Italian and French opera.

The comedy plays on two stereotypical characters: the foolish *padrone* and the clever servant. In Act I, Uberto (bass singer) grows tired of the impertinences of his servant Serpina (soprano), and he orders his valet Vespone (silent actor) to town to find him a wife. In Act II, Serpina bribes Vespone into posing as her suitor, in order to trick Uberto into proposing marriage to her himself. The trick succeeds, and the intermezzo ends with a happy duet.

A performance requires a **string** orchestra of **violins, violas, cello, violone**, and **harpsichord** and runs about 50 minutes.

LAWES, HENRY (baptized 5 January 1596, Dinton, Wiltshire, England–21 October 1662, London). Older brother of **William Lawes**, Henry was known chiefly as the composer of 433 songs, many for various **masques** and other theater productions. He also composed 25 **anthems** and 2 sets of **psalms** (1638, for one voice and **continuo**; 1648, for three voices and continuo).

Lawes may have trained at Salisbury Cathedral, where his father was a lay vicar. He was employed in his 20s by the Earl of Bridgewater, and on 3 November 1626, he became a Gentleman of the **Chapel Royal**. On 6 January 1631, he was made one of Charles I's musicians "for the **lutes** and voices."

During the Commonwealth, Lawes was in demand as a teacher. In 1656, he composed the songs for the first and last acts of *The Siege of Rhodes*.

At the Restoration, Lawes was reinstated to his former positions, and his setting of "Zadok the Priest" was performed at the coronation of Charles II on 23 April 1661.

Henry Lawes is buried in Westminster Abbey.

LAWES, WILLIAM (baptized 1 May 1602, Salisbury, England–24 September 1645, Chester). Brother of composer **Henry Lawes** and of singer John Lawes, William was the leading composer of instrumental music during the reign of Charles I. His collection of 10 **suites** for **viol consort**, *The Royal Consort*, circulated in manuscript until 1680, and he also left 10 other viol consort suites (or "setts," the contemporary term), and at least 16 other **dances** for **harpsichord** or **virginal**. From about 1630 to 1645, Lawes was also a major contributor to the English theater, composing at least 167 songs and 13 **"symphonies"** for **masques**, and he was one of two composers chosen for the masque mounted at the Inns of Court in 1634 by the royalists, *The Triumph of Peace*. He also composed sacred music: about 50 **anthems** and 10 vocal **canons**.

Lawes was probably educated at the Cathedral of Salisbury, but there is no documentary evidence. A posthumous account by an acquaintance of Henry Lawes states that Edward Seymour, Earl of Herford, apprenticed him to the Italian émigré John Coperario (c. 1575–1626). At some point in the 1630s, he began composing for the royal court. In 1642, after civil unrest had made expenditures for music impossible, Lawes joined the king's army, and he was killed at the siege of Chester in 1645.

LEBÈGUE, NICOLAS (c. 1631, Laon, France–6 July 1702, Paris). Although extant documents reveal only two appointments in **Paris**—**organist** at St. Merri from 18 December 1664 and *organiste du Roi* for the year's last quarter starting in 1678—Lebègue was clearly outstanding in the French **keyboard** school. A much earlier document of 1661 from Troyes Cathedral refers to Lebègue as *le fameux organiste de Paris*. Nothing is known of his training or when he moved to Paris. He published three volumes of organ pieces beginning in 1676 and two of **harpsichord** during the 1670s and 1680s, as well as 20 other organ and 7 harpsichord pieces in manuscript. Manuscript copies of his organ works far outnumber those of his contemporaries, and he counted **Nicolas de Grigny** the best among many fine students. He also published a book of **motets** and composed one vespers setting.

LECLAIR, JEAN-MARIE (10 May 1697, Lyons–22 October 1764, Paris). One of the finest **violinists** of the late Baroque, Leclair, like his colleagues **François Couperin** and **Jean-Philippe Rameau**, attempted to fuse characteristics of Italian music with those of the French **dance** tradition deriving from the music of **Jean-Baptiste Lully**. His 48 **solo sonatas** for violin and basso **continuo**, 21 **trio sonatas**, 3 *ouvertures* for violin, and 12 solo violin **concertos** were all published before 1753. He was also a highly trained dancer and contributed music for many **ballets**.

Little is known of his youth and musical training in Lyons, but his name appears on the list of dancers at the Lyons **opera**. On 9 November 1716, he married Marie-Rose Casthagnié, another dancer on the same list. They had no children.

He went to Turin in 1722 and then to **Paris** in 1723 and prepared his first volume of violin **sonatas** for publication under the patronage of Joseph Bonnier. These were very well received, noted for their originality. In 1727, the second volume followed, engraved by Louise Roussel. After Marie-Rose Casthagnié died, Leclair married Roussel on 8 September 1730. She subsequently engraved all Leclair's publications.

In 1728, Leclair made two appearances that established him in the public eye as a great violinist. The first was a series of 12 performances with the **Concert Spirituel** in Paris, playing his own sonatas and concertos. The second was at the court at Kassel, Germany, where he performed along with the virtuoso **Pietro Locatelli** in a kind of competition of French and Italian musical styles.

Leclair's success was recognized officially when he was appointed as *ordinaire de la musique* to King Louis XV, to whom he dedicated his third book of violin sonatas containing his most famous piece, the Sonata Op. 9, No. 6 (1743), which became known as *Le Tombeau* ("The Tomb"). Leclair resigned this appointment in 1737 after a disagreement with another court musician.

Then Leclair went to Holland. From 1738 to 1743, he spent three months per year at the court of Orange where he performed occasionally with Anne, Princess of Orange, daughter of King George II of England and former student of **George Frideric Handel**. The remaining nine months of each year were spent in The Hague as *maestro di capella* for a wealthy businessman, François du Liz. When du Liz went bankrupt in 1743, Leclair returned to Paris. In 1744, he visited the Spanish Prince Don Philippe in Chambéry and, thereafter, made occasional trips to his native Lyons but otherwise remained in Paris in semiretirement. He hoped that the mounting of his first opera, *Scylla et Glaucus*, on 4 October 1746, would launch a new career, as a first opera had transformed Rameau's, but after two months, it was never revived.

In 1748, Leclair was hired by the duke of Gramont to direct his private theater at Puteaux. Sometime around 1758, he and his wife established separate households. Leclair was murdered late one night in October 1764 as he returned to his house in Paris. No one was ever brought to trial.

LEGRENZI, GIOVANNI (baptized 12 August 1626, Clusone near Bergamo, Italy–27 May 1690, Venice). Contributing to all the most important musical genres available, Legrenzi became the most important composer in northern Italy during the last quarter of the 17th century, the period immediately preceding the great **Venetian** instrumental school of **Antonio Vivaldi**, **Giuseppe Torelli**, and **Tomaso Albinoni**, which Legrenzi influenced. He published 10 volumes of sacred music containing **motets**, **litanies**, **antiphons**, at least 13 psalms for five **voices**, *sacri musicali concerti*, and *concerti musicali per uso di chiesa*. He also left three published volumes of secular **cantatas**, and 80 sonatas *da chiesa* and *da camera* in four publications dating from 1655 to 1673. There is a lost volume of **sonatas** for two to seven instruments and one volume of instrumental **dances**. Legrenzi also composed musical drama, 18 **operas** and 7 **oratorios**.

All that is known of his youth is that he was the son of a church **violinist** in Clusone, Giovanni Maria Legrenzi. On 30 July 1645, not yet 19 years old, he became **organist** at the church of Santa Maria Maggiore in Bergamo. He was ordained to the priesthood early in 1651 and, on 2 May, was elected a chaplain of the parish. On 6 September 1653, he was elected first organist at Santa Maria Maggiore, serving there with eminent *maestri di cappella*, such as **Maurizio Cazzati**, until April 1656.

Cazzati may have helped Legrenzi obtain his next post, ***maestro di cappella*** of the Accademia dello Spirito Santo in Ferrara. Although his principal responsibility was the composition of sacred music and oratorios for the academy, in Ferrara, an important musical city, Legrenzi managed to mount his first opera, *Nino il Giusto*, in 1662. To this point, his published music had consisted almost entirely of sacred music.

He left Ferrara in June 1665 and, for five years thereafter, the only evidence of Legrenzi documents positions that he applied for unsuccessfully or refused. A protracted illness prevented him from accepting one of these, an appointment to the court of the French King Louis XIV in 1668.

In 1670, he accepted the post of *maestro di musica* of the Ospedale dei Derelitti in Venice, and in the following year, he was appointed *maestro di coro* of the Congregazione dei Filippini at the church of Santa Maria della Fava, which he held until at least 1680 and where he is buried. On 7 June 1676, he moved from the Derelitti to the Mendicanti in Venice. He missed being appointed *maestro di cappella* at San Marco by one vote in 1676—Natale Monferrato (1603–1685) won—but gained the post of *vice-maestro* on 5 January 1681. While *vice-maestro*, Legrenzi composed about two operas per year.

Legrenzi succeeded Monferrato as full *maestro* on 16 April 1685, his salary eventually rising to 470 ducats, which the procurators awarded to him personally. The composer turned once again to the sacred music that this prestigious appointment required. It is thought, however, that none of the music he composed specifically for San Marco has survived.

Beginning in 1687, Legrenzi began to organize a *sovvegno* or society for the mutual aid of musicians in Venice, at the same time that he had to curtail his musical activities owing to his last illness.

LEIPZIG. Located in the German province of Saxony, the city prospered from trade from the 12th century, grew larger than the capital **Dresden**, and became an important intellectual center through the growing prestige of the University of Leipzig (founded 1409). There was no music curriculum there, but occasionally students enrolled in law were musicians under cover. **Georg Philipp Telemann** was one.

Since the late Middle Ages, the Leipzig town council had sponsored professional music in as many as five churches: Nikolaikirche (founded 1160), Thomaskirche (1212), Paulinerkirche (1229, destroyed 1968), the New Church (1235, bombed in World War II, destroyed 1950), and Petruskirche (1213, destroyed 1886) located outside the city walls. With the introduction of **polyphony**, the Thomaskirche took pride of place among them, and the *Thomaskantor* became a city officer in 1539 when Leipzig turned to Lutheranism. A major musical appointment akin to a *Kapellmeister*, he was responsible for all the liturgical music in the city and ranked as third officer in the school for boys. Prominent cantors during the Baroque include **Johann Hermann Schein** (1616–1630), **Johann Kuhnau** (1701–1722), and **Johann Sebastian Bach** (1723–1750).

Many Lutheran **chorale** books were published in Leipzig. In the 18th and 19th centuries, the important publishers Breitkopf and Härtel (1719) and C. F. Peters (1800) were founded there.

Leipzig had no **opera** but was home to two *collegia musica* founded by Telemann (1702) and **Johann Friedrich Fasch** (1709). These were semi-permanent organizations of professional and amateur music lovers that gave public performances in coffee houses and other informal locales.

After the Baroque, Leipzig played an important role in the **early music revival** through organizations such as the Leipzig Gewandhaus **Orchestra** (founded 1781) and the Singakadamie (1802), which, under the direction of Felix Mendelssohn and others, revived many of J. S. Bach's choral works. In 1859, the Riedel'scher Verein performed the first known complete **Mass in B Minor**.

LE NUOVE MUSICHE **("The New Musics," Giulio Caccini, 1602 [printed 1601] and 1614).** Publications of Italian vocal music in the **monodic** style that also appeared in the first **operas** as **recitative**. In these publications, **Guilio Caccini** includes "arias" (his meaning: strophic songs in **dance meters**), "madrigals" (through-composed, highly **ornamented**, nonmetric works), and other vocal pieces not classified. He was the first to write out the normally **improvised** vocal ornamentations, and his preface contains much useful information about performance practice.

LIBRETTO (It. "little book"). The words to be sung in an **opera**. The earliest operas at the turn of the 17th century established traditions for libretto writing that persisted for the entire Baroque period and beyond.

First, because operas were conceived from the outset as dramatic art, the script had to imitate classical drama. Therefore, opera librettos were always written in poetic forms of various kinds. Operatic **arias** are sung poems.

This required a skilled versifier, and therefore, secondly, the librettist of Baroque operas is never the composer but a classically educated writer. In the Baroque, the "poet" of the opera enjoyed a status as high as the composer, or even, in a case such as **Metastasio**, higher, and the librettist's best work could be set to music many times by different composers during the course of the later Baroque. However, the librettist, while rarely a musician himself, had to understand deeply the musical conventions of the opera, particularly the distinction between aria and **recitative**, so that the composer could satisfy the musical requirements of the drama. Collaboration between librettist and composer was often quite intimate; **George Frideric Handel** often asked his librettists to make changes in the scripts.

Third, however, the librettist almost never invents the plot by himself but always adapts a historical episode of emperors, kings, knights, and other noble personages or a classical myth. The librettists turned this common lore of educated society into operatic verse.

Lastly, it was customary to provide attendees at court operas copies of the libretto so that they might follow the drama more easily. With the coming of public opera beginning in 1637, copies of the libretto being sung were sold to the clientele. For this reason, many Baroque operas survive only in their librettos, since there was no corresponding need to publish the music, whose single copies were often lost.

L'INCORONAZIONE DI POPPEA ("The Coronation of Poppea," Claudio Monteverdi, 1643). **Claudio Monteverdi**'s last **opera**, completed probably with the help of **Francesco Cavalli** and Francesco Sacrati (1605–1650) and premiered at the Teatro Grimani in **Venice** during Carnival of 1642–1643.

Monteverdi's autograph scores do not survive. The sources of *Poppea* are two manuscripts originating in Venice and **Naples**, probably dating some years after the premiere. Both sources are problematic in numerous ways, and therefore, modern performances are reconstructions to some extent and may differ considerably one from another.

The opera's prologue presents a contest where the power of Love wins over Virtue and Fortune. In Act I, the returning Roman general Otho discovers that his lover Poppea has given herself to the emperor Nero, who is utterly infatuated with her. Despite the dangers, Poppea resolves to continue her pursuit. Nero's wife, Octavia, despairs, and Nero's tutor, the philosopher Seneca, tries to persuade Nero to return to his wife. The emperor will hear none of it. Meanwhile, Drusilla, another courtier, presents herself to Otho, who appears to welcome her suit, only to confess to himself that he still loves Poppea.

In Act II, after a love scene, Poppea tells Nero of Seneca's boast that Nero's power devolves from him. Furious, Nero orders Seneca's suicide. Empress Octavia summons Otho and orders him to kill Poppea. Devastated, he tries to obey by eliciting Drusilla's help and disguising himself in her clothing, but at the critical moment, Love prevents him from stabbing Poppea. Otho and Drusilla are both arrested and exiled, as is Octavia.

In Act III, Nero tells Poppea that Octavia was behind the plot, and she rejoices, pointing out that now there is nothing to prevent them from marrying. She is crowned empress, and the opera ends with a love duet for them both.

Poppea has been critically lauded since its revival in the 20th century as one of the greatest operas of any period. Besides his own inestimable melodic gifts and dramatic instincts, Monteverdi had the advantage of Giovanni Francesco Busenello's (1598–1659) **libretto**, one of the best in the history of opera. Despite the lofty setting of ancient **Rome**, every character is entirely human. Not one is free from moral taint. The musical eroticism and portrayal of naked ambition motivates a drama that is utterly realistic.

The opera requires at least three sopranos, two high male altos, a bass, and about a dozen small roles, depending on doubling, as well as a modest Baroque instrumental ensemble. It takes about three hours.

LOCATELLI, PIETRO ANTONIO (3 September 1695, Bergamo, Italy–30 March 1764, Amsterdam). Locatelli's publication of 12 solo **violin concertos**, Opus 3 (1733), called *L'Arte del Violino*, reformed and advanced the technique of playing the violin, especially in France, where his approach persisted until the 19th century. The Opus 3 concertos ask the soloist to execute extremely high left-hand extensions, double and triple stops, a staccato-legato bowing, and, of course, **polyphonic** passages built of compound melodies. The set also contains 24 *capricci*, **improvisatory** passages for violin alone, to be played near the conclusion of the outside movements of each concerto, that stand as models of the late Baroque **cadenza**.

Besides these concertos, Locatelli published 12 **concerti grossi**, 18 **sonatas** for violin, 12 sonatas for **flute**, 10 sonatas for two violins, 6 **trio sonatas**, 6 concertos for four violins, and 6 "theatrical introductions."

Born the first of seven sons of Filippo Locatelli and Lucia Crocchi, Locatelli is first documented as a violinist in the ensemble of Santa Maria Maggiore in Bergamo in April 1710. In January 1711, he was officially appointed third violin, only to be sent to **Rome** that year to study with various violinists associated with **Arcangelo Corelli**. From 1717 to 1723, he played often at San Lorenzo in Damaso for Cardinal Pietro Ottoboni and for the Congregazione dei Musici di Santa Cecilia.

From 1723 to 1729, Locatelli seems to have become an itinerant virtuoso whose movements are not well documented. He may have played at the courts of Mantua in 1725, in **Venice**, and was certainly in Munich (June 1727), Berlin (1728), Frankfurt (1728), arriving in Kassel by December of 1728. He went to Amsterdam by August 1729 at the latest and never left.

Locatelli did not settle in Amsterdam because of its vibrant musical society but rather to enter the business of publishing his works, perhaps trading also in rare books and art. He allowed the famous firm of Roger and Le Cène to handle his **orchestral** music, but Locatelli published at his own expense his own chamber music. Evidently, he was successful, for at his death, he left a considerable store of books and artworks.

He held a regular series of concerts on Wednesdays in his own home, where he played only for and with a small circle of wealthy admirers. Locatelli did not like the limelight.

LOCKE, MATTHEW (c. 1622, Devonshire, England–August 1677, London). Composer of a significant repertory of **consort** music for **viols**, Locke exercised greater influence on the development of music and drama in England. He composed the fourth act of the first English **opera**, *The Siege of Rhodes*, in 1656, and three years later, he revised and expanded James Shirley's **masque** *Cupid and Death*, introducing into it a significant number of **recitatives**, which critics believe to have influenced **John Blow** and **Henry Purcell**.

Locke trained as a chorister at Exeter Cathedral from 1638 to 1641, and then spent much of Charles II's exile period in the Netherlands. He was appointed composer for the King's **Violins** in 1660 and was closely associated with the **Chapel Royal** for the rest of his life. During the early Restoration period, he also contributed instrumental and vocal music for productions at Lincoln's Inn Fields.

LONDON. The history of Baroque music in England's most important musical center begins only after the Restoration of King Charles II in 1660. During the period preceding the English Civil War (1642–1651), the Commonwealth (1649–1653), and the Protectorate under Oliver Cromwell and his son (1653–1659), the glorious Elizabethan tradition of outstanding sacred **polyphony** by **William Byrd**, **Orlando Gibbons**, **Thomas Tomkins**, **Thomas Weelkes**, and their colleagues at the **Chapel Royal** continued under the patronage of James I and Charles I until the war began. Books of English songs and **madrigals** continued to appear. Charles I, a **viol** player, encouraged the composition of **fantasias** for viol **consort** and also established a new ensemble, the **Lutes**, Viols and Voices. His leading composer was **William Lawes**. But the styles of all this prewar music are of the Renaissance; news of **opera** experiments in Italy had not yet arrived.

The Puritans took a dim view of sophisticated polyphony, sacred or secular, and hated the theater, so the Commonwealth was an austere period for music in London.

Charles II had spent much of the war period at the French court, where he heard, it is assumed, a great deal of French repertory and probably some Italian as well. Restored to power in London, he reconstituted the Chapel Royal under **Henry Cooke**. He then began a tradition of English musical theater by licensing two commercial theaters that could produce **masques**. He did not care for the Renaissance **counterpoint** of the viol consort and instead imitated the French court's **orchestra** with his own 24-member **string** ensemble, whose members could play at court and at the theater.

Although lately come, the rise of musical theater in London materially changed the musical culture as it had in cities on the continent. Its greatest Restoration exponent, **Henry Purcell**, altered the course of his career about 1690 from one chiefly devoted to providing **odes** for court and **anthems** for the Chapel Royal to the career of a theater composer, writing operas, masques, incidental pieces, and songs for more than 50 theatrical productions during the last five years of his life.

It is no coincidence that, in the face of such competition, the quality of music at the Chapel Royal and at London churches declined along with the interest in Anglican liturgy through the first half of the 18th century. The only glorious moments for music in church were occasioned by special celebrations, such as the solemnity celebrating the peace Treaty of Utrecht in 1713, for which **George Frideric Handel** wrote a famous **Te Deum**, or the crowning of King George II in 1727, the setting for his **Coronation Anthems**. **William Croft** and **Maurice Greene** carried on as the most significant figures associated with the Chapel Royal.

Meanwhile, the world of theater music in London changed abruptly in 1705 with the performance of the first imported Italian-language opera, Jakob Greber's *Gli Amori d'Ergasto*, which ran for five performances in April. When **Giovanni Bononcini**'s *Camilla* had a resounding success the following season, the strange course of London opera was set for the next 25 years: star singers, foreigners all, performing the music of foreign composers in the Italian language. Handel began his lifelong career in the theaters of London with *Rinaldo* on 24 February 1711.

Following a period of independent productions, the Royal Academy was organized as a joint stock company to produce operas in 1719. It sold subscriptions and, frequently attended by royalty, became quite fashionable in London society. Its period of solvency, from 1720 to 1728, saw *opere serie* of Handel, Bononcini, and **Giovanni Porta** sung by Senesino, Francesca Cuzzoni, and Faustina Bordoni, all international star singers.

On 29 January 1728, *The Beggar's Opera* opened at the Lincoln's Inn Fields Theater and caused a sensation with its English **libretto** and sharp satire of *opera seria*. The failure of the Royal Academy that year was not a direct result, but the coincidence suggests that the craze for Italian opera had begun to fade. Nevertheless, a reconstituted second academy opened in December 1729 and, more remarkably, a rival Opera of the Nobility hired **Nicola Porpora** to compete. Within three years, both had failed. By 1740, most of the foreigners had left, and even Handel was convinced that the reign of Italian opera in London had ended. He spent his remaining active years composing **English oratorios**, while his colleagues **William Boyce** and **Thomas Arne** provided many songs and much incidental music, alongside an occasional masque, for spoken plays in London.

London was the home of John Walsh (1666–1736) and his son John (1709–1766), the leading **printers** of music. The elder Walsh began using faster punches and less expensive pewter plates for engraving about 1700 and built up an empire of music publishing that included songs, instrumental works, instruction books, opera arrangements, and even the complete score to Handel's *Rinaldo*. His relationship with Handel was troubled with accusations of piracy, but the younger Walsh concluded a 14-year exclusive agreement with the composer in 1739.

The **Academy of Ancient Music**, one of the earliest institutions to take an intellectual interest in music history, also resided in London, founded in 1726.

L'ORFEO **(Claudio Monteverdi, 1607).** One of the first **operas** ever composed and, since the **early music revival**, recognized as the first masterpiece of music drama in the Western tradition.

Prince Francesco Gonzaga of Mantua commissioned the opera to be performed during the Carnival season of 1607, and *L'Orfeo* premiered on 24 February at the Accademia degli Invaghiti and repeated at the Mantuan court, where **Claudio Monteverdi** was employed, on 1 March.

Among many reasons for the opera's critical success, three are outstanding. First, Monteverdi and his **librettist**, Alessandro Striggio (1573–1630), created a drama that integrated virtually all of the generic resources of music available at the time: **monodic** singing, instrumental music, **imitative choruses**, **homophonic** choruses, **ostinatos**, strophic songs. All of this was animated with a bewitching variety of instrumental colors: several **continuo** ensembles, solo **strings**, ensemble strings, **harps**, **recorders**, brass. Second, Monteverdi presents in his music an authentic unifying action: the contest of values between feeling and rationality that plays out in the tragedy of Orpheus. Lastly, the opera constantly displays Monteverdi's immense melodic gifts.

After an instrumental **toccata**, the opera's prologue presents the figure of Musica, who states the premise of *dramma per musica* as a manifesto: that music has the power to calm disturbed hearts and to inflame the most frigid spirits, a power to be seen in the story of Orpheus the musician.

Act I presents the newly married Orpheus and Eurydice in great joy and ends with their retiring. In Act II, Orpheus continues to celebrate his great good fortune with his friends, but they are interrupted by a Messenger bringing news of Eurydice's death by snakebite. A prolonged **lament** follows, and the act ends with Orpheus's resolution to go to Hades and retrieve her by the power of his music. In Act III, Orpheus sings to Charon, trying to persuade the boatman to let him cross the River Styx. Charon sleeps instead, but Orpheus crosses, and the act ends with a chorus praising human endeavors. Queen Persephone has heard Orpheus's song, and in Act IV persuades King Pluto to grant Orpheus's desire. He imposes the condition that Orpheus not look back at Eurydice while leading her out of Hades. The love that led Orpheus to rescue Eurydice now overcomes him, he looks at her, and she disappears forever. In Act V, after a long lament by Orpheus, his father, Apollo, descends and promises to make Eurydice ever visible to him in the stars. The shepherds and nymphs rejoice, and there is a concluding **dance**.

The published score of *L'Orfeo* (1609) requires two **harpsichords**, two bass **viols**, two harps, a ten-player string group of **violins**, **violas**, and **cellos**, two *violini piccoli*, two *chitarroni*, two **organs** *di legno*, three violas da gamba, four **trombones**, **regals**, two **cornetts**, two recorders, four **trumpets** required only for the opening toccata, and a five-**voice** chorus of an indeterminate number. Besides the title role, there are 16 brief solo roles, often shared among singers in performance. A performance requires about one hour and three-quarters, plus intermissions.

LOTTI, ANTONIO (1666, Hanover, Germany–5 January 1740, Venice). Last of the great Baroque *maestri di cappella* of San Marco in **Venice**, his legacy of sacred music, including at least 10 **masses** and 2 requiems, remained in the regular repertory of the basilica throughout the 18th century. He could compose in the *stile antico* for liturgy, and his **polyphony** might comprise as many as 10 **voices** full of dissonant suspensions. He was also internationally prominent in the musical theater, having composed at least 24 **operas** (6 survive) and 8 **oratorios** (2 survive), as well as at least 88 secular **cantatas**; a 1705 publication of vocal duets, trios, and "**madrigals**"; a **concerto** for **oboe d'amore**; 6 **sonatas** for **violin** and **continuo**; 6 *sinfonie*; and a half-dozen assorted chamber works.

Antonio Lotti's father, Matteo Lotti, was a *Kapellmeister* in Hanover. Little is known of Antonio's youth, but he studied with **Giovanni Legrenzi** in Venice as early as 1683. Legrenzi became *maestro di cappella* at San Marco in 1685, and thereafter, his prize student rose regularly through the ranks of the basilica: Lotti became a salaried alto singer on 30 May 1689, assistant to the second **organist** on 6 August 1690, second organist on 31 May 1692, and first organist on 17 August 1704. Seven years earlier, in 1697, he was *maestro di cappella* for the church of the Spirito Santo, and the following year, he finished an entire book of masses, presumably for use there and at San Marco. He also composed sacred music for the Ospedale degli Incurabili, although the terms of his appointment there, if any, are not known.

Lotti's opera career began with *Il Trionfo dell'Innocenza* ("The Triumph of Innocence") of 1693, but most of his musical drama dates from the period between 1706 and 1717, which saw the production of at least 16 new operas. He married a prominent opera singer, Santa Stella, but had no children. Granted a leave from his responsibilities at San Marco, he and his wife left for **Dresden** on 5 September 1717. He composed three operas there, one of which, *Giove in Argo* ("Jupiter in Argus"), was eventually revived on 3 September 1719 to open the Hoftheater, Dresden's most important opera venue.

Despite the success of his psalm **motet** *Miserere* of 1733, thereafter sung every Holy Thursday at San Marco for the rest of the century, Lotti failed to win the election to be *maestro di cappella* when the post fell vacant that year. He finally won the appointment on 2 April 1736 and held it until his death.

LOURE. French **dance** of the later 17th and 18th centuries that sometimes appears in instrumental **suites**. In a slow triple **meter** with an upbeat, the loure has phrases of irregular length and a good deal of **ornamentation** in the melody.

LULLY, JEAN-BAPTISTE (28 November 1632, Florence–22 March 1687, Paris). Composer, **violinist**, and **dancer**, Lully fused early traditions of Italian **opera** to French classical drama to invent the ***tragédie lyrique***, which heavily influenced his successors, **Marc-Antoine Charpentier**, **André Campra**, and **Jean-Philippe Rameau**, and maintained a distinct identity for French opera throughout the Baroque period. Besides these 15 operas, Lully composed 30 ballets, 14 *comédies-ballets*, 24 small French-language vocal works, and 9 independent instrumental works. His output in sacred music was small and scattered throughout his career, but his 12 ***grands motets*** exploited **homophonic** choral **textures** and **orchestral** interludes to famous effect. The *Miserere* of 1663, one of the first *grands motets* to open with a five-**voiced** instrumental introduction, was particularly revered. He also composed 10 *petits **motets***, in three voices with **continuo**, devoted to the Virgin Mary and the Blessed Sacrament.

Born Giovanni Battista Lulli, he was the second son of a Tuscan farmer, Lorenzo (1599–1667). Little is known of the son's education. Perhaps he learned the fundamentals of music from the friars of the Via Borgo Ognissanti in **Florence**. Somehow, possibly as early as 1645, he managed to be appointed as a tutor of Italian to Anne-Marie-Louise d'Orléans, cousin of King Louis XIV of France. In February 1646, Lully moved to **Paris**. A source **printed** in 1695 identifies Lully's teachers from this point: the **organists** at the church of St. Louis of Rue Saint-Antoine, Nicolas Métru and Nicolas Gigault, the violinist Jacques Cordier, and the dancer Jean Regnault.

Possibly through Regnault, Lully entered the service of Louis XIV and danced in the *Ballet Royal de la Nuit*, caught the eye of the king, and was appointed *compositeur de la musique instrumentale* on 16 March 1653. His dancing and obvious talent for composition allowed Lully to persuade the king to establish an instrumental ensemble apart from his official one, Les Vingt-quatre Violons du Roi. Lully was able to form the new orchestra, Les Petits Violons, according to his own ideas of ensemble playing, and it would become famous throughout Europe. In 1656, Les Petits Violons made its debut in the ballet *Les Galanteries du Temps*, the earliest surviving ballet composed entirely by Lully.

On 24 July 1662, he married Madeleine Lambert, a composer's daughter 20 years of age. They had six children.

To this point, Lully as composer had contributed chiefly to court ballets. But age began to curtail his dancing, and he retired as a dancer by 1668. In 1664, however, he entered upon a second stage of his career as composer: a collaboration with the great dramatist Jean-Baptiste Poquelin (1622–1673), known by his stage name Moliére, on a series of *comédies-ballets*, comic dramas in which Lully's dance music interweaves with Molière's poetry, beginning with *Le Mariage Forcé* (29 January 1664), including *Le Bourgeois Gentilhomme* (14 October 1670), and concluding with *Psyché* (17 January 1671). Their collaboration ended possibly because of a quarrel over the sharing of profits from performances outside the court at the theater of the Palais Royal.

In the meantime, a number of poets and composers associated with the court attempted to introduce full-blown opera, with **recitatives** replacing all spoken text, to French society. In March 1672, Lully was to able buy the royal privilege of producing "academies for opera . . . in the French language"—essentially a patent for a monopoly granted by Louis XIV—from its original holder, the poet Pierre Perrin (c. 1620–1675), and immediately moved to establish the Académie Royale de Musique. Because the privilege brought no court financing of the new venture, Lully entered into a partnership with long-time acquaintance and theater architect Carlo Vigarani (1637–1713) in August 1672, and together they adapted a tennis court for their productions. They began with *Les Fêtes de L'Amour et de Bacchus*, a pastiche made of Lully's earlier ballet music, and they mounted the first original *tragédie lyrique* in April 1673, *Cadmus et Hermione*. This created a sensation, luring the king to the tennis court to see it. By 28 April 1673, the king authorized Lully to use the Palais Royal theater rent-free, and after the opening of *Alceste* in January 1674, Louis brought the business of *tragédie lyrique* into the court, supported by the court's sets, costumes, and machinery and by funded rehearsals.

The Operas of Jean-Baptiste Lully

Opera	First performance	Librettists and sources
Les Fêtes de l'Amour et de Bacchus	11 November 1672	Philippe Quinault after Molière
Cadmus et Hermione	April 1673	Quinault after Ovid Metamorphoses
Alceste	18? January 1674	Quinault after Euripides Alcestis
Thésée	15 January 1675	Quinault after Ovid Metamorphoses
Atys	10 January 1676	Quinault after Ovid Fasti
Isis	5 January 1677	Quinault after Ovid Metamorphoses
Psyché	19 April 1678	T. Corneille and B. le Bovier de Fontenelle after Apuleius, The Golden Ass
Bellérophon	31 January 1679	Corneille and Fontenelle after Hesiod, Theogeny
Proserpine	3 February 1680	Quinault after Ovid Metamorphoses
Persée	18 April 1682	Quinault after Ovid Metamorphoses
Phaëton	8/9 January 1683	Quinault after Ovid Metamorphoses
Roland	8 January 1685	Quinault after Ariosto Orlando Furioso
Armide	15 February 1686	Quinault after Tasso Gerusalemme Liberata
Acis et Galatée	6 September 1686	Quinault after Ovid Metamorphoses
Achille et Polyxène	23 November 1687	Campistron after Homer Iliad

With such backing, Lully produced a new opera nearly every year until he died in 1687, usually working with the great **librettist** Philippe Quinault (1635–1688). His control of the royal opera privilege virtually eliminated all rivals from Paris, although he did allow provincial opera companies to operate. He also managed the Palais Royal almost as a monopoly, setting high prices for seats. The royal privilege allowed him to earn royalties on his printed librettos and, after 1677, royalties from prints of his music. From then on, he published complete scores of all his *tragédies lyriques*, a phenomenon unknown in the rest of Europe, where opera scores were lucky to survive in manuscript.

In December of 1686, while conducting his **Te Deum** at the Church of the Feuillants, he wounded himself in the foot. The wound became gangrenous, and Lully died on 22 March 1687.

Lully's influence on the high-Baroque style is manifold. His promotion of a highly articulated manner of orchestral playing, with all **string** players using the same bow strokes, remains visible in orchestras today. Without actually inventing it, he made the **French overture** a standard beginning for Baroque operas, including most of **George Frideric Handel**'s, as well as a separate instrumental genre. Finally, his conception of the dramatic role of the **chorus** in *tragédie lyrique* carried into early English operas and reaches its greatest expression in the **English oratorios** of Handel.

Nevertheless, his music shared the fate of most Baroque composers, lost to view after 1750. Today, his operas are rarely mounted because they depend for much of their effect on sumptuous machinery and special effects as well as a large chorus and an expert troupe of dancers, making production costs high, and possibly because their classicism seems too static for modern taste.

LUTE (Fr. *luth*, Ger. *Laute*, It. *liuto*, Sp. *laúd*). A plucked **string instrument**, smaller than most **guitars**, with an egg-shaped body and flat soundboard (belly) decorated with an ornamental *rose* (soundhole), the lute rose rapidly into prominence in the late 15th century as one of the principal beneficiaries, along with the **organ** and **harpsichord**, of the growing interest in composition for instruments at that time. In the Baroque, it lost popularity to those instruments as well as the bowed string instruments, especially the **violin**, as a solo instrument, but continued to flourish throughout the period in Baroque ensembles, particularly as the provider of harmony in a basso **continuo**.

The body of a typical Renaissance lute was formed from separately cut and bent strips of wood (ribs) glued together to form the characteristic egg shape. This kind of construction was intrinsically strong, and so, the ribs could be thin and light, as was the covering soundboard. A separate neck and fingerboard with gut frets is attached to the narrower end of the body and terminates in a slotted *nut* through which pass the strings into the pegbox, usually attached to the neck at an angle approaching 90 degrees. Each string is wound to a rotating peg, which regulates the strings' tension for **tuning**. The strings' other ends are attached to a bridge glued onto the soundboard near the round end of the body.

Such an instrument would be strung with six *courses*, each course being a pair of strings tuned to the same pitch or in octaves. The strings were made of gut. The highest string, called *chanterelle*, was often a single string, and for solo repertory, it was curiously advised that that string be tuned to the breaking point, in order to allow sufficient tension for the lowest pitched strings to be able to sound. In 1664, metal-wound gut strings were advertised in England, and this innovation allowed heavier, shorter-length bass strings to have good resonance with less tension on the top strings.

In the late 16th century, lutes with one to four extra bass strings (*diapasons*) began to appear. Their purpose was to deepen the pitch range of the instrument by playing open (unstopped) strings tuned to important bass pitches. Sometimes these extra courses were gathered in a separate peg box; such lutes are called *double head*. Double-head lutes with 11 courses were common in the Baroque, and a few extant lutes have 12.

Ten-course lute constructed by Thomas Klenck, Hamilton, New York.

The lute player plucks the strings with the right hand while the left hand stops the strings behind the proper fret to produce the length of string for the correct note. The number of frets, at least eight, varied widely according to local tradition and the length of the instrument. Lute music is nearly always written **tablature**, although, in the Baroque period, players could be expected to read a **figured bass** in standard notation.

A typical tuning of a 6-course lute is: G^2 C^3 F^3 A^3 D^4 G^4. In the latter part of the 17th century, a typical tuning for an 11-course lute might be: A^1 D^2 E^2 F^2 G^2 A^2 D^3 F^3 A^3 D^4 F^4.

The Baroque repertory for lute consists mostly in **dance suites**. French composers working in the first half of the 17th century—**Denis Gaultier, Ennemond Gaultier**, and Charles Mouton (1626–1710), among the most important—experimented with various tunings and modes of performance, including the **unmeasured prelude** and the *style brisé*. Thereafter, a revival of interest sprang up in Germany, where many suites were composed by the virtuoso **Sylvius Leopold Weiss**, and a Suite in G Minor was left by **Johann Sebastian Bach**. *See also* KAPSPERGER, GIOVANNI GIROLAMO.

M

MADRIGAL. Originally a refined type of 16th-century Italian lyric poetry, the term quickly came to refer more generally to **polyphonic** musical settings of many kinds of lyric poetry. The madrigal rose quickly in popularity after 1525 and became the most prominent form of secular vocal composition in Italy.

In 1600, the music theorist Giovanni Maria Artusi attacked madrigals of **Claudio Monteverdi** that eventually appeared in the composer's fourth book of Italian madrigals (1603, **Venice**; some had circulated in manuscript earlier). Artusi charged that Monteverdi's music was decadent because it violated syntactic rules of **dissonance** in composition. Monteverdi, speaking through his brother Giulio in the 1607 preface to his *Scherzi musicali*, proposed that modern music must be the servant of the text, the expression of which demanded a *seconda pratica* of compositional syntax, different from the *prima pratica* that was heard in classical church polyphony. The aesthetic claim of the priority of text expression is close to that which grounded the first **operas**, whose **choruses** and ensemble numbers derive much from contemporary madrigalisms.

Monteverdi's fifth book (1605) was the first to require a **continuo** to fill out the necessary harmonies, resembling to some extent the new **monodic** vocal **textures**, and thereafter, the **continuo madrigal** gradually overtook the traditional *a cappella* texture in prominence, eventually giving way to the similarly sounding but more explicitly dramatic **cantata**. By 1650, the madrigal was, except for academic exercises, extinct.

***MAESTRO DI CAPPELLA* (It. "chapel master," Fr. *maître de chappelle*, Ger. *Kapellmeister*, Sp. *maestro de capilla*).** The musician, usually a composer, in charge of all musical activities at an important musical establishment (not always a chapel). Important posts were at the Sistine Chapel in **Rome**, San Marco in **Venice**, the Hofkapelle in **Vienna**, the cathedrals of Seville and Toledo, as well as several in New Spain. During the Baroque, the *maestro di cappella* of a major chapel would provide new sacred music for worship services on a regular basis. The position slowly declined in importance throughout the period as careers in **opera** and other kinds of secular music became more attractive.

MAGNIFICAT. A musical setting of the Gospel canticle from St. Luke 1:46–55, known as the Canticle of Mary, traditionally sung near the conclusion of vespers. During the Baroque, the Magnificat remained an important liturgical genre in Roman Catholic, Lutheran, and Anglican establishments.

Early Baroque settings distinguished the verse pairs of the canticle with strong **cadences** at the end of each one. Later, as in the **"Neapolitan" mass** settings, each pair became a short **aria** with distinct instrumental accompaniment. The **Magnificat** of **Johann Sebastian Bach** is the best example of this type.

The title "Magnificat" is sometimes given to **organ** pieces designed to set the mode for its singing. *See also* PACHELBEL, JOHANN; SCHEIDE-MANN, HEINRICH.

MAGNIFICAT, JOHANN SEBASTIAN BACH, BWV 243. The most famous setting of this text and one of the most popular choral works of **Johann Sebastian Bach**. There are two versions, both in autograph, of essentially the same work with minor variants. The earlier, in E-flat major (BWV 243a), originally had four Lutheran Christmas **chorales** interpolated into its Latin text. The later, more familiar version in D major has no such chorales, thus making it appropriate for any festival vespers. The first performance took place in **Leipzig** during the Christmas Day vespers, 1723.

Bach sets each of the 10 verses of the Magnificat and the 2 verses of the doxology as a short, self-contained movement in the manner of a **"Neapolitan" mass**. He scored it for five vocal soloists (SSATB), five-**voiced** choir, and an **orchestra** of two **flutes**, **oboe** and **oboe d'amore**, **bassoon**, **timpani**, **strings**, and **continuo**. A performance requires about half an hour.

MAÎTRE DE CHAPELLE. See *MAESTRO DI CAPPELLA.*

MANDOLIN. By the 17th century, this plucked **string instrument** had acquired a rounded body and fretted fingerboard similar to that of a **lute** and a pegbox more closely resembling that of the **violin**. Courses ranged from four to six with various **tuning** patterns. (The "Neapolitan" mandolin, whose tuning mimics that of the violin, can be traced only to the mid-18th century.) The mid-17th century produced solo music for the instrument in French and Italian **tablature**, mostly preserved in manuscript. Later, **Antonio Vivaldi** composed **concertos** for mandolin thought to date from 1736, and **Georg Philipp Telemann** occasionally calls for the mandolin in his **church cantatas**.

MANFREDINI, FRANCESCO ONOFRIO (22 June 1684, Pistoia, Italy–6 October 1762, Pistoia). A student of **Giuseppe Torelli** at San Petronio, Manfredini's career centered entirely on Bologna except for the periods

1696–1703, when the **orchestra**'s activities at San Petronio were suspended, and 1712–1723, when he served Antoine I Grimaldi, Prince of Monaco. His reputation rests on his published instrumental works, especially the 12 Opus 3 **concertos**. He also composed 12 **sonatas** for **violin** and **continuo**, another set of 12 concerto-like *sinfonie da chiesa*, 7 **trio sonatas**, a concerto for **oboes** and violins, another for one or two **trumpets**, and another isolated violin concerto. His nine **oratorios** are lost.

MARAIS, MARIN (baptized 31 May 1656, Paris–15 August 1728, Paris). The first of the great French virtuosos of the **viol**, Marais published five books of pieces for viol and **continuo** between 1686 and 1725 in the form of 39 **suites**, including several for two and three viols, 596 pieces in all. There are 45 more in manuscript. Another publication contains some of the first French trio music, *Pièces en Trio pour les Flûtes, Violons et Dessus de Viole* of 1692. He also composed four *tragédies lyriques* after the manner of his teacher **Jean-Baptiste Lully**.

Son of a shoemaker, his uncle Louis supported his training alongside **Michel-Richard de Lalande** at the choir school of St. Germain-l'Auxerrois beginning in 1667. His progress on the viol was so rapid that he was playing in the Opéra **orchestra** under Lully by 1675. In 1679, he was made *ordinaire de la musique de la chambre du roi* ("officer of the king's chamber music") and, in 1706, replaced **André Campra** as conductor of the Opéra orchestra.

MARCELLO, BENEDETTO GIACOMO (24 June or 24 July 1686, Venice–24 July 1739, Brescia, Italy). Scion of one of the lesser aristocratic families of **Venice**, Marcello was admitted to the Maggior Consiglio (Great Council) of the Most Serene Republic on 4 December 1706 and, thereafter, fulfilled the political duties expected of a Venetian noble, serving in various magistracies, as governor of Pola in Istria (1730–1733), and ending his life as financial chamberlain (from 1738) in Brescia (then part of the Republic of Venice).

At the same time, he carried out a remarkable career as a composer, music teacher, and critic. His most influential efforts were, unusual for the time, in sacred music. His 50 Psalms of David, in eight volumes beginning in 1724, were an attempt to cleanse sacred music of **operatic** impurities. (He had made a similar effort in singing style in the second decade of the 18th century.) They have been translated into many languages and continued to be sung in liturgies well into the 19th century. He also composed four **oratorios** and nine **masses**, one of which secured his admission to the Accademia Filarmonica of Bologna in 1711. His main achievements in secular music were: 380 solo **cantatas**, 81 duets, and 7 trios, many composed on his own texts.

His oeuvre of instrumental music is also impressive: 12 **concerti grossi**, 5 other **concertos**, 7 *sinfonie*, 12 **harpsichord sonatas**, some 3 dozen other movements for **keyboard**, and 28 **solo sonatas**, a number of them for **cello** still often performed.

Perhaps Marcello's most popular creation during his own lifetime was his satire of the business of Italian opera, *Il Teatro alla Moda* ("The Stylish Theater"), published anonymously in 1720 and still quite amusing today.

MARINI, BIAGIO (3 February 1594, Brescia, Italy–17 November 1663, Venice). Along with **Dario Castello**, Marini was one of the earliest important composers of music for solo **violin** in the **monodic** *stile moderno*. His *Affetti Musicali* (Opus 1) was published in **Venice** in 1617 and contains *sinfonie*, **canzonas**, **sonatas**, and **dance** movements for one or two violins and **continuo**. His Opus 8, *Sonate, Sinfonie e . . . Retornelli* represents all the important instrumental genres of the early Baroque, and his Opus 22 (Venice, 1655) mentions sonatas *da camera* and *da chiesa* in the title.

On 26 April 1615, Marini was appointed a violinist at San Marco in Venice and thus played under **Claudio Monteverdi**. By 1620, however, he was back in Brescia as *maestro di cappella* at Santa Eufemia, and thereafter, his itinerant career took him to Parma, Düsseldorf, Bergamo, Milan, Ferrara, Vicenza, and Venice at various points.

MARTINI, GIOVANNI BATTISTA (24 April 1706, Bologna–3 August 1784, Bologna). Most often referred to as "Padre Martini," he entered the Conventual Franciscan monastery in Lugo di Romagna in 1721, received minor orders in 1725, ordination in 1729, and thereafter rarely left Bologna, and yet, he was renowned as one of the major musical intellects of the 18th century, who maintained a correspondence with luminaries all over Europe. **Metastasio**, **Jean-Philippe Rameau**, **Pietro Locatelli**, and **Johann Joachim Quantz** are a few of his correspondents. He would number among his students some of the leading composers of the next generation, including **Niccolò Jommelli**, Johann Christian Bach (1735–1782), and Wolfgang Amadeus Mozart (1756–1791).

He wrote five treatises, including one of the earliest histories of music. He composed over 1,500 pieces of music, including over 1,000 **canons**, 3 **oratorios**, 5 **intermezzi**, 32 **masses**, 24 *sinfonie*, 12 **concertos** for various instruments, 96 **keyboard sonatas**, and 5 ensemble sonatas.

In 1725, he became *maestro di cappella* for the church of San Francesco in Bologna and remained there until his death.

MASQUE. An allegorical English court entertainment originating in the 16th century in which speakers, singers, and masked **dancers** alluded to contemporary politics and political figures through the medium of classical mythology. A theatrical genre, the masque required sophisticated poetry, elaborate sets, and significant musical forces. As the tradition developed through the 17th century, it took on characteristics of Italian **opera** and mixed freely with other theatrical genres. Once Italian opera companies gained a foothold in **London** after 1705, the masque faded from view.

The poet laureate Ben Johnson (1572–1637) and architect Inigo Jones (1573–1652) produced a significant body of masques between 1605 and 1631, but very little of the music by Alfonso Ferrabosco (the younger, 1575–1628) survives. Other composers of this period included Giovanni Coperario (a.k.a. John Cooper, c. 1570–1626) and Thomas Campion (1567–1620).

Masque music for the reign of Charles I survives in the autograph manuscript of **William Lawes**, including his *Britannia Triumphans* of 1638, which shows much Italian influence, including an **ostinato aria**. A significant work of the Commonwealth period is *The Siege of Rhodes* of 1656, often called the first English opera, on a text of William Davenant (1606–1668), **Henry Lawes**, **Henry Cooke**, **Matthew Locke**, Charles Colman (died 1664), and George Hudson (died 1672). Locke contributed the first definite English dramatic **recitatives** for *Cupid and Death* of 1653, which is the only completely surviving masque score of the 17th century.

During the 1670s, King Charles II had musicians and theater people brought in from France, opening a new channel of influence. Restoration audiences looked for some kind of musical interlude in every theater production, and between 1663 and 1703, over 40 surviving plays contain extended scenes called "masques." **Henry Purcell** composed a masque for the final act of his **semi-opera** *Diocletian* (1690) and three for *King Arthur* (1691). Such integration exercised an important influence on developing English music drama but also eroded the masque's distinctive dance character, which at the beginning had reigned supreme. **George Frideric Handel**'s masterly *Acis and Galatea* of 1718 is called "masque" in contemporary sources, but there is little of the allegorical and balletic in it. Rather, the term here appears to contrast the pastoral theme and rather comic plot with the Italian *opera seria* dramas of the contemporary London stage.

MASS. The Roman Catholic name for the celebration of the Eucharist; during the Baroque, a musical setting of the ordinary prayers of the Roman liturgy in Greek and Latin languages: Kyrie, Gloria, Credo, Sanctus/Benedictus, Agnus Dei.

The invention of **opera** at the turn of the 17th century forced a bifurcation in sacred music composition. **Giovanni da Palestrina**'s disciples around **Rome** canonized his style and made it a kind of classical language, the *stile antico*, which embodied a sacred semantic distinguished from the new secular music. At the same time, in other localities, new mass compositions began to absorb, slowly, the dramatic ideals and **textures** of opera: solo singers, contrasting textures, instruments. All of these can be heard in the *cori spezzati* ("split choir") repertory associated with **Venice**. The remainder of the Baroque witnessed a bewildering variety and mixture of styles in mass composition, from the strictest *stile antico* to the most operatic **cantata** mass in the "**Neapolitan**" style, which predominated by the end of the period. This type segmented the mass texts, especially the longer ordinaries of the Gloria and Credo, into separate movements for **chorus** or soloists and, except for **imitative** choral passages, is almost indistinguishable in musical style from Baroque secular music. The greatest exemplar is the **Mass in B Minor** of **Johann Sebastian Bach**. *See also* MISSA BREVIS; ORGAN MASS; VERSET.

MASS IN B MINOR. Composed by **Johann Sebastian Bach**, the Mass in B Minor (BWV 232) is one of the largest and most outstanding concerted settings of the Roman Catholic **mass** ordinary in the entire Western tradition. Scored for five-**voice chorus**, vocal soloists, **strings, flutes, oboes, bassoons, trumpets, timpani**, and **continuo**, the work consists of 27 movements and requires about two hours to perform.

Bach did not compose the mass all at once. He wrote the Sanctus in 1724 for the Lutheran Christmas liturgy at the Thomaskirche in **Leipzig**, where he was **cantor**. The Kyrie (three movements) and Gloria (nine movements) were sent in 1733 to petition Friedrich August II, Elector of Saxony, for an honorary court title. (A mass consisting only of the first two Latin ordinary prayers—a *Missa brevis*—was common Lutheran practice.) In the late 1740s, Bach completed the mass by adding the movements of the Credo, Osanna, and Agnus Dei, mostly **parodies** of previously composed movements dating as far back as 1714. Since no performance of the entire mass in Bach's lifetime is known, some critics believe it to be a "speculative" composition, a retrospective summary of what he judged to be his life's best work.

The Mass in B Minor exhibits a great range of compositional form and color, from the intimate Benedictus **aria** for solo flute, tenor, and continuo to tremendous festal choruses requiring every instrument. Much of Bach's revising seems to have been directed at integrating the individual movements into large-scale compositions, particularly in the case of the Gloria and Credo. He removed or truncated many of the articulating ritornellos so that one movement demands the next, and in fact, Bach indicates many links explicitly in the score. The work is both an encyclopedia and tour de force of compositional technique: **cantus firmus**, strict **canon**, **ostinato** bass, *stile antico*, and chromatic **fantasy** merely head the list of devices displayed. Virtuoso solos for every instrument lend great timbral variety, and the difficulty of all the vocal parts make the Mass in B Minor one of the most challenging of choral projects.

The first complete performance did not occur until 1859 in Leipzig, owing perhaps to the lack of a suitable performing edition. The common name "Mass in B Minor" comes from this edition, and does not indicate a unifying **key** of the whole work but rather the key of the first Kyrie. Bach's own inscription on his manuscript reads *Die große katholische Messe* ("The Great Catholic Mass"). The most recent critical edition, edited by Christoph Wolff, was issued by C. F. Peters in 1994. The Mass has been a touchstone of authentic historical performance practice and its attendant controversies over the last half-century.

MATTHESON, JOHANN (28 September 1681, Hamburg–17 April 1764, Hamburg). Possessed of great intelligence and a remarkably broad education in addition to prodigious musical talent, Mattheson is remembered today as one of the most prolific writers on music of the Baroque period. His legacy of treatises, journals, letters, and articles yields a remarkably comprehensive picture of music as it was practiced in the first half of 18th-century Europe. The picture is particularly valuable because Mattheson himself held important positions in the musical world and composed 7 **operas**, 25 **oratorios**, 3 **passions**, 18 Italian **cantatas**, 24 **sonatas**, 13 **suites** for **harpsichord**, and 12 **fugues**. Details of his life come chiefly from his own *Grundlage einer Ehren-Pforte*, a biographical dictionary.

He was the third and only surviving son of a Hamburg tax collector, Johannes Mattheson, and Margaretha Hölling. Johann the son received a liberal education at the Johanneum in **Hamburg** and began musical studies at the age of six. By age nine, he was performing on the **organ** in Hamburg churches and singing with the Hamburg opera, beginning a long association. He befriended **George Frideric Handel** there in 1703 and apparently helped Handel secure a position with the opera **orchestra**.

The key moment of Mattheson's career arrived with the appointment as tutor to the son of Sir John Wich, the English ambassador to Hamburg, in 1704, a job which he performed so impressively that he was made Wich's private secretary in 1706 with a high salary and important diplomatic responsibilities. Mattheson retained this post when the son succeeded his father as ambassador in 1715, even while taking on other posts as director of music at the Hamburg cathedral (1715) and *Kapellmeister* to the Duke of Holstein (1719).

Johann Mattheson's Most Important Writings

Title	Date	Subject matter
Das neu-eröffnete Orchestre	1713	An introduction to contemporary music, including descriptions of current genres and criticism of some traditional theories
Exemplarische Organisten-Probe	1719	A thoroughbass method
Critica musica	1722–1725	The first German music journal, containing debates, chronicles, and excerpts from the letters of famous contemporary musicians
Der musicalische Patriot	1728	A defense of the opera and the operatic influence on church music
Grosse General-Bass-Schule	1731	A thoroughbass method with 48 examples
Kleine General-Bass-Schule	1735	A thoroughbass method with emphasis on improvisation and realization of the figured bass
Der vollkommene Capellmeister	1739	A summary of the musical skills of the *Kapellmeister,* including theories of composition
Grundlage einer Ehren-Pforte	1740	A biographical dictionary of 149 of the best-known musicians of the time

Mattheson married an Englishwoman, Catharina Jennings, in 1709. She died on 8 February 1753. On 25 April 1764, after a funeral with music of his own composition conducted by **Georg Philipp Telemann**, Mattheson's body was buried in the crypt of St. Michael's Church in Hamburg, the organ of which he had paid to restore.

MEDICEAN CHANT. Refers to the Roman Gradual and Antiphonal published by the Medicean press in **Rome** in 1614–1615 (volumes 1 and 2) under the direction of Felice Anerio (c. 1560–1614) and Franceso Soriano (c. 1548–1621) that revised texts and melodies of older manuscript chant books in the wake of the **Council of Trent**. Pope Gregory XIII charged the composer-editors on 25 October 1577 with "revising, purging, correcting, and reforming" the existing chant books, but it is possible that the new edition merely codified contemporary practices, as earlier editions show some of the same changes. Modern chant scholars often charge that the editors, in excising many elaborate melismas and other "superfluities" of the medieval plainchant, applied contemporary humanistic views of how classical Latin ought to work. In any case, the Medicean chant books became the official Roman Catholic editions of plainchant for the entire Baroque.

MESSIAH. An **English oratorio** of **George Frideric Handel**, composed from 22 August to 12 September (**orchestrated** by 14 September) 1741, first performed for a charity concert in Dublin on 13 April 1742, *Messiah* is probably the most famous large piece of music set to English text. Its original version is scored for **strings**, **continuo**, **trumpets**, **timpani**, four vocal soloists (SATB), and four-**voice** choir (in "Lift Up Ye Heads," five). Handel added **oboes**, **bassoons**, and possibly **horns** as doublings for the **London** performances (1743) and altered some of the **arias**, including the vocal solo assignments. The work requires about two and one-half hours to perform.

Messiah is a singular work even within Handel's English oratorios, themselves singular in their midway position between the sacred and secular worlds of art music. The London advertisements termed the work "A New Sacred **Oratorio**" to ward off charges of profaning a sacred subject in the theater. But while almost all his other English oratorios are close to **opera** in aesthetic, having directed plots motivated by named characters singing arias and **recitatives**, *Messiah* is contemplative and abstract. The soloists are anonymous voices, and while there is no doubt that Christ is the subject, the events and ultimate significance of his life, but for a snippet from St. Luke's Gospel, are alluded to without explicit description. Prophecies from the Old Testament dominate the **libretto**.

The libretto was compiled from the King James Bible, with minimal changes, by Handel's collaborator Charles Jennens (1700–1773) and is in three parts. The first features the traditional messianic prophecies of Isaiah (7, 9, 40, and 60), Malachi, and Zechariah and the shepherd scene from the birth narrative of St. Luke's Gospel. The second part describes the **passion** and resurrection obliquely through the "suffering servant" passages of Isaiah (53) and excerpts from Romans and the Psalms. (The tradition of the audience standing for the concluding "Hallelujah" [No. 44] **chorus** because King George II once did is founded on a dubious anecdote in a letter written 37 years after the first London performance.) The final part covers the universal resurrection through 1 Corinthians and Revelation. There are also contributions from Job, Lamentations, and the Gospel of John scattered throughout.

Messiah was revived for London in 1745 and again in 1749, beginning a series of performances for the Foundling Hospital that occurred annually until Handel's death in 1759 and thereafter until 1777. The full score was published in 1767 (London), allowing more frequent local performances throughout the country. The "Commemoration of Handel" at Westminster Abbey in 1784 may have had as many as 500 performers, anticipating a practice, maintained by the growth of amateur choral societies in the 19th century, of using forces far larger than Handel would ever have imagined. Such performances naturally required massive reinforcements of instruments and entire reorchestrations. Wolfgang Amadeus Mozart (1756–1791) performed his own such arrangement in 1789. With growing appreciation of Baroque performance practices in the 20th century, recent professional performances and recordings have returned to a scale that Handel might have recognized. Thus, the performance history of *Messiah* mirrors changing historiographical and aesthetic attitudes about Western classics.

Indeed, *Messiah* governed Handel's very reputation as a composer for more than a century after his death, since, along with *Judas Maccabeus* and *Israel in Egypt*, it was virtually the only work of his in the repertory and performed constantly. The brilliant choruses with sacred text and the famously brief period of composition understandably built an image of spiritual inspiration foreign to Handel. Since the mid-20th century, the image has been filled out. He always worked rapidly; after completing *Messiah* and taking a week off, he completed *Samson* by 29 October. Growing familiarity with other, classically oriented oratorios, the 40 operas, and a wealth of instrumental music has somewhat restored to *Messiah* its peculiar hybrid quality of sacred art as entertainment.

METASTASIO (3 January 1698, Rome–12 April 1782, Vienna). Perhaps the most famous and widely performed of all **opera librettists**. Between 1720 and 1771, he wrote about 60 librettos that were turned into more than 800 operas by more than 300 composers well into the 19th century, including Baldassare Galuppi (1706–1785), **George Frideric Handel**, **Johann Adolf Hasse**, **Niccolò Jommelli**, **Leonardo Vinci**, Christoph Willibald von Gluck (1714–1787), and Wolfgang Amadeus Mozart (1756–1791). The 27 librettos for *opera seria* were the most popular: *Didone Abbandonata* alone was set to music more than 60 times.

Born Pietro Trapassi to parents of modest means, his precocious ability to **improvise** verse impressed Cardinal Pietro Ottoboni who saw to his early education. The young Trapassi was further aided by a distinguished Roman jurist Gianvincenzo Gravina, who adopted him and invented his pen name of Metastasio, which is "Trapassi" with Greek roots substituted for the Latin. In the 1720s, Metastasio worked in a law office in **Naples** while acquiring a growing reputation for writing texts for the music of local composers, including **Nicola Porpora**. His verse attracted the attention of **Apostolo Zeno**, then the leading poet in the operatic reform. When Zeno retired from his post as court poet in **Vienna** and returned to his native **Venice** in 1729, Metastasio was invited to replace him. He assumed the post in August 1730. He had already written *Didone Abbandonata*, *Alessandro nell' Indie*, and *Artaserse*, three of his most popular librettos. He remained in Vienna for the rest of his life.

Metastasio's work represents the culmination of efforts beginning in the late 17th century to reform Baroque opera and return it to the ideals of classical drama. Strictly speaking, these reforms did not succeed entirely, if only because the rigid convention of the *lieto fine*, the happy ending concluding all *opere serie*, excluded authentic tragedy. However, they did produce a set of conventions, realized most consistently and artistically in Metastasio's librettos, that guaranteed dramas of a lean and balanced neoclassical aesthetic, preaching the virtues supposedly resident in noble society. Metastasio's librettos are all moralistic.

A typical libretto of Metastasio casts six roles: a leading couple of nobles, a secondary couple of nobles, and two more supporting characters who might be of lower class. The leading couple, usually a female and male soprano (*castrato*), sings about half of the **arias** in the opera, the secondary couple perhaps three or four each, at least one in each of the three acts. The supporting characters might have one or two each. All these arias had to be varied in verse type and emotional outline, whether violent or reflective, sorrowful or joyful, and distributed in the opera such that, ideally, no opera character sang two arias in succession and no two successive arias were of the same type. The execution of all these conventions in a way that seems natural without occluding the plot line is the source of Metastasio's artistry.

METER. The perceived regular grouping of beats. The beginning of each group is marked by a beat that is accented, somehow made more salient compared to the following beats. In Western tradition generally, and certainly in the Baroque, there are three possible cases for the meter of a piece or passage: duple meter, in which each accented (strong) beat alternates with an unaccented (weak) beat; triple, in which each accented beat is followed by two unaccented beats; and the case of no meter at all, such as in plainchant or **operatic recitative**.

	>		>		>		>		
Duple meter schema:	o	o	o	o	o	o	o	o	etc.

	>			>			>		
Triple meter schema:	o	o	o	o	o	o	o	o	etc.

In modern notation, the composer expresses the prevailing meter of a passage by the higher of the two numerals in the time signature written at the beginning of the score, the number of beats in each measure. Each measure is bounded by a bar line. The lower number indicates the type of note lasting one beat, the unit of counting. The French theoretician Etienne Loulié was one of the first to categorize meter in this way in his *Eléments* of 1696, and that classification became common in the 18th century. It is important to realize, however, that neither time signatures nor bar lines produce the perception of meter. They merely facilitate the reading of scores and parts. Meter must arise from the sound phenomena, and for this reason, it requires several seconds even in music with strong metric profile for the meter to be perceived.

Modern cognitive science more or less agrees that the perception of meter requires two conditions of the music. First, there must be isochronous beats, an abstraction of musical phenomena, most commonly the onsets of notes, even virtual ones at times, spaced equally in time. (This is why recitative has no meter, but rather "free rhythm"; there are no consistent beats.) Second, the musical phenomena must emphasize in some manner every second beat (in duple meter) or every third beat (in triple meter) compared to the other beats. As another way of stating the preceding, some theorists postulate that for meter to be perceived, there must be at least two levels of isochronous beats ordered in a hierarchy.

However, except for recitative, virtually all Baroque music expresses more than two levels of beat in its metric hierarchy. This expression is explicit in the so-called compound meters, or time signatures such as 6/8 or 9/8, where the upper numeral is not a prime number. In these two cases, listeners hear the stream of eighth-note beats as a quick triple meter as every third eighth-note beat is accented. But three eighth-note durations add up to dotted-quarter groups, which themselves are heard as relatively strong and weak beats on a higher level. In a 6/8 time signature, every second of these long beats is strong (accented); in a 9/8 signature, every third. Thus, music in 6/8, such as a **siciliana**, is said to be in triple meter on the low level (eighth note, fast tapping) and duple on the high level (dotted quarter, slow tapping), while music in 9/8 is triple on the low level and triple on the high level.

Figure. Schema of 6/8 compound meter showing low-level beats (bottom staff) and upper-level beats (middle staff)

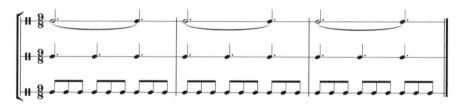

Figure. Schema of 9/8 compound meter showing low-level beats (bottom staff) and upper-level beats (middle staff)

Baroque scores bearing simpler time signatures, however, still have more than two levels of beat. Consider a typical **allemande** meter, with time signature of [C] or 4/4:

Figure. Levels of beat in duple meter, showing strong and weak beat patterns at each level

The distinction of strong and weak beat may be perceived with durations as short as 200 milliseconds. Such beats add up to durations of double or triple their length to create strong and weak beats on the next level and so on until the metric hierarchy is complete. Beats longer than two seconds pass out of working memory before their relative accentuation can be compared in cognition, so the metric hierarchy is limited in abstraction.

Baroque meter is generally conceived as categorical, as either duple or triple on the most salient level, by Baroque music theorists and most modern ones. While efficient, this conception overlooks two essential subtleties. One is the specific metric hierarchy in effect at any moment, how the most salient level is subdivided on the lower levels, how subsumed on the higher, and which of those is actually present in the sound phenomena.

A second subtlety is the relative quality of strength of Baroque meter within the categories. A piece might be strongly duple on a higher level and weakly duple on a lower one, as in most **gavottes** or **French overtures**, or the reverse, as in a duple meter **fugue**. This astonishingly variable mix of qualities derives from the independent nature of the musical phenomena that make a beat seem relatively accented. Long notes are more salient than short ones, loud ones more than soft ones, high-pitched ones more than mid-range notes. Chord changes emphasize beats very strongly, as do tonic **functions**. Entrances or exits of an instrument or singer may accent the beat, too. Because these phenomena are to a large degree independent of one another, composers may concentrate them all together on every other beat to create a powerful duple perception or distribute them among beats for a weak duple or perhaps a momentarily ambiguous meter.

Baroque time signatures evolved significantly in the 17th century from their traditional purpose of indicating the proportional divisions of breve and semibreve notes because instrumental music employed note values much smaller than those. They took on connotations of **tempo** so that a piece with C/ at its head would be slower than one with C, or 3/2 slower than 3/4, but there was much diversity in the practice. The genre of the composition, too, often dictated the form of the time signature so that sacred music of the *stile antico* would prefer signatures with long duration values, mimicking the ancient music that used such values predominantly, whereas **dances** used signatures of short values.

MINUET. Stately aristocratic **dance** in triple **meter**, its origin is unknown, but it begins to appear in French manuscripts of instrumental music about 1660, and composers throughout Europe continued to write minuets into the 19th century. In Baroque music, the minuet appears in the French *ballet de cour* and *tragédie lyrique* and frequently in **suites**, where it usually follows the **sarabande**.

MISSA BREVIS (Lat. "short mass"). A **polyphonic** setting of **mass** ordinaries of short duration. This might be achieved by setting the texts syllabically or by having different parts of longer prayers sung simultaneously by different **voices** in the choir.

In 17th- and 18th-century Lutheran contexts, *Missa brevis* indicates a setting of the Kyrie (in Greek) and Gloria (in Latin). Five such settings, including the first version of the **Mass in B Minor**, were composed by **Johann Sebastian Bach**.

MODE. From the Latin *modus* ("manner"), mode in the Western tradition originally denoted the classification of a plainchant according to its pitch range (*ambitus*) and final pitch (*finalis*). In the late Middle Ages and Renaissance, mode denoted a scale for composition and **improvisation**, distinguished from other modes not by pitch collection but by its tonic, the pattern of intervals made by the scale degrees, and by which of those **pitch-classes** would be prominent in a plainchant melody. By the 17th century, these classifications held little practical value for the new kinds of music based on **functional harmony** and the modern concept of **key**. Mode came to refer to the distinction between Western major and minor scales (e.g., "the minor mode"). However, vestiges of the modal system may be seen and heard into the 18th century in key signatures that do not match their modern key denotations and in older plainchant and **chorale** melodies used as **cantus firmi** in sacred compositions.

MODULATION. The change of **key** or tonal center during the course of a composition. The change must be contained within the continuity of a musical structure, such as a movement, a ritornello, a **chorale**, even a single phrase. That the second movement of a **concerto** may be composed in a key different from the concerto's first movement is not considered modulation because the two movements are not a continuous structure.

The Baroque composer modulates generally by using the same devices as are used to establish any key but orients toward a new **pitch-class** after the original key has been clearly established. He may replace a pitch-class (e.g., F, with its **chromatic** neighbor, for example, F-sharp), thus altering the set of pitch-classes in force and thereby changing the sense of a tonic. Baroque composers usually modulate to "close" keys, that is, keys with similar pitch collections, so that even the chromatic alteration of a single pitch may suffice for a modulation. The composer may **cadence** on the new tonic, thus immediately identifying it as the new tonal center. Often, the simple transposition of a clear tonal melody can reorient the listener's perception to a new tonic pitch-class.

Although a Renaissance composition may sometimes cadence on a pitch other than the primary one of its **mode**, the perception of a new tonal center in force—a modulation—is almost always momentary, replaced by a renewed emphasis on the original tonic. The Baroque style, on the other hand, is the first in the history of Western music to exploit changes of tonal center as a framework for musical structure.

Modulations can build a musical structure in at least two ways. First, the change of key is perceived as a significant articulation, an event that separates the music preceding it from that following it into distinct organizations. This is why listeners may enjoy the rehearing of a long concerto melody and its harmonic accompaniment without any changes in a new key because that is a new harmonic environment, which makes everything in it, in some sense, sound new and different.

Second, Baroque composers universally subscribe to the law of Western musical aesthetics that states that every unified composition must conclude with the same **tonality** with which it began. If a piece begins in D, it must end in D. In this light, a modulation to a new key is analogous to a **dissonance** that must be resolved on a higher structural level. An ABA **da capo aria** in, for example, D major will present its second section in a different key, possibly B minor, which helps to create the sense of a contrasting passage required by the form. But that is why the conclusion of a strong cadence of the B section satisfies on one level, in its key of B minor, but seems unfinished on another, the level of the whole aria. Since the A section began in D major, so must it end, and this aesthetic requires the return of the A section to do so. On the other hand, a singer could satisfactorily perform only the A section and cut the rest because the A section both begins and ends in D major.

Modulations in Baroque music can occur on any level of structure from the musical phrase on upward to organizing a whole movement. As the Baroque progressed, composers learned to exploit changes of key on ever higher levels of structure, one reason why late-Baroque movements are generally longer than early Baroque movements.

MONODY. A term of modern historical musicology that denotes early Italian Baroque compositions for solo **voice** and **continuo** accompaniment. **Giulio Caccini**'s collection *Le Nuove Musiche* (1602) is often cited as one of the earliest archetypical examples. As experiments in textual expression through music, monodies laid the groundwork for both **aria** and **recitative**, the chief **operatic textures** which diverged later in the 17th century by their associations with relatively strong and weak **meter**, respectively.

MONOPHONY (MONOPHONIC). A musical **texture** of a single melody, that is, not more than one note is heard at any moment. Generally, when a melody is presented along with itself at the interval of a perfect octave, such as when men and women sing the same tune precisely together, the texture is still considered monophonic.

MONTEVERDI, CLAUDIO (15 May 1567, Cremona, Italy–29 November 1643, Venice). Although his music faded from view after 1660, in retrospect, Monteverdi must be considered the greatest and most influential composer of the 17th century in Europe. He mastered completely the Renaissance tradition of the Italian **madrigal** and then reformed it entirely around the early Baroque style and established a new tradition of Italian chamber vocal music. His works for the stage, some unfortunately lost, include the first great **opera**, *L'Orfeo*, and vindicated the aesthetic integrity of the notion of *dramma per musica*. He also composed a significant body of sacred music in both *stile antico* and *stile moderno*.

Monteverdi was born the eldest son of Maddalena Zignani and Baldassare Monteverdi, who combined the trades of apothecary, surgeon, and doctor. Little is known of his formal or musical education, but it is inferred from dedications in his published works that he probably studied with the composer Marc'Antonio Ingegneri (1535–1592). Claudio published his first volume of vocal music, a collection of three-**voiced** Latin *Sacrae Cantiunculae*, in 1582, at age 15, a precocity unheard of at the time. At 23, he was appointed *suonatore di vivuola* ("**viol** player") to Duke Vincenzo Gonzaga of Mantua and moved there in 1590 or 1591.

On 20 May 1599, he married a singer at the Mantuan court, Claudia Cattaneo, with whom he had four children, three of whom survived to adulthood. His wife died on 10 September 1607, a heavy loss. He did not marry again and was ordained to the priesthood on 16 April 1632. Monteverdi's time at the court of Mantua was also troubled by the duke's failure to pay him regularly, even after Monteverdi was promoted to the top position as *maestro di cappella* on 26 November 1601. The duke also neglected the timely payment of pensions, which would annoy the composer until the end of his life.

His Mantuan years, however, saw Monteverdi achieve an international reputation as composer, chiefly owing to the publication and republication of his first five books of Italian madrigals. These involved him in a famous aesthetic controversy of the time. A music theorist from Bologna, one Giovanni Maria Artusi, published a critique of certain novelties of the musical syntax arising from experiments in musical text expression in "The Imperfections of Modern Music" (1600) and in particular cited passages from Monteverdi's madrigals in Book IV (published 1603) and Book V (1605, e.g., "Cruda Amarilli"; pieces from both books had circulated in the 1590s). When Monteverdi published his Book V in 1605, he not only included madrigals that required an instrumental basso **continuo**, thus explicitly advancing his progressive cause, but also a postface in which he defended his musical syntax on the grounds that it was a new language, *lo stile moderno*, not to be confused with the traditional *stile antico* characterized by the careful **counterpoint** of sacred music.

At Mantua, Monteverdi also composed one of the most important works in the history of music, his first opera, *L'Orfeo*. In 1600, Duke Vincenzo traveled to **Florence** to attend the wedding of Maria de' Medici and Henri IV of France, where **Jacopo Peri**'s opera *Euridice* was performed. It is highly probable that Monteverdi was among the musicians who accompanied the duke. Prince Francesco Gonzaga commissioned Monteverdi's opera for the Carnival season, and it was premiered on 24 February 1607 for the Accademia degli Invaghiti, an intellectual society, and then for the court of Mantua on 1 March. This was followed by other dramatic works: the *Ballo delle Ingrate* to accompany a play by Gabrielle Chiabrera, and then another opera based on the myth of the minotaur, *Arianna*. *Arianna* premiered on 28 May 1608 to great acclaim, but unfortunately, only the famous **lament** "Lasciatemi morire" survives from it.

The last landmark composition of Monteverdi's Mantua years is the first collection of sacred music, the so-called **Vespers of 1610**. In September of that year, he went to **Rome**, ostensibly to secure a place at the seminary for his son Francesco, but biographers believe that in presenting the Vespers personally to Pope Paul V, Monteverdi thought that he might secure there an appointment better than his post at Mantua.

That post suddenly became tenuous when Duke Vincenzo died on 18 February 1612. Cutbacks in music making at the court probably caused Monteverdi's dismissal on 29 July. Then, the new Duke Francesco died on 22 December, further reducing Monteverdi's chances of being rehired. Then his fortune turned. The position of *maestro di cappella* at San Marco in **Venice**, one of the most prestigious in Europe, opened up when Giulio Cesare Martinengo (born c. 1568) died on 10 July 1613. Monteverdi applied for the position on 1 August, providing a new **mass** and taking the required audition test. He was appointed on 19 August at a salary of 300 ducats. He arrived to take up residence in Venice in October, but he lost most of his possessions to highwaymen en route.

At San Marco, Monteverdi reformed the chapel organization, acquired new works for its library, including music of **Giovanni da Palestrina** and Orlando di Lasso (1532–1594), and hired new musicians. On 24 August 1616, the procurators of San Marco raised Monteverdi's salary to 400 ducats. His extant letters express contentment with his new working conditions. Nevertheless, he was apparently concerned about his financial security, as shown by numerous attempts to collect pensions promised him by the Gonzagas of Mantua and a trip to try to acquire a canonry in his birthplace, Cremona, in September 1627.

Monteverdi died on 29 November 1643 and was buried in the furthest chapel in the north transept of the church of Santa Maria Gloriosa dei Frari with full civic honors of the Republic of Venice.

Monteverdi's compositions fall into three groups: secular vocal music, chiefly Italian madrigals, works for the stage, and sacred music.

There are over 265 secular vocal compositions, the majority of which appear in his nine publications of Italian madrigals spanning his entire career. They reflect Monteverdi's early mastery of the late Renaissance style, which is then gradually replaced in favor of the new **textures** of *dramma per musica*, first in Book V, which is the first of his collections to demand a continuo accompaniment, and then in Book VII, which gives the voices the textural prominence typical of opera.

Monteverdi's stage works probably include at least seven full-length operas, of which only three survive: *L'Orfeo* (1607), *Il Ritorno d'Ulisse in Patria* ("The Return of Ulysses to His Homeland," 1640), and *L'Incoronazione di Poppea* ("The Coronation of Poppea," 1643), the last two stimulated by the new business of public opera that began in Venice in 1637. These works alone suffice to place Monteverdi in the company of the greatest musical dramatists of the Western tradition. He also composed at least 11 other smaller works: *balli*, **intermedi**, and *mascherate*.

Chronology of Monterverdi's Madrigal Publications

Madrigali, libro primo	Venice, 1587	Italian madrigals for five voices
Il secondo libro de madrigali	Venice, 1590	Italian madrigals for five voices
Il terzo libro de madrigali	Venice, 1592	Italian madrigals for five voices
Il quarto libro de madrigali	Venice, 1603	Italian madrigals for five voices
Il quinto libro de madrigali	Venice, 1605	Italian madrigals for five voices and basso continuo
Il sesto libro de madrigali con uno dialogo	Venice, 1614	Italian madrigals for five and seven voices and basso continuo
Concerto: settimo libro de madrigali con altri generi di canti	Venice, 1619	Secular vocal music for one to six voices and basso continuo
Madrigali guerrieri, et amorosi . . . Libro ottavo	Venice, 1638	Secular vocal music for one to eight voices and basso continuo
Madrigale e canzonetti . . . Libro nono	Venice, 1651	Secular vocal music for two to three voices and basso continuo

Monterverdi's Principal Works for the Stage

Title	Librettist	First performance
L'Orfeo	Alessandro Striggio	24 February 1607, ducal palace, Mantua
[Arianna]	Ottavio Rinuccini	28 May 1608, ducal palace, Mantua
[Le Nozze di Tetide]	S. Agnelli	Intended 1617, no record
[La Finta Pazza Licori]	G. Strozzi	Intended 1627, incomplete
[Proserpina Rapita]	G. Strozzi	1630, Venice
Il Ritorno d'Ulisse in Patria	G. Badoaro	1640, Carnival, teatro San Cassiano, Venice
L'Incoronazione di Poppea	G. F. Busenello	1643, Carnival, teatro San Giovanni e Paolo, Venice

Note: Bracketed works are lost.

Monteverdi's sacred music, consisting of some 105 Latin **motets**, 32 Italian *madrigali spirituali*, 3 masses, and the Vespers of 1610, received less attention despite its superb quality only because the musical culture of Europe in general was moving away from sacred music. It was published chiefly in three collections: the 1610 **print** containing the Vespers (including two versions of the **Magnificat**) and *Missa In illo tempore*; the large collection *Selva Morale e Spirituale* of 1641; and a posthumous collection of 1650, as well as in anthologies that appeared throughout his professional career.

Many of the motets exploit the **monodic** and concertante idioms of opera and are thus typical of early Baroque trends in Italian and German sacred music. At the same time, Monteverdi seemed anxious to show that he also commanded the *stile antico* approved by the **Council of Trent**. All three masses are exemplars, and along with the *Missa In illo tempore*, he took the trouble to print separately the 10 **subjects** of Nicholas Gombert's (c. 1495–c. 1560) motet **parodied** in his own music. The Vespers of 1610 is unique in 17th-century sacred music because it synthesizes all available idioms sacred and secular in a single monumental composition.

Because he had to provide new music for important festivals during his long tenure (1613–1643) as *maestro di cappella* at San Marco Basilica in Venice, it is thought that much of his sacred music must be lost.

Because his work grounded the success of the early Baroque operatic aesthetic, and because, like that of all his contemporaries, it was put aside in favor of newer fashions after his death, his influence on the Baroque might be considered absolutely fundamental and yet anonymous. The Italian 20th-century composer Gian Francesco Malipiero (1882–1973) made Monteverdi's name one of the earliest recognized by the **early music revival** by editing a complete edition of his works begun in 1928. Although these editions are revised according to Malipiero's taste, many are still in circulation, even though many Monteverdi works are now available in critical editions informed by historical research.

MOTET. A **polyphonic** composition for unaccompanied choir setting a Latin sacred, often biblical, text. This is the most common connotation, but in the Baroque, motets may employ the **operatic** *stile moderno* and have instruments.

The advent of opera at the turn of the 17th century made permanent the fissure between sacred and secular musical languages that had been deepening throughout the 16th century and split motet composition into two paths. Composers, particularly those working near **Rome**, could follow the legendary **Giovanni da Palestrina** and uphold the fixed ideals of the *stile antico* and the *a cappella* sound, or they could write "motets" with the new operatic **textures**. Contemporary terminology becomes confused and imprecise at this juncture; "motet" in the 17th century might refer to any vocal composition associated with liturgy, while the settings of sacred texts in operatic manner might be called "concerted motets," "**sacred concertos**," or "**sacred symphonies**." In these works, beginning with Ludovico Viadana's *Cento Concerti Ecclesiastici* ("One Hundred Church Concertos") in 1602 and followed on by many publications of **Claudio Monteverdi**, **Alessandro Grandi**, **Heinrich Schütz**, and others, solo voices and instruments combine to make a complete harmonic texture. The ensemble might be as simple as one singer and **continuo** or as elaborate as double or triple **choir** with a large instrumental group. In the late 17th century, motets, such as those of **Alessandro Scarlatti**, become like spiritual operas in their use of **recitative** and **da capo aria**. In general, semantic referents, such as traditional chant melodies, are abandoned, although German Lutheran composers wrote **chorale motets** using their own traditional **chorale** melodies as **cantus firmi**. Some Baroque motets, such as those of **Antonio Lotti** and Schütz (*Cantiones Sacrae*, 1625; *Geistliche Chormusik*, 1648) combine traditional *stile antico* textures with secular harmonic effects. This strain culminates in the six motets of **Johann Sebastian Bach** (BWV 225, 227–231).

French composers did not adapt operatic techniques until the approximately 100 motets of **Guillaume Bouzignac** in the 1630s. Thereafter, they readily assumed secular elements, culminating late in the century in the *grand motet* at the court of Versailles and the *petit motet* composed for less ostentatious circumstances, such as convents. These genres continued to follow the secular trends until the French Revolution.

MUFFAT, GEORG (baptized 1 June 1653, Mégève, Savoy [modern southeastern France]–23 February 1704, Passau, Germany). Training under two of the most signal composers of the late 17th century, **Jean-Baptiste Lully** and **Arcangelo Corelli**, Muffat brought the so-called French and Italian styles to Austria and Germany, where he spent most of his career. His 15 **orchestral suites** (in two sets, 1695 and 1698) model the French manner, while the 12 **concerti grossi** (1701) bring out the typical Corellian **textures** and contrasts of small and large groups. He also composed 5 **sonatas** for **strings** and **continuo**, a single **violin** sonata, 3 lost **operas**, and a volume of **organ** music containing 12 **toccatas**, a **chaconne**, a **passacaglia**, and an **aria** with **variations**. His 1699 treatise, the *Regulae Concentuum Partiturae*, is one of the best on continuo playing.

Muffat studied with Lully and his contemporaries in **Paris** from 1663 to 1669. Then he held posts in Molsheim (from 1671), Prague (1677), and Salzburg, where he was appointed organist and chamber musician to the

Archbishop Max Gandolf in 1678. In the early 1680s, he was granted leave to study in **Rome**, where he met Corelli. He returned to Salzburg in September 1682. In 1690, he became *Kapellmeister* for Johann Philipp, bishop of Passau. *See also* MUFFAT, GOTTLIEB.

MUFFAT, GOTTLIEB (baptized 25 April 1690, Passau, Germany–9 December 1770, Vienna). Protégé of **Johann Joseph Fux**, the son of **Georg Muffat** became a leading composer for **organ** and **harpsichord** in **Vienna** in the first half of the 18th century. His oeuvre, all composed before 1741, consists of about 350 works, including 72 **versets**, 12 **toccatas**, and 2 **masses** for organ, 6 **suites** for harpsichord, and the following generic **keyboard** pieces: 27 toccatas, 21 *capricci*, 16 **preludes**, 2 **chaconnes**, 32 *ricercari*, 19 **canzonas**, 5 **fugues**, and 4 **partitas**.

Gottlieb Muffat began his study with Fux in 1711 and, thereafter, never left the imperial court, rising through the ranks, with support from Fux, until he became first organist in 1741. He retired with a pension in 1763.

MUSETTE. (1) A bagpipe instrument popular in France in the 17th and 18th centuries. A *bellows* under the arm supplies air for the *chanter*, a wooden tube with fingering holes that determines the pitch of the melodic part played over the steady drone pitch or pitches, usually C^2 or G^2. A second chanter, added in the early 18th century, extended the melodic range to D^6. **Sonatas** and **suites** for musette were published by **Joseph Bodin de Boismortier** and other woodwind composers, and it was not unusual to hear the instrument in stage works of **Jean-Baptiste Lully**, **André Campra**, and **Jean-Philippe Rameau**.

(2) A movement in a **keyboard** suite composed to sound like a musette owing to an unmoving bass (drone), usually a tonic **pedal point**. **Johann Sebastian Bach**'s third "English" suite contains an example.

MUSICAL OFFERING (original title: *Musicalisches Opfer*; Johann Sebastian Bach, BWV 1079). A unique publication dedicated to Frederick the Great, King of Prussia, in 1747, and containing 2 **ricercars** for **keyboard**, a **trio sonata**, and 10 **canons** all based on a **chromatic subject** composed by the king. Bach had the work engraved at his own expense.

The idea for the Musical Offering arose out of a visit by **Johann Sebastian Bach** to the Prussian court where his son **Carl Philipp Emanuel** was court **harpsichordist**. King Frederick, a fine **flutist** and composer, asked "the old Bach" to **improvise** a **fugue** on his theme. According to newspaper accounts, Bach did improvise a three-**voice** fugue on the spot, astonishing the entire court thereby, and then promptly stated that he was unhappy with his improvisation and would engrave a proper fugue to do justice to the royal theme.

The resulting **print** is a **contrapuntal** tour de force typical of Bach's late work. The royal theme appears in all the pieces, including a six-voice ricercar (the antique name for **imitative** composition, replaced by "fugue") and all manner of canons, including **puzzle canons**, perpetual canons, and canons by contrary motion (theme in **inversion**). The complete performance might take one hour or so, depending upon repetitions.

N

NAPLES. Naples and its territories were ruled by foreign viceroys for almost the entire Baroque, first by Spain from 1503 to 1707 and then by Austria from 1707 to 1734. The change of power in 1707 interrupted the career of **Alessandro Scarlatti**, who was forced from Naples to **Rome** for a time, but otherwise foreign domination appears to have provided the political stability that allowed Naples its rise to prominence in the world of music.

One stable institution was the Chapel of the Royal Palace. Charged with providing the liturgical music for the viceroy and court, in 1614, the ensemble consisted of a comparatively large choir of seven sopranos, four altos, three countertenors, six tenors, and six basses accompanied by six **violins**, two **organists**, and one each of **cornetto**, **trombone**, **lute**, and **harp**. The size of this ensemble remained about the same throughout the 17th century. These musicians performed in other kinds of music in the city, including **operas** mounted at the royal palace and at Teatro di San Bartolomeo.

The only rival of the Chapel of the Royal Palace for sacred music was the Oratorio dei Girolamini. Established at the request of the original oratorian, St. Philip Neri of Rome, as the Congregazione dell'Oratorio in 1586, it became independent with a new name in 1612 and was the primary location in Naples for **oratorios** and other devotional music.

Naples boasted a number of conservatories for musical training. Some were eventually merged with the Royal College, but an important independent one was the Conservatorio dei Poveri di Gesù Cristo, founded in 1599. From the mid-17th century onward, its teachers were reputed to be among the best in Naples. In the 18th century, it could count **Leonardo Vinci** and **Giovanni Pergolesi** among its prize students.

Foremost, however, was the reputation of Naples as a center of opera, indeed, as the source in Baroque times of a particular style of "Neapolitan" opera, the identity and existence of which remains controversial today. The earliest known opera performed in Naples was *Didone* in September 1650. The composer is unknown, but the **libretto** is the same as that of a 1641 *Didone* of **Venice**'s **Francesco Cavalli**, and for some years, the only operas seen in Naples were imported from Venice, including a 1651 performance of

Claudio Monteverdi's *L'Incoronazione di Poppea*, one of only two surviving sources for that masterwork.

The next important period in Neapolitan opera would be the tenure at Teatro San Bartolomeo of Scarlatti, who spend 20 years, off and on, in Naples and composed 40 operas for the city. He also introduced works of his outstanding Italian colleagues: **Giovanni Legrenzi**, **Giovanni Bononcini**, **Bernardo Pasquini**, and **Antonio Draghi**, among others.

Finally, the same theater saw the first full-length music drama of the 18th century's finest librettist, the *Didone* of **Metastasio**, with music by Domenico Natale Sarro (1679–1744).

NEAPOLITAN MASS. A Baroque type of **mass** setting that segments the texts of the five proper prayers—Kyrie, Gloria, Credo, Sanctus, and Agnus Dei—so that each is set as a complex of several movements, as in a late-Baroque **church cantata**. Commonly, each prayer begins and ends with a **chorus**. Between these, other choruses and solo **arias** are heard. The instrumental accompaniment may be as simple as a pipe **organ** in the church or a large **orchestra**. By far the most famous example is the **Mass in B Minor** of **Johann Sebastian Bach**.

NEUMEISTER, ERDMANN (12 May 1671, Weissenfels, Germany–18 August 1756, Hamburg). Poet and theologian, he wrote nine cycles of **church cantata** texts for all Sundays and many feasts of the Lutheran liturgical year. His second such cycle legitimized the alternation of **aria** and **recitative**, as in Italian **opera**, for Lutheran Church cantatas. **Johann Sebastian Bach** drew on the fourth cycle for his Cantatas BWV 18, 24, 28, 59, and 61.

NIEDT, FRIEDRICH ERHARD (baptized 31 May 1674, Jena, Germany–13 April 1708, Copenhagen). A rather obscure composer who nevertheless wrote five theoretical treatises of unusual influence. His rules for **continuo** playing were evidently used in teaching by **Johann Sebastian Bach**, and two volumes of his *Musicalische Handleitung* ("Musical Handbook") were published and promoted by **Johann Mattheson**.

NOTES INÉGALES (Fr. "unequal notes"). The practice of transforming the typical **meter** of an **allemande**, duple on both high and low levels (e.g., 4/4), into the meter of a **gigue**, duple on the high but triple on the low level (e.g., 12/8), by playing successive pairs of short notes (e.g., eighth notes) in a duration ratio of 2:1 or, more rarely, 1:2, rather than 1:1 as indicated by standard notation practices. Thus, literally equal notes become unequal in duration. Making an *allemande giguée* or *allemande en gigue* in this way seems to have been a typical performance practice in 17th-century **lute** and **keyboard suites**.

O

OBOE (Fr. *hautbois,* **Ger.** *Hoboe***).** The most important woodwind of the Baroque, it saw rapid technical advancement in the early 17th century among the major instrument-making families of France, the Philidors, the Chédev-illes, and the **Hotteterres**, with Jean Hotteterre recognized by many as the creator of the modern oboe. The instrument, a slender wooden tube whose column of air is activated by the player's blowing forcefully through a bound double reed, distinguished itself from its ancestor the shawm by allowing the player more direct contact with the reed, a reshaping of its conoidal bore, and by reforming the size and placement of the finger holes to allow a complete set of **diatonic** and **chromatic** pitches through two octaves.

Like the **transverse flute**, the oboe has no significant repertory in the first half of the 17th century, probably because neither it nor the shawm could negotiate the kinds of chromatic melodies composed in the manner of the *seconda pratica* for the **violin** and **recorder**.

In the latter half of the century, the oboe began to be heard in the musical theater, perhaps as early as **Jean-Baptiste Lully**'s *L'Amour Malade* of 1657. Brought to England during the Restoration, it appears to have won favor almost immediately, and **Henry Purcell** used it frequently after 1690, demonstrating its expressive range especially in his **ode** *Come Ye Sons of Art* (1694).

In the 18th century, the oboe came into its own as the principal woodwind instrument for the **orchestra**. **George Frideric Handel** often had the oboe double the leading violin melodies when he composed for orchestra and gave the instrument beautiful solo parts in **arias**. In Italy, the 24 **concertos** for oboe of **Tomaso Albinoni** (in his Opus 7 of 1715 and Opus 9 of 1722) is one of the first large collections for the instrument, and his **Venetian** colleague **Antonio Vivaldi** also wrote many oboe concertos. The First **Brandenburg Concerto** of **Johann Sebastian Bach** has a trio of oboes, and in the Second, it holds its own among a diverse **concertino** group, to say nothing of the many solos in his **church cantatas** and **passions**.

Baroque oboe.

Baroque composers also wrote **sonatas** explicitly for the oboe, as well as many more sonatas that may be played by the oboe as one choice among several treble instruments. *See also* OBOE DA CACCIA; OBOE D'AMORE.

OBOE DA CACCIA (It. "hunting oboe"). A "tenor **oboe**" of range F^3 to A-flat^5 ending in a large open bell. The origin of the name is obscure. **Johann Sebastian Bach** called for the oboe da caccia in about 30 of his compositions, including the **St. Matthew Passion**.

OBOE D'AMORE (It. "oboe of love"). An **oboe** pitched at an interval of a minor third below the oboe, therefore of range A^3 to C-sharp^6, it can have a pear-shaped bell. It is often featured as a solo instrument in Baroque **arias**.

ODE. Vocal music of the English court, similar to the Italian **cantata** in form, setting a text that celebrates, most frequently, the birthday of the monarch, the return of the monarch from a journey ("welcome song"), or the feast of St. Cecilia (November 22), patron saint of music. Except for its function of praise, there is no connection with the ode of antiquity.

Although not called an ode, the tribute music of **Orlando Gibbons** for King James I upon his arrival in Edinburgh in 1617, "Do not repine, fair sun," clearly adumbrates the function. The oldest extant ode text dates from 1635, Ben Jonson's "A New-Yeares-Gift Sung to King Charles," and became a source for later ones well into the Restoration period. The earliest extant Restoration odes were composed for New Year's Day of 1666: "Good morrow to the year" of **Henry Cooke** and "All things their certain periods have" of **Matthew Locke**. Composers who followed them in the ode tradition include **Pelham Humfrey, John Blow, Henry Purcell, Jeremiah Clarke, William Croft, Maurice Greene**, and **George Frideric Handel**.

The ode typically began with an instrumental introduction in the form of a **French overture** or an Italian *sinfonia*. Thereafter, the text could be sung to a mixture of **recitatives** and **arias** for soloists and numbers for **chorus**. The Gentlemen and Boys of the **Chapel Royal** with a considerable instrumental ensemble, often the King's Band of 24 **violins**, performed the ode for the assembled court on ceremonial occasions.

From 1715, the composition of the ode text was the duty of the poet laureate, one that appears to have been roundly hated by the poets. Court odes fell out of fashion by the early 19th century.

OPERA. The Baroque form of sung drama, which has evolved continuously until the present day. Invented in **Florence** in the closing years of the 16th century, opera became the quintessential Baroque composition, spawning new secular genres, reforming older, even sacred ones, and transforming the aesthetics of music in general, including its role in society.

"Opera" in Latin means "works" (the plural of *opus*) and in Italian may mean "work" or "task." The term, perhaps originating in England to describe the new music drama from Italy, was not common in the 17th century. Instead, one spoke of *dramma per musica* ("musical drama") or *favola in musica* ("fable in music") or *rappresentazione in musica* ("dramatization in music").

Opera is utterly distinct from earlier forms of sung drama, such as the liturgical **passion** play, because the opera composer exploits the symbolic properties of musical expression to convey the dramatic elements of character, passion, motivation, and action. In this sense, the composer is at least as much of a dramatist as the writer of the words, the **librettist**, with whom he collaborates. Baroque librettists were usually extremely skilful versifiers, constructing Baroque librettos largely of various poetic forms, and although not musicians, they had to understand the musical conventions that the composer would use to set the verses.

Chief among such conventions was the distinction between music that could set dialogues, exchanges of information, and rapidly changing character feelings on one hand and music that set a sustained emotional expression of a single character on the other. The former type became known as **recitative** and is founded on a musical **texture** of one singer accompanied by a progression of **functional harmonies** without **meter**. This allows the natural speech rhythms of the text to be sung plainly and yet not without musical expression, which comes from the chords chosen by the composer and from the speed of the elocution as well as other local rhythmic effects.

Music to sustain a single expression became known as **aria** (It. "air"). An aria establishes a strong meter on a motor rhythm, which makes possible an integrated and sophisticated musical structure that employed periodic phrasing, **ostinato**, **modulation** patterns, ritornellos, solo instruments, and other means of high-level formal articulations.

Baroque operas may also include **choruses** (arias for a large group, all singing the same text), **dances**, spoken text (in the German *Singspiel* and English **masque**, where it replaces recitative), and instrumental pieces, such as **overtures** to announce the beginning of the opera and *sinfonie* to articulate scene changes and the passage of time in the plot. Other traditional elements of the theater were important, too. Some operas were more famous for their scenery than for their narratives or music: machines that allowed deities to ascend to the heavens, storms, ships on the sea, and other spectacles. The performance of **George Frideric Handel**'s first **London** opera, *Rinaldo* (1711), called for a flock of live birds to be released into the audience.

But all forms of Baroque opera depend on the recitative/aria distinction. Indeed, the history of opera in the Baroque is the history of this distinction becoming ever clearer. Early in opera's history, the sense of meter was carefully graduated, so that arias might develop seamlessly out of recitatives and dissolve back into them, whereas by the last quarter of the 17th century, the meter was either strong or absent, making the distinction continually more rigid and, in general, rendering the music of recitative more workmanlike and less interesting than aria music, except in dramatic *accompagnato* recitatives.

As the aria's relative importance increased, so did the fame of the virtuoso singers who sang them. Baroque opera became the first socially approved professional career for women in music. Soprano singers such as Faustina Bordoni (1697–1781, wife of **Johann Adolf Hasse**) and Francesca Cuzzoni (1698–1778) engaged in notorious rivalries and commanded higher pay than the composers or librettists, whom the singers occasionally intimidated into rewriting arias more to their liking. Even more famous were the male sopranos and altos, the *castrati*. Senesino (1680–1759), **Farinelli**, and their like may be counted as the first performing superstars of the Western musical tradition.

The first operas were composed for the Medici court in Florence. *Dafne*, with music by **Jacopo Peri** and a libretto by court poet Ottavio Rinuccini (1562–1621), was performed during Carnival season in 1598. Its music is lost but for six fragments. During the celebrations for the wedding of Maria de' Medici and King Henry IV of France, a second opera by Rinuccini, *Euridice*, with music by Peri and **Giulio Caccini** was performed on 6 October 1600. Such celebrations had long been the scene of plays with music called "**intermedi**" interpolated between the acts, and Florence was also home to the **Camerata**, a group of humanistic intellectuals who speculated about the role of music in Greek classical drama. The precise relation of such thinking and the first operas is disputed, but it seems clear that, unlike the evolution of most genres in the history of music, opera was a conscious invention that demanded the new application of tried musical techniques.

The earliest opera regarded today as a masterwork is *L'Orfeo*, first performed on 24 February 1607 for Duke Vincenzo Gonzaga of Mantua, with a libretto of Alessandro Striggio (c. 1573–1630) and music of **Claudio Monteverdi**. Here arias and recitatives of great metric subtlety are integrated with Greek-style choruses, instrumental interludes, and effective staging, all animated by Monteverdi's superior melodic gifts.

In 1637, a troupe of musicians based in **Rome** arrived in **Venice**, rented the theater at San Cassiano parish, mounted Francesco Manelli's (c. 1595–1667) opera *Andromeda*, and sold tickets to a paying public. Two years later, **Francesco Cavalli**, a native Venetian, mounted his own *Le Nozze di Teti e* *di Peleo* at San Cassiano, while Manelli's troupe opened the theater of Santi Giovanni e Paolo. Thereafter, Carnival season in Venice was always marked by public operas, sometimes six in mutual competition, for over a century.

From this auspicious beginning, public opera spread over Italy and then over Europe, at first carried by traveling companies, such as opened San Cassiano, and then by more permanent resident establishments. Florence, **Naples**, and Rome became operatic centers. In 1646, Cavalli's *Egisto* was heard at the royal court of France, and by 1673, **Jean-Baptiste Lully** had composed the first *tragédie lyrique*, a particularly French music drama that, while founded on basic principles of Italian opera, remained distinct throughout the Baroque. In 1656, *The Siege of Rhodes* was mounted in London, and the Restoration period brought the first operatic experiments in masque, followed by the **semi-operas** of **Henry Purcell** and his colleagues. From about 1680, hundreds of cities and towns in Europe heard their first operas, often in Italian, sometimes in translation: Berne and Hanover in 1678, Amsterdam in 1680, Krakow in 1682, **Hamburg** and **Leipzig** in 1693, Berlin in 1700, Copenhagen in 1703, London in 1705, Lisbon in 1720, Seville in 1729, and Moscow in 1731. In public opera houses, the Italian import was modified to accommodate local tastes.

In Venice, home of the first public operas, the business continued to thrive throughout the Baroque. At times, there were as many as nine competing opera theaters operating in the island city. When one failed, soon enough another would be founded to take its place. To stay in business, the late 17th-century **Venetian opera** provided comedy and peculiar effects that would attract audiences but often resulted in ridiculous dramas. Efforts by reformers, such as **Apostolo Zeno**, in Venice and Rome at the end of the century led to the more respectable *opera seria*.

Because each opera was created for a particular state occasion, court entertainment, or to make money, when an opera was revived, it was almost always altered to conform to the new occasion of its revival. New singers required that arias be altered or even borrowed from other operas. Scenes could be added or cut, with new music demanded. Baroque operas were not considered by their creators or their audiences to be fixed works of art.

The invention of opera at least encouraged mightily, if it did not spawn, three fundamental changes in European musical culture. First, the success of public opera in Venice from 1637 on opened up a new career path for composers: in theory, they could earn a livelihood on the proceeds from operatic productions. In fact, virtually no Baroque composer lived entirely without patronage from the nobility or the church, but a few, notably **Antonio Vivaldi**, George Frideric Handel, and **Jean-Philippe Rameau**, came very close. Second, public opera made secular art music available to a broader segment of society and at the same time suggested that a musical event was worth attending for its own sake, not simply as an appendage to liturgy or court function. From here, it is a short step to public instrumental concerts and musical institutions such as the **Concert Spirituel** that arrived on the scene in the 18th century. Finally, opera changed the conception of music as an art. It did not lose its older purposes of contemplating God or human love but acquired, through opera, a new one as a dramatic agent, capable of narrative. *See also* *OPERA BUFFA.*

OPÉRA-BALLET. A type of French musical drama that followed the decline of the *tragédie lyrique* upon the death of **Jean-Baptiste Lully** in 1687. An *opéra-ballet* consists of a prologue and three or four acts, called *entrées*, each of which has its own cast and its own plot that relates rather vaguely to the title of the whole work. Each *entrée* contains at least one ***divertissement*** of **airs** and **dances**.

The history of the *opéra-ballet* falls into two phases distinguished by the character of the **libretto**. The first phase began with **André Campra**'s *L'Europe Galante* of 24 October 1697 and lasted until about 1720, dominated by Campra and Michel Pignolet de Montéclair (1667–1737). Critics immediately recognized that they were no longer mythological classic tragedies but contemporary stories set in real places: the French countryside, **Hamburg**, even the Grimani palace in **Venice** in Campra's *Les Fêtes Vénitiennes* (1710). Characters were petty aristocrats, ladies, and amorous adventurers. Comedy displaced tragedy. Such themes fed directly into the budding *opéra comique*.

The second phase opened in 13 July 1723 with the first performance of *Les Festes Grecques et Romaines*, a *ballet-héroïque* of François Colin de Blamont (1690–1760). While the comic element was not expunged entirely, serious classical themes returned to dominate, preparing the way for the mythological **operas** of **Jean-Philippe Rameau** beginning in 1733, several of which were called *ballets-héroïques*.

OPERA BUFFA. An Italian comic music drama. Although many of the **Venetian operas** of the late 17th century are comedies, the term is usually applied to **operas** dating from the 1720s and later that come out of the **intermezzo** tradition. In contrast to the plots of ***opere serie***, *opera buffa* stories are usually contemporary and involve lower-class as well as upper-class characters who sing shorter and simpler types of **aria** in order to accommodate the pace of comedy. The **librettos** are often written in local dialect rather than literary Italian in order to heighten the comic tone; the first Neapolitan operas of **Leonardo Vinci**, starting in 1719, are fine examples. **Giovanni**

Pergolesi's *La Serva Padrona* of 1733 created a popular sensation and aesthetic controversy.

In the Baroque, *opera buffa* was considered a lower form of opera, and virtually none of the major opera composers besides Vinci—**Alessandro Scarlatti, Johann Adolf Hasse, George Frideric Handel**—composed any. In the classical period, however, particularly in the work of Wolfgang Amadeus Mozart (1756–1791), it is central.

OPÉRA COMIQUE. French music drama dating from the early 18th century that might include popular tunes set to new words, spoken dialogue, witty and **improvisational** repartee, **arias**, and **recitatives**, arranged to appeal to a much broader, less sophisticated audience than would be attracted to the more traditional *tragédie lyrique*. The Théâtres de la Foire of St. Germain and St. Laurent housed a company called Opéra-Comique from 1714 until 1762.

The French word *comique*, difficult to translate, includes comedy in its connotation but is not limited to it. According to Diderot's *Encyclopédie*, the *comédie* portrays the human condition. *See also* CAMPRA, ANDRÉ.

OPERA SERIA. The predominant form of Baroque **opera** from the early 1690s to the end of the 18th century. In the 18th century, the term *melodramma* was more common, but *opera seria* distinguished this kind of opera from comic forms (*opera buffa*). The **libretto** of an *opera seria*, always written in Italian, contains verses of various types, with **recitatives** set in free verse (*versi sciolti*). The plot is almost always drawn from the ancient histories of Greece and **Rome**, occasionally from medieval stories, or from mythology. Typically, the *opera seria* portrays rulers, heroes, and heroines involved in a love interest connected to some moral dilemma. The tone is serious throughout, even tragic, but disaster is always averted through the ruler's virtuous choice of duty over self-interest, and so, the custom of the *lieto fine* ("happy ending"), common enough in the 17th century, became obligatory.

In the 1690s, characteristics of the typical **Venetian opera** were simplified in *opera seria*, largely through the enormously influential librettos of Vincenzo Grimani (c. 1652–1710), **Apostolo Zeno**, and **Metastasio**. Casts are limited to half a dozen noble characters of more or less equal weight, each character having at least one **aria**, almost always a **da capo aria**, in each of the three acts. These are very often **exit arias**, ending with the singer leaving the stage after making a dramatic statement through the aria, accompanied by applause. Some theories advised that plots should always connect scenes by *liaisons*, having at least one character remain on stage as new ones are introduced.

Plots must be fashioned to alternate two kinds of writing: dialogues of factual plot information and resultant reactions by various characters; and emotional reflection by the single character most affected by the course of events, in the manner of a soliloquy apart from the action. These libretto passages are set to recitative music and solo aria, respectively, and in the 18th century the division was further dramatized by the aria soloist coming to the front of the stage and assuming an appropriate posture that moved very little, while the remaining cast, if any, remained in position. An *opera seria*, after opening with an instrumental **French overture** or Italian-style *sinfonia*, presents one recitative-aria pairing after another for the rest of the evening. Operas with 30 arias are not uncommon.

Arias for more than one singer (duet, trios, etc.) are rare, usually pairs of lovers or perhaps a trio of characters suffering the same loss, so that the affect among them can be identical. Variety in the relentless succession of arias arises from the different aria types composed. Eighteenth-century writers mention the *aria di bravura* for virtuoso singers at critical moments in the story, the *aria cantabile* for gentler emotions, the *aria patetica* for sorrow, the *aria parlante* for defiance, and so on. Aria texts are highly stylized poems, abstract, and usually without any specific reference to events or characters in the opera, which allowed the fairly common substitution of arias from one opera into another in order to suit the qualities of a particular singer or meet some other local contingency. The last number would usually portray all the characters singing a united sentiment together in a *coro*. *See also* UNITIES.

OPUS 3 (Antonio Vivaldi, 1711). Collection of 12 **concertos** published by Roger of Amsterdam that made **Antonio Vivaldi**'s reputation international and featured the fast movement–slow movement–fast movement pattern of the concerto tradition that persists in some form to the present.

The concertos require from one to five solo **string** players accompanied by a basso **continuo** and an **orchestra** of first and second **violins**, **violas**, and bass (**cellos**). Each work lasts from 7 to 15 minutes.

While the slow movements are usually *cantilene* for the solo instruments, often over an **ostinato** bass, the fast movements usually exploit a ritornello as the structural principle.

Vivaldi's Opus 3 constitutes some of the most influential instrumental music of the 18th century. **Johann Sebastian Bach** arranged no fewer than five of these works for **organ**.

OPUS 6 (Arcangelo Corelli, 1714). A collection of 12 **concerti grossi** published by Roger of Amsterdam. **Arcangelo Corelli** was already a legend by this time, and Opus 6 almost instantly became a classic, studied and per-

The 12 Concertos of Vivaldi's Opus 3

1	Concerto for Four Violins in D Major	Allegro / Largo e spiccato / Allegro	RV 549
2	Concerto for Two Violins and Cello in G Minor	Andante e spiccato / Allegro / Larghetto / Allegro	RV 578
3	Concerto for Solo Violin in G Major	Allegro / Largo / Allegro	RV 310
4	Concerto for Four Violins in E Minor	Andante / Allegro assai / Adagio / Allegro	RV 550
5	Concerto for Two Violins in A Major	Allegro / Largo / Allegro	RV 519
6	Concerto for Solo Violin in A Minor	Allegro / Largo / Presto	RV 356
7	Concerto for Four Violins and Cello in F Major	Andante / Adagio / Allegro / Adagio / Allegro	RV 567
8	Concerto for Two Violins in A Minor	Allegro / Larghetto / Allegro	RV 522
9	Concerto for Solo Violin in D Major	Allegro / Larghetto / Allegro	RV 230
10	Concerto for Four Violins and Cello in B Minor	Allegro / Largo-Larghetto-Largo / Allegro	RV 580
11	Concerto for Two Violins and Cello in D Minor	Allegro-Adagio-Allegro / Largo e spiccato / Allegro	RV 565
12	Concerto for Solo Violin in E Major	Allegro / Largo / Allegro	RV 265

formed continuously even after the end of the Baroque. Its modest technical demands and flexible performing requirements make its music ideal for student orchestras and amateur chamber ensembles.

All the **concertos** require two **violin** soloists and one **cello** soloist, accompanied by basso **continuo** and, traditionally, a *ripieno* of first and second violins, **violas**, and cellos or **basses** of indeterminate number. Each complete concerto requires from 10 to 15 minutes to perform.

The collection is divided into two groups. The first eight concertos are entitled: *Concerti grossi con duoi Violini, e Violoncello di Concertino obligati, e duoi altri Violini, Viola e Basso di Concerto Grosso ad arbitrio, che si potranno radoppiare . . . Opera Sesta. Parte Prima* ("Concerti grossi for two violins and cello required, and two other violins, viola and bass of the **orchestra** as desired, which may be doubled . . . Opus six. First part."). These concertos begin with a slow **prelude** and then alternate slow and fast **tempos** throughout. Although some movements employ **dance** rhythms, none is so entitled, and most are abstract in character, with much **imitative texture**. No. 8 is the famous **Christmas Concerto**.

The last four are entitled: *Preludii, Allemande, Corrente, Gighe, Sarabande, Gavotte e Minuetti . . . Parte seconda per Camera* ("Preludes, **allemandes, correntes, gigues, sarabandes, gavottes,** and **minuets** . . . second part for the chamber."). The dance movements continue to exploit the contrast of soloists and full ensemble typical of the concerto grosso with much less imitative texture.

ORATORIO. A sacred drama set to music, whose appearance at the turn of the 17th century coincides with the invention of **opera** and whose aesthetics and conventions closely parallel that genre. At first heard in prayer halls of certain Roman churches (oratories), oratorios soon joined the opera in aristocratic salons, theaters, and concert halls but used no staging or scenery. Instrumental accompaniment ranges from **continuo** alone to large **orchestral** forces. A **chorus** for both commentary and character portrayal (e.g., the people of Israel), is typical, particularly of oratorios after 1700, perhaps the most distinctive element of the genre. Vocal soloists sing individual character roles. The plots are most often adaptations of Bible stories, particularly Old Testament, and hagiographies, with **librettos** of moral or allegorical character a distinct minority.

The name derives from the Congregazione dell'Oratorio, a religious order founded by St. Philip Neri (1515–1595) dedicated to renewal of contemplative prayer for the laity, whose oratory services were animated by sacred music. In February 1600, the oratory at the Chiesa Nuova in **Rome** saw the first performance of **Emilio de' Cavalieri**'s *Rappresentatione di Anima et di Corpo*, a Neoplatonic allegory of Soul, Body, Pleasure, Earthly Life, and other representations set to **recitative**, with intermittent choruses. The same kind of work, although only 49 lines and 12 minutes in length, is Pietro Della Valle's (1586–1652) *Oratorio della Purificazione* of 1640, the first instance of the term applied to a piece of music, not on the score but in a letter of Valle. In the first half of the 17th century, however, traditional **contrapuntal** music (*stile antico*) continued to set oratorios along with the newer recitative **texture**.

In the second half of the 17th century, oratorios were preferred in those cities where the theaters closed for the solemn season of Lent. In Rome, oratorios could be mounted not only in places of prayer but also in the salons of wealthy patrons, such as Cardinals Benedetto Pamphili (1653–1730) and Pietro Ottoboni (1667–1740). Other Italian cities with active oratorian societies included Bologna, Modena, **Florence,** and **Venice.** In **Vienna,** the first oratorio libretto, *Il Sacrifizio d'Abramo* ("The Sacrifice of Abraham," 1660), was written by the Emperor Leopold I (reigned 1658–1705) himself, inaugurating a rich tradition of oratorio composition distinguished by the *sepolcro,* a one-act drama on themes of Christ's **passion**, always performed on Holy Thursday or Good Friday, with costumes and scenery.

The music of these later oratorios resembled opera and **cantata** closely, with recitative and **aria** alternation as the basic scheme. Texts were in Italian (*oratorio volgare*) or Latin (*oratorio latino*). The Latin librettos often drew their material from one of the Lenten readings at **mass**. Italian poetry was typically 350–400 lines and required from one and one-half to two hours to sing. Less dramatic, more contemplative subjects could be much shorter. Latin librettos were usually prose, often excerpted from the Vulgate Bible, and a narrator (*testo*) often took the role of evangelist. **Giacomo Carissimi** wrote 11 influential Latin works that included a significant choral role, but choruses are rare in the 20 or so extant oratorios of his much younger colleague **Alessandro Scarlatti**, replaced by an occasional *coro*, an ensemble of the vocal soloists. In France, however, Carissimi's student **Marc-Antoine Charpentier**, composer of 35 oratorios, sometimes called *histoires sacrées*, in French and Latin, expanded the number of choruses and employed them as commentators and dramatic agents.

In German-speaking lands, sacred dramas remained bound to Lutheran liturgies until very late in the Baroque. Italianate oratorios were preceded by various traditions of liturgical drama—*actus musicus*, **historia**, and **oratorio passion**—with strictly biblical librettos (e.g., **Christmas Oratorio** of **Heinrich Schütz**). Biblical dramas presented outside the liturgy often provoked controversy. In England, **George Frideric Handel** managed to overcome such objections with his **English oratorio**. Handel's personal amalgam of Italian operatic conventions, the English language, and the English cathedral choir tradition, and his international reputation, particularly through *Messiah*, provided the model for oratorio composition that remained more or less consistent through an age of expanding orchestras and choruses and changing musical languages until the present. *See also* LANDI, STEFANO.

ORATORIO PASSION. German tradition of liturgical drama originating in the mid-17th century and continuing into the 18th, at which point such works are usually called "**passions**." The oratorio passion stems directly from the German *historia*, a musical recitation of biblical passages telling of Christ's passion, birth, or resurrection. When other biblical texts, **chorale** texts, and, later, spiritual poetry were added as commentary on the Gospel passages, the result is the oratorio passion. The earliest known example is **Thomas Selle**'s *Passio secundum Joannem cum Intermediis* (1643).

ORCHESTRA. The familiar large ensemble of **string instruments**, woodwinds, brass, and percussion did not exist at the beginning of the Baroque, but by the end of the period, something close to the classical **symphony** orchestra was a common feature of the **opera** house and even, on occasion, in other musical institutions, such as the **Concert Spirituel** in **Paris** or the various *collegium musicum* organizations in the major cities of the continent. Thus, the Baroque was the cradle of the modern orchestra.

The early Baroque did know large ensembles of instruments in the production of certain court spectacles, such as **Claudio Monteverdi's** *L'Orfeo* or the performance of polychoral works at San Marco in **Venice**. On 21 May 1685, the procurators at San Marco established the maximum ensemble at 34 players: 8 **violins**, 11 violettas (**violas**), 2 *viole da braccio*, 3 **violones**, 4 **theorbos**, 2 **cornetts**, a **bassoon**, and 3 **trombones**. Such large forces might be considered orchestras, but they were neither permanent nor standard combinations of instruments.

The trend toward a consistent ensemble began perhaps with the opening of public opera in Venice in 1637, where a small group of string instruments, **continuo** instruments, and occasional woodwinds would be required on a regular basis during the opera season. It became apparent early on that string instruments were best suited for accompanying singers because they could provide harmonic filler without a distracting timbre yet produce a louder and warmer sound than continuo alone to add variety and fill the theater. In this way, string instruments acquired their traditional role as the mainstay of the orchestra.

Increasing the size of the ensemble without increasing unduly the number of **voices** in the musical **texture** meant using several instruments of the same type, especially string instruments, to share a single melody or part. The question of how many players were assigned to the violin parts or **cello** parts in Baroque ensemble music has been very difficult to trace and seems to have varied according to place and circumstance. One source of evidence is the records showing many more musicians being paid for a performance than the number of instruments in the score. Generally, the practice of part sharing gradually increased through the Baroque. Two developments of the mid-17th century might be singled out as particularly important influences in this regard.

The first would be the development of the **concerto grosso** tradition in Italy, whereby the sonic contrast between a small group of virtuoso soloists (*soli*) and a larger group (*ripieni*) would require at least that the solo player and *ripieni* players share the same melodies even if the *ripieni* added only one player per part.

The second would be the international fame of the French string ensemble called Les Vingt-quatre Violons (The Twenty-Four Violins) of King Louis XIV's court under the direction of **Jean-Baptiste Lully**. By 1686, this orchestra consisted of six violins, four first violas (*hautecontre*), four second violas (*taille*), four third violas (*quinte*), and six *basses di violon* or large cellos. Lully reformed the performance practices of this permanent string band by forbidding all individual **improvisation** or **ornamentation** and insisting that bowing be uniform, with the stronger down-bow coordinated with the strong **metric** accents of his **dances**. The result was a large group of 24 musicians playing with a clear and robust uniform articulation that astounded foreign listeners and made a convincing case for the sharing of parts in a large ensemble. Because Les Vingt-quatre Violons provided the music for **ballets**, operas, and other spectacles, it could influence similar productions elsewhere.

In the 18th century, opera orchestras in **London** and Paris continued to employ several violins, violas, cellos, and string basses as the mainstay. A 1704 document states the Paris Opéra orchestra consisted of nine violins, eight violas (in three sections), eight cellos, eight wind players, and one set of **timpani**. The surviving orchestra parts to the productions of **Johann Adolf Hasse**'s operas in 1737 at the **Dresden** court's summer residence in Hubertusburg, which had a comparatively small stage, reveal an ensemble of two **transverse flutes**, two **oboes** (**chalumeau** doubled), and two **horns**, all playing independent parts, plus six violins, two violas, two cellos, one string bass, and two bassoons, all playing shared parts, with **lute** and **harpsichord** to fill out the continuo. Imaginative composers, such as **George Frideric Handel**, would vary the orchestration required from **aria** to aria, with the continuo alone as a minimum, the full ensemble as a maximum, and various other combinations between them. Oboes and bassoons often doubled the appropriate string melodies in opera *sinfonie* and in many arias to enrich the timbre, and they became the standard orchestra winds. Transverse flutes, **recorders**, **trumpets**, horns, trombones, **harps**, and timpani added distinct timbres for particular symbolic or dramatic effects (e.g., **flutes** for mourning, trumpets and drums for military triumph).

In contexts apart from the opera house, such as **concertos** that might be heard in a court or aristocratic salon or *collegium musicum*, performance practices probably varied considerably. Whether **Johann Sebastian Bach** or **Antonio Vivaldi** would have used more than one player for the *ripieno* parts and, if more than one, how many, in their concertos is still controversial.

ORGAN. The oldest **keyboard** instrument of the Western tradition, the pipe organ was introduced into Roman Catholic churches by the 10th century. At the beginning of the Baroque period, other instruments had infiltrated Christian liturgies, but the pipe organ dominated sacred music and remained the only officially recognized legitimate instrument in most traditions. Baroque organ builders are counted among the greatest in the history of the instrument, and the organs of Gottfried Silbermann (1683–1753), Arp Schnitger

(1648–1719), Christian Müller (1690–1763), and others remain among the most complex machines of their time. Virtually every significant Baroque composer, except specialists in non-keyboard instruments, such as **Arcangelo Corelli** or **Antoine Forqueray**, composed for it and compiled by far the largest and richest organ repertory of any period in history.

The pipe organ has three essential components: pipes, a windchest, and a keyboard. The pipes sit upon a container of pressurized air ("windchest," supplied by a bellows) connected to a lever system or keyboard. The organ produces tones when the player depresses a key on the keyboard, which then opens one (or more) valves at the base of a pipe(s), allowing the pressurized air to vibrate the column of air within the pipe(s). The number and arrangement of these components in each organ is unique. Organ building recognizes the particular needs of each church as well as national traditions and terminologies that have developed through history.

Each pipe's pitch is determined by its length. The pitch range of a whole set of similar pipes, called a "rank," is indicated by the length of the rank's longest pipe. The standard is 8′ ("eight-foot stop"), the approximate length of the pipe producing the pitch C^2. All 8′ stops produce their notes at concert pitch; 4′ stops sound one octave higher, 2′ two octaves higher, and so forth; 16′ stops sound one octave lower, 32′ two octaves lower.

A rank sounds only when its connection to the windchest is activated by pulling a wooden rod near the manuals (keyboard) called a "stop."

The 15th and 16th centuries saw a number of technical developments in building that would flower fully in the Baroque. One was the distinction of two basic types of pipe, open cylinders (flutes) and pipes fitted with flappers (reeds), which greatly affected the timbre (kind of sound produced). Timbre was further controlled by the pipe's diameter to length ratio (scale), its material (type of metal or wood), by tapering or closing the pipe, and by using the pipe in combination with others, particularly mutation stops, which include non-octave partials: a 2 2/3′ stop sounds one octave and a perfect fifth above concert pitch.

A second critical development for the Baroque organ in northern Europe was the so-called *Werkprinzip* (Ger. "division principle"), a modern term that describes the construction of a large pipe organ by combining several collections of ranked pipes, or divisions, each with its own physical location, set of pipes, windchest, and manual. Each of these divisions may be played alone or in combination with the others, and the separate manuals are terraced together to allow this simultaneous playing of the divisions. (One division is played by the feet on a pedalboard below the manuals.) The English-language names for divisions are: *great* (Ger. *Hauptwerk*), the main division that characterizes the entire organ; *positive* or *choir* (Ger. *Brustwerk*), often containing lighter

Tracker pipe organ at Colgate University constructed by Holtkamp Organ Company, 1976. The great division is located in the center, the swell division in the shutter box to the right, the positive division cantilevered on the left, and the pedal division with the largest pipes in the rear.

Three-manual keyboard and pedalboard of the Holtkamp organ.

sounding (flute) pipes; *swell* (Ger. *Oberwerk*), enclosed within a shuttercase that opens and closes during playing to regulate volume; and *pedal*, which has the largest pipes and therefore lowest pitches, the bass section of the organ.

Each division of a Baroque organ normally contains several (or many) ranks. These ranks may be of similar type so that the division has a particular timbre or range of timbres, such as mostly flutes, or the ranks may be quite mixed. The player may pull any combination of stops (registration) in the division. Playing a single composition with more than one division active is very common, allowing contrasts of timbre from different divisions as well as from within a single division. Couplers combine ranks from separate divisions onto a single keyboard, creating even more possible combinations of timbre.

Because the design of individual pipes, ranks, and divisions was so variable, organ construction could easily accommodate local or national preferences in liturgical usage and musical style, and often reflected local history. In France, the divisions often included prominent **cornett** stops and mixtures (specialized groupings of different ranks) that could bring out a plainchant melody. A registration typical of the "classical French organ" consisted of highly contrasting timbres and volumes that favored particular melodies of a **contrapuntal texture**, as opposed to a more blended approach. In England, organs could have manuals capable of many timbres, but there were no pedalboards until 1790, meaning that the English repertory, including **George Frideric Handel**'s unique set of organ **concertos**, has no bass melody independent of the hands. Italian organs are recognizable by a particular combination of pipes that remained fairly consistent from the late 16th to the 19th century, played often by a single manual and a short pedalboard of 12 to 17 keys.

The Baroque organist was the principal musician of most churches, often in a highly respected and well-paid position. In Roman Catholic churches during the Baroque, the organist might accompany liturgical plainchants with **improvised** harmony, play the **continuo** accompaniment to **sacred concertos**, **sacred symphonies**, **Neapolitan masses**, and **motets**, and play **versets** that might replace certain prayers of the liturgy. In Lutheran churches, the organist introduced the service with an organ **prelude**, led the congregation in singing **chorales**, and accompanied **church cantatas**, sacred symphonies, sacred concertos, **passions**, and motets. Anglican churches would hear the organist play **voluntaries** and accompany the singing of **anthems** by the **choir**.

Some early Baroque genres of composition for organ sprang directly from 16th-century practices of improvising on church melodies for liturgy: **toccata**, prelude, **chorale fantasia**, **chorale partita**. Others genres developed 16th-century techniques of **ostinato**: organ **passacaglia**, **chaconne**, **ground**; and **imitation**: **ricercar** and especially **fugue**. The organ would be the natural continuo instrument for any nonliturgical composition heard in church, such as an **oratorio**, **church sonata**, or **Christmas concerto**. The most prominent names in the repertory of Baroque organ music might include, from Italy, **Girolamo Frescobaldi** and Claudio Merulo (1533–1604); from the Netherlands, **Jan Pieterszoon Sweelinck**; from England, **John Blow**, **Henry Purcell**, **William Croft**, and George Frideric Handel; from France, **Jehan de Titelouze, Nicolas de Grigny, Nicolas Lebègue**, and members of the **Couperin** family; from Germany, **Johann Jacob Froberger**, **Samuel Scheidt, Dietrich Buxtehude, Johann Kuhnau, Johann Pachelbel, Georg Philipp Telemann**, and **Johann Sebastian Bach**. Bach's position is singular: no other composer dominates an instrumental repertory as does his organ music.

ORGAN MASS. A liturgical genre by which **organ versets** substitute for chanted portions of the ordinary and proper prayers of the **mass**. The earliest versets are found in the Faenza Codex (Italy, c. 1400). In 1600, Pope Clement VIII's *Caeremoniale Episcoporum* ("Bishops' Ceremonial") ratified this long-standing practice. At that time, the organ typically played 19 versets for the complete organ mass: 5 for the Kyrie, 9 for the Gloria, 2 for the Sanctus, 1 for the Benedictus (entire text), and 2 for the Agnus Dei. The document also called for soft organ music during the Elevation (Consecration) and at the end of mass. The Credo could not be performed *alternatim* after the **Council of Trent**. The division of proper chants varied widely; the Offertory enjoyed particular freedom of treatment.

Publications of organ masses peaked in the 17th century. Particularly important are **Girolamo Frescobaldi's** *Fiori musicali* (1635), Antonio Croci's (died after 1641) *Frutti musicali* (1642), Guillaume Gabriel Nivers's (1632–1714) *2e Livre d'Orgue* (1667), **Nicolas Lebègue's** *Second Livre d'Orgue* (1678?), André Raison's (c. 1650–1719) *Livre d'Orgue Contenant Cinque Messes* (1688), **Nicolas de Grigny's** *Premier Livre d'Orgue* (1699), and, above all, **François Couperin's** *Pièces d'Orgue Consistantes en Deux Messes* (1690).

ORGELBÜCHLEIN (Ger. "Little Organ Book"). Famous collection of **chorale preludes** composed by **Johann Sebastian Bach** almost certainly during his Weimar years, probably from 1713 to 1716. The collection is unfinished. The autograph indicates Bach's intention to provide 164 chorale preludes along the plan of a Lutheran hymnal, with 60 proper **hymns** preceding the 104 common ones. He finished 46. Their short length, one or two pages of score, excluded the kind of setting in which each phrase of the **chorale** initiates a brief **fugue**, but all other types of chorale prelude are represented, the majority of the pieces presenting the tune unadorned in the highest **voice**. The pedal is obbligato in all of them, and there is a wide variety of **texture** and **contrapuntal** effect, including double **canons**. According to the title page, Bach intended the collection to be played and studied by beginners, but many of the pieces are quite difficult by modern standards.

ORNAMENTATION. The decoration of a written-out melody in performance, almost always by fragmenting long notes into notes of shorter duration.

Ornamentation in the solo parts of **arias** and **concertos** was generally **improvised** completely. In **da capo arias**, it was customary, or even obligatory, to decorate the sung melodies in the return of the (A) section. In concertos, particularly the slow movements, a ritornello or a melody that was merely slow might be ornamented in similar fashion. In **sonatas**, ornamentation might occur with the repeated sections of a **binary form**.

Some ornaments became so common that composers would indicate their occurrence in their scores by conventional signs. Trills, mordents, appoggiaturas, turns, and many others all acquired such signs. French **harpsichord** and **organ** music includes many such signs, the proper execution of which is an essential part of that repertory's performance. On the other hand, **Johann Sebastian Bach** included precisely notated and finely detailed ornamental patterns right into his melodies, which prompted some critics to complain that he left nothing for performers to invent.

Ornamentation remains a controversial aspect of performing Baroque music today. Disputes typically concern the amount of ornamentation for a given type of composition and the precise way to execute ornamental signs in the composers' scores. *See also* D'ANGLEBERT, JEAN HENRY.

Figure. Some common ornament symbols written out in standard notation by Johann Sebastian Bach for his son Wilhelm Friedemann

OSTINATO (It. "stubborn"). General term for the compositional technique of repeating an element many times while the other **voices** in the music make a constantly changing **counterpoint**. In the Baroque, the ostinato is most commonly heard as a basso ostinato, a repeating bass melody, which in turn usually generates a repeating harmonic progression. In the 17th century, this kind of ostinato is ubiquitous, and it acquired more particular names with national flavors, often associated with the **dances** that the bass melody originally accompanied: **chaconne**, **passacaglia**, **folia**, and **ground**.

When composers at that time were looking for means to extend the forms of **arias** and instrumental compositions, the ostinato provided a way of uniting an opulence of expressive melodic variation in a steady pulse. It proved an excellent basis for instrumental **variations** where the unifying sound was much more harmonic than melodic. It was popular for arias in the **Venetian opera**, French *tragédie lyrique*, and English operas of **Henry Purcell**. *See also* CANTUS FIRMUS.

OUVERTURE. See FRENCH OVERTURE.

OVERDOTTING. *See* DOUBLE DOTTING.

OVERTURE. An instrumental composition that begins an **opera**, **oratorio**, or other kind of music drama. The overture appears to derive from the Renaissance court practice of playing a fanfare to accompany the entrance of a dignitary, and in the earliest operas, the opening instrumental piece resembles such flourishes (e.g., the **Toccata** of *L'Orfeo* of **Claudio Monteverdi**, 1607). In the first half of the 17th century, the overture, more commonly called *sinfonia avvanti l'opera* ("**symphony** before the opera") or something similar, often consisted of three slow phrases, but there was much variety.

By the turn of the 18th century, the overture practice reduced to two choices: the **French overture** that **Jean-Baptiste Lully** had developed for his *tragédie lyrique* or the Italian *sinfonia*, a three-movement composition in fast-slow-fast pattern common in the Neapolitan opera at the end of the 17th century.

P

PACHELBEL, JOHANN (baptized 1 September 1653, Nuremberg–buried 9 March 1706, Nuremberg). Known by millions today, unfairly, as the composer of one work, the **Canon** in D for three **violins** and **ostinato** bass, Pachelbel was a prolific composer of such renown in the late 17th-century musical life of central Germany that his home city, Nuremberg, waived the normal practice of inviting prominent candidates to be examined for its most important musical position, **organist** of Sebalduskirche, and simply asked Pachelbel, then town **organist** at Gotha, to take the job.

Pachelbel's compositions fall into two large groups: compositions for the liturgy, either Roman Catholic or Lutheran, and secular music for **keyboard**.

In the liturgical genres, he composed at least 11 **sacred concertos**, 2 **masses**, 9 German **motets** and 2 Latin motets (almost all for double **chorus**), and 13 *ingressus* **antiphons** and 13 **Magnificats** for vespers services. These vocal works show Pachelbel's mastery of all the traditional sacred **contrapuntal textures** as well as the *stile moderno* derived from Italian **opera**. His reputation, however, mainly sprang from his organ music, and especially his treatment of the German **chorale**. There are 20 three-**voice** settings with the chorale as **cantus firmus**, 3 four-voice settings with cantus firmus, 8 chorale **fugues**, 10 sets of **chorale partitas**, and 35 chorale settings of various other types and techniques. In addition, there are 98 "Magnificat" fugues organized according to all the traditional church **modes**, designed to introduce the singing of the Magnificat at vespers in Nuremberg.

His secular keyboard music includes 3 **ricercars**, 6 **fantasias**, 6 **chaconnes**, 7 independent **preludes**, 5 preludes and fugues, 15 independent **toccatas**, 2 toccatas and fugues, and 29 independent fugues. There are also about 20 keyboard **suites** and some 19 secular German **arias**.

Johann Pachelbel received his early education at the St. Lorenz school in Nuremberg and then entered the university at Altdorf in June 1669 but because of finances had to transfer to the Gymnasium Poeticum at Regensburg, where he qualified for a scholarship and was allowed to study music under Kaspar Prentz outside the normal curriculum.

In 1673, he became deputy organist at Stefansdom in **Vienna**, where he possibly studied with **Johann Caspar Kerll** and doubtless learned much about Catholic liturgical music. He then moved to Eisenach in Thuringia, becoming organist on 4 May 1677. The next year, Pachelbel left for Erfurt, possibly because the mourning for his patron's brother, Prince Bernhard of Saxe-Jena, reduced musical activities. He began a 12-year residence at the Predigerkirche at Erfurt on 19 June 1678.

Pachelbel married Barbara Gabler on 25 October 1681, but she and their son were carried off in a plague of September 1683. He then married Judith Trommert on 24 August 1684, and together they had five sons and two daughters. Wilhelm Hieronymus Pachelbel became a well-known musician in Germany, and another son, Charles Theodore, brought his father's music to the American colonies. During this period, in Thuringia, Pachelbel taught music to Johann Christoph Bach, who would later teach **Johann Sebastian Bach**.

He took up a new post as organist at the Württemberg court in Stuttgart on 1 September 1690, but a French invasion forced him back to Thuringia, and he became the town organist for Gotha. He remained there, refusing one invitation to return to Stuttgart and another to move to Oxford, until the invitation from his home city of Nuremberg came shortly after the death of Sebalduskirche organist Georg Kaspar Wecker on 20 April 1695.

PADILLA, JUAN GUTIÉRREZ DE (c. 1590, Málaga, Spain–c. 22 April 1664, Puebla, Mexico). *Maestro de capilla* at Jérez de la Frontera (1613–1616), Cádiz Cathedral (1616–1620), and Puebla Cathedral in Mexico (1629–death), where he established a first-rate choir and instrumental ensemble. He wrote some 50 sacred vocal works in *stile antico*, including works for *cori spezzati*, several **masses**, and many vernacular *villancicos* to be sung on church festival days.

PALESTRINA, GIOVANNI PIERLUIGI DA (between 3 February 1525 and 2 February 1526, Palestrina near Rome–2 February 1594, Rome). Composer of 104 **masses**, at least 375 **motets**, 68 **polyphonic** offertories, 65 **hymn** settings, 35 **Magnificats**, in addition to **lamentations**, *madrigali spirituali*, and secular vocal works, his oeuvre is one of the largest of his time. His sincere efforts at intelligible diction in his polyphony and its association with the **Council of Trent** were exaggerated into legends early on, as when **Agostino Agazzari** wrote in 1607 that his *Missa Papae Marcelli* had convinced the council delegates not to abolish polyphony from Catholic liturgy. With such fame, it was natural that Palestrina should be the model for those who wished to learn the traditional **counterpoint** of the church: he is the teacher in **Johann Josef Fux**'s *Gradus ad Parnassum* (1725), the most influential such textbook for the 18th and 19th centuries. And so, he became an icon of "classical polyphony," or the *stile antico*, a musical language frozen in time, particularly after the invention of **opera** at the close of the 16th century.

PARIS. The few great names of French Baroque music who were not born in Paris—**Jean-Baptiste Lully, Jean-Philippe Rameau,** and **Jean-Marie Leclair,** among the most prominent—soon found their way there. The rest were born and remained there because Paris, including its royal palace at nearby Versailles, was by far the most important musical center in France for the Baroque.

Paris offered manifold opportunities for the church composer, which in the second half of the 17th century became more important while declining in other lands as Lully legally monopolized the composition of **opera** and stage music for himself. The churches of Notre Dame, St. Germain-l'Auxerrois at the Louvre, the Sainte Chapelle, and the chapel of the Tuileries were all attended by the royal families of Louis XIII and Louis XIV. In addition, after their recall to the country in 1603, the Jesuits provided musical employment through their various colleges and churches. **Marc-Antoine Charpentier** worked at two of them. The church of St. Gervais must also be counted as one of the most significant, since members of the **Couperin** family, including **François** "*le grand*," were **organists** there.

After *dramma per musica* was introduced to France in 1646, the idea of sung drama and French ballet fused in the *comédie-ballet* in the 1650s and then into a distinctly French opera, the *tragédie lyrique*, in the early 1670s. Lully excluded almost all competition in this magnificent genre until his death in 1687, but thereafter, royal patronage for opera declined while commercial competition among theater groups grew, making the opera careers of **André Campra** and Rameau possible. In the early 18th century, there were four public theaters in Paris: the prestigious Opéra, the Comédie-Française, the Comédie-Italienne, and the unofficial but very popular Opéra-Comique.

Under the spiritual influence of Madame de Maintenon, Louis XIV rarely attended the opera in his last years but continued to employ singers and chamber musicians at Versailles, among them the daughters of **Michel-Richard de Lalande,** Jeanne and Marie-Anne, the **viol** players **Antoine Forqueray** and **Marin Marais,** and **harpsichordists Elisabeth Jacquet de La Guerre** and François Couperin.

Aristocrats in Paris also maintained salons for entertainment and prestige, often providing performances in the courtyards of their townhouses. Charpentier and Rameau both benefitted for years from such patronage. Anne Danican Philidor (1681–1728) expanded this notion of the informal concert into something more public and much grander, the **Concert Spirituel,** founded in 1725.

PARODY. Technique by which a composer employs a preexisting composition to create a new one, using its melodic ideas, **imitative** patterns, harmonic structures, and so forth, to whatever extent he sees fit. The concept of borrowing music to begin a new piece is as old as Western music and exists in most other traditions in some form, but in the Baroque, "parody" usually refers to the practice of reconfiguring a **polyphonic** composition. The two composers most frequently associated with parody today are **Johann Sebastian Bach** and **George Frideric Handel**, but that is perhaps because most research into the practice is fairly recent so that the extent to which less famous Baroque composers parodied themselves and each other is not yet known. Bach parodied his secular **cantatas** to create **church cantatas** with new texts and parodied both kinds to build such large works as the **Christmas Oratorio** and the **Mass in B Minor**. Handel also reconfigured his own works frequently and occasionally used entire movements of other composers without substantial change, most famously in his **English oratorio** *Israel in Egypt*.

Music historians and critics who came of age with romantic prejudices about artistic originality were once embarrassed when they realized the great extent to which Bach and Handel parodied their own works and those of others. More recently, studies have shown that parody often demanded more effort from the composer than the creation of a new work from scratch. The Baroque composer and critic **Johann Mattheson** considered parody a way for one composer to compliment the **invention** of another.

PARTITA. (1) A **variation** or set of variations on an **ostinato** bass or on a **dance**. The term often appears in Italian **keyboard** and **lute** literature of the late 16th and 17th century and persists to denote variations on **chorales** in the **organ** literature of **Johann Sebastian Bach** and his German contemporaries.

(2) A **suite** of dance movements. This meaning dates from at least 1649 in the title of a manuscript collection of **Johann Jacob Froberger**, *Libro secondo di toccate . . . gigue et altre partite*, and becomes the dominant meaning in the 18th century, the most famous examples being the Partitas for Solo **Violin** (BWV 1002, 1004, 1006) and the partitas of the *Clavier-Übung*, Part I (BWV 825–830), of J. S. Bach.

PASQUINI, BERNARDO (7 December 1637, Massa Valdinievole near Pistoia, Italy–22 November 1710, Rome). Pasquini made his reputation as a **keyboard** player nearly as great as that of his contemporary **Arcangelo Corelli** on the **violin**. Little is known of his education, but he made his way to **Rome** by 1650 and thereafter never left, eventually rising to the services of Queen Christina of Sweden, the Cardinals Ottoboni, Chigi, and Pamphili, and

Prince Giambattista Borghese. From 1666, when he became **harpsichordist** to Prince Borghese, Pasquini was a leading musician of the city, collaborating with Corelli, **Alessandro Scarlatti**, and **George Frideric Handel**, and acquiring many students. Along with Corelli and Scarlatti, Pasquini was inducted into the Arcadian Academy of Rome on 26 April 1706.

Pasquini composed 18 **operas**, 17 **oratorios**, about 60 **cantatas**, and a significant body of keyboard music: 33 **toccatas**, 17 **suites**, 22 "**arias**" for keyboard, 13 **partitas** and **variation** sets, 4 **organ sonatas**, 14 sonatas for single harpsichord, and 14 for two harpsichords.

PASSACAGLIA (Fr. PASSACAILLE). A term often used synonymously with **chaconne**, the passacaglia seems to have originated in the early 17th century as **improvisations** between the verses of Italian songs over a common harmonic progression. **Girolamo Frescobaldi** seems to have first published the word in his *Partite Sopra Passacagli* for **keyboard** in 1627. Subsequently, the term appears in **variation** sets for **guitar** and **lute** as well.

In France, it appears much less often than "chaconne," but **Jean-Baptiste Lully**'s passacaille from his *tragédie lyrique* Armide provided a famous model for the 18th century.

In Germany, the repeating bass of the passacaglia became the basis for improvisations and brilliant figurations in **organ** compositions. The most famous example is the Passacaglia and **Fugue** in C Minor of **Johann Sebastian Bach** (BWV 582).

PASSEPIED. In the late 16th and early 17th century, a quick duple-**meter dance** in three-bar units. However, this meaning was supplanted by the passepied of the court of King Louis XIV, a quick triple-meter dance in four-measure phrases with steps identical to those of the **minuet**. In this form, it was danced in many French **operas** and ballets through the end of the Baroque. The passepied also appeared in instrumental **suites** throughout the later Baroque, beginning with an anacrusis of one beat in a fast 3/8 meter.

PASSION. A setting of one of the four Gospel accounts of Christ's suffering and death on the cross. The genre sprang from a traditional practice of reading or chanting the passion accounts during Holy Week—St. Matthew on Palm Sunday, St. Mark on Tuesday, St. Luke on Wednesday, St. John on Friday—and it retained its liturgical function until the late 18th century.

Despite Martin Luther's (1483–1546) reservations about performing the passion texts and compiled *summae*, the **monophonic** and **polyphonic** passion was widely practiced in Protestant Germany. Two German-language **responsorial** passions, St. Matthew and St. John, attributed to Johann Walther

(1495–1570), Luther's most important musical collaborator, exercised great influence on the Lutheran passion until well into the 18th century.

The north German Hanseatic cities contributed the next innovation by modeling the passions after Italian **operatic** practices: **Thomas Selle**'s St. John Passion of 1643 provides a **continuo** throughout the score as well as melodic instruments to accompany Christ and the narrator. **Heinrich Schütz** invented his own recitation tones, having the character of **recitative**, for his three passions, and others added instrumental *sinfonie*. The "**oratorio passion**" also added nonbiblical texts drawn from **hymns**, spiritual verse, and other sources that subdivided the Gospel into episodes. After the publication of **Erdmann Neumeister**'s operatic **cantata** texts after 1700, the recitation tones could be abandoned in favor of free recitative, with **arias** for the poetic texts. **Reinhard Keiser**'s St. Mark Passion (c. 1710), performed by **Johann Sebastian Bach** at Weimar, is such an oratorio passion and could have provided the model for Bach's own **St. John** and **St. Matthew Passion**, which are the culmination of the genre and own permanent places in the choral concert repertory.

The early 18th century saw the conversion of the liturgical passion into secular form completed. In Protestant Germany, poets wrote passion texts that could replace the biblical accounts: Christian Friedrich Hunold's (1680–1721) *Der blutige und sterbende Jesus* ("Jesus, bloody and dying"), set by Keiser in 1704, omitted the narration altogether, and Barthold Heinrich Brockes's (1680–1747) *Der für die Sünden der Welt gemarterte und sterbende Jesus* ("Jesus, martyred and dying for the sins of the world") uses expressive paraphrase and became very popular, set by Keiser (1712), **Georg Philippe Telemann** (1716), **George Frideric Handel** (1717), and **Johann Mattheson** (1718), among others. In Catholic **Vienna**, the *sepolcro* (passion stories) followed the opera completely, even to the point of staging a scene at Christ's tomb. Performances of the *sepolcro* took place only on Holy Thursday or Good Friday, thus retaining a link with the liturgical tradition.

PASTICCIO. A musical drama patched together with **arias** and **recitatives** drawn from various existing **operas** by various composers, tied together with either an extant **libretto** or one newly written for the occasion. The singers for the *pasticcio* usually chose the arias.

The practice dates from the late 17th century, but the term appears only about 1730. Most of the leading *opera seria* composers in the first half of the 18th century participated in the construction of *pasticci* at one time or another.

PAVAN (PAVANE). Stately, duple-**meter dance** of Italian origin, whose popularity peaked in the 16th century but persisted into the 17th century, appearing in French and English **suites**. It is often paired with a **galliard** based on the same melodic idea as begins the pavan.

PEDAL POINT. A sustained pitch, usually in the bass, around which other **voices** continue to move at the speed normal for the composition. The term probably derives from the practice of **organists improvising** over a bass tone played on the pedal division, just before an important **cadence**. They occur frequently in Baroque compositions, particularly in **preludes, fantasias, toccatas**, and other instrumental works.

PEPUSCH, JOHANN CHRISTOPH (1667, Berlin–20 July 1752, London). Today, Pepusch is most famous as the composer of the **overture** of *The Beggar's Opera* and possible arranger of some of its songs, and he did compose about 10 **masques** and other works for the stage, but in his own day, he was highly regarded as a composer of instrumental music: over 180 **sonatas** for various instruments, mostly **violin**, about 12 **concerti grossi**, and 43 **trio sonatas**. He also composed a **Magnificat**, 3 **motets**, 5 **odes**, 14 English-language **cantatas**, and over 15 **anthems**. A scholar who, along with **William Croft**, received an honorary doctorate of music from Oxford University in July 1713, he left a **thoroughbass** method book and *A Treatise on Harmony*, both dating from 1730.

Pepusch was employed at the Prussian court from age 14, but left in 1697, visited Holland, and settled in **London** after September 1697. By 1708, he was employed by the Queen's Theatre at the Haymarket, where he met his future wife, the soprano Margherita de l'Epine. From 1717 to 1725, he provided music for the Duke of **Chandos** at Cannons. By 1729, he seems to have retired from active composition to devote himself to antiquarian interests, including the direction of the **Academy of Ancient Music**, and by 1732, he ceased to be active in the theater. In 1738, along with **George Frideric Handel, Thomas Arne**, and **William Boyce**, he founded the Society of Musicians, later the Royal Society.

Pepusch married l'Epine sometime between 1718 and 1723. They had one son, baptized 9 January 1724.

PERGOLESI, GIOVANNI BATTISTA (4 January 1710, Iesi delle Marche, Italy–16 March 1736, Pozzuoli near Naples). He died at the early age of 26 and, therefore, left a comparatively small body of music, but Pergolesi's compositions for musical theater exercised an extraordinary influence on the history of musical style. Although four of his **operas** are traditional *opere serie*, it is the other works, two *commedie musicali* and three comic **intermezzi**, especially *La Serva Padrona* (1733), that are regarded as popularizing the comic genres at the expense of *opera seria* and thus ushering in the dramatic aesthetics of the classical style.

Pergolesi also composed six **concertos** for various combinations of instruments, two **oratorios**, two **masses**, eight psalms, at least six chamber **cantatas**, and a setting of the **sequence** *Stabat Mater* that remains popular today.

Giovanni Battista Pergolesi was the third child of a surveyor, Francesco Andrea Draghi-Pergolesi. His two brothers and sister died in infancy, and Giovanni himself is described by contemporaries as a sickly person. His father's connections with the Iesi nobility allowed Giovanni to go to **Naples** and study at the Conservatorio dei Poveri di Gesù Cristo between 1720 and 1725. He may have studied composition with **Leonardo Vinci** until October 1728 and then with **Francesco Durante**. Documents attest to an extraordinary ability to **improvise** on the **violin**.

Pergolesi broke into musical drama with his oratorio, *Li Prodigi della Divina Grazia nella Conversione di San Guglielmo Duca d'Aquitania* ("The Miracles of Divine Grace at the Conversion of St. William, Duke of Aquitaine") in summer of 1731 and, in January 1732, staged his first opera, *Salustia*, in Naples.

In 1732, at age 22, Pergolesi was appointed *maestro di cappella* to Prince Ferdinando Colonna Stigliano of Naples, and his first comedy, *Lo Frate 'Nnamorato* ("The Friar in Love") followed on 27 September 1732. A revival in 1748 was extremely popular.

In spring 1734, the Prince of Stigliano was obliged to withdraw to **Rome** when the Bourbons took over Naples. There, Pergolesi's Mass in F impressed the Romans with the **Neapolitan mass** setting of separate movements within prayers. After that, the composer became *maestro di cappella* for another Neapolitan nobleman, Marzio Domenico IV Carafa, Duke of Maddaloni, by June 1734, when the entourage returned to Naples.

In summer 1735, Pergolesi became seriously ill, probably with the tuberculosis that killed him the following year. His last comedy, *Il Flaminio* ("The Fleming") was produced at the Teatro Nuovo in Naples that fall. Early the following year, he moved to the Franciscan monastery in Pozzuoli founded by his patron's family. The *Stabat Mater* appears to have been his last composition.

PERI, JACOPO (20 August 1561, Florence or Rome–12 August 1633, Florence). Composer of the first known **opera**, the pastoral *Dafne* (1597), and of the earliest complete opera to survive, *Euridice* (1600). Because he was one of the principal musicians in the earliest experiments in music drama, Peri's career materially influenced the formation of the early Baroque style. He collaborated in five other music dramas, the last of which, *La Flora*, was first performed at the Pitti Palace in **Florence** on 14 October 1628. There are also 3 sacred dramas, music for about 10 **intermedi**, and a publication of 32 compositions for one to three voices and **continuo** (1609). Evidently, composition was not natural or easy for him; his fame derived from his dramatic singing. The **librettist** Marco da Gagliano claimed that Peri's music could not be fully known until it was heard sung by the composer himself.

Jacopo Peri's first important teacher was the composer Cristofano Malvezzi (1547–1599), who thought so well of Peri that he included two of the youth's compositions in his own publications of 1577 and 1583. The abbey of the Badia Fiorentina employed him as **organist** from 1 February 1579 until April 1605. In the meantime, he had composed music for an intermedium to a comedy by Giovanni Fedini in 1583 and was appointed at the Medici court in 1588, performing mostly as a singer. It is possible that Peri was a member of the Florentine **Camerata**, and he definitely met with the intellectuals associated with Jacopo Corsi (1561–1602) who planned the earliest music dramas in Florence in the 1590s, collaborating with the dramatist Ottavio Rinuccini (1562–1621) and the musicians **Giulio Caccini** and **Emilio de' Cavalieri**.

After the premiere of *Euridice* in 1600, Peri continued to collaborate in various kinds of music drama, maintaining contacts and working on projects not only in Florence but also in Mantua and **Rome** as well. Many of these projects were never completed, and some that were completed were never performed.

In 1630, Peri became so seriously ill that on 15 March he prepared his will. He lived three and one-half more years and was buried in the Church of Santa Maria Novella.

PERTI, GIACOMO ANTONIO (6 June 1661, Crevelcore near Bologna, Italy–10 April 1756, Bologna). During a 60-year reign as *maestro di cappella*, Perti made the basilica of San Petronio in Bologna into one of the outstanding musical establishments in Baroque Italy. He trained **Giuseppe Torelli** and **Giovanni Battista Martini**, among many others, and left a large body of sacred music: 28 **masses**, 120 psalm settings, 55 **motets**, 83 **versets**, and perhaps as many as 25 **oratorios**. There is evidence also for more than 30 **operas**, but most of the music is lost.

Perti began musical study with his uncle Lorenzo, and saw his first compositions performed at the church of San Tomaso al Mercato in Bologna in 1678. The next year, he composed an oratorio, *Santa Serafia*, and one act of an opera. He succeeded his uncle as *maestro di cappella* at the cathedral of San Pietro in 1690, then to the same post at *San Petronio* in 1696, where he remained for the rest of his life.

PIANO. *See* FORTEPIANO.

PIANOFORTE. *See* FORTEPIANO.

PIPE ORGAN. *See* ORGAN.

PITCH-CLASS. The set of all pitches having octave relationships and bearing the same letter name (e.g., all the As or all the B-flats on the piano **keyboard**).

PITCH STANDARDS. *See* BAROQUE PITCH.

POLONAISE. Stately **dance** in triple **meter** that developed in 16th-century Poland but became popular and throughout western Europe and stylized in dance **suites** of **Georg Philipp Telemann, Johann Sebastian Bach, François Couperin**, and other composers of Germany and France.

POLYCHORAL TEXTURE. *See CORI SPEZZATI.*

POLYPHONY (POLYPHONIC). A musical **texture** of more than one simultaneous melody or **voice** (i.e., any music that is harmonized). In some contexts, polyphony denotes much more specifically the *stile antico* style of **a cappella** singing perfected in the late 15th and 16th centuries.

PORPORA, NICOLA (17 August 1686, Naples–3 March 1768, Naples). Internationally famous as an **opera** composer and singing teacher, Porpora's career touched many of the most important opera cities of Europe and crossed the paths of numerous luminaries of the opera world. His oeuvre of instrumental music—12 **sonatas** for solo **violin**, 6 *sinfonie*, 6 sonatas for two violins and two **cellos** with **continuo**, another **solo sonata** for cello, 2 **concertos**, 2 **harpsichord fugues**, and an **overture** for **orchestra**—is not trivial, but Porpora's strength and interest was in vocal music: 43 operas, 4 *pasticcios*, 12 **serenatas**, 132 secular **cantatas**, 5 **masses**, 10 **oratorios**, 35 psalm settings, 3 **Magnificats**, 2 **Te Deums**, 9 solo **motets**, and 13 Marian **antiphons**.

His influence persisted after his death not so much through his compositions as through his methods of teaching voice. He taught two famous *castrati*, **Farinelli** and Caffarelli (1710–1783), and the vocal exercises published by Porpora continued to be used through the 19th century.

Son of a bookseller, Carlo Porpora, and his wife Caterina, Nicola Porpora attended the Conservatorio dei Poveri di Gesù Cristo from 29 September 1696. At age 22, he composed his first opera, *L'Agrippina* (1708), but after that, the presence in **Naples** of the great **Alessandro Scarlatti** prevented advancement in the theater. But in 1711, he was employed as *maestro di cappella* for Prince Philipp Hesse-Darmstadt, then residing as military commander in Naples, and then for the Portuguese ambassador in **Rome** from June 1713. From 1715 to 1722, he was a teacher at the Conservatorio di San Onofrio.

Then Scarlatti left Naples for Rome in 1719, and Porpora responded with a new opera, *Faramondo*. For the birthdays of Empress Elizabeth in 1720 and 1721, he composed two serenatas, collaborating with the brilliant young **librettist Pietro Metastasio** for the first time and introducing his brilliant vocal student, Farinelli, auspicious occasions for Baroque opera.

Porpora and Farinelli then scored two successes with operas in Rome in 1721 and 1722. Porpora tried to expand his reach, producing operas in Munich (1724) and visiting **Vienna** before settling in **Venice**, where his operas were featured at the famous Teatro San Giovanni Grisostomo. By this point, Porpora was engaged in competition with the leading opera composers of the continent, first **Leonardo Vinci** in Venice through 1730 and, thereafter, with **Johann Adolf Hasse**.

In 1733, Porpora received an invitation to compose for the Opera of the Nobility, a company set up in **London** to rival **George Frideric Handel**'s Royal Academy. He began with the successful *Arianna in Naxo* in December 1733 and followed up with three more *opere serie* and one oratorio, but despite having the finest singers at its disposal, including Farinelli for a time, the new company could not defeat Handel.

Porpora returned to Venice in summer 1736. He then received a commission from the new theater in Naples, Teatro San Carlo, so he returned to his home city, and by the summer of January 1739, he was *maestro di cappella* at the Conservatorio di Santa Maria di Loreto. For a while, the commissions continued to arrive, and Porpora continued to tour: to Venice in October 1741 to produce *Statira*, to London in 1742 for *Temistocle*.

In 1747, he was brought to **Dresden** to be the singing teacher to the electoral princess of Saxony, who then managed to have him appointed *Kapellmeister* in 1748, despite the presence of Hasse. But Hasse won in the end; he was promoted to *Oberkapellmeister*. After receiving a pension, Porpora left for Vienna in 1752. There, he gave singing lessons but became ill. He returned to Naples and to his old job at the Conservatorio di Santa Maria but had to resign in September 1761. His retirement was spent in considerable poverty.

PORTA, GIOVANNI (c. 1675, the Veneto region, Italy–21 June 1755, Munich). Porta was commissioned to open the company in which **George**

Frideric Handel would find fame, the Royal Academy in **London**, on 2 April 1720, with *Numitore*. He composed about 30 other **operas**, mostly for **Venice**. As *maestro di coro* at the Ospedale della Pietà in Venice, he composed much sacred music for the famous female **chorus** and **orchestra** to perform: at least 19 **masses**, 22 psalm settings, a **Te Deum**, 8 **motets**, and 4 **passions** survive.

Porta studied with **Francesco Gasparini** and perhaps was attached to the household of Cardinal Ottoboni in **Rome** from about 1706 to 1710. He was *maestro di cappella* at the Vicenza Cathedral from 1710 to 1711 and then at the Verona Cathedral from 1714 to 1716. His tenure at the Ospedale ran from 1726 to 1737. Then he became *Hofkapellmeister* at the court of Elector Karl Albrecht in Munich, remaining there until his death.

PRAETORIUS, MICHAEL (February 1571, Creuzburg an der Werra, near Eisenach, Germany–15 February 1621, Wolfenbüttel). Composer of over 1,000 works based on Protestant **hymn** tunes and the popular *Terpsichore* **dances** of 1612 for instrumental ensemble. Only in his last publications, the *Polyhymnia*, did Praetorius move away from the **chorale** and begin to incorporate into his music the **textures** coming out of the Italian experiments with music drama. His importance for the Baroque in Germany lies in his systematic organization and exhaustive arrangements of the chorale repertory, creating a curriculum in **functional harmony** that exploits **chromatic** resources and a tradition of chorale usage for Lutheran composers. Beyond that, his theoretical work ***Syntagma Musicum*** documents the state of art music at the beginning of the Baroque.

After the humanist fashion of the time, Michael Schultheiss adopted a Latinized name. Praetorius began his formal education at the Lateinschule at Torgau in the 1570s and then continued at the University of Frankfurt in 1582. His first musical post was as **organist** of the Marienkirche in Frankfurt from 1587 to 1590. He moved to Wolfenbüttel in the early 1590s and became organist of Duke Heinrich Julius of Brunswick-Wolfenbüttel in 1595. In 1602, he was given a raise and, in September 1603, married Anna Lakemacher. They had two sons.

In 1604, he was appointed *Kapellmeister* to the duke. The following year he published the first of his nine volumes of chorale arrangements, the *Musae Sioniae*, continuing until 1610. Once, while traveling with the duke in 1605, the party was attacked, and Praetorius defended his patron so bravely that the duke rewarded him with 2,000 thaler and a future gift of land.

When the duke died suddenly in 1613, Praetorius was invited to spend the mourning period in **Dresden** by the Elector Johann Georg of Saxony. He stayed two and one-half years, met **Heinrich Schütz**, and acquainted himself with his Italianized style. Visits to Magdeburg, **Leipzig**, Nuremberg, and Bayreuth in 1618 and 1619 in the company of Schütz and **Samuel Scheidt** are documented. Thereafter, his health declined. He left a considerable fortune upon his death, much of which went to charitable causes.

PRELUDE (PRELUDIO, PREAMBULUM). The term connotes a piece of instrumental music that precedes either a liturgy or another piece of music somehow more substantial than the prelude. Such musical introductions probably come from 16th-century practices of **improvising** to cover liturgical actions, or, in secular contexts, to check the intonation of an instrument and to warm up the player. The weakness or even absence of **meter** in Baroque preludes is a vestige of this origin in instrumental improvisation and is responsible for their introductory character, particularly evident in the **unmeasured preludes** of French **suites**. In 17th-century preludes, the introductory nature is also marked when the prelude ends with a half **cadence**, on dominant harmony, with the resultant harmonic tension demanding the next movement. In the 18th century, preludes were more often metrically strong and harmonically self-contained compositions.

In the Baroque, the most important kinds of prelude include those that stand at the head of a suite, that act as introductory movements in a 17th-century **concerto** or **sonata**, **chorale preludes** designed to introduce a **hymn** in a liturgy, and the pairing of a prelude with a **fugue** in the **keyboard** repertory, mostly German, the preeminent examples of which are the preludes and fugues for **organ** by **Johann Sebastian Bach** and his two books of the *Well-Tempered Clavier.*

PRIMA PRATICA **(It. "first practice").** Refers to the traditional musical aesthetic of high Renaissance **polyphony** that prefers a **counterpoint** of strictly controlled **dissonances** in a largely consonant **texture**. The expression appears in 1607 in the famous response of **Claudio Monteverdi** to criticisms of Giovanni Maria Artusi about his **madrigals**.

PRINTING. During the Baroque, the great increase in the household consumption of music for **keyboard**, chamber music, and songs encouraged technological advances that gradually made printing music, rather than copying manuscripts, the principal means of disseminating music for the first time. Composers famous for instrumental music, such as **Arcangelo Corelli** and **Antonio Vivaldi**, made their reputations with publications. Only works intended for a specific occasion—**operas, cantatas, oratorios**, some pedagogical works—were produced in manuscript because there was no need for many copies, although for honorific or commemorative purposes even these might be printed. **Jacopo Peri**'s *Euridice*, **Claudio Monteverdi**'s *L'Orfeo*, and **Johann Sebastian Bach**'s early **church cantata** *Gott ist mein König* BWV 71 were all published. Still, the great majority of Bach's oeuvre, as well as **George Frideric Handel**'s and most other Baroque composers, survived in manuscript. Corelli was the great exception: his six publications Opera 1 through 6 represent almost all his known work.

There were three printing technologies available to the Baroque. The oldest, dating from the earliest music prints in the 15th century, was the woodblock, whereby a reverse image of the entire page of music in relief would be cut into a block of wood or metal. This labor-intensive method was employed mostly for short musical examples in music theory treatises.

The second, developed during the 16th century and used widely during the Baroque, was the technology of movable type. Each unit of type contained the image of a note of specific duration (breve, semibreve, etc.) placed on a bit of musical staff to indicate the pitch. A music font consisted of one metal type piece for each duration at every available pitch. Thus, as in word printing, the typesetter could set the notes in order as the composer required and print them at a single impression. The type could be rearranged for each new page, unlike woodblocks, which had a single dedicated use.

Setting the increasingly varied and florid instrumental rhythms of the Baroque challenged the movable type method. The solution was the third technology, pioneered by Simon Verovius in **Rome** in 1586, when he published the two earliest books of engraved music. In engraving, a metal sheet would be cut with a reverse image of the desired music, a concept analogous to the woodblock. Engraving, however, was much cheaper and faster than cutting a woodblock because of standardized cutting tools called *punches* for each type of note. A special cutter first scored the metal with straight lines to make the staves, and then punches added the note heads, accidentals, time signatures, and words, if necessary. The engraver needed only to add by hand the note stems, ties, slurs, and special articulations. Estienne Roger of Amsterdam and John Walsh of **London** were among the first to exploit these techniques at the opening of the 18th century and also converted from copper sheeting to pewter, which was softer, thus increasing the speed of engraving and production. After this, printing music with movable type gradually declined.

PURCELL, HENRY (10 September 1659?, London–21 November 1695, Westminster, London). Composer who is generally acknowledged as the finest setter of English text, sometimes called the greatest native English composer, his oeuvre may be divided into three generic areas. He composed the instrumental incidental music to over 40 plays between 1680 and 1695, as well as 14 **fantasias**, 3 **overtures**, 5 **pavans**, 24 **sonatas**, and much **harp-**

sichord music. His musical dramas were composed later, including one complete **opera** and five **semi-operas**, mostly after 1688. The third group, sacred music, was composed throughout his career: 56 masterly **verse anthems**, 18 full **anthems** (all before 1682), 4 Latin psalms, 34 other sacred songs, a morning and evening **service**, and a few works for **organ**.

Purcell learned music as a chorister at the **Chapel Royal** in **London** from the late 1660s until December 1673, when he was hired as keeper of the king's instruments. He probably studied with **John Blow** and Christopher Gibbons (1615–1676), composers associated with the Chapel Royal. On 10 September 1677, Purcell succeeded **Matthew Locke** as composer-in-ordinary to the king and, in 1679, was appointed organist to Westminster Abbey when Blow stepped down, apparently to create an opening for Purcell, and then, on 14 July1682, was appointed as organist to the Chapel Royal. He retained these positions for his whole life.

In 1680, Purcell married Frances Peters. Their first son, born on 9 July 1681, died one week later, but Frances, born in 1688, and Edward, born in 1689, survived into adulthood.

As a court composer, Purcell was responsible for providing the required ceremonial music, including birthday **odes**, welcome songs, anthems, **voluntaries**, and other music for coronations. Under King Charles II, who ruled until 1685, and James II, until 1688, these duties kept Purcell busy and provided adequate income. Attempts to introduce Italian- and French-style opera into England early in the Restoration period had failed, but after the Glorious Revolution had exiled James and brought King William III and Queen Mary II to the throne in 1689, the musical establishment at court was reduced considerably, and this may have caused Purcell to seek more income outside from the stage.

He had supplied vocal music for a tragedy of Nathaniel Lee, *Theodosius*, in 1680. In 1689, Purcell worked with the future poet laureate of England, Nahum Tate, to produce his only true opera, ***Dido and Aeneas***. The only known performance was given at a girls' boarding school in Chelsea run by a dance master, Josiah Priest, traditionally dated 1689. However, in the same year, he was commissioned by the Theatre Royal to compose music for the semi-opera *The Prophetess, or the History of Dioclesian* (usually referred to today as *Dioclesian*). Because it was highly unusual at that time for the music of a semi-opera to be composed by one man, the commission implies that Purcell, perhaps owing to *Dido and Aeneas*, had become the leading composer in England by age 30.

The poet John Dryden, who had once proclaimed that the English language and opera were incompatible, offered Purcell the chance to set his semi-opera *King Arthur*. It premiered in late spring 1691 and was so popular that it continued to be performed into the 18th century. This triumph was followed by another on 2 May 1692, *The Faerie Queen*, based on Shakespeare's *A Midsummer Night's Dream*, commissioned by the Theatre Royal. The management continued to use Purcell's music for as many of their productions as possible. In 1695, Purcell composed the music for his last major work, the semi-opera *The Indian Queen*.

Purcell seems to have died of a sudden illness or infection, since his will is dated the day of his passing.

Purcell's music, especially the earlier instrumental music, often experimented with unorthodox **chromaticism** and **dissonance** but always shows a mastery of **contrapuntal** art. He exploited particularly well a favorite compositional technique of the 17th century, the **ostinato** bass (in English, the **ground** bass); *Dido and Aeneas* alone has three ostinato **arias** in 45 minutes of music. His ability to reflect faithfully the natural diction of the English language in his rhythm remains unsurpassed and was studied by figures as great and diverse as **George Frideric Handel**, Edward Elgar (1857–1934), and Benjamin Britten (1913–1976).

PUZZLE CANON. Self-standing **canon** in which the Latin prescription (canon) only hints at the solution of the canon (i.e., the pitch interval and time interval required for the following voices to enter). *See also* MUSICAL OFFERING.

Q

QUANTZ, JOHANN JOACHIM (30 January 1697, Oberscheden, Hanover, Germany–12 July 1773, Potsdam). Renowned as a **flutist** in his own time, Quantz composed over 300 **concertos** and over 235 **sonatas** for that instrument, as well as other assorted flute (**transverse**) compositions, 16 concertos for other instruments, 60 **trio sonatas**, and a very few vocal short vocal works, including 22 **hymns**. Quantz is chiefly remembered today, however, for his manual on flute playing, *Versuch einer Anweisung die Flöte traversiere zu spielen* (1752), because the book explains not only how to play the transverse flute but also many other aspects of Baroque performance practice.

Quantz received his early training from relatives, achieving proficiency on **string instruments**, **oboe**, and **trumpet**. He was appointed oboist to the Polish Chapel of Augustus II, Elector of Saxony and King of Poland in 1718. He saw little opportunity for advancement as oboist, however, so in 1719, he took up the transverse flute, taking a few lessons from a French virtuoso Pierre-Gabriel Buffardin (c. 1690–1768).

The cosmopolitan Saxon court in **Dresden** exposed Quantz to the latest trends in the composition of concertos, sonatas, and **operas**. He then took a three-year tour of Italy, France, and England from 1724 to 1727, studying with **Francesco Gasparini** in **Rome** and meeting, among other luminaries, **Alessandro Scarlatti**, **Johann Adolf Hasse**, and **George Frideric Handel**.

In May 1728, Quantz impressed Prince Frederick of Prussia while on a state visit to **Berlin**. After that, Frederick, an amateur flutist himself, took occasional lessons from Quantz, and when Frederick acceded to the throne in 1740, he hired Quantz with an extremely attractive offer. Quantz moved to Berlin in 1741 and spent the remainder of his career instructing the king and composing flute music for him.

QUATTRO STAGIONI. *See FOUR SEASONS, THE.*

R

RAMEAU, JEAN-PHILIPPE (baptized 25 September 1683, Dijon, France–12 September 1764, Paris). One of the most important French composers in Western music history, and in modern times the most influential theorist of Western harmony, Rameau's eccentric career falls into three spheres of activity: the composition of five important collections of **harpsichord** works beginning in 1706; a large number of books and essays in music theory, beginning with his revolutionary *Traité de l'Harmonie*, published in 1722; and over 30 **operas** and other works for the stage, placing him, along with **Jean-Baptiste Lully**, as a primary exponent of French Baroque opera. The first of these operas, *Hippolyte et Aricie* of 1733, Rameau did not produce until the astonishing age of 50. He also composed nine secular **cantatas**, at least three *grands motets*, and the five chamber collections known as *Pièces de clavecin en concert*.

Details about Rameau's life before 1722, when he moved permanently from Dijon to **Paris**, are sketchy, partly owing to his own reticence. He was the seventh child and eldest surviving son of Jean Rameau, **organist** in Dijon, and Claudine Demartinécourt. He may have studied music with the organist at the Sainte Chapelle in Dijon, Claude Derey, and he eventually enrolled in the Jesuit Collège des Godrans, where he first encountered musical theater. In 1701 or 1702, he spent a brief time in Italy and then took up the post of organist of the Clermont Cathedral in May 1702. Next, he moved to Paris in 1706, became organist at the Jesuit Collège Louis-le-Grand and to the Pères de la Merci, and published *Premier Livre de Pièces de Clavecin*. In 1709, he returned to Dijon to succeed his father as organist of Notre Dame and then to Lyons in 1713 to be chief organist of the city. In 1715, he was reappointed at Clermont Cathedral, where he began work on the *Traité de l'Harmonie*.

His first decade in Paris was consumed with publishing his new book, which would become famous all over Europe, two more collections of **keyboard** music in 1724 and 1729, and teaching. Oddly, Rameau was not able to secure a major position as organist anywhere in Paris until 1732, when he became organist at Sainte Croix-de-la-Bretonnerie.

He married a talented singer, 19-year-old Marie-Louis Mangot, on 25 February 1726. She would bear him four children and sing in some of his operas.

Rameau's first attempt at a full-scale opera, *Hippolyte et Aricie*, opened in 1733 and immediately ignited that kind of intellectual controversy that could only happen in France. His proponents, the *ramistes*, admired the opera's adventurous harmonies and more realistic dramaturgy, while the opposing *lullistes*, motivated perhaps by jealousy and fear that their namesake might be eclipsed, railed against its Italianisms and harmonic complexity. The contro-

Rameau's Works for the Theater

Opera	First performance	Librettists and sources
Hippolyte et Aricie	1 October 1733	Simon-Joseph Pellegrin
Samson	Music lost	Voltaire
Les Indes Galantes	23 August 1735	Louis Fuzelier
Castor et Pollux	24 October 1737	Pierre Joseph Bernard et alia
Les L Les Fêtes d'Hébé	21 May 1739	Antoine Gautier de Montdorge
Dardanus	19 November 1739	Charles-Antoine Le Clerc de La Bruère
La Princesse de Navarre	23 February 1745	Voltaire
Platée	31 March 1745	Adrien Joseph Le Valois d'Orville after J. Autreau
Les Fêtes de Polymnie	12 October 1745	Louis de Cahusac
Le Temple de la Gloire	27 November 1745	Voltaire
Les Fêtes de Ramire	22 December 1745	Voltaire, rev. Jean-Jacques Rousseau
Les Fêtes de l'Hymen et de l'Amour	15 March 1747	Cahusac
Zaïs	29 February 1748	Cahusac
Pigmalion	27 August 1748	Ballot de Sovot after A. Houdar de La Motte
Les Surprises de l'Amour	27 November 1748	Bernard
Naïs	22 April 1749	Cahusac
Zoroastre	5 December 1749	Cahusac
Linus	Most music lost	La Bruère
La Guirlande	21 September 1751	Jean-François Marmontel
Acante et Céphise	18? November 1751	Marmontel
Daphnis et Eglé	29 or 30 October 1753	C. Collé
Lysis et Délie	Music lost	Marmontel
Les Sibarites	13 November 1753	Marmontel
La Naissance d'Osiris	12 October 1754	Cahusac
Anacréon	23 October 1754	Cahusac
Anacréon	31 May 1757	Bernard
Les Paladins	12 February 1760	Jean-François Duplat de Monticourt? after La Fontaine
Les Boréades	None	Cahusac
Nélée et Myrthis	None	Cahusac
Zéphyre	None	Cahusac
Io	None	Cahusac

versy persisted through the 1730s and encompassed Rameau's second opera, *Les Indes Galantes*, which saw 64 performances in two years, and especially his fifth, *Dardanus*. From the perspective of nearly three centuries, it has become clear that these operas owe much to Lully's practice of *tragédie lyrique*, and critics generally point to Rameau's first works of the 1730s as his finest.

From sometime in the mid-1730s until 1753, Rameau was attached to the household of one of the richest men in France, Alexandre Le Riche de La Poupelinière. La Poupelinière, a financier, was a great patron of the arts and all manner of writers, actors, and cultural figures would meet at his house. The attachment advanced Rameau's operatic career considerably, since he met some of his many **librettists** there.

After a fallow period in the early 1740s, Rameau seems to have caught the attention of the French court. In 1745, he received three commissions for theater works, including the opera for the Dauphin's wedding, *La Princesse de Navarre*, with a libretto of Voltaire. On May 4, he was rewarded with an annual pension of 2,000 livres and the title *compositeur de la musique de la chambre du roy*, a singular honor for a musician not officially appointed at the court. These commissions began a train of nine works for the stage composed between 1745 and 1749. Rameau's operas so dominated Paris at this time that the management of the Paris opera felt compelled to restrict the offerings of Rameau to only two operas per year, in order to give younger composers a chance.

Despite his fame as a thinker about music, Rameau was never elected to the Académie Royale des Sciences, a disappointment. Five months before his death, however, he did receive a patent of nobility from the king, and he died a comparatively wealthy man three weeks after falling ill with a fever. Many memorial services in Paris, Dijon, and other provincial cities followed. The first, at the Pères de l'Oratoire on 27 September 1764, included as many as 180 musicians and was attended by over 1,000 mourners.

RAPPRESENTATIONE DI ANIMA E DI CORPO (Emilio de' Cavalieri, 1600, Rome). Emilio de' Cavalieri's *Dramma per musica* published in 1600, first performed in February of that year in the Oratorio della Vallicella in **Rome**. There are 11 named roles for soloists and three- to four-**voiced** vocal ensembles, accompanied by "a good quantity of" **continuo** instruments and **strings**. There are 91 numbered sections organized into a prologue and three acts, lasting a total of about 80 minutes.

The **libretto** by Agostino Manni presents a Neoplatonic allegory in which spiritual values triumph over the pleasures of the world. The musical **textures** employed, mostly *stile recitativo* with interpolated **choruses** and two *sinfonie*, are those of the first **operas**, but its time and place of first performance and moralizing tone have led many historians to consider it the first **oratorio**, despite staging and colorful costumes.

RECITATIVE. Music for **opera** designed to set dramatic dialogue or text expressing rapidly changing feelings in a single character or factual plot information. The musical **texture** consists of a single vocal line accompanied by harmonic progressions supplied by the basso **continuo**. There is little or no **meter** and, therefore, no mid- or high-level musical structure. Rhythms derive directly from the natural accent patterns of the text as if spoken, and there is seldom any text repetition as in **arias**. The effect is that of a heightened speech, and the interest and structural integrity of the recitative depends entirely on the semantics of the text.

The term *lo stile recitativo* was first used by the Italian theorist Giovanni Battista Doni (1594–1647) in his *Annotazioni* of 1640.

In early Baroque operas, recitative could have widely varying character, ranging from something like simple speaking with pitch to florid melodic structures approaching that of an aria, depending upon the strength of the meter and harmonic rhythm provided by the accompaniment. As the distinction between aria and recitative grew stronger later in the period, recitative devolved into a device mainly used to advance the plot of the opera: the *secco* recitative. An occasional textual passage demanding stronger and yet variable emotional expression could be set as an *accompagnato*, a recitative accompanied by the **orchestra**.

Recitatives can be found not only in Baroque operas, but in any of the genres derivative of opera, especially **cantata**, **church cantata**, **serenata**, **oratorio**, and **passion**.

RECITATIVO ACCOMPAGNATO. See *ACCOMPAGNATO*.

RECORDER (Fr. *flûte à bec*, **Ger.** *Blockflöte*, **It.** *flauto dolce*). Wooden **flute** played straight out from the lips, as a **clarinet** or **oboe** is played, not sideways, as the **transverse flute** is played. In the 17th century, the recorder of three jointed sections replaced the single piece of wood common before. The cylindrically bored head joint contains the whistle mouthpiece or *fipple*; the middle joint has six finger-holes drilled into the top side and one thumb-hole on the underside; this tapers to the foot joint, which has a seventh finger-hole.

The Baroque recorder was made in a variety of sizes and pitch ranges, permitting a most mellifluous **consort**. The most typical sizes are:

sopranino–F^5 to G^7
soprano or descant–C^5 to D^7
alto or treble–F^4 to G^6
tenor–C^4 to D^6
bass–F^3 to G^5
great bass–C^3 to D^5

Alto recorder.

Recorder players read traditional notation. The parts for sopranino, descant, and bass recorders are typically written one octave below their sounding pitches. All the **pitch-classes** of the **chromatic** scale are available. Fingering systems have changed little since the Renaissance.

By the turn of the 18th century, the alto (treble) recorder had become the standard solo instrument for which **sonatas, concertos,** and solo roles in **arias** were composed. In Italy, **Alessandro Scarlatti, Benedetto Marcello,** and **Antonio Vivaldi** contributed to the **solo sonata** repertory, and Vivaldi composed recorder concertos as well. In France, **Joseph Bodin de Boismortier,** Jacques Aubert (1689–1753), and Jacques-Christophe Naudot (c. 1690–1762) are the principal names. In England, there are the sonatas of **William Croft** and important solos in the **odes** and **operas** of **Henry Purcell**. In Germany, major contributions come from **Johann Mattheson** (his Opus 1 sonatas), **Georg Philipp Telemann,** and **Johann Sebastian Bach,** who included solo recorders in his Second and Fourth **Brandenburg Concertos,** 20 of his **church cantatas,** the Easter **Oratorio,** and the **St. Matthew Passion.** **George Frideric Handel** called for them in many of his operas and **English oratorios** and wrote four sonatas for recorder in his Opus 1, which are typical of the age in that they may be played not only by alto recorder but by oboe, **violin,** or other suitable treble instrument.

REGALS. Table-top **organ** that produces tones by forcing air from attached bellows over one or more sets of beating metal tongues (reeds). Documentary evidence for regals dates from 1511. In the Baroque, it was used mostly for secular music, sometimes specified as a **continuo** instrument for specific characters in **operas** or **oratorios** (e.g., Charon in **Monteverdi's** *L'Orfeo*).

REINCKEN, JOHANN ADAM (baptized 10 December 1643?, Deventer, Netherlands–24 November 1722, Hamburg). Although only a few of Reincken's compositions survive, including two **chorale fantasias,** eight **harpsichord suites,** and a collection of six **sonatas** and suites for viola da gamba and **continuo,** he was one of the most important **organists** of the north German school of the middle Baroque. After studies in Deventer, Reincken moved to **Hamburg** to study with **Heinrich Scheidemann,** and after a brief return to Deventer, became Scheidemann's assistant at the Catharinenkirche in late 1658. Reincken succeeded him as organist in 1663 and married one of his daughters in 1665.

From 1671 to 1674, he supervised the rebuilding of the organ at the Catharinenkirche, and Reincken, along with **Dietrich Buxtehude**, became one of the century's leading experts on organ construction.

In 1678, Reincken collaborated with city fathers to found the Hamburg **opera**, which earned him controversy. In April 1705, some church elders moved to replace him with **Johann Mattheson** but failed. Reincken died a comparatively wealthy man.

RESPONSORY. Prayers traditionally chanted at the Liturgy of the Hours (Divine Office) in the Roman Catholic tradition. The simplest form is in three parts: the respond sung by the **choir**, the psalm verse sung by the cantor, and the *repetendum*, the last segment of the original respond, sung by the choir. In the Baroque, composers employed at Catholic chapels or cathedrals set traditional responsory texts, with or without the traditional plainchant melodies, in *stile moderno*, with an accompaniment of basso **continuo** at the least.

RHETORIC. The science of persuasive speaking and writing, derived from classical sources such as Aristotle, Cicero, and Quintilian, was frequently cited by Baroque music theorists and critics as an analogue to the processes of musical composition. Examples among many include the *Musica poetica* of Joachim Burmeister (1564–1629, 1606), the *Musurgia Universalis* of **Athanasius Kircher** (1650), and *Der vollkommene Capellmeister* of **Johann Mattheson** (1739). In such works, the techniques of musical composition appear to parallel the fundamental strategies of composing and presenting an argument: *invention*, the overall planning of the composition, including the number of movements, **tempo**, **keys** and **modes**, and principal motives; *disposition*, the orderly introduction of the ideas (exhortation), the increase of tension (narration), and the worthy conclusion; *elocution*, the use of rhetorical figures and devices such as musical contrast (antithesis) or insertion (parenthesis); and *delivery*, the selective emphasis of text by musical means. The degree to which composers consciously applied rhetorical principles in the act of composing is unknown. *See also AFFEKTENLEHRE*; BERNHARD, CHRISTOPH.

RICERCAR (It. pl. *ricercari*). Sixteenth-century term of disputed origin and meaning indicating an instrumental composition that, when intended for **organ**, might have been used as a **prelude** in Christian liturgies in Italy and German-speaking countries.

By the early Baroque, ricercar usually denoted a **keyboard** composition organized on the principle of **imitation**, a direct ancestor of the keyboard **fugue**. The master of the form is generally acknowledged to be **Girolamo**

Frescobaldi, particularly in his publication *Recercari et canzoni* (1615), in which various imitative **subjects** may appear sequentially or introduced all at once at the beginning, in the manner of a double or triple fugue, and *Fiori musicali* (1635), whose ricercars were to be played as a substitute for the Offertory antiphon of the Roman Catholic rite, thus continuing the ancient tradition. Italian and German composers continued to title imitative pieces "ricercar" through the 17th and early 18th century, and **Johann Sebastian Bach** called the six-**voice** monothematic fugue in his **Musical Offering** a "ricercar," although by then the word was certainly archaic.

RIPIENO (It. "full"). Term referring to the total ensemble, or in modern terms, to the **orchestra**, of a Baroque **concerto**.

ROME. One could argue in a number of ways why Rome was the most important city for Baroque music. First, as the capital of the Papal States and home of the pope, Rome had held for centuries the most important positions in sacred music of the Catholic tradition and boasted some of that tradition's greatest names, including **Giovanni da Palestrina** and Orlando di Lasso (c. 1530–1594). But the invention of **opera** at the beginning of the Baroque made the distinction between sacred and secular styles very plain. The papal choir and its directors chose to remain faithful to the *stile antico*. Thereafter, the chapel needed less and less new sacred music, so that after about 1620, production stopped, and the prestige and attraction of such posts declined rapidly. Outside the papal chapel, however, there were many other churches and religious confraternities offering opportunities to compose sacred music in the *stile moderno*, and during the 17th century, Rome produced more sacred music than any other city in Europe.

Second, one of these outlets was the **oratorio**, the genre of sacred drama that was born in Rome with the performance of **Emilio de' Cavalieri**'s *Rappresentatione di Anima e di Corpo* in 1600. **Giacomo Carissimi** composed his most important oratorios there, and later in the century, religious confraternities and great families sponsored the production of oratorios, especially during those periods when the opera was closed.

Third, because the papacy was a powerful but not hereditary monarchy, the competing great families maintained a constant presence in Rome: the Colonna, the Borghesi, the Chigi, the Ruspoli, the Barberini, the Rospigliosi, the Pamphili, the Orsini, and the Ottoboni. Heads of these families were cardinals with contacts at the important churches that employed musicians but who also provided sumptuous private musical entertainment in their own houses: oratorios, instrumental ensembles, even operas on occasion. These families could maintain famous composers in their households with generous compensation. Carissimi, **Girolamo Frescobaldi**, **Arcangelo Corelli**, and, briefly, **George Frideric Handel** are among the luminaries who benefitted from this arrangement.

The most frequent musical entertainment at such houses was the Italian chamber **cantata**; Rome was by far the center of cantata composition in the 17th century. In fact, Rome was odd among Italian cities in that the production of the various species of musical drama spinning off of opera—cantata, **serenata**, oratorio—was greater than the production of opera itself. The environment for opera was not always secure in the 17th century; one could never be sure when the election of a new pope who disapproved of theater would close everything down. Rome did not have a public opera house until the Teatro Tordinona opened in 1671, only to be closed by the pope four years later.

Toward the end of the century, the situation become more stable, and new opera houses, such as the Teatro Capranica and Teatro delle Dame, were opened. In addition, on occasion, the great families mounted operas for private viewing in their own household while authorities looked the other way. Most of the important figures in Italian *opera seria* composed for Roman audiences at some point in their careers: **Antonio Vivaldi**, **Antonio Caldara**, **Nicola Porpora**, **Leonardo Vinci**, and of course **Alessandro Scarlatti**.

At the beginning of the Baroque, Rome was an important center of music publishing. Indeed, the first **prints** of music to use engraving came from Rome. However, costs were high, and by the end of the 17th century, music publishing had virtually ceased.

RONDEAU (RONDO). Structure of at least five sections that alternates a refrain (A section) with contrasting sections or couplets. The origin of the idea is difficult to trace, as it is a strategy based on perceptual similarity and so employed in many guises. In the Baroque, rondeau forms may be heard in 17th-century **opera arias** and other vocal works and especially in French **keyboard** music. The **suites** of **François Couperin** and **Jean-Philippe Rameau** often include a rondeau. The French rondeau, the invention of which is sometimes attributed to **Jean-Baptiste Lully**, employs two couplets, and the resulting structure is A B A C A. The Italian or chain rondeau works this way: A B A C A D . . . A.

ROSARY SONATAS (Heinrich Ignaz Franz von Biber, 1676; a.k.a. Mystery Sonatas). Set of 16 programmatic **sonatas** for **violin**, probably performed by the composer **Heinrich Ignaz Franz von Biber** during the October services for the rosary traditional at the Salzburg Cathedral. In the one surviving manuscript, each sonata is accompanied by an engraving depicting one of the Joyful, Sorrowful, or Glorious Mysteries, 15 in all, plus an additional **passacaglia** with an image of a guardian angel and child. This unaccompanied passacaglia is an enormous work, a set of **variations** over 65 repetitions of the traditional descending bass tetrachord (8-7-6-5).

Of the 16 sonatas, 14 require *scordatura*, or variant **tuning** of the violin **strings**, which makes possible new combinations of multiple stops on the violin. Thus, the tuning for each of the 15 Rosary Sonatas is unique. The set includes many **ostinato** variations and **dance** movements.

ROSSI, SALOMONE (19 August 1570, Mantua–c. 1630, Mantua). Composer who first set ancient Jewish liturgical texts to **operatic** idioms. His collection *Ha-Shirim Asher Li'Shlomo* (1622) contains 33 works composed in the manner of Italian **madrigals** for three to eight **voices**. Attacked by orthodox Jews, Rossi's works nevertheless encouraged many imitators in Italy, France, and the Netherlands. He also published collections of *sinfonie e gagliarde* for instrumental ensemble and **continuo** in 1607 and 1608.

S

SACKBUT. *See* TROMBONE.

SACRED CONCERTO. A setting of a Christian text, usually biblical, for voices and instruments, dating from early to mid-17th century in Italy and German-speaking lands. Seventeenth-century collections adopted the **textures** and techniques of Italian **opera**, the sacred concertos of **Heinrich Schütz** (also called *Symphoniae Sacrae*) being among the greatest exemplars. The use of sacred concertos in worship appears to have paralleled that of **motets**. *See also CENTO CONCERTI ECCLESIASTICI;* DU MONT, HENRY; MONTEVERDI, CLAUDIO; RECITATIVE; SACRED SYMPHONY; SCHEIN, JOHANN HERMANN.

SACRED SYMPHONY (Lat. *Symphonia sacra*). Term used synonymously with but less frequently than "**sacred concerto**" in early 17th-century Italy and Germany. Important collections are the 1597 *Sacrae Symphoniae* of **Giovanni Gabrieli** and the *Symphoniae Sacrae* (1629, 1647) of **Heinrich Schütz**.

SARABANDE (It. *sarabanda*, Eng. "saraband," Sp. *zarabanda*). Triple-**meter dance** introduced to Europe through the repertory of the Spanish **guitar** in the early 17th century. A fast type was preferred in England and Italy, but a stately slower type found a place in the French *ballet de cour* and in the instrumental **suites** of France and Germany, in which it usually appeared after the **courante**. After 1630, the sarabande acquired, particularly in France, a specific rhythmic stamp typified by this pattern:

Figure. Typical rhythmic pattern for the sarabande.

SCARLATTI, ALESSANDRO (2 May 1660, Palermo–22 October 1725, Naples). The most significant composer of *opera seria* of his generation and perhaps the most prolific **opera** composer of all time. The manuscript of his last opera, *La Griselda* (1721), bears the notation "Opus 114," although only something over 60 of Scarlatti's operas have survived. Once reputed to have founded the "Neapolitan" school of opera and to have invented both the **da capo aria**, the **accompagnato**, and the Italian opera **overture**, more recent scholarship has shown the inventions to have preceded him and the native Neapolitans **Leonardo Vinci**, Leonardo Leo (1694–1744), and **Nicola Porpora** to have as good a claim on a specifically Neapolitan brand of opera. Nevertheless, Scarlatti was the dominant composer in **Rome** and **Naples** in the last two decades of the 17th century. As expressed in a letter to his sometime patron the Grand Duke Ferdinando de' Medici, his aims in opera were "naturalness, charm, and, at the same time, expression of the passion with which the characters speak."

Because he was attached at times to the Congregazione dell' Oratorio di San Filippo Neri and churches in Rome, Scarlatti also composed a significant body of sacred music, much of it in *stile antico*. There are 10 extant complete **masses** (including one requiem) and over 70 **motets** and other Latin settings, including two **Magnificats** and a *Stabat Mater*. The 25 extant **oratorios**, mostly commissioned for performance during Lent in Rome, are completely operatic in style.

Scarlatti was also the most prolific and last important composer of Italian chamber **cantatas**, over 600 of them, mostly for soprano voice with simple **continuo** accompaniment.

Alessandro Scarlatti was the second son of Pietro Scarlata and Elenore d'Amato, both musicians in Palermo. In 1672, the family fled a famine in Sicily and went to Rome. Alessandro married Antonia Maria Vittoria Anzaloni on 12 April 1678, and they lived in an apartment in the Bernini palace. Scarlatti appears to have made friends in high places easily: the Duke of Paganica commissioned from him oratorios, the powerful Cardinal Benedetto Pamphili (1653–1730) asked him to set his own poetry, and the exiled Queen Christina of Sweden (1626–1689) appointed him *maestro di cappella*. One of his earliest operas, *Gli Equivoci nel Sembiante* (1679), made his name both in Rome and without.

He composed six operas for various private houses in Rome between 1679 and 1683, but because of Pope Innocent XI's general opposition to opera (he ruled 1676–1689), opportunities were limited to private performances in wealthy households. Scarlatti was persuaded to move to Naples in 1684, where he composed the bulk of his operas, including one to a **libretto** of the Grand Duke of Tuscany Ferdinando de' Medici in 1688, for the royal chapel and the Teatro San Bartolomeo. Sacred works also were occasionally required of him. His son, the future outstanding **keyboard** composer, **Domenico Scarlatti** was born on 26 October 1685. On 1 March 1689, he was appointed *maestro di cappella* at the Conservatorio of Santa Maria di Loreto but was dismissed on 15 July because he overstayed a leave of absence taken in Rome.

In Rome, he became the protégé of Cardinal Pietro Ottoboni (1667–1740). Scarlatti set Ottoboni's libretto *La Statira* in 1690, and the cardinal's influence secured an appointment for the composer on 9 January 1703 as assistant to the elderly *maestro di cappella* Giovanni Bicilli at the Congregazione dell' Oratorio, despite significant opposition owing to Scarlatti's reputation for absenteeism. From 31 December of that year, he became assistant to the *maestro* of the Capella Liberiana at Santa Maria Maggiore.

By 1700, his reputation had spread through much of Italy, with many performances of his operas in Palermo and **Florence** owing to various family connections. Already in 1684, he had been admitted to the Congregazione di Santa Cecilia, along with **Arcangelo Corelli**, and on 26 April 1706, along with Corelli and **Bernardo Pasquini**, to the Arcadian Academy of Rome. Cardinal Ottoboni succeeded in securing for Scarlatti an entrée into the **Venetian opera**, but Scarlatti's efforts there, including *Il Mitridate Eupatore* of 1707, an opera admired by **George Frideric Handel**, were not well received, perhaps owing to the composer's being Sicilian, perhaps owing to the nature of Scarlatti's dramatic art. *Il Mitridate Eupatore* was cast in five acts like the French *tragédie lyrique*, and its uncompromising seriousness evidently did not appeal to Venetian taste.

He returned to Rome in 1707 but discovered that he could not earn as much there as he could from his former positions in Naples. With political stability restored in Naples, Scarlatti secured the support of the new Austrian ambassador to the Holy See, the librettist Vincenzo Grimani (1652–1710), to win back his former position as *maestro* of the royal chapel in 1708. There, he composed his last operas. His obituary in the *Aviso di Napoli* of 30 October 1725 stated that to Scarlatti "music owes so much for the many works with which he enriched it."

Scarlatti's works went out of fashion very quickly after he died and have yet to see a sustained revival despite his stature in the history of opera.

SCARLATTI, DOMENICO (GIUSEPPE) (26 October 1685, Naples–23 July 1757, Madrid). Sixth child of the great **opera** composer **Alessandro Scarlatti** and Antonia Anzaloni, Domenico composed 13 operas of his own from 1703 to 1718, 23 other dramatic works extending to 1728, about 70 chamber **cantatas**, 3 **masses**, 14 Latin **motets**, and 17 *sinfonie*, but his modern reputation rests on the roughly 550 **harpsichord sonatas**, mostly composed later in life in the service of the royal courts of Portugal and Spain. Domenico's first widely circulated publication, the *30 Essercizi* of 1737, impressed **keyboard** players all over the continent with its exploitation of virtuoso keyboard effects such as crossed hands and rapidly repeated tones. Scalatti's harpsichord sonatas (which he called *essercizi*) are composed in a single movement in **binary form**, within which no consistent harmonic pattern occurs, except that the opening and closing **keys** are identical. No small part of their renowned caprice derives from Scarlatti's abandonment of the Baroque principle of motor rhythm. Instead, one hears sudden changes from fast pulses to slow, unprepared **dissonances** undergirded by slow harmonic rhythm, and occasionally even silent pauses in the flow of the music. Rhythmic continuity arises instead from consistent binary phrases, usually two bars, often articulated by Scarlatti's characteristic literal repetitions, often twice, of motivic patterns allied with clear harmonic **functions**. Critics have cited this periodicity as an important source of the classical style rhythm practiced in the second half of the 18th century.

Scarlatti's works were catalogued by the 20th-century harpsichordist Ralph Kirkpatrick (1911–1984). His "K" numbers represent a disputed attempt at chronological order, but they remain the best-known index of Scarlatti's music and replace an earlier numeration, Longo numbers.

Details about Domenico's youth and education from contemporary biographers are obscure. In 1700, Alessandro arranged for Domenico to be specially appointed as *clavicembalista di camera* ("chamber harpsichordist"), in addition to the more regular post of **organist** and composer of the Cappella Reale in **Naples**, indicating perhaps that Domenico's flair for the harpsichord was already evident.

In 1705, Alessandro had Domenico join him in **Rome** and then sent him to **Venice**, but nothing is documented about the son's activities in either place. From Rome comes the famous, if unsupported, story about the keyboard competition between Domenico and **George Frideric Handel** set up by Cardinal Pietro Ottoboni (1667–1740), in which it is said that Domenico recognized Handel's primacy on the organ but that the harpsichord competition ended in a tie. The two admired each other throughout their careers.

Perhaps as early as 1708, Domenico served the exiled Queen Maria Casimira (1641–1716) of Poland in Rome as *maestro di cappella*, and then he succeeded to the same post at the prestigious Cappella Giulia at St. Peter's after the death of Tommaso Baj (c. 1650–1714) on 22 December 1714. He composed his most significant sacred work, including a 10-**voice** *Stabat Mater*, at this time. His operas were occasionally staged at the Teatro Capranica, along with those of his father.

Sometime before 1719, through connections with the Portuguese ambassador in Rome, Domenico was appointed *mestre de capela* to King João V of Portugal (ruled 1706–1750), and he arrived in Lisbon on 29 November 1719, charged with tutoring the king's brother Don Antonio. A more important pupil, however, was the talented Princess Maria Barbara. Scarlatti composed sonatas (*essercizi*) for her and for Don Antonio; it is possible that these represent the first batch of about 550 that he would compose for harpsichord solo. On 19 January 1729, Maria Barbara married Ferdinando (1713–1759), heir to the throne in Spain, and soon Scarlatti followed his royal student, by her father's command, to the Spanish court.

In the meanwhile, Scarlatti may have journeyed to Palermo, Sicily, in December 1722, and to Rome and Naples in 1724 and 1725. He was certainly in Rome in January 1727, when he was ill and granted leave by the Portuguese king for his recovery. His music was performed for the princess's betrothal ceremony on 11 January 1728 in Lisbon, but Scarlatti's presence at the occasion is not confirmed.

On 15 May that year, Scarlatti married Maria Catalina Gentili in Rome. They had six children before she died on 6 May 1739. Scarlatti then married Anastasia Ximenes of Cádiz, who bore him four children.

At the Spanish court, free from the obligations of a *maestro di cappella*, Scarlatti could enjoy a fairly quiet and leisurely life of teaching and performing for and with the royal family, free to compose his harpsichord sonatas. When Ferdinando acceded to the Spanish throne in 1746, their resident singer **Farinelli** convinced them to establish a court opera, but Scarlatti was not asked to compose for it and left instead during the 1750s to copy systematically his collected sonatas. The manuscripts indicate that he composed them to the very last days of his life.

SCHEIDEMANN, HEINRICH (c. 1595, Wöhrden, Holstein, Germany–26 September 1663, Hamburg). Pupil of **Jan Pieterszoon Sweelinck** and colleague of **Thomas Selle** and **Matthias Weckmann**, Scheidemann became an esteemed figure in the early north German **organ** school. No other contemporary is better represented in the sources. He made a particular specialty of **chorale** arrangements, of which 24 to 30 survive, and organ settings of the **Magnificat** in the eight traditional church **modes**. Also surviving are 12 **preludes**, 2 **canzonas**, a **fugue**, and 2 **toccatas** for organ. For **harpsichord** are 12 **courantes**, 5 **allemandes**, and other **dance** movements with **variations**. He also composed 34 sacred songs with simple accompaniment.

Heinrich Scheidemann's father, David, also an organist, moved the family to **Hamburg** by 1604. Heinrich went off to Amsterdam from November 1611 to November 1614 to study organ with Sweelinck. He is next documented assuming his father's post as organist at Catharinenkirche in Hamburg by 1629 (from 1625 according to one source). He remained there until he died of plague in 1663. *See also* CHORALE FANTASIA.

SCHEIDT, SAMUEL (baptized 3 November 1587, Halle, Germany–24 March 1654, Halle). After studying with **Jan Pieterszoon Sweelinck** in Amsterdam, he returned to Halle in 1609 as court **organist** to the Margrave Christian Wilhelm, rising to *Kapellmeister* in late 1619 or early 1620. Scheidt suffered unemployment and other professional misfortune during the Thirty Years War but remained in Halle and resumed his official duties as *Kapellmeister* in 1638 for Duke August of Saxony. His most famous work is the three-volume collection of 57 **chorale preludes, fugues, canons**, and other organ pieces in *Tabulatura Nova* of 1624. He harmonized 100 **chorales** in four **voices** in the *Görlitzer Tabulatur-Buch* of 1650. He also composed 176 **sacred concertos** published in four volumes (1631, 1634, 1635, 1640) and over 80 other sacred vocal works, mostly in the Italian concerted style with **continuo**.

His secular works, of which but a fraction survives, includes some 70 **dances** scored for **strings** and 50 "**symphonies**" for three voices, probably intended as interludes or introductions to his sacred concertos. *See also* CHORALE CONCERTO; CHORALE FANTASIA.

SCHEIN, JOHANN HERMANN (20 January 1586, Grünhain near Annaberg, Germany–19 November 1630, Leipzig). He was appointed *Kapellmeister* for the court of Duke Johann Ernst the Younger (1594–1626) at Weimar beginning 21 May 1615, then summoned to try out to be cantor at the Thomaskirche in **Leipzig** on 21 May 1615. He was accepted, preceding **Johann Sebastian Bach** by a century, and finished his life there.

Schein's secular music includes an important collection of instrumental music, the *Banchetto Musicale* ("Musical Banquet," 1617) containing 20 **suites**; the first published collection of **continuo madrigals** in German, the pastoral *Hirten Lust* ("Shepherds' Joy," 1624); and three other collections of **polyphonic** songs (*Venus Kräntzlein*, 1609; *Musica boscareccia*, three volumes, 1621, 1626, 1628; and *Studenten-Schmauss*, 1626).

His sacred compositions include *Cymbalum Sioniae* (1615), a collection of 30 Latin and German **motets**; *Opella Nova*, the first large publication of German **sacred concertos** with **continuo** (Part I, 1618, 31 works; Part II, 1626, 28 works); *Fontana Israel* (1623), 30 *madrigali spirituali*; and 130 **chorale** arrangements in *Cantional oder Gesangbuch Augspurgischer Confession* (1627). *See also* CHORALE CONCERTO.

SCHÜTZ, HEINRICH (baptized 9 October 1585, Köstritz [now Bad Köstritz], Germany–6 November 1672, Dresden). Recognized by 1690 as the greatest German composer of the 17th century, his talent was spotted by the Landgrave Moritz of Hesse-Kassel (1572–1632), who took over Schütz's education in 1599 and sent him to **Venice** to study with **Giovanni Gabrieli** from 1609 to 1612. In 1615, he joined the court of the Elector of Saxony Johann Georg (1585–1656) in **Dresden** and remained there for the rest of his life, except for another trip to Venice from 1627 to 1629 to study with **Claudio Monteverdi** and a sojourn with the Crown Prince Christian (1577–1648) of Denmark from 1633 to 1635 to avoid the disastrous effects of the Thirty Years War.

Schütz's surviving secular works include only his Opus 1, a collection of 19 Italian **madrigals** (published 1611) composed while studying with Gabrieli, and a strophic song, but he did compose at least one **opera**, *Dafne* (1627, lost), and other smaller dramatic works.

Schütz's sacred music commands all the various idioms that were available to composers in the first half of the 17th century, although he rarely used **chorales**. His major publications fall into four categories (the SWV *Schützwerkeverzeichnis* catalog numbers generally follow his publications and so give a rough chronological order).

Simple arrangements of psalm paraphrases by Cornelius Becker (1561–1604) appeared as *Psalmen Davids* (1628, 90 works; 1661, enlarged, 159 works). **Motets** that approximate the *stile antico* in **texture** but are filled with **chromaticisms** and other expressive syntax from Italian madrigals were published as *Cantiones Sacrae* (1625, four voices and **continuo**, 41 works) and *Geistliche Chormusik* (1648, five **voices** and continuo, 29 works). Small-scale **sacred concertos** for solo voices and instruments were published as *Symphoniae Sacrae* (Part 1, 1629, 20 works; Part 2, 1647, 27 works) and *Kleine Geistliche Conzerte* (Part 1, 1636, 24 works; Part 2, 1639, 32 works). Large-scale sacred concertos employing solo voices, instruments, and *cori spezzati* (Lat. "split choirs") on the Venetian model of Gabrieli appeared in *Psalmen Davids* (1619, 26 works) and *Symphonie Sacrae* (Part 3, 1650, 21 works).

Schütz also composed a funeral service, the *Musicalische Exequien* (1636), three **passions** on Gospels from St. Matthew, St. Luke, and St. John (all 1666), and three **oratorios**: on the resurrection (*Historia Auferstehung*, 1623), the Seven Last Words (c. 1650), and the **Christmas Oratorio** (1660).

SCORDATURA **(It. "untuned").** The term refers to a variant **tuning**, usually of the **violin**, whereby the **strings** are not tuned in perfect fifths but with other intervals to facilitate playing in particular **keys**. *See also* ROSARY SONATAS.

SECCO **RECITATIVE** (or *recitativo secco*, It. "dry recitative"). Type of **recitative** common in *opera seria* and other dramatic genres of the later Baroque. The musical **texture** consists of a singer accompanied by harmonic progressions from the basso **continuo**, often only a **harpsichord**. The function of this recitative is to provide factual information to advance the plot, and the music is of little intrinsic interest. Later, Baroque **opera** composers sometimes assigned the composition of recitatives to their students.

SECONDA PRATICA (It. "second practice"). Refers to a musical aesthetic that prizes expression of the text, even at the price of strident **dissonant** harmonies, over syntactic purity, that is, strictly controlled **dissonances** in a largely **consonant texture**. The expression appears in 1607 in the famous response of **Claudio Monteverdi** to criticisms of Giovanni Maria Artusi about his **madrigals**.

SELLE, THOMAS (23 March 1599, Zörbig near Bitterfeld, Germany–2 July 1663, Hamburg). Educated at **Leipzig**, he made his career as cantor at various churches in northwest Germany, from 12 August 1641 at the Johanneum in **Hamburg**. Although he published seven collections of songs and light secular works, he is remembered for his sacred music. His own compilation comprises 281 sacred settings of Latin and German texts. His St. John **Passion** (1641, rev. 1643) is the first passion to use instrumental interludes.

In Hamburg, Selle worked with **Matthias Weckmann** and **Heinrich Scheidemann**. Both he and Scheidemann were victims of the 1663 plague.

SEMI-OPERA. Modern term for English spoken plays integrated with instrumental pieces and songs. During the Baroque, they were called "dramatick **operas**" and were the chief form of musical theater after the Restoration (1660) and before the introduction of Italian opera in 1705. Instrumental music called the "first" and "second music" precedes the opening curtain, which reveals a prologue to the play, sometimes including singing and **dancing**. This is often followed by an **overture**. Songs may be performed between the acts, or within them, but only by minor characters.

SEPOLCRO. Form of music drama developed at the imperial court in **Vienna**. The earliest known example is *Santi Risorti* ("Risen Saints," 1643) of Giovanni Valentini (c. 1582–1649). Thereafter, the tradition slowly fused with the Italian **oratorio** tradition, brought by the resident Italian composers of the imperial court, such as **Antonio Draghi** and **Antonio Caldara**.

The **librettos** always treated themes of Christ's **passion**, and the completed *sepolcro* was performed on Holy Thursday or Good Friday in a single act with scenery depicting the tomb of Christ. Singers, in full costume, often performed penitential acts, such as carrying a cross.

SEQUENCE. A melodic or harmonic pattern repeated while being transposed at a consistent interval upward or downward.

Example. George Frideric Handel, *Messiah*, "O thou that tellest," mm. 43–48

If the interval of transposition and all intervals within the pattern are precisely replicated, the sequence is called "**chromatic**" and will cause a change of **key** with each repetition. This type is rare in Baroque music. Much more common is the tonal sequence, whereby the interval of transposition and intervals within the pattern are consistent only in their numerical parts (e.g., transposition by thirds, whether major or minor) to keep the music within a single key. Baroque composers, however, may partially chromaticize the patterns to create lower-level "keys" within a high-level single key, as the example shows.

Sequences that transpose the pattern upward in pitch are called "ascending sequences"; those that transpose the interval downward are called "descending sequences."

If only a single prominent melody is consistently transposed, it is a melodic sequence. If only the harmonic pattern is transposed, it is a harmonic sequence. If both are consistently transposed, very common, it is a melodic/harmonic sequence.

SERENATA. A form of musical drama that first appeared in Italy and **Vienna** about 1660, remained popular until about 1800, and, like other genres descending from **opera**, consisted of a succession of **arias**, **recitatives**, and occasional **choruses**. The serenata was usually performed outdoors, by night, with artificial illumination, often sponsored by a noble patron or learned society to mark some important event: a birth or birthday, wedding, military victory, peace treaty, or other civic celebration. The music consisted of about a dozen arias separated by recitatives, divided into two short acts, accompanied not by **continuo** as in a **cantata** but by an **orchestra**, sometimes ostentatiously large. Scenery and machines were deployed in the public performance space. Costumed singers were often personifications of virtues, vices, or elements, as in early **oratorios** or in the prologues of early Italian operas. Thus, there was little plot; the appearance of the event being celebrated formed the climax of a typical **libretto**.

The serenata influenced similar entertainments in other parts of Europe, except France. In England, it merged with the court **ode** by the beginning of the 18th century, about the same time that "secular" cantatas celebrating civic events appeared in Germany. Important early composers of the serenata include **Antonio Cesti** and **Alessandro Stradella**. Librettos, being topical, could not be used again, with the exception of some by the great opera librettist **Metastasio**, who wrote rather generic serenatas that could be set by different composers for different occasions.

SERVICE. Anglican term referring to musical settings for one or more of the following liturgies: Morning Prayer (matins); Evening Prayer (evensong); Holy Communion; the Burial Service. The elements of each service are united by their **mode** or **key** and by their manner of composition: a complete setting of the liturgy was called a "full service"; one employing simple **homophonic textures**, a short service; one composed with elaborate **contrapuntal** textures, a great service; and one that exploited soloists, a verse service. Such compositions came from the pens of Baroque English composers such as **Thomas Tomkins**, **Thomas Weelkes**, **Orlando Gibbons**, **John Blow**, **William Croft**, and **Maurice Greene**, all connected with the **Chapel Royal**.

SICILIANA. A **dance** type sometimes found in Baroque instrumental **suites** and **arias** of Baroque **operas**. The relation between these is not clear, but both are characterized by compound **meters** of 6/8 or 12/8 and long-short patterns of durations in a stately **tempo**. Sicilianas were associated with pastoral scenes, prominent examples being the *pastorale ad libitum* final movement of the **Christmas Concerto** of **Arcangelo Corelli** and the Pifa or "Pastoral Symphony" (No. 13) and the aria "He shall feed his flock" (No. 20), both from *Messiah* of **George Frideric Handel**.

SINFONIA. In the 17th century, *sinfonia* could refer to an instrumental composition of almost any type. The word derives from the Greek *syn* and *phone*, meaning "sounding together." In an independent collection, it could denote chamber music for one instrument with accompaniment or several instruments, a usage therefore indistinguishable from the **sonata** or **trio sonata**. Music theorist and composer Adriano Banchieri (1568–1634) noted that his *Sinfonie ecclesiastiche* (1607) might also be called **canzonas**.

It might also denote the first piece in a **suite** or collection of **keyboard** movements. The title of **Johann Sebastian Bach**'s so-called three-part **inventions** is *Sinfonie*.

In the context of **operas** or **oratorios**, the *sinfonia* is almost always a single, independent instrumental movement designed to suspend the action for a moment of reflection, as in the *sinfonia* after the messenger's announcement in **Claudio Monteverdi**'s *L'Orfeo*, to cover a change of scenery, to set a scene musically, as in the opening pastoral movement in the second part of Johann Sebastian Bach's **Christmas Oratorio**, or to indicate the passage of time or symbolize an event not expressed directly by the **libretto**, as in **George Frideric Handel**'s *Saul*, where **symphonies** (Handel uses the English equivalent) paint the battle scenes and the funeral procession. In the 18th century, *sinfonia* referred more and more consistently to the introductory music to an opera (**overture**).

SINGSPIEL (Ger. "singing play," pl. *Singspiele*). A musical drama setting a **libretto** in the German language. In most *Singspiele*, the **arias** or songs are separated by spoken dialogue rather than **recitative**. *See also* KEISER, REINHARD.

SOLO CONCERTO. A **concerto** for **orchestra** and a single soloist. In the Baroque, the favorite solo instrument by far was the **violin**, and many preeminent composers of concertos were all fine violinists: **Arcangelo Corelli**, **Giuseppe Torelli**, **Tomaso Albinoni**, **Antonio Vivaldi**, **Pietro Locatelli**, **Giuseppe Tartini**, **Jean-Marie Leclair**, **George Frideric Handel**, and **Johann Sebastian Bach**, among many others. Later in the period, composers increasingly wrote concertos for other instruments, especially **harpsichord**, **oboe**, and **flute**. Handel's most famous contribution to the genre are his concertos for pipe **organ** (manuals only), which he performed during the intermissions of his **operas** and **English oratorios**.

SOLO SONATA. A **sonata** for a single melodic instrument, such as **violin** or **flute**, and basso **continuo**. Less frequently, a sonata for a **keyboard** instrument, such as **harpsichord, organ, clavichord,** or **fortepiano**.

The solo sonata is fundamentally a two-**voiced texture**: the melodic line for the featured instrument and the bass line of the continuo. If the bass melody is to be brought out properly, a violoncellist or **bassoonist** should be included in the continuo, and so, the solo sonata actually requires three players. However, in modern performances, the keyboard player often covers the bass melody without other support.

In the solo sonata, the internal harmonies are **improvised** by the keyboard, **lute**, or **guitar** player from the **figured bass** given in the continuo part. The solo sonatas of **Johann Sebastian Bach** are exceptional: he supplies a completely written out *obbligato* harpsichord part, without figured bass, so that the resulting texture is three-voiced **counterpoint**: featured instrument, right hand of the keyboard, bass line.

SONATA (from It. *suonata*, "played"). The term is commonly understood today to refer to a composition for solo **keyboard**, usually **harpsichord** or **fortepiano** (e.g., "harpsichord sonata"), or for a small number of melodic instruments with keyboard accompaniment (e.g., "sonata for **violin** and harpsichord"). Either composition would have three or four movements of contrasting **tempo**. "Sonata," however, only attained a meaning even this precise toward the end of the Baroque. Not until 1732 could **Johann Gottfried Walther** write in his *Musikalisches Lexikon* that "the sonata is a piece for instruments, especially the violin, of a serious and artful nature, in which adagios and allegros alternate."

Because the turn of the 17th century saw such an explosion of experiments in composition for instruments, there was no such international standardization of terms. In Italy, origin of most of the earliest sonatas until about 1650, "sonata" was used to describe a new instrumental work no more frequently than was **canzona**, *sinfonia*, and **concerto**, and **capriccio, fantasia, ricercar,** and **toccata** might also denote pieces the music of which is indistinguishable from other pieces called "sonata." "Sonata" itself had various denotations. It could be in the title of an instrumental collection, such as Giovanni Battista Buonamente's (d. 1642) *Quinto Libro de Varie Sonate* of 1629, of which none of the individual works is called "sonata." Or it might refer to a borrowed **ostinato** melody, as in the "Sonata sopra Sancta Maria" from **Claudio Monteverdi**'s **Vespers of 1610**, even when it is sung, as in this case, thus defying the usual defining contrast of sonata with the genre of **cantata** (It. "sung").

In the early Baroque, two types of sonata might be distinguished. The older type derived from instrumental transcriptions of 16th-century French *chansons* and were often appropriately called "canzonas." The canzonas of the *Symphoniae Sacrae* of **Giovanni Gabrieli** have the **texture** of Renaissance **motets**, even though conceived for instruments, often organized into contrasting groups, after the *cori spezzati* tradition of San Marco in **Venice**. This type of sonata declined after 1620. The newer type sprang from the experiments in new **monodic** textures and **opera**, as in the publications of **Dario Castello** of 1621 and 1629. These works link traditional passages of **dance** rhythms and brief **fugal** expositions with rhapsodical instrumental **recitatives** in which the **meter** virtually disappears, all bound into a single uninterrupted movement, a tiny abstract opera.

This type of sonata itself breaks into two later types. The single movement with contrasting subsections continues into the 18th century in the works of Marco Uccellini (c. 1603–1680), **Giovanni Battista Vitali**, **Dietrich Buxtehude**, Johann Gottfried Walther, and many others. As late as 1703, Sébastien de Brossard (1655–1730), in his *Dictionnaire de Musique*, notes its origin in dramatic music—"to all sorts of instruments what the cantata is to the voice"—and its free form—"according to the composer's fancy." The second type, favored in **Rome** and made famous by **Arcangelo Corelli**, has several self-contained movements of contrasting tempo, including **preludes** and dance movements. This is the tradition, found in the late Baroque sonatas of **Antonio Vivaldi**, **Tomaso Albinoni**, **Benedetto Marcello**, **Pietro Locatelli**, **Francesco Geminiani**, **Georg Philipp Telemann**, **Johann Sebastian Bach**, and **George Frideric Handel**, most commonly brought to mind by "Baroque sonata."

Three common classifications of sonata are the **solo sonata** for one melodic instrument and keyboard accompaniment. The solo instrument, especially in 17th-century sonatas, is most commonly the violin, but sonatas for **oboe**, **flute** (both **transverse** and **recorder**), and violoncello were other popular choices. The **trio sonata** requires two high-pitched instruments, again usually violins, and **continuo** accompaniment. The ensemble sonata may require any number of instruments together, usually with continuo. Some title pages of sonatas indicate that they might be performed with alternative instruments. Handel's sonatas for recorder, for example, may be performed by transverse flute, oboe, or violin instead.

Sonatas along with cantatas were the preeminent form of chamber music in the Baroque, and another classification purports to describe their use. The *sonata da chiesa*, often of four movements, **contrapuntal** in texture, in slow-fast-slow-fast order, was thought appropriate for Catholic liturgies, where they might replace **organ** solos or accompany the Elevation of the Eucharist. The *sonata da camera*, on the other hand, was characterized by dance movements. This distinction, however, mostly disappears from contemporary sources by the 18th century and is inconsistent even in the 17th.

Last to attain normative status was the solo keyboard sonata. **Domenico Scarlatti** composed about 550 of these, which he called *essercizi*, almost all in one movement in **binary form**. *See also* DURANTE, FRANCESCO.

SONATA DA CAMERA. *See* SONATA.

SONATA DA CHIESA. *See* SONATA.

SPINET. A smaller kind of **harpsichord**, the spinet was developed in Germany and Italy at the turn of the 17th century and, by that century's end, replaced the **virginal** as the chief household **keyboard** instrument.

Like the harpsichord, the spinet produces tones when the player depresses a key that is really a lever and causes a *jack* equipped with a *plectrum* to rise and pluck a string under tension. It differs, in modern terminology, in that the stringing is at an oblique angle to the keyboard, running left to right. Larger spinets, called "bentsides," often have a wing shape to accommodate the longer strings. There is no direct relation to the modern small upright piano marketed in the 1930s as a "spinet."

During the Baroque, spinets could be used as practice or composing instruments and to play harpsichord music of limited pitch range.

SPLIT CHOIR. *See* CORI SPEZZATI.

STANLEY, JOHN (17 January 1712, London–19 May 1786, London). Blind from age two, under the tutelage of **Maurice Greene** at St. Paul's Cathedral, Stanley became an outstanding **violinist** and **organist**, eventually becoming an important figure in English public music. By 1724, he was already organist at All Hallows Bread Street Church near St. Paul's and then, in 1726, at St. Andrew's in Holborne. During the 1720s and 1730s, he composed his 30 **keyboard voluntaries**, the music for which he is best known today. In 1738, he married Sarah Arlond, who brought him a dowry of 7,000 pounds. After 1750, he began to direct the **English oratorios** of **George Frideric Handel** and, after Handel's death in 1759, took on the Lenten programs at Covent Garden, contributing three **oratorios** of his own. He also composed a **masque**, an **opera**, a pastoral, at least 16 court **odes**, 15 **cantatas**, 9 **anthems**,

6 **concertos** for seven instruments, 6 concertos for **harpsichord** solo, and 14 **sonatas** for **flute** and violin.

STEFFANI, AGOSTINO (25 July 1654, Castelfranco Veneto, Italy–12 February 1728, Frankfurt). A composer who, as diplomat, helped to secure the elevation of the city of Hanover to electorate status and, as churchman after his ordination in 1680, rose to the rank of apostolic vicar for northern Germany and also left a legacy of about 14 **operas**, 3 lighter stage works, 10 psalm settings, a *Stabat Mater* (his greatest work in his own estimation), a few instrumental works, and about 75 chamber **cantatas** for two **voices**, almost all composed before 1702, the music for which he was most famous in his time.

Steffani's musical career began as a soprano at the church of Il Santo in Padua, and he sang in a Carnival opera of **Venice**, probably Carlo Pallavicino's (c. 1640–1688) *Demetrio* in 1666. The Elector Ferdinand Maria (1636–1679) of Bavaria took him to Munich, where he studied with **Johann Caspar Kerll**. He visited **Rome** in 1672 for more education and had his first sacred music published. In July 1674, he was appointed court **organist** in Munich. In 1678 and 1679, he visited **Paris** and heard a *tragédie lyrique* of **Jean-Baptiste Lully**, and in January 1681, his first opera, *Marco Aurelio*, was mounted in Munich.

He made his first contact with Hanover on a diplomatic mission and was appointed *Kapellmeister* by Duke Ernst August (1629–1698) in summer 1688. In the 1690s, Steffani was occupied increasingly by diplomatic work concerning the status of Hanover and the War of the Spanish Succession. In 1703, he entered the service of Elector Palatine Johann Wilhelm (1658–1716), in Düsseldorf, and thereafter composed very little music. He continued to take an interest, however, and was even elected president of **London**'s **Academy of Ancient Music** on 1 June 1727.

***STILE ANTICO* (It. "ancient style").** Term used in Italian Baroque theory and criticism to designate the style of high-Renaissance **polyphony**, or "classical polyphony," as epitomized in the music of **Giovanni da Palestrina**. It was opposed to the *stile moderno*, which referred to the new **textures** and musical syntax appearing in secular genres, particularly **opera**. *See also PRIMA PRATICA.*

***STILE MODERNO* (It. "modern style").** Term used in Italian Baroque theory and criticism to designate the musical **textures** and syntax arising at the turn of the 17th century relating to **opera**. The *stile moderno* was contrasted with the 16th-century *stile antico*. *See also SECONDA PRATICA.*

ST. JOHN PASSION (Johann Sebastian Bach, BWV 245, 1724). Scored for four-**voice choir**, vocal soloists, and an **orchestra** of **strings** and **continuo** with obbligato instruments: two **flutes**, two **oboes**, two **oboes da caccia**, **oboe d'amore**, **lute**, two **violas d'amore**, and viola da gamba (the precise scoring of each number is not clear because no score survives from the earliest version). The 67 numbered movements are divided into Parts I and II, and require about an hour and 45 minutes to perform. The work is universally recognized as one of the great exemplars of the **passion** tradition.

Johann Sebastian Bach first performed this passion at vespers on Good Friday, 7 April 1724, at the Nikolaikirche, **Leipzig**. The **libretto** of this version contains chapters 18 and 19 of St. John's Gospel, two interpolations from St. Matthew, which describe Peter's remorse and the miraculous events following Christ's death, and poetic commentary drawn from various sources, including a famous libretto of Barthold Heinrich Brockes (1680–1747). Bach sets these various texts to five kinds of music: **recitative** for the Gospel, except where speeches by the Apostles or the crowd require a "**madrigal**" **chorus**; **arioso** for the poetry immediately reacting to the Gospel passages, followed immediately by an **aria** for sustained reflective commentary; and simple, four-voice **chorale** settings for poems that express a more collective response.

Bach performed the St. John Passion again in 1725, 1732, and 1749, altering the work each time, adding or substituting new movements and changing texts. *See also* ST. MATTHEW PASSION.

ST. MATTHEW PASSION (Johann Sebastian Bach, BWV 244, 1727). Scored for double four-**voice choir**, vocal soloists, and a double **orchestra** of **strings** and **continuo** with obbligato instruments: two **transverse flutes**, two **oboes**, two **oboes d'amore**, two **oboes da caccia**, and viola da gamba. The 78 separate numbers are divided into Parts I and II and require over two and one-half hours to perform. **Johann Sebastian Bach**'s own family members referred to the work as "the great **passion**." Felix Mendelssohn believed it to be "the greatest of all Christian works," and most critics consider it the greatest exemplar of the passion tradition.

The **libretto** presents two kinds of text: the Gospel narrative from chapters 26 through 27 of St. Matthew's Gospel and poetic commentary by Picander (pen name of Christian Friedrich Henrici, 1700–1764). Bach sets these to five kinds of music: **recitative** for the Gospel, except where speeches by the Apostles or the crowd require a "**madrigal**" **chorus**; **arioso** for the poetry immediately reacting to the Gospel passages; followed immediately by an **aria** for sustained reflective commentary; and simple, four-voice **chorale** settings for poems that express a more collective response. Thus, the passion story is punctuated by spiritual reflection expressed through poetry and music of great variety at every episode. The entire action is framed by three massive choral numbers at the very beginning, at the end of Part I, and at the end of Part II, which bring the level of exegesis to that of Christ's sacrifice considered *in toto*.

Evidence suggests that Bach first performed the St. Matthew Passion as part of a Good Friday vespers on 11 April 1727, Parts I and II surrounding a sermon. He revised the entire score in 1736, and this is the version almost always performed today. The work was entirely neglected after Bach's death until Mendelssohn's revival in Berlin on 11 March 1829. Most of the arias were left out, but this performance, nevertheless, ignited the explosive Bach revival of the mid-19th century. *See also* EARLY MUSIC REVIVAL; ST. JOHN PASSION.

STRADELLA, ALESSANDRO (3 April 1639, Nepi near Viterbo, Italy–25 February 1682, Genoa). Before his murder in Genoa at age 42 for unknown reasons—rumors implicate a jealous rival—Stradella's vocal music was in constant demand by patrons in **Venice**, **Rome**, Modena, and Genoa. There survive 309 authenticated compositions, including about 27 **operas**, **serenatas**, and other works for stage, 7 **oratorios**, 8 **madrigals**, 36 **arias**, 13 vocal duets, a trio, and 174 **cantatas** (123 for solo voice and **continuo**). His 1669 opera *Il Trespolo Tutore* for Genoa is an early example of *opera buffa*. He composed 26 **sonatas** *da chiesa* and a single set of **variations**. His sacred music includes a Marian antiphon and 14 **motets**.

Stradella lived in Rome as a youth, certainly from 1653 to 1660. After the premiere of an oratorio on 11 March 1667, he received commissions from the Venetian Michiel Polo and the Roman family Pamphili. By the mid-1670s, he was composing for the exiled Queen Christina of Sweden (1626–1689). Threatened by imprisonment for dubious dealings as a marriage broker, Stradella went to Venice in February 1677. There, he became the tutor to the mistress of Venetian noblemen Alvise Contarini (1601–1684), Agnese Van Uffele, with whom he ran off to Turin in June. Contarini eventually forced Stradella to marry her, but after he signed the contract, he was nearly killed by assailants. Nothing more is known of Uffele. Stradella went to Genoa in early 1678 and was appointed to lead the opera **orchestra** and prepare the female singers. Commissions continued to arrive, and he composed operas and oratorios feverishly in these years.

STRICT IMITATION. Type of **imitation** by which the melodic intervals of the **subject**'s entrances subsequent to the first entrance are preserved so that the copy is true. Traditionally, only the numerical part of the interval is judged: the melodic interval from the tonic to the third degree in a minor **key** counts as identical to the interval from the tonic to the third degree in a major key, even though the first interval is a minor third and the second a major third.

STRING BASS. *See* VIOLONE.

STRING INSTRUMENTS. Instruments producing tones by vibrating and amplifying strings fall into two large groups during the Baroque: plucked instruments and bowed instruments.

The plucked instruments include the **lute, archlute, theorbo, guitar, mandolin,** vihuela, and **harp**.

The names of the bowed string instruments derive from the Italian word "*viola*," which denotes two broad classes of bowed instruments used widely in Baroque music. The class more familiar to modern audiences has no frets on the fingerboards, and the smaller members may be played *da braccio* (It. "by the arm"), that is, resting on the chest or shoulder of the player and held up by the arm.

Italian term	Translation	Modern term
viola	—	viola
violino	It. "little viola"	violin
violone	It. "big viola"	string bass, double bass
violoncello	It. "smaller big viola"	cello

The less familiar *da gamba* instruments (It. "by the leg") are all held between the knees and bowed with an underhand grip. Today these are called "**viols**" in English.

STROPHIC ARIA. An **aria** setting a strophic poem, of which the music for each strophe is identical. Sometimes the strophes are separated by instrumental ritornellos. Before the development of larger and more musically integrated aria forms, such as the **da capo aria**, the strophic aria was the predominant form in early Baroque **operas**. *See also* CAVALLI, FRANCESCO; VENETIAN OPERA.

STROZZI, BARBARA (6 August 1619, Venice–11 November 1677, Padua). A remarkable case of a 17th-century woman surviving, unmarried, apparently on the patronage deriving from her musical performances and publications. Barbara Strozzi was the adopted, possibly illegitimate, daughter of the poet Giulio Strozzi (1584–1652), whose own birth required legitimization. Although not an aristocrat, Giulio moved in academic and aristocratic circles and introduced his talented daughter to meetings of the Accademia degli Unisoni of **Venice**, where she performed. Barbara published a book of **madrigals** in 1644, and then, after her father's death, five volumes of **cantatas** and **arias**, one volume of sacred music, and a single **motet**. The dedicatees of these volumes, indicating possible patronage, include the Emperor Ferdinand II of Austria (1578–1637), Archduchess Maria of Innsbruck (1584–1649), and a future doge of Venice. She had four children, at least three of whom took religious orders.

STYLUS PHANTASTICUS **(Lat. "fantastic style").** Generic term for instrumental genres, such as the **toccata**, having an **improvisatory** character.

SUBJECT. The melody of an **imitative texture**, overlapped with itself.

SUITE. A collection of instrumental **dances** of varying types composed in the same **key** and often in **binary form**. Baroque composers wrote suites for **keyboard**, **lute**, **guitar**, small instrumental ensembles, and **orchestras** throughout the period. Suites take their place with **sonatas**, **concertos**, **preludes**, and **fugues** as one of the preeminent Baroque instrumental genres. Famous examples include the **Partitas** for Solo **Violin** (BWV 1002, 1004, 1006) of **Johann Sebastian Bach**, as well as his "English" Suites (BWV 806–811), his "French" Suites (BWV 812–817), the *Clavier-Übung*, Part I (BWV 825–830), the suites for solo violoncello (BWV 1007–1012), and the four *Ouverturen* for orchestra (BWV 1066–1069), the **Water Music** of **George Frideric Handel**, the Terpsichore dances of **Michael Praetorius**, and most of the **harpsichord** music of **Johann Jokob Froberger, Nicolas Lebègue, Jean Henry D'Anglebert, François Couperin**, and **Jean-Philippe Rameau**.

Suites may be classified by their performance medium—harpsichord suites, lute suites, orchestra suites (often called *ouvertures* when they begin with a **French overture**)—or by the kinds of dances included in them. The "standard" or "classical" suite composed before 1650 contained an **allemande**, a **courante**, and a **sarabande**; after 1650, a **gigue** became the fourth traditional dance. Other kinds of dances—**gavotte, bourrée, minuet, loure**, and so forth—might be added to these *ad libitum*, and the whole is often preceded by a prelude, in strict **meter** or **unmeasured**. This "classical" suite enjoys a historiographical preeminence probably owing to the prestige of the suites of J. S. Bach, but the Baroque is filled with other suites not conforming to this pattern, such as Handel's Water Music. The great French *clavecinistes* of the late 17th and early 18th centuries often gave their dance movements referential titles, such as the sarabande "La Majestueuse" (Fr. "the majestic woman") in François Couperin's first suite, and omitted the name of the dance type, even though the rhythmic character clearly identifies the movement as a gavotte or sarabande.

The tradition of grouping different types of dances together comes directly from Renaissance practices and, in the Baroque, appears early in the 17th century in all countries. The international popularity of dances is easily seen in the *Terpsichore* dances of Michael Praetorius, a German, of 1612, who wrote in his preface that most of the 400 melodies that he harmonized in the collection were given him by a Frenchman, Antoine Emeraud, who was dancing-master to the Duke of Brunswick. Another important early collection is **Johann Hermann Schein**'s *Banchetto Musicale* (The musical banquet, 1617), 20 suites each containing a **pavan, galliard**, courante, allemande, and *triplum*. In France, most suites before 1650 were lute suites, but harpsichord suites exploded into prominence after 1650, and most French harpsichord music for the next 75 years would be composed in the form of suites.

Ensemble suites, which functioned as a type of chamber music, can be found in the 17th-century Italian *sonata da camera*, which, while not called "suite," is a collection of dance movements organized by **tonality**. In France, ensemble suites were easily constructed by anthologizing the music of **Jean-Baptiste Lully**, who wrote virtually no suites per se but had composed hundreds of dances for his *ballets de cour* and *tragédies lyriques*. Other ensemble suites were composed explicitly for **consorts** of **viols** by Jean de Sainte-Colombe (died before 1701), **Marin Marais**, and François Couperin in his *Pièces de Violes avec la Basse Chifrée* (1728). Couperin also composed ensemble suites entitled *Les Nations* (1726).

In Germany, **Georg Philip Telemann** and J. S. Bach were among those who composed *ouvertures* for orchestra, French overtures that are often three or four times as long as any of the dance movements that follow. These suites were intended for semipublic performance and were of the "nonclassical" type containing an unpredictable assortment and order of dance movements. Handel's Water Music and Music for the Royal Fireworks (1749) are other famous examples.

SWEELINCK, JAN PIETERSZOON (May 1562, Deventer, Netherlands–16 October 1621, Amsterdam). He lived almost all his life in Amsterdam and was **organist** at the Oude Kerk certainly from 1580 (possibly earlier) until his death. Famous as a teacher, indeed known as "the maker of organists" in north Germany, his students included **Samuel Scheidt**, **Heinrich Scheidemann**, and others who formed the so-called north German organ school. Although vocal music predominates in his oeuvre, including 37 **motets** published as *Cantiones Sacrae* (1619) and 153 **psalms**, Sweelinck influences the Baroque mostly through his **keyboard** works, including 32 **fantasias** and **toccatas** and 12 **chorale** settings. The fantasias, in particular, constructed on a single theme often treated in **diminution** and **augmentation** and interspersed with **fugal** episodes, are considered to be an important step in the development of the monothematic fugue predominant in the high Baroque.

SYMPHONY. (1) English equivalent for *sinfonia*. (2) An instrumental composition for **orchestra**, usually in several sections or self-standing movements, often intended for public performance. Coming to prominence in the classical period (after 1750), the symphony originated in the late Baroque, when **opera overtures** and other self-contained instrumental movements began to be performed independently. The opera overtures of **Alessandro Scarlatti**, often in three sections, and **Johann Adolf Hasse** are thought to have directly influenced the multi-movement classical form. Giovanni Battista Sammartini's (c. 1700–1775) 20 symphonies composed before 1740 have three movements.

SYNTAGMA MUSICUM **(Michael Praetorius).** Voluminous work of music theory by a leading composer, **Michael Praetorius**, valuable for its comprehensive documentation of the state of the art of music at the beginning of the Baroque in Germany.

Volume I: *Musicae Artis Analecta* (1614–1615)—a discussion of liturgical music, replete with quotations from many sources, including Martin Luther's (1483–1546) chief musical advisor, Johann Walther (1495–1570).

Volume II: *De Organographia* and *Theatrum Instrumentorum* (1618)—an illustrated encyclopedia of musical instruments. Its thorough technical description of the **organ** was the model for Baroque organ construction in the early 20th century, *Orgelbewegeung*, part of the **early music revival**.

Volume III: *Termini Musici* (1618)—a dictionary of musical terms and concepts, including notation, transposition, polychoral writing, and early basso **continuo**.

A fourth volume, never completed, was to have covered musical composition.

TABLATURE (It. *intavolatura*). A system of musical notation designed for a specific instrument, most commonly the **organ, harpsichord, lute,** or **guitar**. The more familiar standard musical notation places symbols representing note durations on a graded staff representing note pitches and derives from singing, where the object is to symbolize the sound itself. Tablature instead represents the physical action and position of the player required to produce the desired sound. The lines in a lute tablature, for example, represent the **strings** of a lute in a particular **tuning**, and letters (*alfabeto* system) or numerals above the lines tell the player which fret to stop at any given moment.

The earliest known tablature is the Robertsbridge Codex (c. 1360). In the Baroque, tablature continued to be the standard way of notating music for lute, guitar, and related instruments. **Keyboard** tablature declined in favor of the conventional notation, although it continued to be used until the end of the period.

Lute tablature in modern edition.

TARTINI, GIUSEPPE (8 April 1692, Piran, Istria [modern Slovenia]–26 February 1770, Padua). In an age when composing for the church or the theater was the sure path to success, Tartini refused to do either and embarked upon an idiosyncratic career establishing an international reputation as **violinist** and philosopher of music, writing five treatises contesting the ideas of **Giovanni Battista Martini, Jean-Philippe Rameau**, and Jean-Jacques Rousseau (1712–1778), among others, and leaving an oeuvre concentrated on the violin: about 135 solo violin **concertos**, about 135 violin **sonatas** with **continuo**, 30 unaccompanied sonatas, and about 40 **trio sonatas**. He also composed 2 **flute** concertos, 2 concertos for viola da gamba, 4 **motets**, and 20 Italian sacred songs. Most of his living was made as a freelance violinist. In the late 1720s, he founded his own school of violin playing, the first of its type, known as "school of the nations" because it attracted students from all over Europe.

Tartini's parents desired that he enter the church, but while a law student at the University of Padua, he married Elisabetta Premazore on 29 July 1710. Compelled to leave Padua, he took refuge for three years in the convent of San Francesco d'Assisi, where he studied the violin without a teacher. By 1714, he was a violinist in the Ancona **opera** and spent the next years playing at various theaters in northeastern Italy. On 16 April 1721, he was appointed *primo violino e capo di concerto* at San Antonio of Padua. From 1723 to 1726, he was in Prague, in service to the Kinsky family, where he met **Johann Joseph Fux**, **Antonio Caldara**, and **Sylvius Weiss**, among other luminaries. Then he returned to Padua, started his school, and about 1730, brought out his first published volume of violin works. About 1740, he suffered a stroke that adversely affected his playing, and he devoted more and more time to music theory in his last years.

TE DEUM. Short title of the **hymn**, *Te Deum Laudamus* (Lat. "We Praise You God"), also known as the Ambrosian Hymn, after the tradition that Saints **Ambrose** and **Augustine** composed it on the occasion of the latter's baptism in 387

In the Roman Catholic rite, Te Deum is sung at the end of matins on feast days and through the next eight days. It may also be sung on solemn occasions, such as the pope's blessing after **mass** or the divine office. The chant melody varies in different sources.

Baroque-style settings of the Te Deum, with instrumental soloists and **continuo** for choral and solo vocal movements, were important at the French court. *See also* CHARPENTIER, MARC-ANTOINE; HANDEL, GEORGE FRIDERIC.

TELEMANN, GEORG PHILIPP (14 March 1681, Magdeburg, Germany–25 June 1767, Hamburg). Almost entirely self-taught, endowed with a brilliant mind and facility for composition, Telemann became one of the most prolific composers in Western musical history. While cantor for the city of **Hamburg** from 17 September 1721 until the end of his life, it is believed that Telemann composed about 1,700 **church cantatas**, of which 1,400 survive, about 12 liturgical cycles. Four cycles were published, highly unusual at the time, and in general, his cantatas circulated widely and continued to be heard in Protestant churches throughout Germany until the century's end. He wrote over 45 liturgical **passions** (23 survive) as well as 5 other **oratorio passions** and 7 sacred **oratorios**. He also composed about 15 **motets** with **continuo**, a **Magnificat**, and several Latin **masses** and psalm settings. His repertory of secular music is nearly as impressive: over 30 **operas**, 90 songs,

132 ensemble **suites** or **French overtures**, 53 **solo concertos**, 52 **concertos** for multiple soloists, 18 for **orchestra**, and over 60 **solo sonatas**. For **keyboard**, he composed 28 **fugues**, 36 **fantasias**, and 18 other works.

At the request of lexicographers **Johann Mattheson** and **Johann Gottfried Walther**, Telemann left three autobiographical statements, dated 1718, 1729, and 1740.

A few singing lessons and two weeks of **organ** instruction taken at the age of 10 apparently comprise all of Telemann's formal education in music. He taught himself composition by transcribing scores, as well as **recorder**, zither, and **violin**, which became his principal instrument. By age 12, he had already completed several motets, **arias**, instrumental works, and one opera, *Sigimundus*. His mother, alarmed that Georg might forgo a more secure livelihood for music, confiscated his instruments and forbad further study, to no avail: Telemann's teacher at school, Casper Calvoer of Zellerfeld, encouraged his obvious musical aptitude by introducing him to the relationships of music and mathematics. Already, he was providing the local church with a motet for each Sunday.

In 1697, he entered the prestigious Gymnasium Andreanum in Hildesheim and graduated third in his class in 1701. In the meantime, he had taught himself **thoroughbass** composition and the instruments **flute**, **oboe**, **chalumeau**, viola da gamba, **violone**, and bass **trombone**. Then, he entered the University of **Leipzig** to study law. But, according to Telemann's own account, his roommate chanced upon one of his psalm settings, and after it was performed, the mayor of Leipzig hired Telemann to compose music for the city's two principal churches, the Thomaskirche and Nikolaikirche. Then he founded the Leipzig **Collegium Musicum** (to be directed after April 1729, long after Telemann had left the city, by **Johann Sebastian Bach**), with 40 student musicians, and gave public concerts of instrumental music. In 1702, Telemann was appointed music director of the city's Opernhaus auf dem Brühl, composing four operas for it and four more for the court of Weissenfels.

In June 1705, he left Leipzig to become *Kapellmeister* to Count Erdmann II of Promnitz at Sorau, Lower Lusatia (now Żary, in Poland), and began to study intensively the works of **Jean Baptiste Lully** and **André Campra** to learn the popular French style. In December 1708, he became secretary and concertmaster to Duke Johann Wilhelm of Saxe-Eisenach. In 1712, he moved again, to become the director of music in Frankfurt and *Kapellmeister* for the city's Barfüßkirche. From this period, comes a significant portion of Telemann's instrumental repertory.

On 13 October 1709, he married Amalie Louise Juliane Eberlin, lady-in-waiting to the Countess Promnitz. They had one daughter together, but his wife died in January 1711. In his autobiography, Telemann confesses a religious awakening at this time. On 28 August 1714, he married the daughter of a Frankfurt councilman, Maria Catharina Textor. They had eight sons and a daughter together, and yet the marriage seems to have broken up by 1736, when Maria Catharina left Telemann for a convent in Frankfurt.

On 10 July 1721, the Hanseatic city-state of Hamburg invited Telemann to become the city's cantor. He accepted and was installed on 17 September. This position demanded all of Telemann's prodigious productivity. He was responsible for all the music in the city's five churches. He was required to compose two new cantatas for each Sunday, one to be sung before the Gospel reading and another after, as well as a new passion for Lent, in addition to various occasional works for civic celebrations. He directed the city's *collegium musicum*, and these public concerts became so popular that their number had to be doubled from weekly to twice weekly. If all this were not enough activity, in 1722, he became director of the Hamburg Gänsemarkt Opera, where he performed operas by **Reinhard Keiser**, **George Frideric Handel**, and himself, among others. Some in Hamburg objected to his connection with the opera, and friction increased to the point where, in 1722, Telemann applied for the position of cantor in Leipzig to replace the deceased **Johann Kuhnau**. He was the Leipzig city council's first choice, but he declined their offer after Hamburg offered him a higher salary to stay, leaving Leipzig with J. S. Bach as their third choice.

Telemann had intellectual interests beyond composition. He published poetry, anthologized between 1723 and 1738 in C. F. Weichmann's *Poesie der Niederlander*. He undertook the publishing of 43 collections of his own music and often engraved the plates himself. Some of these, like J. S. Bach's publications, are conceived as encyclopedic surveys of genres and techniques of his own time, especially the *Essercizii Musici* (1739), *Musique de Table* (1733), and *Der getreue Music-Meister* (1728). For the Societät der musikalischen Wissenschaften (Society of Musical Sciences), he wrote a theory of enharmonic and **chromatic** relationships, the *Neues musikalisches System* (1752).

In the mid-1740s, Telemann seems to have withdrawn into semiretirement. By then, he was, along with Handel, the most famous German musician alive. From October 1737 to May 1738, he had visited **Paris**, acquiring publication rights there, and had his Psalm 72 performed twice within three days by over 100 musicians of the **Concert Spirituel**. Yet he still provided the required passion for Hamburg every year until his death and, in fact, increased his output of sacred music late in life when new sacred poetry arrived on the scene.

Telemann died in his home of "a chest illness" on 25 June 1767. The *Staats- und Gelehrte Zeitung des Hamburgischen unpartheyischen Correspondenten* simply wrote that "his name is his eulogy."

TEMPERAMENT. *See* TUNING.

TEMPO (It. "time"). The perceived speed of the beats or pulse of the music (e.g., "fast movement," "slow movement"). More precisely, tempo is the perceived speed of the stream of pulses central to the perceived **metrical** hierarchy, the phenomena to which a listener taps the foot or snaps fingers, called the *tactus* in modern perception science. The duration of these beats ranges from approximately 200 ms (very fast tempo) to 1200 ms (very slow tempo).

By the early Baroque, the very fast note values of the new instrumental idioms had made the traditional terminology used to describe mensural rhythm and notation obsolete and so forced the Latin term *tempus* to evolve in meaning from its traditional, precise denotation of whether the breve (the double whole note in modern notation) should be subdivided into two or three equal durations to a vague connotation of the speed and mood of the music. Thus, in the first half of the 17th century, tempo words meaning "fast" or "slowly" appeared at the head of the score or part for the first time in the history of Western music. By 1695, the theorist Daniel Merck (c. 1650–1713) could provide the following list of tempo markings, roughly ordered from slow to fast tempi, in his *Compendium Musicae Instrumentalis Chelicae* (1695):

> *grave*
> *adagio*
> *largo*
> *presto* or *allegro*
> *vivace*
> *prestissimo*

The convention, still valid to some extent today, of using Italian words to indicate the composer's desired tempo derives from the fact that the changes in the musical language requiring tempo words occurred in Italy at the beginning of the Baroque.

The tempo word, however, was not the only determinant of the tempo for a Baroque musician. The metric signature (time signature), genre of the composition, especially if it were a **dance** piece or sacred piece, and the predominant duration values appearing in the score all influenced the performance tempo.

TENEBRAE (Lat. "shadows," "darkness"). A special liturgy combining the offices of matins and lauds sung for Thursday, Friday, and Saturday (or their previous evenings) of Holy Week in the Roman Catholic Rite. A total of 15 psalms are sung, a candle being extinguished after each until "shadows" remained. Baroque composers, such as **Marc-Antoine Charpentier** and

François Couperin, set these psalms in *stile moderno* with basso **continuo** accompaniment.

TEXTURE. Description of the interrelationships among the simultaneous melodies of a passage or composition. Texture may be specified according to the number of melodies, or **voices**, present (e.g., two-voice texture, six-voice **fugue**, etc). **Monophony** is a texture of one voice only. **Polyphony** indicates two or more voices.

Texture may also describe the relative salience of voices. **Homophony** indicates a texture analogous to figure and ground in painting, where one melody attracts attention most of the time while others are accompanimental. **Counterpoint**, by contrast, is the art of combining voices of more or less equal salience.

Less precisely, texture may also describe a particular generic or instrumental idiom (e.g., **operatic** texture, **guitar** texture).

THEORBO. In effect a bass **lute**. All the courses (double **strings**) of the theorbo are longer than those of the lute, and there is a second pegbox containing at least six additional courses running outside the fingerboard (*diapasons*) sounding deep bass pitches. In the Baroque, a typical **tuning** could be:

$A^1 \ B^1 \ C^2 \ D^2 \ D^2 \ F^2 \ G^2$ (open strings)
$A^2 \ D^3 \ F^3 \ A^3 \ D^4 \ F^4$ (stopped strings, over fretted fingerboard)

Deborah Fox playing the theorbo.

Often, the highest two courses were tuned downward one octave because their extra length would not allow the tension necessary to tune them as lute courses. This longer length and altered tuning, as well as its larger body, distinguish the theorbo from the **archlute**.

Three early sources attribute the invention of the theorbo to Antonio Naldi (d. 1621) of **Florence** before 1592.

Solo music for theorbo was published in **tablature** from time to time in the first half of the 17th century. The theorbo was much more widely used throughout the Baroque, however, as a harmony instrument for a **continuo** ensemble. The theorbo player would then have to read the bass melody in standard notion and **improvise** the harmonic accompaniment from the **figures**.

THE SIEGE OF RHODES. Believed to be the first fully sung **opera** in England, this stage work was mounted at Rutland House, **London**, in September 1656. The **libretto** is by William Davenant (1606–1667), once poet laureate of England. The vocal music was composed by **Henry Lawes** (first and fifth acts), **Henry Cooke** (second and third acts), and **Matthew Locke** (fourth act). George Hudson (?–1672) and **Charles Coleman** contributed instrumental music. Only the libretto survives.

The drama is based on the actual siege of the island of Rhodes, held by the Knights of St. John, by the sultan Solyman and the Turkish fleet. Called a "heroic opera," themes of personal courage and conjugal fidelity are strong.

THOROUGHBASS. The art of composing, usually extemporaneously, a harmonic progression upon a given bass melody to provide the harmonic organization for a piece of Baroque music. The **figured bass** is a specific notation system of this art, and the **continuo** is the typical ensemble that would perform its realization, but thoroughbass refers to the general idea of harmonic structure that derives from a bass melody. In that regard, thoroughbass embodies more efficiently than any other aspect of Baroque music the fundamental change in the musical language that began in the 16th century and was virtually complete by the turn of the 18th century: the conception of harmonic successions as a confluence of melodies evolving to one of harmonic successions with syntactic integrity in their own right, with each chord being a discrete vertical (synchronic) unit.

Every Baroque **keyboard** performer had to have some skill in thoroughbass in order to realize continuo parts, and composition teachers often found it the most efficient way to impart the mysteries of Baroque harmonic syntax, which would often differ in their particulars according to region, period, and the disposition of the teacher. **Carl Philipp Emanuel Bach** reported that his father, **Johann Sebastian Bach**, insisted "his pupils . . . begin their studies by learning pure four-part thoroughbass" (Lester, *Compositional Theory in the Eighteenth Century*, 65).

The Baroque produced many instruction manuals for thoroughbass. Three of the most important are **Johann David Heinichen**'s *Der General-Bass in der Composition* (**Dresden**, 1728), **Friedrich Erhard Niedt**'s *Musicalische Handleitung* (**Hamburg**, 1706) and François Campion's (c. 1685–1747) *Traité d'Accompagnement et de Composition* (**Paris**, 1716).

TIENTO (from Sp. *tentar*, "to try out"). Like the Italian **toccata**, the *tiento* resists any definition of form but is a Spanish **organ** genre that takes advantage of the instrument's capacities in **imitative** and freely **improvisational textures**. Its most famous composers, Antonio de Cabezón (c. 1510–1566) and Manuel Rodrigues Coelho (c. 1555–1635), belong to the Renaissance, but the tradition persisted until the early 18th century, particularly in the work of **Juan Bautista José Cabanilles**.

TIMPANI (sing. *timpanum*; also "kettledrum"; Fr. *timbales*; Ger. *Pauken*). An ancient kind of drum formed by a bowl-shaped resonating chamber, the top of which is covered with a head of calfskin or plastic, during the Baroque the timpani rose to become the essential percussion instrument for an **orchestra**, particularly for theatrical, outdoor, or festival music. Most often, Baroque scores call for a pair of them, with drumheads 50–55 centimeters in diameter (modern timpani are larger, 61–75 cm). By mechanisms that control the tension of the drumhead, timpani are **tuned** to specific pitches at the interval of a perfect fourth in the bass register (e.g., D^3 and A^2) and thus can reinforce the dominant and tonic **functions** essential to Baroque harmony.

Evidently, timpani were used frequently in stage productions from the earliest **operas** and **masques**, its music rarely notated but **improvised** by following the lowest **trumpet** part. **Jean-Baptiste Lully** is traditionally credited with making the timpani a member of the orchestra for his *tragédies lyriques*, beginning with *Thésée* of 1675. **Henry Purcell** employed them in *The Fairy Queen* (1692), and thereafter, the inclusion of timpani in large orchestral works became common in England and Germany.

TITELOUZE, JEHAN DE (c. 1562, St. Omer, [modern] France–24 October 1633, Rouen). The first significant composer of **organ** music in France, Titelouze was appointed organist at the cathedral in Rouen in 1588 and never left the post. He published volumes of organ **versets** in 1623 and a set of **preludes** on the eight church **modes** to precede the **Magnificat** in 1626. *See also* PACHELBEL, JOHANN.

TOCCATA (It. "touched"). Instrumental composition originating in the 16th century. "Toccata" connotes rhapsodic passagework and **improvisation**, although many works so entitled have passages of **strict imitation**. When played on the **organ**, the toccata might have been used as a **prelude** or **verset** in Christian liturgies in Italy and German-speaking countries during the Baroque. The earliest **printed** collections appear in 1591 and 1593 in Italy.

The dominant figures in the 17th century were **Girolamo Frescobaldi**, particularly in *Recercari et canzoni* (1615) and *Fiori musicali* (1635), whose innovations were brought northward to Austria by **Johann Jacob Froberger**, and **Jan Pieterszoon Sweelinck**, who taught members of the so-called north German organ school. In their work, however, the toccata declines in importance.

The organ toccatas of **Dietrich Buxtehude** and **Johann Sebastian Bach** sometimes contain contrasting sections of improvisatory and **fugal** character. Others begin with a long improvisatory passage linked to a concluding fugal section or separate fugue, thus contrasting free and strict compositional methods. *See also* CANZONA; RICERCAR.

TOMKINS, THOMAS (1572, St. Davids, Pembrokeshire, England–buried 9 June 1656, Martin Hussingtree, Worcester). Prolific composer of widely circulated Anglican **anthems** (over 120) and **service** music, about 28 **madrigals**, 11 **fantasies** and about 12 other **dances** for **keyboard**, and 5 fantasias and 11 **pavans** for **viol consort**, he studied with **William Byrd** and was a Gentleman of the **Chapel Royal** from at least 1620.

TONAL CENTER. *See* TONALITY.

TONALITY. (1) The structural principle found all over the world by which the pitches of a piece of music are hierarchically ordered, or organized, around a single **pitch-class**, called a "tonal center." The tonal center is perceived as a reference point for melody and, when appropriate, harmony. The "tonality" of a passage of Baroque music names the pitch-class acting as this reference point (tonic), which is the same as naming the **key** or **mode**, in effect.

(2) The syntactic system of Western harmony from c. 1600–present, in this dictionary called "**functional harmony**," in older sources is often called "tonality" or "tonal harmony." In this sense, early Baroque music may be considered a mix of tonal and modal harmony, with the tonal becoming ever stronger as the period advances.

TORELLI, GIUSEPPE (22 April 1658, Verona–8 February 1709, Bologna). Best known today as a composer of instrumental music for **strings**, Torelli was credited by **Johann Joachim Quantz** in 1752 for inventing the **concerto** with his publication of *Sinfonie a 3 e Concerti a 4*, Opus 5 (Bologna, 1692). Among his published works are 10 **trio sonatas**, 18 *sinfonie*, 12 concertos for two **violins**, 12 concertos for one violin and one violoncello, 12 **concerti grossi**, 12 other concertos for various instruments, over 30 works for solo **trumpet**, and over 30 other unpublished **sonatas**, *sinfonie*, and concertos. There are also a few **arias** and **cantatas** and one **oratorio**, *Adam auss dem irrdischen Paradiess verstossen* ("Adam Expelled from Earthly Paradise").

Giuseppe Torelli was born the sixth of nine children to Stefano and Anna Boninsegna Torelli. By 15 May 1676, he is recorded as having played violin for vespers at the church of Santo Stefano in Verona and, by August 1684, was engaged as violinist at the cathedral. The next month, he moved to Bologna, having been admitted to the Accademia Filarmonica on 27 June 1684. He was appointed to the regular chapel on 28 September 1686 and then to *compositore*, probably by 1692. Torelli composed a number of *sinfonie* for the city's feast of San Petronio between 1692 and 1708, but he was in demand as a violinist in neighboring cities and was frequently absent from San Petronio.

In January 1696, the chapel ensemble was disbanded temporarily for lack of funds, so Torelli moved north to Ansbach in Bavaria, Germany. By 1698, he had secured an appointment as *maestro di concerto* for the Margrave of Brandenburg at Ansbach. In 1699, he is recorded in **Vienna**, and the following year, he appears to have applied to the margrave for permission to return to Italy. He is next recorded in 1701 back in San Petronio in Bologna as a member of the newly reconstituted *cappella musicale*, directed by **Giacomo Antonio Perti**. Owing to Perti's influence and his own international reputation, Torelli was granted a special appointment that allowed traveling.

Torelli was buried by the Confraternity of the Guardian Angel in Bologna.

TORREJÓN Y VELASCO, TOMÁS DE (baptized 23 December 1644, Villarrobledo near Albacete, Spain–23 April 1728, Lima, Peru). *Maestro de capilla* of Lima Cathedral from 1 January 1676 until his death, Torrejón set Pedro Calderón de la Barca's (1600–1681) play *La Púrpura de la Rosa* ("The Crimson of the Rose," 1660) to music in 1701 for the viceroyal court in Lima and created the New World's first **opera**. He also composed 20 extant *villancicos* (4 polychoral), 4 **motets** (2 polychoral), and a **Magnificat** for 12 **voices**.

TRAGÉDIE-BALLET. See BALLET DE COUR.

TRAGÉDIE EN MUSIQUE **(Fr. "tragedy in music").** *See TRAGÉDIE LYRIQUE.*

TRAGÉDIE LYRIQUE **(Fr. "musical tragedy").** French form of music drama established in the early 1670s by the composer **Jean-Baptiste Lully**, working with the **librettist** Philippe Quinault (1635–1688) and usually enjoying the support of King Louis XIV (ruled 1661–1715). The first original collaboration was *Cadmus et Hermione* of April 1673. Insofar as it attempts to project a drama sung throughout with instrumental accompaniment, distinguishes **recitative** from **aria**, and employs **choruses** and instrumental interludes, the *tragédie lyrique* (also called *tragédie en musique*) shows its ancestry in the earliest Italian court **operas**. However, specific national features deriving from French traditions of classic theater, the ***ballet de cour***, and *comédie-ballet* lend this form of opera a character that would remain distinct, especially from the newer Italian public operas after 1637, until at least the end of the 18th century.

The plots of the *tragédie lyrique*, always cast in five acts (or a prologue and four acts), are typically mythological in order to accommodate deities and various allegorical figures glorifying the French régime as well as spectacular scenic effects. Conflicts of love, military glory, and virtue formed the narrative line, and the *deus ex machina* usually made everything turn out well.

The French recitative is not nearly as *secco* (It. "dry") as the late 17th-century Italian version. More like the earlier, original Italian concept, the French recitative has more perceptible **meter** and melodic integrity, richer instrumental accompaniment, although less adventurous harmony, and can slip smoothly into the arias (Fr. *airs*), which, again as in early Italian opera, are generally short, simple in form and melodic line, avoiding Italian vocal virtuosity. The libretto is usually written entirely in *vers libres* ("free verse"), which also aided the transitions between recitative and aria. In Lully's operas, scenes are organized around tonal centers, and changes of **key** accompany changes of scene.

Because *tragédie lyrique* enjoyed lavish state support, the spectacle was not constrained by economy as was the Italian public opera. Every act contained ***divertissements*** with elaborate and allegorical **dances** derived from the plot, accompanied by a chorus standing to the side or back of the stage, lending its Greek-style commentary. Spectacular machines creating astounding stage effects and brilliantly costumed singers were commonplace.

After the death of Lully in 1687, the king's interest in opera declined, and centralized control over the enterprise dissolved. Privileges to perform operas were granted to many provincial cities, and new composers, notably **Marc-Antoine Charpentier** and **André Campra**, composed successful operas. Inevitably, Italian influences began to creep into the *tragédie lyrique*, particularly after the music of **Antonio Vivaldi** became well known after the publication of his **Opus 3** in 1711. Controversies over the relative merits of the two opera traditions began in the early decades of the 18th century and continued intermittently until the famous Querelle des Bouffons in the 1750s, which affected the greatest composer of *tragédie lyrique* in the 18th century, **Jean-Philippe Rameau.**

TRAITÉ DE L'HARMONIE **(Jean-Philippe Rameau, 1722).** The most influential music theory to come out of the Baroque, **Jean-Philippe Rameau**'s first of seven musical treatises proposes the first comprehensive account of harmonic syntax. In its essentials, it remains the heart of instruction in Western harmony courses everywhere. Within the decade of its publication, other theorists, such as **Johann David Heinichen**, were revising theories of **counterpoint** and **thoroughbass** according to Rameau's new concepts of chord forms, and by the end of the century, the entire discipline of music theory had been transformed.

Although writers had been aware of the essential identity of harmonic **inversions** (e.g., a chord comprised of C E G, building from the bass upward, versus one of E G C) since the late 16th century, Rameau was the first to extend this recognition to seventh chords, allowing him to account for various unsolved problems involving **dissonances**, and, most importantly, to argue that roots of all chords are the source of a particular chord's character and function within the harmonic progression. (A root is the **pitch-class** first named when the pitch-classes of a chord are arranged as a sequence of thirds, e.g., in a C E G triad, C is the root; in a D F A C seventh chord, D is the root; in the arrangement F D C A, an inversion, D is still the root.) This fundamental approach allows Rameau to open the discussion of other issues in harmonic theory entirely new to the 18th century: how a **key** is defined, the role of **consonance** and dissonance in that definition, the roles of the different chords according to their positions in the scale, and the harmonic structure of **cadences**.

Rameau graphed his harmonic analyses as notes representing the roots of triads and seventh chords written on an added musical staff below the original music. This is the "fundamental bass." The roman numerals so familiar to modern students of harmony began to be added by his disciples beginning in 1766 but did not become common until the 19th century. Neither did Rameau speak of triads, which instead in his book are *accords parfaits* (consonant harmonies). The other chord type is the seventh, or dissonant harmony.

Rameau considered himself a scientist and, following the lead of his countryman René Descartes (1596–1650), attempted to make of harmony an entirely rational system based on first principles. His full title is *Traité de l'Harmonie Reduite à ses Principes Naturels* ("Treaty of Harmony Reduced to its Natural Principles"). His argument derives from the natural harmonics arising for the Pythagorean division of a string. The argument does not succeed. For example, Rameau cannot explain the simple element of the minor triad having such a fundamental role in music because the minor third is not a simple Pythagorean ratio. Fortunately, Rameau allowed his experience as one of the greatest musicians and composers of his age to supervene logic when necessary. His harmonic theory is eminently practical, as nearly three centuries of applying it attest.

TRANSVERSE FLUTE or TRANSVERSE (It. *traverse*, Fr. *traversière*).
What is today commonly called the "Baroque flute" is a wooden instrument played sideways in a manner similar to playing the modern silver flute. Boxwood was typical, although other hardwoods such as ebony might be used.

The 17th century saw a significant standardization in **flute** making, much of which is attributed to the family of Jean **Hotteterre** (c. 1610–1692). A variety of pitch ranges was replaced by one dominant one, the transverse flute beginning on D^4 and extending for two octaves. A variety of bores was replaced by the cylindrical-conical bore, by which the transverse was made in three sections fitting together to form the whole instrument. The first, or head, joint had a cylindrical bore, while the following two sections had a conical bore, which allowed the finger holes to be drilled more closely together for greater facility, especially with **chromatic** pitches. Lastly, a single key stopping the seventh hole allowed easy production of the E-flat^4 and became widespread.

In the 1720s, the middle section was divided into two, and these could be exchanged with other joints of different sizes, allowed the player to adjust the fixed pitch of the transverse in order to accord with local **tuning** standards. These replacement parts were known as *corps de rechange*.

The best source of knowledge about Baroque transverse technique is **Johann Joachim Quantz**'s *Versuch einer Anweisung die Flöte traversière zu Spielen* ("Attempt at an Instruction of How to Play the Transverse") of 1752.

Transverse wooden flute.

The Baroque repertory for transverse flute is a curiosity of contrasts. Because the technical advances that allowed the transverse to negotiate Baroque instrumental idioms did not arrive until the late 17th century, there is very little 17th-century repertory for the instrument at all. Once those advances were in place, however, the instrument became fashionable, and there was an explosion of composition to satisfy the new virtuosos of the instrument, particularly in France, where the advances had occurred, beginning with Michel de la Barre's (c. 1675–1745) *Pièces pour la Flûte Traversière avec la Basse-Continue* of 1702, the first solo transverse music ever published. **François Couperin** called for the transverse in his *Concerts Royaux* of 1722, as did **Jean-Philippe Rameau** for his *Pièces de Clavecin en Trio* of 1741, considered by some to be one of the best collections of chamber music for the instrument. **Michel Corrette**, **Joseph Bodin de Boismortier**, Jacques **Hotteterre**, and **Jean-Marie Leclair** also contributed to the new repertory.

Italians composed many **sonatas** and **concertos** for the transverse—**Antonio Vivaldi**, **Tomaso Albinoni**, **Leonardo Vinci**, **Francesco Geminiani**, among others—although much of their music is designated for generic treble-pitched instruments, of which the transverse is one option.

In Germany, there were the compositions of the specialist Quantz and of his student and patron King Frederick the Great of Prussia (1712–1786) and a great deal of chamber music and some concertos of **Georg Philipp Telemann**. Today, the transverse is perhaps most frequently heard in the small but outstanding solo repertory of **Johann Sebastian Bach**, including three sonatas for flute and **harpsichord** (BWV 1030–1032), three sonatas for flute and **continuo** (BWV 1033–1035), one for flute, **violin**, and continuo (BWV 1038), one for two flutes and continuo (BWV 1039), one unaccompanied **partita** (BWV 1013), and the Second **Overture** (BWV 1067), as well as in solo roles for **arias** in **church cantatas** and the two **passions**.

TRIO SONATA. A **sonata** for two treble (high-pitched) instruments, very often two **violins**, and basso **continuo**. The name comes from the three-**voiced** musical **texture**: the two treble melodies and the bass melody of the continuo, all independent. If the bass melody is to be brought out properly, a cellist or **bassoonist** should play the continuo part along with the **harpsichord**, **theorbo**, or **guitar** player, and so, the trio sonata actually requires four players.

The trio sonata was a very popular form of Baroque chamber music, and virtually all important composers of instrumental music after 1650 composed them. The first four of the six famous publications of **string** music of **Arcangelo Corelli**, beginning in 1681, are trio sonatas and established his international reputation. To these sets is often attributed the well-known if overemphasized distinction between the *sonata da camera* (Corelli's Opus 2), which comprises three to five **dance** movements, often in **binary form**, and the *sonata da chiesa*, which has four movements of more learned **counterpoint** in a slow-fast-slow-fast order.

The trio sonata texture could be translated into a **keyboard** idiom. The six trio sonatas (BWV 525–530; three movements each, fast-slow-fast) for **organ** of **Johann Sebastian Bach** are extraordinary examples, in that right hand, left hand, and feet must negotiate demanding and independent melodies simultaneously.

TROMBONE (It. "large trumpet," Ger. *Posaune*). This brass wind instrument derivative of the **trumpet** attained its familiar slide, which changes the effective length of the tubing, late in the 15th century. The Baroque instrument is quite similar to the modern but generally has a smaller bore and less flare to the bell. The Baroque trombone may come in various sizes.

In late Renaissance sacred music, the trombone was often used to double the melodies of **motets** and **masses**, giving support to the singers, and this tradition survived through much of the Baroque (e.g., **Cantata** BWV 4 of **Johann Sebastian Bach**, 1708). Obbligato trombones could occasionally be heard in **sacred symphonies**, such as *Saul, was verfolgst du mich* of **Heinrich Schütz**, or in **operas**, to symbolize the underworld, as in **Claudio Monteverdi**'s *L'Orfeo*, but **George Frideric Handel**'s scoring for them in *Saul* and *Israel in Egypt* notwithstanding, unlike the trumpet and **horn**, trombones were never regular members of a Baroque **orchestra**. There is virtually no solo music for trombone from the period.

TRUMPET (Fr. *trompette*, Ger. *Trompete*, It. *tromba*). In the 16th century, the city of Nuremburg, Germany, emerged as the most important center for the making of brass instruments, maintaining this position throughout the Baroque, and about this time, the Schnitzer and Neuschel families, among others, gave the trumpet its most familiar and fairly consistent form. The "natural" trumpet has no valves, which meant that different pitches must be culled by the player's lips and force of breath from the partial frequencies (overtones or harmonics) of the instrument's fundamental pitch derived from the length of tubing.

The Baroque trumpet consisted of two sections of cylindrical brass tubing with two bends (*bows*) and a third section, the bell. The sections fit into one another, and the joins might be insulated with beeswax. The Baroque mouthpiece had a rim, flatter and wider than the modern one, and there is a sharp edge between the cup and the throat. The edge gave the trumpet a

Natural trumpet. Modern copy by Robert Barclay. Photo by Miles Dudgeon.

more brilliant timbre and made the adjustment of pitches easier. This basic construction could take several forms: a single coil of tubing (long trumpet), several coils of tubing made into a circle, several coils made into two circles, and the German slide trumpet (*Zugtrompete* or *tromba da tirarsi*) attached a slide to the mouthpiece. The bore and length of the tubing is the same in each case.

The most common **keys** for English and German trumpets were D and E-flat (the keys of the two versions of the **Magnificat** of **Johann Sebastian Bach**), and in fact, a great deal of Baroque ensemble music that includes trumpets is in D major. However, small lengths of tubing could be inserted between the mouthpiece and main body to allow performance in other keys.

The trumpet had long symbolized military and political power, and princes of Europe maintained ensembles of trumpeters and **timpanists** for ceremonial occasions. Trumpet guilds guarded standards of performance and a certain exclusion, creating a socially distinct group of musicians.

By the early 17th century, however, the trumpet had begun to figure in art music. **Michael Praetorius** set the Christmas carol "In Dulci Jubilo" for a choir accompanied by six trumpets in his 1618 publication *Polyhymnia Panegyrica et Caduceatrix* (No. 34). The city of Bologna became famous for a tradition of fine trumpet music. **Maurizio Cazzati** published an important collection, his Opus 35, in 1665, and **Giuseppe Torelli** and Domenico Gabrieli (1651–1690) carried the Bolognese tradition to the end of the century. In turn-of-the-century **Venetian opera**, a "trumpet aria" came to be expected. In France, trumpets sounded great fanfares in the spectacular scenes of **Jean-Baptiste Lully**'s **operas** and to amplify more glorious texts, such as the **Te Deum**, in the sacred music of **Marc-Antoine Charpentier**.

In the 18th century, the trumpet was the mainstay of any kind of festival music, sacred or secular, almost always paired with timpani. **George Frideric Handel** took the French practice of fanfare writing and made it his own in the **Water Music Suite**, in his **Coronation Anthem** "Zadok the Priest," and in many triumphant moments of his **English oratorio choruses**. J. S. Bach took full advantage of a strong tradition of trumpeting already present in **Leipzig** and composed some of the finest trumpet music for his **church cantatas**, the Second **Brandenburg Concerto**, the **Christmas Oratorio**, and the **Mass in B Minor**. These scores pose challenges even to modern trumpet players.

TRUMPET MARINE (Fr. *trompette marine*, Ger. *Trumscheit*, It. *tromba marina*). A bowed instrument of a single **string**, about two meters in length, consisting of a solid neck attached to an open-ended resonator, on which sits a bridge that is excited by the vibration of the bowed string. **Jean-Baptiste Lully** used it in the fourth entrée of his ballet *Xerxes* (1660) and **Alessandro Scarlatti** in the fourth act of his **opera** *Il Mitridate Eupatore* (1707). Rarely employed, it fell into obsolescence by the mid-18th century.

TUNDER, FRANZ (1614, Bannesdorf near Fehmarn, Germany–5 November 1667, Lübeck). An important composer in the developing north German **organ** school, Tunder may also have founded the Lübeck tradition of *Abendmusiken*, developed by his successor **Dietrich Buxtehude**. His surviving compositions are few: 14 organ works, mostly **chorale fantasias** and other settings, and 17 vocal works, about one third of which are German **chorale** settings.

Tunder may have been in **Florence** in the late 1620s and possibly studied with **Girolamo Frescobaldi**. Then Tunder became organist to the court of Duke Friedrich III of Holstein-Gottorp in December 1632. In 1647, he took the post of organist at the Marienkirche in Lübeck.

TUNING. Techniques of adjusting or playing an instrument to produce the precise pitches proper for harmony varied widely during the Baroque by time, place, and the instrument concerned. In general, there were two approaches— unequal and equal temperament—with the former at first predominant but slowly giving way to the latter in pre-tuned instruments as the Baroque period passed.

Both equal and unequal temperament are compromises of "pure" or Pythagorean tuning, which holds that the frequency ratios of consonant intervals should be made of small integers (e.g., octave ratio = 2:1; perfect-fifth ratio = 3:2; major-third ratio = 5:4, etc). The intrinsic fault of pure tuning for Western music is that, if one generates all the required pitches from a starting pitch frequency by the 3:2 ratio for perfect fifth (C x 3/2 = G; G x 3/2 = D, etc.), the resulting scale has pure fifths but impure thirds: the interval C to E has not the 5:4 (or 1.25) Pythagorean ratio but the ratio 81:64 (or 1.266) so that a harmony made out of such a third sounds harsh. On the other hand, tuning all the notes of the C scale in Pythagorean ratios to C itself results in very impure intervals within the scale (e.g., the major third F-A has a ratio of 1.20 rather than 1.25).

Various methods of unequal temperament compromise pure tuning by distributing the intrinsic impurities among the most commonly used harmonies in a given **tonality** while retaining some pure intervals. When a **harpsichord** is tuned to C, all the harmonies in C major and in closely related **keys** sound euphonious, although not quite pure, and each key will have its own unique, albeit very subtle, intervallic character. Distant keys, such as G-flat major, may be unusable because the important intervals within their scales are too impure. This may be one reason why early Baroque **keyboard** music does not **modulate** far from its original tonality and that such tonalities require either no accidentals, or at most two, in their signatures.

Equal temperament takes this compromise one step further, by distributing the intrinsic impurities so that the frequency ratios of every half-step within the instrument are identical. The only Pythagorean intervals are the octaves. Again, beginning from C, this method results in C major sounding less euphonious than an unequal temperament because there are no pure intervals at all. C major also has no particular interval character vis-à-vis the other keys, because all the ratios within the other keys are exactly the same as in C. The advantage of equal temperament is that all keys sound tolerably well, and all manner of **chromatic** and distant **modulations** are possible.

Singers and instruments without fixed pitches, such as unfretted **strings**, typically modify the frequencies of pitches in performance to fit the harmonic context as well as possible, so that the C^4 of a C-major context has a slightly different frequency from a C^4 of an A-flat-major context, even in the same composition. *See also WELL-TEMPERED CLAVIER.*

U

UNITIES. The unities of time, place, character, and action, a dramatic theory derived from Aristotle's *Poetics* and applied to French **opera** and many Italian operas after 1690. A well-formed drama should take place within 24 hours in a limited space, such as a palace or small neighborhood. All the important characters should appear early on, preferably within the first act. Unity of action, the least precise criterion, suggests that the events of the plot follow logically one upon another without interruptions and perhaps underlies the *opera seria* practice of the *liaison*, retaining at least one character in every scene to connect to the following scene.

UNMEASURED PRELUDE. An **improvisatory prelude** standing as the first movement of a **dance suite**, usually French, for **lute** or **keyboard**. These are most common in the latter half of the 17th century. The absence of rhythmic symbols above the lute **tablature** indicates that the player is to supply his own; in keyboard works, the same effect—an absence of **metric** structure—is expressed by sequences of whole notes, sometimes slurred, without bar lines. How these notations were realized by their originators is unknown, but it is thought by many that the result was a prelude of arpeggiated chords organized by harmonic progression and not any pattern of durations.

V

VARIATIONS. Genre that formalizes one of the most fundamental and common techniques of composition found throughout the music history of the world, that of presenting a good complete melody and then re-presenting it a number of times, with each iteration of the melody revealing some new element—variation—of the melody that alters it without obscuring its identity. Typically, at first, such changes are small but gradually accumulate to the point where the main melody of the last variation may bear little apparent resemblance to the original melody.

In the Baroque, such variation sets gradually transform **improvisation** traditions of the Renaissance for **keyboard** and **lute** until rhythmic and harmonic idioms of the Baroque musical language dominate. Typically, the original melody is in **binary form**, often in **dance** rhythm, often a popular tune not by the composer of the variations. While retaining the harmonic progression and binary form of the original, successive variations change the melody by techniques of **diminution**, **augmentation**, translation into the parallel **mode** (major or minor), added **contrapuntal** melodies, and **tempo**.

Occasionally, a set of variations based upon a famous **ostinato** pattern, such as *La Folia*, proceeds by varying the bass melody rather than the soprano or by retaining only the original harmonic progression to bind the individual variations together. The greatest example of this type is the **Goldberg Variations** by **Johann Sebastian Bach**.

In any case, a set of Baroque variations is quite discontinuous on the high level of structure. Each variation is melodically and harmonically a complete structure weakly associated with the other variations by similarity of melodic/harmonic form rather than a continuous harmonic syntax. Thus, the number of variations in a set is not standard, and in performance, almost any variation may be omitted without harming the coherence of the whole composition. See also PARTITA; VARIATION-SUITE.

VARIATION-SUITE. A **suite** in which each of the **dances** begins with a variant of the same melody, rhythmically transformed to fit the character of the particular dance in which that variant is heard. **Variation**-suites are common in the 16th and 17th centuries.

VENETIAN OPERA. The term refers not so much to a particularly musical style of **opera** but rather the historical phenomenon of opera in **Venice**, beginning with the opening of the Teatro San Cassiano in 1637, through the rise and fall through bankruptcy of many other public opera houses in the city until well into the 18th century. During this period, Venice was the primary venue for public Italian opera in Europe. Only **Paris**, with its *tragédie lyrique* largely funded by the state, might be comparably famous for its opera. A number of Europe's leading opera composers during this period were Venetians or made their living in Venice, sometimes even as *maestro di cappella* of San Marco: **Claudio Monteverdi, Francesco Cavalli, Antonio Lotti, Antonio Vivaldi, Antonio Caldara**. Other composers spent time there to promote their operas during Carnival season: **Alessandro Scarlatti, Johann Adolf Hasse, Nicola Porpora, Leonardo Vinci**, and **George Frideric Handel**. Thus, although one cannot speak of a particular sound of Venetian opera as distinct from those composed in **Florence** or **Naples**, its influence was so great that certain practices were often imitated elsewhere.

Venetian opera houses operated for profit and without external support. Producers, therefore, aimed first at minimizing expenses: **choruses** were reduced or eliminated; instrumental ensembles were simplified, sometimes to a small group of **strings** and **continuo**; scenery was reused. They aimed next at maximizing opera's appeal: much was borrowed from the popular dramatic tradition of the Italian *commedia dell'arte*, including plot lines and characters not limited to the educated elite, fewer and shorter **recitatives** and more **arias**, the length of which slowly increased in the later 17th century with the prestige of star singers. Complicated, sometimes barely credible plots running several lines at once allowed a great variety of aria types: love arias of course but also love duets, **laments**, mad scenes, scenes showing a character falling asleep to twist the plot, and varieties of comic arias.

In 1691, the Venetian noble Giovanni Carlo Grimani (1648–1714) and his librarian **Apostolo Zeno** founded the Accademia degli Animosi (Academy of the Spirited) dedicated to making opera more rational, according to aesthetics of ancient drama, such as the Aristotelian **unities**. They took as contemporary models the French classical tragedies of Pierre Corneille (1606–1684) and Jean Racine (1639–1699), and Zeno became one of the leading **librettists** of this reform opera that led to *opera seria*.

VENICE. The capital city of La Serenissima Repubblica (the Most Serene Republic) rose to prominence in sacred music in the 16th century, later than most other Italian city-states, but then developed spectacularly into the second most important musical center in Europe after **Rome** through the Baroque.

The nerve center of art music in Venice was the doge's chapel at San Marco, not, as was usual elsewhere, the cathedral at San Pietro di Castello. Most of the *maestri di cappella* during the Baroque were Venetians, long familiar with the republic's peculiar civic ceremonies and liturgies: Giovanni Croce (1603–1609), Giulio Cesare Martinengo (1609–1613), Giovanni Rovetta (1644–1668), **Francesco Cavalli** (1668–1676), Natale Monferrato (1676–1685), **Giovanni Legrenzi** (1685–1690), Giovanni Battista Volpe (1690–1691), Gian Domenico Partenio (1692–1701), Antonio Biffi (1702–1732), **Antonio Lotti** (1736–1740), Antonio Pollarolo (1740–1746), and Giuseppe Saratelli (1747–1762). The great exception was the Mantovan **Claudio Monteverdi** (1613–1643). At the turn of the 17th century, San Marco could have at its disposal a choir of 30 and an instrumental ensemble of 20. With such large ensembles and two **organs**, San Marco made such a specialty of colorful **motets** and **mass** movements for *cori spezzati* (It. "split choirs") that, even without originating in Venice, polychoral music became virtually synonymous with the "Venetian school" of church music and was occasionally employed by composers as late and far flung as **Johann Sebastian Bach** and **George Frideric Handel**.

A peculiarly Venetian venue for sacred music were the four *ospedali* of the Incurabili, Mendicanti, Derelitti, and Pietà. Orphanages that sheltered mostly illegitimate girls, they trained their inmates in singing, organ playing and, by the late 17th century, **string** playing and were renowned all over Europe for the quality of their music. **Sacred concertos**, **oratorios**, and instrumental **concertos** by **Francesco Gasparini** and **Antonio Vivaldi** survive from the Pietà. Other venues for music included convents, monasteries, trade guilds, and the *scuole grandi* ("great schools"), religious confraternities analogous to those found in most Italian cities during the Baroque. These organizations and less formal gatherings of great Venetian families were well supplied by the publications of Giovanni Legrenzi and **Tomaso Albinoni**.

With the opening of Europe's first commercial **opera** house at San Cassiano in 1637, the city's best musical talent increasingly preferred working in the theater to composing for the church. Accordingly, the production of new sacred works for San Marco had dropped off sharply by the end of the 17th century. By the mid-1640s, there were six public theaters for the **Venetian opera**. As the century wore on, unpopularity closed some while new ones opened in a newly dynamic market for operatic music. Cavalli, Legrenzi, and Lotti, all *maestri di cappella* at San Marco, among many others, composed operas for these theaters.

Venice began the Baroque as the leading publisher of music in Europe, having held that position since Ottaviano Petrucci (1466–1539) developed the first method for **printing polyphony** in 1501. In 1577, Antonio Gardano

(1509–1569) brought out the first printed musical score, a book of **madrigals** by a deceased *maestro di cappella* of San Marco, Cipriano da Rore (c. 1515–1565). By the turn of the 18th century, however, advances in engraving technique adopted in England and Holland forced Venetian printing into economic decline, and even Vivaldi sent his **Opus 3** concertos to Etienne Roger in Amsterdam.

VERSE ANTHEM. An **anthem** featuring vocal solos, usually in some pattern of alternation with the full **choir**. The concept coincides with the first major collections of English anthems. The first verse of the anonymous *Now Let the Congregation* in the Wanley Partbooks (c. 1546–48) is apparently for alto solo, followed by the same verse for full choir.

Early Baroque verse anthems most often begin with introductory **organ** solos, followed by a verse for vocal solo(s) with instrumental obbligatos, closing the first section with a verse for full **chorus**, with instruments doubling the vocal parts. Solo/chorus pairs proceed in through-composed manner for as long as the text demands.

The revival of the **Chapel Royal** after the Restoration of Charles II occasioned more elaborate instrumental settings. A **string** ensemble might further articulate a larger structure by playing ritornellos between the sung verses. Sometimes these are called "**symphony** anthems."

VERSET. Organ piece that substitutes for a chant in Roman Catholic liturgy. It may use the original chant melody as a **cantus firmus** or as a **subject** of **imitation**, or the music may be entirely original. *See also* CANZONA; COUPERIN, FRANÇOIS; *FIORI MUSICALI*; FRESCOBADLI, GIROLAMO; ORGAN MASS; RICERCAR; TOCCATA.

VESPERS OF 1610 (*VESPRO DELLA BEATA VERGINE*). The greatest sacred composition of the 17th century is a setting of a Roman Catholic vespers composed by **Claudio Monteverdi** and published in **Venice** in 1610. The scoring of the 13 movements (not including an alternate, simpler six-**voiced Magnificat** and a six-voiced *Missa In Illo Tempore* **printed** with them) varies from a **monody** for solo tenor and **continuo** to a polychoral psalm for 10 **voices** in 2 **choirs** with accompaniment. A historical performance requires in addition eight vocal soloists and two **violins**, three **violas**, one bass violin, one **double bass**, three **cornettos**, one large cornetto, three **trombones**, one contrabass trombone, two tenor **recorders**, and two **transverse flutes** or shawms. However, a number of modern editions make possible performances with modern instruments. Jeffrey G. Kurtzman has published the most recent and authoritative critical performing edition (Oxford, 1999). Monteverdi's

13 movements require about 90 minutes to perform in concert; a liturgical performance might require an amount of additional chant, depending upon how certain controversial matters were resolved.

Monteverdi's Vespers include settings of the **response** *Domine ad adiuvandum*, five psalms (109, 112, 121, 126, and 147), the **hymn** *Ave Maris Stella*, the Magnificat, and five **sacred concertos** setting biblical texts (except *Audi coelum*, not biblical). He included no antiphons to frame the psalms and Magnificat, presumably because they would be chosen according to the feast. But some scholars believe that sacred concertos should replace the antiphons; others believe they are independent compositions. Pitch is another controversy. Some movements are notated in *chiavi alte* ("high clefs"); evidence suggests that these should be transposed down a perfect fourth. Unresolved questions include when to use the instruments when they are not obbligato and how many singers to use on a part in a given movement and the best order of movements.

Published 13 years after the performance of **Jacopo Peri**'s *Euridice* and three years after Monteverdi's own **opera** *L'Orfeo*, the Vespers is a unique synthesis of two styles concurrent in early 17th-century Italy: the *stile antico*, the high Renaissance **polyphony** promoted by the **Council of Trent**, and the *stile moderno*, emphasizing the expressivity of the solo voice against a framework of **functional harmony**. The psalms and Magnificat present this synthesis most clearly. The **cantus firmus** of the ancient psalm tones sounds slowly at times against virtuosic solo singing reminiscent of opera, at times against highly **contrapuntal** choral writing reminiscent of the glories of the Venetian school.

VIADANA, LUDOVICO (c. 1560, Viadana near Parma, Italy–2 May 1627, Gualtieri near Parma). *See CENTO CONCERTI ECCLESIASTICI.*

VIENNA. With the exception of the Austrian **Johann Joseph Fux**, Vienna had no exceptional Baroque composers that the city could call its own, and yet, owing to the sophisticated musical tastes of its emperors, Vienna became one of the most important centers for every kind of Baroque music from early in the period. **Francesco Cavalli, Antonio Cesti, Johann Jacob Froberger, Johann Adolf Hasse,** and the **librettist Metastasio** are among the luminaries associated with the imperial court before 1750.

The accession of Emperor Ferdinand II (1578–1637) in 1619 brought an interest in the new Baroque experiments to the throne, and his marriage to Eleonora Gonzaga of Mantua established links to musical centers in Italy. Important productions of **opera** and **oratorio** date from the 1640s: revivals of Cavalli's *Egisto* in 1642, his *Giasone* in 1650, a possible performance of **Claudio Monteverdi**'s *Il Ritorno d'Ulisse in Patria*, which preserved one of the opera's few existing copies, and the premiere, reported all over the continent, of Cesti's *Il Pomo d'Oro*. This most magnificent opera celebrated the marriage of the emperor Leopold I (1640–1705) and required two days, July 12 and 14 of 1668, and 22 scene changes for its complete performance. The peculiarly Viennese type of oratorio, the *sepolcro*, dates from this period.

Leopold's love of music was extraordinary even for an age of many musically inclined autocrats. He composed music, including full-length operas to librettos by one of his court composers **Antonio Draghi**, and his wide support of Italian music is documented by his surviving library of scores.

After the repulse of the Turks in 1683, Emperor Charles VI (1685–1740) reigned over a court more magnificent than ever. Fux was appointed court composer in 1698 and worked with an expanded Hofkapelle ("imperial chapel"). Charles promoted him to *Hofkapellmeister* in January 1715 and then brought in, over Fux's opposition, **Antonio Caldara** as *vice-Kapellmeister* in the spring of 1716, and the two supplied a great deal of sacred music, much of it in *stile antico*, for the imperial chapel. Caldara also was involved in the founding of the Cecilian Society, an organization founded in Vienna in 1725 for the preservation of Roman Catholic traditions of sacred music, which spawned influential chapters all over Europe during the 18th and 19th centuries.

Fux and Caldara also provided operas regularly, and in residence since 1718 was one of the most important opera reformers of the age, **Apostolo Zeno**. Zeno was succeeded by an even greater librettist, Metastasio, in 1730, who began to work with Hasse intermittently in 1731. Hasse finally joined the court permanently in 1763, and the two worked even more closely together thereafter.

VILLANCICO. Appearing in the 15th century as a type of secular song, in the latter half of the 16th century, devotional poetry began to predominate. During the Baroque, the **polyphonic** *villancico*, using Spanish or other vernacular language, substituted for **motet** composition. In 17th-century Spain and New Spain, cathedral chapel masters were expected to compose new *villancicos* each year for certain feasts, such as Corpus Christi and Christmas, and for matins of local saints' days as well, at which they replaced the Latin **responsories**. As a result, many hundreds were composed, but many were lost and few are available in modern edition. The musical form varied, but most examples contain a refrain (*estribillo* or *responsión*) alternating with several stanzas. The particular folk element composed into the music specified the type further: *negrilla, calenda, gallego, jácara*.

VINCI, LEONARDO (1690 or 1696?, Strongoli, Calabria, Italy–27 or 28 May 1730, Naples). Despite a career that began rather late within a short life, Vinci quickly joined his rivals **Nicola Porpora** and **Johann Adolf Hasse** as one of the leading **opera** composers on the continent during the 1720s. His music was intensely popular in **Naples**, his home base, and **Rome** but was also heard in Parma and **Venice**.

Vinci began his opera career with comedy and must be counted as one of the main popularizers, along with his student **Giovanni Battista Pergolesi**, of the *opera buffa* genre that would eventually dislodge *opera seria* from its prestigious position by late in the 18th century. His comedy *Li Zite 'ngalera* of 1722 is the oldest surviving score of a Neapolitan comedy. Recognized in his own time was Vinci's capacity to compose captivating melodies depending not so much on the continuity of Baroque motor rhythm but on the periodic phrase modeled on **dance** forms. However, Vinci also succeeded in the more prestigious and cosmopolitan *opera seria* (most of those composed for Naples also have comic **intermezzi** between acts). He collaborated regularly with the great **librettist Metastasio**, beginning with *Didone Abbandonata* (Rome, 1726) and *Siroe Re di Persia* (Venice, 1726), and was the first to set many of Metastasio's other early librettos.

Beside his 31 operas, Vinci composed 3 other minor stage works, 12 chamber **cantatas**, 5 **motets**, and a Kyrie and Gloria **mass** pair for eight **voices**.

Vinci entered the *Conservatorio dei Poveri di Gesù Cristo* in Naples on 14 November 1708. In 1718, he served as ***maestro di cappella*** to Prince Sansevero of Naples.

Vinci's first opera, the comedy *Lo Cecato Fauzo* ("The Fake Blind Man") opened on 19 April 1719 at the Teatro dei Fiortentini in Naples to broad acclaim. He followed it with another success and became the principal composer of the theater for the next three years. His *Publio Cornelio Scipione*, which opened in Naples on 4 November 1722, at once established Vinci in the front ranks of *opera seria* composers, so great was its success.

In 1724, Vinci produced his first opera for Rome. The success of *Farnace* secured for Vinci an invitation to compose a new opera every year except for 1725, a papal Holy Year that closed the theaters. So Vinci instead composed two operas that year for Venice, whose success led to an invitation from Parma. In the season of 1726–1727, Vinci composed three new operas: *Astianatte* for Naples, *Didone Abbandonata* for Rome, and *Siroe Re di Persia* for Venice. In October 1725, Vinci was appointed to succeed **Alessandro Scarlatti** as pro-vice-*maestro di cappella* for the royal chapel in Naples.

In his last years, Vinci supplied operas for various commissions and theaters in Naples, Parma, and Rome. He also served as *maestro di cappella* for the monastery of St. Catherine's at Formiello, for which he composed his few motets and mass movements. In the season of 1729–1730, he was the principal composer of the Teatro delle Dame in Rome, producing two operas there. Chroniclers report an intense rivalry with Nicola Porpora, who also mounted two operas at the Teatro Capranica, which Vinci allegedly tried to sabotage.

Vinci died in Naples. Contemporaries report rumors that he was poisoned in retribution for an illicit love affair.

VIOL (also, viola da gamba; It. "leg viol"). Refers to a family of variously sized bowed **string instruments**, very popular from the 16th to the mid-18th century, that were held between the legs in a manner reminiscent of playing the modern **cello**. The right hand held the bow, and the left stopped the strings on the fingerboard, which had frets made of stretched gut that determined precisely, as on a **guitar**, the lengths of the stopped strings and, therefore, the pitches of the notes played.

Viols varied widely in size and shape, but the most common sizes were the treble (high) viol, tenor viol, and bass viol, all standard members of the ensemble known as the viol **consort**. Alto and small tenor viols were rare, and the very high *pardessus* was not invented until the 18th century.

The viol was typically constructed of thin pieces of light wood so that the instrument, although large, was light in weight. Deeply cut ribs, a flat back except where it attached to the neck, a slightly arched top (belly) made of bent staves that covers the ribs entirely without edging are all typical features. A single flat batten reinforced the back. The bridge holding the strings above the body might be quite high, but the neck to which the fingerboard was attached sloped toward the bridge so that the space between the strings and the fingerboard was small, allowing the player to stop the strings quickly and easily.

Viols typically have six strings, except the bass viol, which often has seven, and these are **tuned** as follows:

treble viol	D^3 G^3 C^4 E^4 A^4 D^5
tenor viol	G^2 C^3 F^3 A^3 D^4 G^4
bass viol	D^2 G^2 C^3 E^3 A^3 D^4

Bass viol constructed by Thomas Klenck, Hamilton, New York.

The proportions of the instrument sizes accord more closely with their tunings than the modern string instrument family of **violin**, **viola**, cello, and string bass. This, and the lightness of construction, accounts in great measure for the resonant and consistent timbre through all the viol family.

The viol player grips the bow with the palm upward and wrist below the stick, opposite to the bow hand of the violin, viola, and cello player. For this reason, bow articulation is also opposite: the "up bow" is the stronger of the two strokes. The bow is typically convex, and the player tenses the bow hair with the middle finger placed directly on the hair while playing. With the left hand, the player holds the finger down just behind a fret to produce the desired pitch and leaves it there until required to move it. These "holds" facilitate fast passagework. Whether players used vibrato or not is controversial.

The repertory for the viol consort consisted mostly of collections of **dances** and **contrapuntal fantasias** and *ricercari* and reached its zenith in the late 16th century. Viols are required in the famous **intermedi** of the Medici in **Florence** and for the ensemble of **Claudio Monteverdi's** *L'Orfeo*. During the 17th century, however, the viols, especially the treble, were gradually replaced by the more penetrating violin, probably owing to its greater suitability for the solo repertories of **concertos** and **sonatas**. In England, isolated from the Italian **operatic** fashions, viol consort music survived much longer in the work of **William Lawes**, **Matthew Locke**, and others until the Restoration.

In the later Baroque, viols, especially the bass, continued to be employed as members of mixed ensembles and occasionally as solo instruments. France in particular became known for virtuoso viol playing, and many players went there to study with **Marin Marais** or one of the **Forquerays**. **Johann Sebastian Bach** used the viol as a solo instrument in a number of his **church cantatas** (e.g., BWV 106, 198) as well as for two **arias** of the **St. Matthew Passion**, and he also composed three **solo sonatas** for viola da gamba (BWV 1027–1029).

VIOLA. The technological history of the viola matches closely that of the **violin**. The principal difference is that its size cannot be in the same proportion as has the violin to its pitch range—a perfect fifth lower—and at the same time be played *da braccio*, resting on the chest or shoulder, for it would be too long a stretch for the arm. As a result, some compromise between optimum length, instrument resonance, and practicality must be brokered, causing violas to vary significantly in length.

In the Baroque, the viola is confined almost entirely to playing the middle **voices** of an **orchestral** ensemble. Although all violists know the G Major Concerto of **Georg Philipp Telemann**, there is almost no other Baroque solo repertory. *See also* VIOLA DA BRACCIO; VIOLA D'AMORE.

VIOLA DA BRACCIO. Often appearing as a synonym for **viola**, the term also distinguishes the class of bowed **string instruments** that are playing resting on the chest or shoulder from those that are played between the legs, the *viole da gamba*.

VIOLA DA GAMBA (It. "leg viola"). *See* VIOL.

VIOLA D'AMORE. A bowed **string instrument** about the size of the **viola** and similarly played under the chin, but constructed more like a **viol**, with characteristic flat back and wide ribs, and usually seven strings supported by the bridge. The most characteristic feature of the viola d'amore, however, is the set of seven more strings running under the fingerboard and passing freely through the bridge. These vibrate and, therefore, resonate when energized by the sound waves produced by the instrument as its normal strings are stopped and bowed. These are commonly called "sympathetic strings" and give the instrument its characteristic ring.

The viola d'amore has no standard **tuning**. It was often tuned according to the piece to be played. Some notation for the instrument represents the actual pitch; other notation is more like **tablature**, indicating the finger position according to a specified tuning.

A large number of surviving instruments shows that it was in demand at the close of the 17th century and through the 18th, but the repertory is limited because it was not a standard member of the string **orchestra** or other common ensemble. **Antonio Vivaldi** composed eight **concertos** for it, and **Georg Philipp Telemann** also employed it as a solo instrument, but the viola d'amore is most frequently heard today in a performance of the bass **arioso** "Betrachte, mein Seel" and the following **aria**, "Erwäge," from Part II of the **St. John Passion** of **Johann Sebastian Bach** and also in some of his **church cantatas**.

VIOLIN. The preeminent bowed **string instrument** of the Baroque, the high standards of violin making had been pretty well settled in late 16th century Italy, where Andrea Amati (b. 1511–1577) and Gasparo da Salò (1540–1609) established their workshops in Cremona and Brescia respectively. The Baroque period saw a few small improvements: the lengthening of the fingerboard to accommodate playing in high positions, the invention of the mute in the 17th century, and the replacement of entirely gut strings with gut strings wound with wire, usually silver, which improved their response, beginning about 1700. Like the modern violin, the average length of the Baroque instrument was about 35.5 cm., but there was great variety in the height and placement of bridges.

Some of the greatest violin makers in the history of Western music flourished during the Baroque: Nicolo Amati (1596–1684) and his disciples Antonio Stradivari (1644–1737) and the five makers of the Guarneri family, including Giuseppe Guarneri del Gesù (1698–1744), all of Cremona, and Jacob Stainer (1617–1683) of the Austrian Tyrol, as well as many other less famous masters.

Making the bow, which set the strings of a violin vibrating, was a separate art practiced by a different set of craftsmen. In the 17th century, the bow was generally convex (opposite to the modern type) and of many different lengths to suit the kind of music played. Later in the century, bows began to be straighter and longer. The frog, the part of the bow that holds the horsehair away from the stick, was at first immovable and maintained the hair at a fixed tension. These were generally replaced after 1700 by moveable frogs, so that hair tension might be regulated. The earliest frog with a screw mechanism, common in modern bows, is dated 1694. The brazilwood called pernambuco, prized for its weight and flexibility, is found in some Baroque bows, but most were made of snakewood and common brazilwood. Baroque bows were generally lighter than modern bows, with a balance point closer to the hand.

From the beginning of the Baroque, the violin was far and away the favorite solo instrument for **sonatas** and **concertos**. It became the mainstay of virtually all **orchestral** ensembles of any size, and it dominated the chamber genres, especially the **trio sonata**, the combination of two violins and **continuo** being the most common. Violin solos in vocal music begin in the **continuo madrigals** and **sacred concertos** of **Claudio Monteverdi, Heinrich Schütz**, and their contemporaries; in **opera** and **oratorio arias** they are innumerable. Only the **organ** and **harpsichord** can compete for richness of repertory.

Most Baroque composers were at least proficient on the violin, and virtually all wrote sonatas, concertos, and other solo music for the violin, with the exception of virtuosos of other instruments, such as **Jacques Gautier** or **Domenico Scarlatti**. Today, the violin works of **Arcangelo Corelli, Antonio Vivaldi** and his **Venetian** colleagues, **George Frideric Handel**, and especially **Johann Sebastian Bach** are commonly heard in the concert and recital halls. *See also* GEMINIANI, FRANCESCO; LECLAIR, JEAN-MARIE; MARTINI, GIOVANNI BATTISTA.

VIOLINO PICCOLO **(It. "small violin").** A **violin** smaller than normal size and consequently **tuned** to a higher range of pitch, usually a perfect fourth higher. Although not commonly required for Baroque music, some famous examples include a virtuoso solo part in the **aria** "Wann kommst du, mein Heil?" from **Cantata** BWV 140 of **Johann Sebastian Bach**, the solo part in his First **Brandenburg Concerto** (tuned a minor third higher), and the *violini piccoli alla francese* listed in the score for **Claudio Monteverdi**'s *L'Orfeo*, probably tuned a perfect octave higher.

VIOLONCELLO. *See* CELLO.

VIOLONE (It. "large viol"). Today, the term connotes the Baroque ancestor of the modern **string** bass or double bass. During the Baroque, "violone" could refer to instruments in a range of sizes and types, from a bass viola da gamba or **viol**, which would be the lowest pitched member of a viol **consort**, fretted and played with an underhand bow grip, to a large unfretted instrument more like the modern string bass. Such instruments could have from four to six strings. Typical **tunings** include:

$G^1 \ C^2 \ F^2 \ A^2 \ D^3 \ G^3$ and $D^1 \ G^1 \ C^2 \ E^2 \ A^2 \ D^3$

The violone could appear in a large **continuo** ensemble, reinforcing the bass melody along with the **cello**, and was a regular member of a Baroque **orchestra** or large string ensemble. There is virtually no Baroque solo music for the instrument.

VIRGINAL. Second in importance only to the **harpsichord** for secular **keyboard** music of the Baroque, the smaller and cheaper virginal was depicted

Virginal constructed by Thomas Klenck, Hamilton, New York.

in 16th- and 17th-century painting much more frequently, suggesting greater popularity as a household instrument. Its name may derive from an association with women players. Most Baroque secular keyboard music of the 17th century may be played on this instrument.

Like the harpsichord, the virginal produces tones when the player depresses a key that is really a lever and causes a *jack* equipped with a *plectrum* to rise and pluck a **string** under tension. It differs, in modern terminology, in that the stringing is perpendicular to the direction of the keys, with the longest bass register strings closest to the player. Thus, the case of the virginal may take various forms, with rectangles supposed to be the oldest, joined later by various polygonal shapes. Virginals almost always have a single keyboard and one set of strings; it is not possible to vary the timbre, as may be done on many harpsichords.

Construction of virginals gave way to the bentside **spinet** at the close of the 17th century, except in Italy.

VITALI, GIOVANNI BATTISTA (18 February 1632, Bologna–12 October 1692, Bologna). Vitali's 12 volumes of instrumental music contributed significantly to the repertory and development of the solo **violin sonata** and **trio sonata**, and many of them were reprinted repeatedly. He also composed two volumes of sacred music (Opus 6 and Opus 10) and one famous pedagogical work: the *Artifici Musicali* of 1689, which presents 60 compositions constituting an encyclopedia of **contrapuntal** technique. It may be the earliest such publication in the Baroque and adumbrates the **Musical Offering** of **Johann Sebastian Bach**.

Vitali studied with **Maurizio Cazzati** and played **cello** at San Petronio in Bologna before moving to Modena in 1674 to become *vice-maestro di cappella* for Duke Francesco II d'Este. He was promoted to *maestro* in 1684 but then demoted to *vice* with the arrival of **opera** composer Antonio Gianettini (1648–1721). Vitali remained at this post until his death.

VIVALDI, ANTONIO (4 March 1678, Venice–28 July 1741, Vienna). Known as "the red priest" in his own day for his fiery red hair, today Antonio Vivaldi is remembered chiefly as a composer of **concertos** for **orchestra** and solo instruments, establishing the norms for that genre that would persist until the present. His programmatic *Le Quattro Stagioni* (*The Four Seasons*) are the most famous of his more than 500 such works. In his own day, however, Vivaldi was at least as active in the world of Italian **opera**, composing about 55 of them himself and producing others. Other dramatic works include 4 **oratorios**, 41 solo **cantatas**, and 8 **serenatas**. His chamber music is made up of 70 **solo sonatas**, mostly for **violin**, and 28 **trio sonatas**. He also left a considerable body of sacred music: 33 psalms and **Magnificats**, 28 **motets** for solo voice and instruments, a complete **mass**, and 6 other mass movements, including the frequently performed **Gloria in D**.

Vivaldi was born the eldest of nine children of Giovanni Battista Vivaldi (1655–1736), a violinist at Basilica San Marco in **Venice**. He took the tonsure on 18 September 1693, trained for the Roman Catholic priesthood, and was ordained on 23 March 1703. However, a condition that Vivaldi himself described as *strettezza di petto* ("tightness of the chest"), probably bronchial asthma, had the curious effect of preventing his celebrating the mass from 1706 onward yet allowing his extensive teaching, publishing, and traveling about Italy to oversee his operatic productions.

While training for the priesthood, he probably learned the fundamentals of violin from his father and occasionally substituted for him at San Marco. Son Antonio's performance as an extra violinist at the basilica for Christmas 1696 is his first documented public appearance. Thereafter, he developed into a violinist of international reputation, with technical capacities that founded much of the innovation of his solo violin concertos.

Vivaldi's income as a musician came from three different kinds of activity, which constantly intertwine chronologically: as a salaried violin teacher at the famous Pio Ospedale della Pietà, as an independent opera composer and impresario, and as a composer of instrumental publications for sale.

The Pietà was one of four institutions Venice dedicated to the care and upbringing of abandoned, orphaned, or poor children. The Pietà in particular became famous for its musical training of girls with musical ability, highly unusual in Europe. Their public performances, usually from behind a screen, attracted both Venetian nobility and foreign travelers at the turn of the 18th century. Vivaldi was appointed master of violin teaching in 1703 by **Francesco Gasparini**, and his intermittent and at times tumultuous relationship with the governors of the Pietà would last until nearly the end of his life. His duties included teaching the young girls on various **string instruments**, maintaining the instruments, directing ensembles, and composing music for them.

The governors renewed his contract every year until 1709, when he was dismissed for reasons unknown, possibly just because his position was discontinued as a savings measure. But he was reappointed in September 1711. He composed a number of sacred works, including a mass and an oratorio and at least 30 motets, for the Pietà in 1715, and the governors awarded him a bonus of 50 ducats. Then the governors again voted against retaining him in March 1716, only to rehire him as "master of concerts" two months later. He composed a new oratorio, *Juditha Triumphans*, that same year. Then in April 1718, Vivaldi did not apply for reappointment at the Pietà, perhaps because he had been invited to Mantua to compose operas.

From 1723 to 1729, Vivaldi composed about 140 concertos for the Pietà on commission and rehearsed them with the girls when he was in Venice.

The governors hired him again, this time as *maestro di cappella* in 1735 but, tiring of his many travels, dismissed him in March 1738. The last transaction between Vivaldi and the Pietà was the sale of 20 concertos in May 1740.

His earliest known opera, *Ottone in Villa*, opened in the city of Vicenza in May 1713. Thereafter, he was associated with the public theater at Sant' Angelo in Venice. In 1718, he oversaw a production of his *Armida al Campo d'Egitto* in Mantua, and composed three more operas for the Carnival seasons of 1719 and 1720. The Hapsburg governor of Mantua, Prince Phillip of Hesse-Darmstadt, appointed Vivaldi *maestro di cappella di camera*. This title seems to have been honorary, since he was almost certainly in **Rome** for the Carnival seasons of 1723 and 1724, although he did compose several cantatas and serenatas for Prince Philipp. In Mantua, at some point during this period, he accepted a contralto Anna Girò as a student, and from this point, she along with her sister often performed in Vivaldi's operas, even traveling with him to

Antonio Vivaldi's principal publications

Opus	Title	Date/publisher	Contents
Opus 1		1705, Sala in Venice	12 trio sonatas
Opus 2		1709, Venice	6 solo sonatas for violin
Opus 3	L'Estro Armonico (The harmonic inspiration)	1711, Roger in Amsterdam	12 concertos for solo instruments and orchestra
Opus 4	La Stravaganza (Extravagance)	1711, Roger in Amsterdam	12 concertos for solo instruments and orchestra
Opus 5	VI Sonate	1716, Roger in Amsterdam	6 trio sonatas
Opus 6	VI Concerti a 5 Stromenti	1719, Roger in Amsterdam	
Opus 7	Concerti a 5 Stromenti	1720, Roger in Amsterdam	
Opus 8	Il Cimento dell'Armonia e dell' Inventione (The test of harmony and invention")	1725, Roger in Amsterdam	12 concertos for solo instruments and orchestra, including The Four Seasons
Opus 9	La Cetra (The lyre)	1727, Roger in Amsterdam	
Opus 10	VI Concerti	1729, Roger in Amsterdam	Concertos for solo flute or piccolo and orchestra
Opus 11	6 Concerti	1729, Roger in Amsterdam	
Opus 12	6 Concerti	1729, Roger in Amsterdam	

Vienna on his last journey. Evidence can neither confirm nor deny the rumors of an improper relationship between Anna Girò and Vivaldi.

From 1733 to 1735, Vivaldi composed operas for the Teatro Sant' Angelo and for another Venetian venue, Teatro San Samuele, working with the brilliant young Venetian poet Carlo Goldoni (1707–1793). He was offered a chance to compose operas for the Carnivals of 1737, 1738, and 1739 in Ferrara, but the Archbishop Tommaso Cardinal Ruffo forbad Vivaldi to enter the city, possibly on account of Anna Girò. *Siroe* was therefore mounted in his absence and failed in 1737, and the other two operas were never put on.

Vivaldi's solo sonatas, trio sonatas, and concertos for various instruments and orchestra began to appear in **print** by 1705 (see table).

Vivaldi's **Opus 3**, *L'Estro Armonico*, marks a turning point not only in his career but also for all Baroque instrumental music. Venice had been the center of music printing since the beginning of the 16th century but no more. With Opus 3, a major Venetian composer looked outside the city to publish his work because of the superiority of Roger's music engraving over the block printing traditional in Venice and perhaps because of the wider exposure to the northern music market. In any case, Opus 3 could be the most famous collection of instrumental music of the high Baroque. It proved the structural power of the ritornello form, established the fast movement–slow movement–fast movement as the principal model for concerto writing, and made Vivaldi's name internationally famous.

The publications Opus 5 through Opus 7 indicate no dedicatee, which usually named a financial supporter, so it is likely that the publisher Roger engraved them at his own expense, so confident was he of Vivaldi's popularity. This kind of contract was rare at this point in the history of music publishing.

Vivaldi's publications comprise but a small fraction of his instrumental music; most of it circulated in manuscript. In fact, by 1729, Vivaldi had decided that it was more profitable for him to sell his instrumental music as manuscripts, and so there are no publications of his late music.

A chance to perform at Vienna's Kärntnertortheater seems to have inspired Vivaldi's last journey in 1740, but the death of Emperor Charles VI in October shut down all the theaters throughout the Carnival period of 1741. Vivaldi stayed on, perhaps too sick or poor to return to Venice. His last documented professional act was the sale of some concertos to one Count Antonio Vinciguerra of Collalto. On 27 or 28 July, he died and was buried as a pauper in the Spittaler Gottsacker, a hospital burial ground in Vienna.

Like almost all his contemporaries' music, Vivaldi's was soon forgotten after his death and remained virtually unknown until the 20th century. Because **Johann Sebastian Bach** had transcribed five of the Opus 3 concertos, the Bach revival generated serious interest in Vivaldi. In 1947, Ricordi began a printed edition of his complete works, and the explosive popularity of the recording of *The Four Seasons* made by Louis Kaufman (1905–1994) in 1948 (Grand Prix du Disque in 1950) brought Vivaldi into the modern concert hall. The preferred method of identifying a Vivaldi composition today is the Ryom (RV) number, derived from the most recent version of Peter Ryom's catalog first published in 1973. *See also* EARLY MUSIC REVIVAL.

VOICE. In theoretical or analytical contexts, a melody of a musical **texture**.

VOLUNTARY. A free composition or **improvisation**, usually for pipe **organ**, played before or after an Anglican **service**, at the Offertory of Holy Communion, or after the psalms or second lesson at Morning and Evening Prayer. The term dates to the Mulliner Book (c. 1550–1575) and has loose associations with **fugal** writing, but its use varies widely in the sources. In the Baroque, **Matthew Locke**, **John Blow**, **Henry Purcell**, **Maurice Greene**, **William Croft**, and **John Stanley** are the principal composers.

WALTHER, JOHANN GOTTFRIED (18 September 1684, Erfurt, Germany–23 March 1748, Weimar). Cousin and friend to **Johann Sebastian Bach** and composer, according to his own record, of 92 vocal works and 119 **keyboard** works, his **organ** music is based mostly on **chorales**, and the chorale **variations** especially are highly regarded.

Walther is remembered chiefly for a musical dictionary, his *Musicalisches Lexicon, oder Musicalische Bibliothec*, published in **Leipzig** in 1732. This is the first book in any language to list both musical terminology along with biographies of notable musicians, past and present. It presents an invaluable picture of musical life and thought in 18th-century Germany.

According to his autobiography in **Johann Mattheson**'s *Grundlage einer Ehren-Pforte*, Walther studied music from age four and, in summer 1702, was appointed organist at the Thomaskirche in Erfurt. After studying law briefly at the university there, he decided to devote himself to music and to music theory particularly. He was befriended by Andreas Werckmeister (1645–1706), a leading German theorist, in 1703.

On 29 July 1707, Walther received a more prestigious appointment that he would retain until his death, as organist of the Stadtkirche in Weimar under Duke Wilhelm Ernst. Bach arrived the following year. When Bach left for Cöthen in 1717, however, Walther was not promoted as his successor.

WATER MUSIC (George Frideric Handel). The popular name for three collections of **orchestral** music by **George Frideric Handel**, some or all of which may have been performed by Handel as entertainment for royal parties upon barges on the Thames River. Each collection is unified by its orchestration and **key**:

First **Suite**–F major–**oboes** I and II, **horns** I and II, **bassoons, violins** I and II, **violas,** basso **continuo.**
Second Suite–D major–**trumpets** I and II, oboes I and II, horns I and II, bassoons, violins I and II, violas, basso continuo.
Third Suite–G major–**transverse flutes** I and II, oboes I and II, violins I and II, violas, basso continuo.

The designations of order and "suite" are traditional, but the autograph of the music does not survive, and so it is difficult to ascertain the original orders and usages of the music. Many of the movements of the "suites" bear no title and do not fall into any of the traditional Baroque **dance** types. Still, the Water Music probably contains the best-known orchestral dances to come out of the Baroque.

There are three documented excursions on the Thames where royalty heard Handel's music: 1715, 1717, and 1736, but there is no specific correlation between these events and the particular movements or even collections of the Water Music.

About 50 minutes are required for a complete performance, depending upon the observance of the repeat signs.

WECKMANN, MATTHIAS (1616?, Niederdoria near Mühlhausen, Germany–24 February 1674, Hamburg). Although his surviving music consists of only 12 **sacred concertos**, 11 chamber **sonatas**, 6 **partitas** for **keyboard**, 5 **canzonas**, and 9 sets of chorale **variations**, Weckmann, as one of the best students of **Heinrich Schütz**, influenced several important composers working in mid-17th-century Germany. His **organ** variations in particular show a mastery of the most learned **contrapuntal** techniques as well as sensitivity to the **chorale** melodies.

Weckmann's father, Jacobus, a clergyman, took Matthias to **Dresden** to study with Schütz about 1627. Schütz, in turn, brought him to **Hamburg** to study with Jacob Praetorius (1586–1651) and **Heinrich Scheidemann**. He spent the years 1642 to 1646 playing for the royal chapel in Denmark. In 1649, he was appointed inspector of the chapel of the Elector of Saxony in Dresden. About this time, he began lifelong friendships with **Christoph Bernhard** and **Johann Jacob Froberger**.

In 1655, he won the competition to become organist at the Jacobkirche in Hamburg, where **Thomas Selle** was cantor, and founded a *collegium musicum* there in 1660, and thereby introduced the city to the latest music from the leading musical centers of Europe.

WEELKES, THOMAS (baptized 25 October 1576–buried 1 December 1623, London). Composer, student of **William Byrd**, and **organist** at Chichester Cathedral from between October of 1601 or 1602 until 16 January 1617, when he was dismissed for drunkenness. He composed nine **services**, the most for a single major composer of his time, and completed nearly 50 **anthems**, about 90 **madrigals**, 2 **voluntaries** for **keyboard**, and about 10 works for **viol consort**.

WEISS, SILVIUS LEOPOLD (October 1686, Breslau [now Wroclaw], Poland–16 October 1750, Dresden). One of the greatest **lutenists** of music history, Weiss spent most of his career in the court of the Elector of Saxony at **Dresden**, from 1718 to his death, but his fame created demand for performances and instruction at the courts of **Vienna**, Munich, Prague, and Berlin, among other places he visited. His legacy of compositions is the largest in the history of the lute, more than 600 works: hundreds of **dances** organized into **suites** ("**sonatas**") following the "classic" suite pattern of **allemande, courante, bourrée, sarabande, minuet,** and **gigue,** often preceded by an **unmeasured prelude. Johann Sebastian Bach** arranged No. 47 as a **violin** sonata with **harpsichord** (BWV 1025).

Silvius was trained by his father, the lutenist Johann Jacob Weiss (c. 1662–1754), and performed for Emperor Leopold I at age seven. Silvius began composing as early as 1706. From 1710 to 1714, he was in **Rome** in the service of Polish Prince Alexander Sobieski, whose mother employed both **Alessandro** and **Domenico Scarlatti.** Doubtless, Weiss also knew **Arcangelo Corelli** in Rome. He then served Carl Philipp, imperial governor of the Tyrol, probably from 1715 to 1717, at which point he went to Dresden with a considerable salary increase. About this time, he married Maria Elizabeth (c. 1700–1759), and they had 11 children.

WELL-TEMPERED CLAVIER **(Johann Sebastian Bach BWV 846–893; Ger.** *Das wohltemperierte Clavier***).** Didactic collection of **keyboard preludes** and **fugues** composed by **Johann Sebastian Bach.** "*Wohltemperierte*" or "appropriately **tuned**," probably refers to a system of tuning the keyboard known as equal temperament, such that within a single tuning the playing of music in all 24 **keys,** 12 major and 12 minor, made possible by the **chromatic** pitch collection of the Western tradition is possible. "Clavier" is the German generic term for keyboard, and the somewhat constrained pitch range of the music suggests that Bach tried to make it playable on **organ** and **clavichord** as well as **harpsichord.** Today, the works are most commonly performed on the harpsichord and modern piano and are indispensable in the pedagogies of both instruments as well as others for which transcriptions have been made.

There are actually two collections, known as Book I and Book II, of the *Well-Tempered Clavier.* The final version of Book I dates from 1722 and the Book II from about 1742, but many of the pieces in the books are known to have been composed earlier than those terminus dates.

Both collections have the same format, adapted from a collection of Johann Caspar Ferdinand Fischer (c. 1670–1746) entitled *Ariadne* that first appeared in 1702. There are 24 pairs of preludes and fugues, one for each key and

mode, presented in chromatic pitch order: C major, C minor, C-sharp major, C-sharp minor, D major, and so forth.

Bach's didactic purpose in making these collections included giving the student practice in playing in all keys (even though Baroque composers rarely, if ever, used many of them), and to demonstrate the art of fugue composition. Most of the fugues are composed for three or four **voices**; there is one fugue for two voices (Book I: E minor) and two for five **voices** (Book I: C-sharp minor and B-flat minor). In addition, every style of fugue known to Bach is represented: the *stile antico* **ricercar subject**, the chromatic subject, techniques of **inversion**, **diminution**, and **augmentation** all find their places. There is much **invertible counterpoint**, fugues where the similarity of subject and **countersubject** is such that the piece seems to be composed on a single idea, and discursive fugues where the distinctive countersubject comes to dominate the composition. The preludes comprise an encyclopedic collection of pieces apparently designed to acquaint the student with everything the fugues could not cover: **dance** movements, brilliant arpeggiated passagework, **fantasias**, which themselves include fugal passages, **trio sonata textures**, *style brisé*, and other types that defy classification.

The *Well-Tempered Clavier* is one of the few works of J. S. Bach that needed no revival. Composers admired the work so much as a teaching tool for counterpoint that it was kept in circulation in manuscript during the century following Bach's death, when most of his music was unknown. Wolfgang Amadeus Mozart (1756–1791) was introduced to it in 1782, and Ludwig van Beethoven (1770–1827) studied it throughout his life. The first **printed** edition appeared in 1801–1802.

Z

ZACHOW, FRIEDRICH WILHELM (baptized 14 November 1663, Leipzig, Germany–7 August 1712, Halle). Teacher of **George Frideric Handel**, Zachow was **organist** at the Marienkirche Church in Halle from 11 August 1684 until his death. Surviving from an apparently large oeuvre are about 30 **cantatas** in various forms from **sacred concerto** to **operatic**, a **chorale mass**, 3 Latin **motets**, about 50 **keyboard chorales**, and about 20 assorted keyboard works.

ZARZUELA. A light form of Spanish musical drama developed by the playwright Pedro Calderòn de la Barca (1600–1681) in the 1650s. There are two acts in a pastoral or rustic setting, and the tone tends to the comic, with simplified poetry. **Juan Hidalgo** composed the music for the oldest surviving zarzuela score, *Los Celos Hacen Estrellas* ("Jealousy Makes Stars," 1672), to a **libretto** by Juan Vélez de Guevara (1611–1675).

ZELENKA, JAN DISMAS (baptized 16 October 1679, Lounovice, modern Czech Republic–22 or 23 December 1745, Dresden). A composer who, unusual for his time, did not write **operas** but instead produced at furious pace a large volume of Roman Catholic sacred music during the 1720s that maintained many of the *stile antico* **contrapuntal** traditions. He also left a small oeuvre of instrumental music: six ensemble **sonatas**, five **capriccios**, a **concerto**, a **symphony**, and an **overture**.

Zelenka arrived at the court of **Dresden** as a **violone** player about 1710. From 1716 to 1719, he studied in Italy. When the Dresden opera closed in 1720, the energy of the court's composers turned to sacred music, whence comes most of Zelenka's **masses**, psalm settings, and other sacred works. He was appointed *vice-Kapellmeister* in 1721. After **Johann David Heinichen** died in 1729, Zelenka stepped in and filled many of his duties, but the Elector Friedrich August II, instead of promoting Zelenka to *Kapellmeister*, passed him over in favor of **Johann Adolf Hasse** in 1731. Zelenka's compositional activity fell off sharply afterward.

ZENO, APOSTOLO (11 December 1668, Venice–11 November 1750, Venice). Along with **Metastasio**, one of the most important **opera librettists** of the Baroque, whose words were set to music by **Alessandro Scarlatti, Antonio Lotti, Antonio Vivaldi, Johann Adolf Hasse, Nicola Porpora, Giovanni Bononcini, George Frideric Handel**, and any composer of standing in the opera world. Most of his 42 librettos were set many times; *Lucio Vero*, first composed by Carlo Francesco Pollarolo (c. 1653–1723) and produced on 26 December 1699 in **Venice**, was set 25 more times until 1789 by **Tomaso Albinoni, Francesco Gasparini, Reinhard Keiser, Niccolò Jommelli** (twice), and others.

No small part of Zeno's importance derives from his efforts, as founder of the Accademia degli Animosi (Academy of the Spirited) in 1691, to reform the often ridiculous dramas of the **Venetian opera** by streamlining the casts and making the plots exemplars of the triumph of virtue, important characteristics of the ***opera seria***. Nevertheless, his own first libretto of 1696, *Gli Inganni Felici* ("The Happy Deceptions"), still contained much comedy and far-fetched misunderstandings, and Zeno complained even in his late career of the constraints that singers and impresarios imposed on true drama.

He held only one post as court poet, at the imperial court in **Vienna** from 1718 to 1729, when he was replaced by Metastasio. Most of his 17 **oratorio** librettos, 11 of them set by **Antonio Caldara**, date from this period. After returning to Venice, he sent one last libretto, *Enone* of 1734, to Vienna and then devoted himself to other more scholarly pursuits: the history of literature and antiquarian collections.

Bibliography

CONTENTS

INTRODUCTION

Since the entries of the dictionary can provide only the most basic information about any item in the vast body of European Baroque music, the bibliography directs the reader to sources of more detailed and deeper treatments.

Beginning with the most general references about music and cultural or political history taken separately, the listing proceeds through general histories of music and histories, dictionaries, bibliographies, and collections of Baroque music. Then come biographies, studies of specific genres of Baroque music (e.g., oratorio), and studies of instruments and their traditions. The last sections, not being strictly bibliographical, are more general: discographies and electronic sources. Inevitably, some items do not fall neatly into any category or might have fit sensibly into more than one: for example, *Dance and Music in French Baroque Theatre: Sources and Interpretations* might have been listed in the "Surveys of Baroque Music" rather than "Generic

Studies of Baroque Music" / "Suite and Dance," where it is found, since dance is the nearly exclusive topic of the book. To avoid double listings and include as many sources as possible, I hope that the reader may check all plausible subheadings.

The criteria for inclusion begin with the obvious ones of the authors' and publishers' reputations in the various subfields of Baroque music. Beyond that, I and the series editor preferred to include more recent works rather than older ones, works in English, and books rather than articles. There are exceptions made to each of these criteria at times, of course. Some specialized areas have been but little studied as yet, and one must take what one can get. Classic studies and standard references deserve a place almost regardless of their age, especially in matters of music criticism and analysis, where the most valuable is not always the most recent. Not listed are doctoral dissertations because they are not nearly as accessible to readers as books, but they nevertheless contain many excellent specialized studies of Baroque music. To find them, please consult Cecil Adkins, *Doctoral Dissertations in Musicology*, listed in the "General References on Music," and at http://www.music.indiana.edu/ddm/. Not listed are items written in languages other than those of standard Western musicology: English above all, German, French, Italian, Latin, and Spanish.

For English speakers, the most useful of the "General References" to be found in most libraries are *The New Grove*, a music encyclopedia of 29 volumes, recently revised and updated, the *RILM* index of periodical literature, the *RISM* catalog of musical sources, and *Baker's* biographical dictionaries. Those who can read German should see the new edition of *Musik in Geschichte und Gegenwart*.

Knowledge of European political and cultural history is indispensable to a thorough understanding of its music. "Studies of European History That Include the Baroque" lists modern and easily accessible books covering the principal political, cultural, and religious institutions of early modern Europe, including the Protestant Reformation, whose precipitating events happened well before the beginning of the Baroque but whose influence on music throughout the period is immense.

"Histories of Music Comprising Baroque Music" is a selection of books about historical topics, such as the history of keyboard music, history of music theory, or history of music printing, which devote significant coverage to Baroque music, even though the Baroque may not be the primary focus of the book. These works provide another means, specifically oriented to a particular aspect of music history, to learn about musical traditions and practices preceding the Baroque and those that continued to influence the history of music afterward.

"Surveys of Baroque Music" focuses exclusively on Baroque music. These works range from the very broad, such as George Buelow's *A History of Baroque Music*, to the very specific, such as Eugene Enrico's *The Orchestra at San Petronio in the Baroque Era*.

The list also includes works that may not treat Baroque music directly but rather illuminate a musical, cultural, religious, or intellectual tradition that affected it, such as George Houle's *Meter in Music, 1600–1800* and Albert Cohen's *Music in the French Royal Academy of Sciences: A Study in the Evolution of Musical Thought*.

"Bibliographies and Dictionaries That Include Baroque Music" includes four kinds of related references: narrative surveys of repertories, such as Arnold Corliss' *Organ*

Literature; catalogs of musical scores and parts, such as David Fuller and Bruce Gustafson's *A Catalogue of French Harpsichord Music, 1669–1780*; dictionaries oriented toward Baroque music, such as James Robert Davidson's *A Dictionary of Protestant Church Music*; and traditional bibliographies oriented toward Baroque music, such as Carol MacClintock's *Readings in the History of Music in Performance.*

"Important Primary Sources" includes writings on music originating in the Baroque period, mostly by composers. They include theoretical works, handbooks or manuals of composition, criticism, and encyclopedias of music. The original dates of publication are given, and, wherever possible, the publication data of an English translation.

"Baroque Music Anthologies" and "Collected Works of Composers" contain modern editions of important repertories of Baroque music, that is, scores and parts. The first lists anthologies of music by various composers, such as the famous *Denkmäler der Tonkunst in Österreich* (Monuments of Austrian Music). The second lists the many sets of complete works by single composers. When there is more than one set, all are listed. In general, the more recent ones have had recourse to more sources and, therefore, have been carried out more thoroughly with modern text-critical methods, but older ones can offer an interesting picture of the early music revival in those times when they were released. It is important to note that this section is ordered by the family name of the composer, not the editor of the set, even if the composer's name is not the first item in the bibliographical entry.

"Biographies of Musicians and Composers and Studies of Specific Works" lists studies of composers, with a subheading for each one with three or more entries so that one may search fairly easily by composer rather than the author of the study. Items about less significant personages or books that cover several composers, such as Joshua Rifkin's *North German Baroque Masters: Schütz, Froberger, Buxtehude, Purcell, Telemann*, are grouped together under "Others," listed alphabetically by author as usual. In recent years, there has appeared a great number of books devoted to single works, such as the Mass in B Minor of J. S. Bach, and these are duly listed under the composer's subheading, especially if there is a corresponding entry in the historical dictionary. Of particular interest to scholars are the "Guides to Research" for individual composers, usually published by Garland Press but occasionally by Routledge and others. The Cambridge Handbooks are also excellent bibliographical references.

A great many excellent studies on Baroque music have concentrated not on single composers but on a single genre of composition: opera, cantata, oratorio, suite, and so forth. These are listed in "Generic Studies of Baroque Music," which has subheadings organized by genre name. A study combining a single composer and a single genre, however, such as Pieter Dirksen's *The Keyboard Music of Jan Pieterszoon Sweelinck*, is found in the biographical section.

"Baroque Musical Instruments" also includes subheadings for each instrument family: keyboard, strings, winds. "Others" contains more general studies of Baroque performance practice and a few modern how-to books on ornamentation and playing the figured bass.

The bibliography concludes with two general sections, "Discographies" and "Internet Resources." The latter does not include the many general references that may provide information about Baroque music but only broad musicological indices, such as *RISM: International Inventory of Musical Sources after 1600*, or new resources specifically tailored to Baroque topics, such as, Yo Tomita's *Bach Bibliography*, found at http://www.qub.ac.uk/~tomita/bachbib/.

GENERAL REFERENCES ON MUSIC

Adkins, Cecil, and Alis Dickinson. *Doctoral Dissertations in Musicology.* 2nd ser. 1st cumulative ed. Philadelphia: American Musicological Society / Basel, Switzerland: International Musicological Society, 1990. Supplements, 1991–.

Benjamin, Thomas. *The Craft of Tonal Counterpoint.* New York: Routledge, 2003.

Duckles, Vincent H., and Ida Re, eds. *Music Reference and Research Materials: An Annotated Bibliography.* 5th ed. New York: Schirmer, 1997.

Finscher, Ludwig. *Musik in Geschichte und Gegenwart: allgemeine Enzyklopädie der Musik.* 2nd ed., rev. ed. 20 vols. Kassel, Germany: Bärenreiter, 1994–2004.

Kennedy, Michael, and Joyce Bourne. *The Oxford Dictionary of Music.* 2nd ed. Oxford: Oxford University Press, 1994.

Mesa, Franklin. *Opera: An Encyclopedia of World Premieres and Significant Performances, Singers, Composers, Librettists, Arias and Conductors, 1597–2000.* Jefferson, NC: McFarland, 2007.

Porte, Jacques. *Encyclopédie des Musiques Sacrées.* 3 vols. Paris: Édition Labergerie, 1968–70.

Randel, Don Michael. *The New Harvard Dictionary of Music.* Cambridge, MA: Belknap Press of Harvard University Press, 1986.

Répertoire International de Littérature Musicale. *RILM Abstracts of Music Literature.* Vol. 1–. New York: International *RILM* Center, 1967– .

Répertoire International des Sources Musicales [RISM]. Munich: G. Henle, 1960–.

Sadie, Julie Anne, and Rhian Samuel. *The New Grove Dictionary of Women Composers.* London: Macmillan, 1994.

Sadie, Stanley, ed. *The New Grove Dictionary of Music and Musicians.* 29 vols. New York: Macmillan, 2001.

———. *The New Grove Dictionary of Musical Instruments.* 3 vols. London: Macmillan, 1984.

Sadie, Stanley, and Jane Bellingham. *The Illustrated Encyclopedia of Opera.* Rowville, Victoria, Australia: Five Mile, 2004.

Slonimsky, Nicolas. *Baker's Biographical Dictionary of Musicians.* New York: Schirmer, 1991.

Slonimsky, Nicolas, and Laura Diane Kuhn. *Baker's Biographical Dictionary of Musicians.* 6 vols. New York: Schirmer, 2001.

Wade-Matthews, Max. *The World Encyclopedia of Musical Instruments.* London: Lorenz, 2000.

Wiering, Frans. *The Language of the Modes: Studies in the History of Polyphonic Modality.* New York: Routledge, 2001.

STUDIES OF EUROPEAN HISTORY THAT INCLUDE THE BAROQUE

Asch, Ronald G., and Adolf M. Birke, eds. *Princes, Patronage, and the Nobility: The Court at the Beginning of the Modern Age, c. 1450–1650.* Oxford: Oxford University Press, 1991.

Casey, James. *Early Modern Spain: A Social History.* New York: Routledge, 1999.

Chaunu, Pierre, ed. *The Reformation.* New York: St. Martin's, 1986.

Church, William F. *The Impact of Absolutism in France: National Experience under Richelieu, Mazarin, and Louis XIV.* New York: John Wiley, 1969.

Corp, Edwart T. *A Court in Exile: the Stuarts in France, 1689–1718.* Cambridge: Cambridge University Press, 2004.

Deward, Jonathan. *The European Nobility, 1400–1800.* Cambridge: Cambridge University Press, 1996.

Elliott, John Huxtable. *Imperial Spain, 1469–1716.* New York: New American Library, 1977.

Fraser, Antonia. *Charles II: His Life and Times.* London: Weidenfeld and Nicolson, 1979.

Haskell, Francis. *Patrons and Painters: A Study in the Relations between Italian Art and Society in the Age of the Baroque.* 2nd ed. London: 1980.

Hayburn, Robert F. *Papal Legislation on Sacred Music 95 A.D. to 1977 A.D.* Collegeville, MN: Liturgical Press, 1979.

Hersey, George L. *Architecture and Geometry in the Age of the Baroque.* Chicago: University of Chicago Press, 2001.

Hillebrand, Hans J., ed. *Oxford Encyclopedia of the Reformation.* New York: Oxford University Press, 1996.

Ingrao, Charles W. *The Hapsburg Monarchy, 1618–1815.* Cambridge: Cambridge University Press, 1994.

Jones, Martin D. W. *The Counter-Reformation: Religion and Society in Early Modern Europe.* Cambridge: Cambridge University Press, 1995.

Leppert, Richard D., and Susan McClary, eds. *Music and Society: The Politics of Composition, Performance, and Reception.* Cambridge: Cambridge University Press, 1987.

Monod, Paul Kleber. *The Power of Kings: Monarchy and Religion in Europe, 1589–1715.* New Haven, CT: Yale University Press, 1999.

Monter, E. William. *Frontiers of Heresy: The Spanish Inquisition from the Basque Lands to Sicily.* New York: Cambridge University Press, 1990.

Mullett, Michael. *James II and English Politics, 1678–1688.* London: Routledge, 1994.

O'Malley, John W., Gauvin A. Bailey, and Giovanni Sale. *The Jesuits and the Arts, 1540–1773.* Philadelphia: Saint Joseph's University Press, 2005.

Reid, Jane Davidson. *The Oxford Guide to Classical Mythology in the Arts, 1300–1990.* New York: Oxford University Press, 1993.

Scott, H. M., ed. *The European Nobilities in the Seventeenth and Eighteenth Centuries.* Vol. 1, *Western Europe.* London: Longman, 1995.

Strong, Roy. *Art and Power: Renaissance Festivals, 1450–1650.* Berkeley: University of California Press, 1984.

Sturdy, David J. *Louis XIV*. New York: St. Martin's, 1998.
Vierhaus, Rudolf. *Germany in the Age of Absolutism*. Translated by J. B. Knudsen. New York: Cambridge University Press, 1988.
Woolsey, Charles. *Colbert and a Century of French Mercantilism*. New York: Columbia University Press, 1939. Reprint, London: F. Cass, 1964.
Ziegler, Gilette. *At the Court of Versailles*. Translated by Walter Taylor. New York: Dutton, 1966.

HISTORIES OF MUSIC THAT INCLUDE THE BAROQUE

Apel, Willi. *The History of Keyboard Music to 1700*. Translated and revised by Hans Tischler. Bloomington: Indiana University Press, 1972.
Badin, Paul. *Ricercar*. Coaraze: Amourier, 2000.
Baldauf-Berdes. *Women Musicians of Venice: Musical Foundations, 1525–1855*. Oxford: Clarendon, 1993.
Benoit, Marcelle. *Versailles et les Musiciens du Roi, 1661–1733: Étude Institutionelle et Sociale*. Paris: Picard, 1971.
Berdes, Jane L. *Women Musicians of Venice: Musical Foundations, 1525–1855*. Oxford: Clarendon, 1993.
Berger, Karol. *Musica Ficta*. Cambridge: Cambridge University Press, 1987.
Bianconi, Lorenzo, and Biagio Pestelli, eds. *Opera Production and Its Resources*. Translated by Lydia G. Cochrane. Part 2, vol. 4 of *The History of Italian Opera*. Chicago: University of Chicago Press, 1987.
Blume, Friedrich. *Protestant Church Music: A History*. Revised by Ludwig Finscher. Translated by F. Ellsworth Peterson. New York: Norton, 1974.
Bowers, Jane, and Judith Tick. *Women Making Music: The Western Art Tradition, 1150–1950*. Urbana: University of Illinois Press, 1986.
Burkholder, J. Peter, Donald J. Grout, and Claude V. Palisca. *A History of Western Music*. 8th ed. New York: Norton, 2010. 1st ed. 1960.
Caldwell, John. *English Keyboard Music before the Nineteenth Century*. Oxford: Blackwell, 1973.
Carreras López, Juan José, and Bernardo José García García. *The Royal Chapel in the Time of the Hapsburgs: Music and Ceremony in the Early Modern European Court*. Woodbridge, UK: Boydell, 2005.
Christensen, Thomas S. *The Cambridge History of Western Music Theory*. Cambridge: Cambridge University Press, 2001.
Dahlhaus, Carl. *Studies on the Origin of Harmonic Tonality*. Translated by Robert O. Gjerdingen. Princeton, NJ: Princeton University Press, 1990.
Griffiths, Paul. *A Concise History of Western Music*. Cambridge: Cambridge University Press, 2006.
Grout, Donald J. *A Short History of Opera*. 2nd ed. New York: Columbia University Press, 1965.
Haar, James. *European Music, 1520–1640*. Woodbridge, UK: Boydell, 2006.

Harper, John. *The Forms and Orders of Western Liturgy from the Tenth to the Eighteenth Century: A Historical Introduction and Guide for Students and Musicians.* Oxford: Clarendon, 1991.

Härtwig, Dieter. *Der Dresdner Kreuzchor Geschichte und Gegenwart, Wirkungsstätten und Schule.* Leipzig, Germany: Evangelische Verlag-Anst., 2006.

Herl, Joseph. *Worship Wars in Early Lutheranism: Choir, Congregation, and Three Centuries of Conflict.* Oxford: Oxford University Press, 2004.

Hudson, Richard. *The Folia, the Saraband, the Passacaglia, and the Chaconne.* Musicological Studies and Documents 35. Neuhausen-Stuttgart, Germany: American Institute of Musicology, 1982.

Hyatt King, Alec. *Four Hundred Years of Music Printing.* London: British Museum, 1964.

Keefe, Simon P. *The Cambridge History of Eighteenth-Century Music.* Cambridge: Cambridge University Press, 2009.

Keller, James M. *Chamber Music: A Listener's Guide.* New York: Oxford University Press, 2011.

Kirby, Frank E. *A Short History of Keyboard Music.* New York: Schirmer, 1966.

Kirkendale, Warren. *The Court Musicians in Florence during the Principate of the Medici.* Florence, Italy: Leo S. Olschki, 1993.

Lang, Paul Henry. *Music in Western Civilization.* New York: Norton, 1941.

Launay, Denise. *La Musique Religieuse en France du Concile de Trente à 1804.* Paris: Société Française de Musicologie, 1993.

Lester, Joel. *Compositional Theory in the Eighteenth Century.* Cambridge, MA: Harvard University Press, 1992.

Lewis, Anthony, and Nigel Fortune, eds. *Opera and Church Music, 1630–1750.* Vol. 5 of *New Oxford History of Music.* London: Oxford University Press, 1975.

Lippmann, Edward. *A History of Western Musical Aesthetics.* Lincoln: University of Nebraska Press, 1992.

Long, Kenneth. *The Music of the English Church.* London: Hodder and Stoughton, 1991.

Mann, Alfred, ed. *The Great Composer as Teacher and Student: Theory and Practice of Composition: Bach, Handel, Haydn, Mozart, Beethoven, Schubert.* New York: Dover, 1994.

———. *The Study of Fugue.* New Brunswick, NJ: Rutgers University Press, 1958. Reprint, New York: Dover, 1987.

Marshall, Robert, L., ed. *Eighteenth-Century Keyboard Music.* New York: Schirmer, 1994.

Meier, Bernhard. *The Modes of Classical Vocal Polyphony: Described according to the Sources.* Translated by Ellen S. Beebe. New York: Broude, 1988.

The New Oxford History of Music. 10 vols. London: Oxford University Press, 1954–90.

Pahlen, Kurt, et al. *The World of the Oratorio: Oratorio, Mass, Requiem, Te Deum, Stabat Mater, and Large Cantatas.* Portland, OR: Amadeus, 1990.

Pierre, Constant. *Histoire du Concert spirituel 1725–1790.* Paris: Société Française de Musicologie, 1975.

Pirotta, Nino. *Music and Culture in Italy from the Middle Ages to the Baroque: A Collection of Essays*. Cambridge, MA: Harvard University Press, 1984.

Rice, Paul F. *The Performing Arts at Fontainebleau from Louis XIV to Louis XVI*. Ann Arbor, MI: UMI Research Press, 1989.

Robbins Landon, H. C., and John Julius Norwich. *Five Centuries of Music in Venice*. New York: Schirmer, 1991.

Routley, Erik. *A Short History of English Church Music*. London: Mowbrays, 1977.

Salmen, Walter, ed. *The Social Status of the Professional Musician from the Middle Ages to the 19th Century*. Translated by Herbert Kaufman and Barbara Reisner. Sociology of Music 1. New York: Pendragon, 1982.

Selfridge-Field, Eleanor. *Song and Season: Science, Culture, and Theatrical Time in Early Modern Venice*. Stanford, CA: Stanford University Press, 2007.

Shaw, H. Watkins. *Eighteenth-Century Cathedral Music*. London: Hodder and Stoughton, 1970.

Silbiger, Alexander, ed. *Keyboard Music before 1700*. New York: Schirmer, 1995.

Simpson, Claude M. *The British Broadside Ballad and Its Music*. New Brunswick, NJ: Rutgers University Press, 1966.

Smither, Howard E. *A History of the Oratorio*. 3 vols. Chapel Hill: University of North Carolina Press, 1977.

Spink, Ian. *Restoration Cathedral Music, 1660–1714*. Oxford: Clarendon / New York: Oxford University Press, 1995.

Spink, Ian, and Nicholas Temperly, eds. *The Blackwell History of Music in Britain*. Oxford: Blackwell, 1900–.

Strunk, Oliver, and Leo Treitler. *Source Readings in Music History*. 1950. Rev. ed., New York: Norton, 1998.

Swain, Joseph P. *Harmonic Rhythm: Analysis and Interpretation*. New York: Oxford University Press, 2002.

Taruskin, Richard. *Oxford History of Western Music*. 6 vols. New York: Oxford University Press, 2005.

Ulrich, Homer. *A Survey of Choral Music*. New York: Harcourt Brace Jovanovich, 1973.

Ursprung, Otto. *Die katholischen Kirchenmusik*. Handbuch der Musikwissenschaft 9. Potsdam, Germany: Akademische Verlagsgesellschaft Athenaion, 1931.

Weber, William. *The Rise of Musical Classics in Eighteenth-Century England: A Study in Canon, Ritual, and Ideology*. Oxford: Clarendon, 1992.

Weiss, Piero, and Richard Taruskin, eds. *Music in the Western World: A History in Documents*. New York: Schirmer, 1984.

Walker, Paul Mark. *Theories of Fugue from the Age of Josquin to the Age of Bach*. Rochester, NY: University of Rochester Press, 2000.

White, John D. *Theories of Musical Texture in Western History*. New York: Garland, 1995.

Wright, Craig M., and Bryan R. Simms. *Music in Western Civilization*. Belmont, CA: Thomson/Schirmer, 2006.

SURVEYS OF BAROQUE MUSIC

Anderson, Nicolas. *Baroque Music*. London: Thames and Hudson, 1994.

Anthony, James R. *French Baroque Music from Beaujoyeux to Rameau*. Rev. ed. Portland, OR: Amadeus, 1977.

Baldwin, David. *The Chapel Royal: Ancient and Modern*. London: Duckworth, 1990.

Bartel, Dietrich. *Musica Poetica: Musical-Rhetorical Figures in German Baroque Music*. Lincoln: University of Nebraska Press, 1997.

Benoit, Marcelle, ed. *Dictionnaire de la musique en France aux XVIIe et XVIIIe siècles*. Paris: Fayard, 1992.

Bianconi, Lorenzo. *Music in the Seventeenth Century*. Translated by David Bryant. Cambridge: Cambridge University Press, 1987.

Bjurström, Per. *Feast and Theatre in Queen Christina's Rome*. Stockholm: Bengtsons, 1966.

Boyd, Malcolm, and Juan José Carreras, eds. *Music in Spain during the Eighteenth Century*. New York: Cambridge University Press, 1998.

Buelow, George J. *A History of Baroque Music*. Bloomington: Indiana University Press, 2004.

——, ed. *The Late Baroque Era: From the 1680s to 1740*. Englewood Cliffs, NJ: Prentice-Hall, 1994.

——. "Symposium on Seventeenth-Century Music Theory: Germany." *Journal of Music Theory* 16 (1972): 36–49.

Bukofzer, Manfred F. *Music in the Baroque Era from Monteverdi to Bach*. New York: Norton, 1947.

Butt, John. *Music Education and the Art of Performance in the German Baroque*. Cambridge: Cambridge University Press, 1994.

Butt, John, and Tim Carter, eds. *The Cambridge History of Seventeenth-Century Music*. Cambridge: Cambridge University Press, 2005.

Carter, Tim. "A Florentine Wedding of 1608." *Acta Musicologica* IV (1983): 89–107.

——. *Music in Later Renaissance & Early Baroque Italy*. London: Batsford, 1992.

Chater, J. "Musical Patronage in Rome at the Turn of the Seventeenth Century: The Case of Cardinal Montalto." *Studi Musicali* XVI (1987): 179–227.

Christensen, Thomas Street, and Peter Dejans. *Towards Tonality: Aspects of Baroque Music Theory*. Leuven, Belgium: Leuven University Press, 2007.

Cohen, Albert. *Music in the French Royal Academy of Sciences: A Study in the Evolution of Musical Thought*. Princeton, NJ: Princeton University Press, 1981.

Cowart, Georgia. *The Origins of Modern Musical Criticism: French and Italian Music, 1600-1750*. Ann Arbor, MI: UMI Research Press, 1981.

Culley, Thomas D. *Jesuits and Music: A Study of the Musicians Connected with the German College in Rome during the 17th Century and of Their Activities in Northern Europe*. Sources and Studies for the History of the Jesuits 2. Rome: Jesuit Historical Institute, 1970.

Dufourcq, Norbert, ed. *La musique à la Cour de Louis XIV et de Louis XV, d'après les "Mémoires" de Sourches et Luynes, 1681–1758*. Paris: Picard, 1970.

Enrico, Eugene. *The Orchestra at San Petronio in the Baroque Era*. Washington, DC: Smithsonian Institution Press, 1976.

Gambassi, Osvaldo. *La Cappella Musicale di S. Petronio: Maestri, Organisti, Cantori e Strumentisti dal 1436 al 1920*. Florence, Italy: Leo S. Olschki, 1987.

Hammond, Friderick. *Music and Spectacle in Baroque Rome*. New Haven, CT: Yale University Press, 1994.

Harris-Warrick, Rebecca, and Carol G. Marsh. *Musical Theatre at the Court of Louis XIV: "Le Mariage de la Grosse Cathos."* Cambridge: Cambridge University Press, 1994.

Heartz, Daniel. "The Concert Spirituel in the Tuileries Palace." *Early Music* XXI (1993): 241–8.

Herissone, Rebecca. *Music Theory in Seventeenth-Century England*. New York: Oxford University Press, 2000.

Hill, John Walter. *Baroque Music: Music in Western Europe, 1580–1750*. Norton Introduction to Music History. New York: Norton, 2005.

Hilton, Wendy. *Dance of Court and Theater: The French Noble Style, 1690–1725*. London: Dance Books / Princeton, NJ: Princeton Book Co., 1981.

Hogwood, Christopher. *Music at Court*. London: Folio Society, 1977.

Houle, George. *Meter in Music, 1600–1800: Performance, Perception, and Notation*. Bloomington: Indiana University Press, 1987.

Isherwood, Robert M. *Music in the Service of the King: France in the Seventeenth Century*. Ithaca, NY: Cornell University Press, 1973.

Jorgens, Elise Bickford. *The Well-Tun'd World: Musical Interpretations of English Poetry, 1597–1651*. Minneapolis: University of Minnesota Press, 1982.

Kevorkian, Tanya. *Baroque Piety: Religion, Society, and Music in Leipzig, 1650–1750*. Aldershot, UK: Ashgate, 2007.

Lester, Joel. *Between Modes and Keys: German Theory, 1592–1802*. Harmonologia Series 3. Stuyvesant, NY: Pendragon, 1989.

Monson, Craig A. *Disembodied Voices: Music and Culture in an Early Modern Italian Convent*. Berkeley: University of California Press, 1995.

The New Grove French Baroque Masters. New York: Norton, 1986.

The New Grove Italian Baroque Masters. New York: Norton, 1984.

The New Grove North German Baroque Masters. New York: Norton, 1985.

Orrey, Leslie. *Programme Music: a Brief Survey from the Sixteenth Century to the Present Day*. London: Davis-Poynter, 1975.

Palisca, Claude. *Baroque Music*. 2nd ed. Englewood Cliffs, NJ: Prentice-Hall, 1981.

Price, Curtis A., ed. *The Early Baroque Era: From the Late 16th Century to the 1660s*. Music and Society. Englewood Cliffs, NJ: Prentice Hall, 1993.

Riviera, Benito V. *German Music Theory in the Early 17th Century: The Treatises of Johannes Lippius*. Studies in Musicology 17. Ann Arbor, MI: UMI Research Press, 1980.

Rosand, Ellen, gen. ed. *Baroque Music*. Vols. 5–6 of *The Garland Library of the History of Western Music*. New York: Garland, 1985.

Sadie, Julie Anne. *Companion to Baroque Music*. Berkeley: University of California Press, 1998.

Schulenberg, David. *Music of the Baroque*. New York: Oxford University Press, 2001.

Selfridge-Field, Eleanor. *Pallade Veneta: Writings on Music in Venetian Society, 1650–1750*. Venice: Fondazione Levi, 1985.

——. *Venetian Instrumental Music from Gabrieli to Vivaldi*. Oxford: Blackwell, 1975. Reprint, New York: Dover, 1994.

Spink, Ian, and Nicholas Temperly, eds. *The Blackwell History of Music in Britain*. Vol. 3, *The Seventeenth Century*. Oxford: Blackwell, 1992.

Stauffer, George B. *The World of Baroque Music: New Perspectives*. Bloomington: Indiana University Press, 2006.

Strohm, Reinhard, ed. *The Eighteenth-Century Diaspora of Italian Music and Musicians*. Turnhout, Belgium: Brepols, 2001.

Walker, Paul, ed. *Church, Stage, and Studio: Music and Its Contexts in Seventeenth-Century Germany*. Ann Arbor, MI: UMI Research Press, 1989.

Williams, Peter, ed. *Bach, Handel, Scarlatti: Tercentary Essays*. Cambridge: Cambridge University Press, 1985.

——. "The Snares and Delusions of Musical Rhetoric: Some Examples from Recent Writings on J. S. Bach." In *Alet Musik: Praxis und Reflexion*, edited by Peter Reidmeister and Veronika Guttmann, 230–40. Winterthur, Switzerland: Amadeus, 1983.

BIBLIOGRAPHIES AND DICTIONARIES THAT INCLUDE BAROQUE MUSIC

Arnold, Corliss R. *Organ Literature: A Comprehensive Survey*. Metuchen, NJ: Scarecrow, 1995.

Baron, John H. *Baroque Music: A Research and Information Guide*. New York: Garland, 1993.

Bieri, Martin. *Ricercare: Verzeichnis cantus-firmus-gebundener Orgelmusik*. Wiesbaden, Germany: Breitkopf and Härtel, 2001.

Borren, Charles van den. *The Sources of Keyboard Music in England*. Translated by James E. Matthew. London: Novello, 1913. Reprint, various.

Bowers, Roger. *English Church Polyphony: Singers and Sources from the 14th to the 17th Century*. Aldershot, UK: Ashgate/Variorum, 1999.

Daniel, Ralph T. *The Sources of English Church Music, 1549–1660*. London: Stainer and Bell for the British Academy, 1972.

Davidson, James Robert. *A Dictionary of Protestant Church Music*. Metuchen, NJ: Scarecrow, 1975.

Day, Cyrus Lawrence, and Eleanore Boswell Murrie. *English Song-Books, 1651–1702, and Their Publishers*. 1940. Reprint, Philadelphia: West, 1977.

Gustafson, Bruce, and David Fuller. *A Catalogue of French Harpsichord Music, 1669–1780*. New York: Oxford University Press, 1990.

Hays, Alfreda. *Passion Settings of the German Baroque: A Guide to Printed Editions*. New York: American Choral Foundation, 1975.

Hill, George R., and Norris L. Stephens. *Collected Editions, Historical Series and Sets and Monuments of Music: A Bibliography.* Berkeley, CA: Fallen Leaf, 1997.

Johnson, Cleveland. *Vocal Compositions in German Organ Tablatures, 1550–1650: A Catalogue and Commentary.* New York: Garland, 1989.

Lippmann, Edward A. *Musical Aesthetics: A Historical Reader.* Vol. 1, *From Antiquity to the Eighteenth Century.* Stuyvesant, NY: Pendragon, 1986.

Little, Meredith. *Le Danse Noble: An Inventory of Dances and Sources.* Williamstown, MA: Broude, 1992.

MacClintock, Carol. *Readings in the History of Music in Performance.* Bloomington: Indiana University Press, 1979.

Monson, Craig. *Voices and Viols in England, 1600–1650: The Sources and the Music.* Ann Arbor, MI: UMI Research Press, 1982.

Schwartz, Judith L., and Christena L. Schlundt. *French Court Dance and Dance Music: A Guide to Primary Source Writings, 1643–1789.* Stuyvesant, NY: Pendragon, 1987.

Swain, Joseph P. *Historical Dictionary of Sacred Music.* Lanham, MD: Scarecrow, 2006.

Vinquist, Mary, and Neal Zaslaw, eds. *Performance Practice: A Bibliography.* New York: Norton, 1971.

Walker, Diane Parr, and Paul Walker. *German Sacred Polyphonic Vocal Music between Schütz and Bach: Sources and Critical Editions.* Warren, MI: Harmonie Park, 1992.

Yeats-Edwards, Paul. *English Church Music: A Bibliography.* London: White Lion, 1975.

IMPORTANT PRIMARY SOURCES

Arbeau, Thoinot. *Orchésographie.* 1589. Translated by Mary Stewart Evans. New York: Dover, 1967.

Artusi, Giovanni Maria. *L'Artusi, ovvero Delle Imperfettioni della Moderna Musica* [Artusi, or On the Imperfections of Modern Music]. Venice: 1600. In *Source Readings in Music History*, translated by Oliver Strunk, 393–402. New York: Norton, 1950.

Bach, Carl Philipp Emanuel. *Versuch über die wahre Art das Clavier zu spielen.* 1753. Translated by William Mitchell as *Essay on the True Art of Playing Keyboard Instruments.* New York: Norton, 1949.

Bacilly, Bénigne de. *Remarques Curieuses sur l'Art de Bien Chanter.* Translated by Austin B. Caswell as *A Commmentary upon the Art of Proper Singing.* Brooklyn, NY: Institute of Mediaeval Music, 1968.

Bernhard, Christoph. "The Treatises of Christoph Bernhard." Translated by Walter Hilse. *The Music Forum* 3 (1973).

Brossard, Sébastien de. *Dictionnaire de Musique.* Paris: 1703. Translated by Albion Gruber. Henryville, PA: Institute of Mediaeval Music, 1982.

Couperin, François. *L'Art de Toucher le Clavecin* [The Art of Playing the Harpsichord]. Paris. 1716. Translated by Mevanwy Roberts. Leipzig, Germany: Breitkopf und Härtel, 1933.

D'Alembert, Jehan le Rond, and Denis Diderot. *Encyclopédie, ou Dictionnaire Raisonné des Sciences, des Arts et des Métiers*. Paris: 1751–1765.

Descartes, René. *Compendium Musicae*. Ms., 1618. Published, Utrecht, Netherlands: 1650. Translated by Walter Robert as *Compendium of Music*. N.p. : American Institute of Musicology, 1961.

Fux, Johann Joseph. *Gradus ad Parnassum*. Vienna: 1725. Partial English translation by Alfred Mann as *The Steps to Parnassus*. New York: Norton, 1943.

Galilei, Vincenzo. *Dialogo della Musica Antica et della Moderna* [Dialogue on Ancient and Modern Music]. Florence: 1581. Translated by Claude V. Palisca. New Haven, CT: Yale University Press, 2003.

Heinichen, Johann David. *Neu erfundene und gründliche Anweisung . . . des General-Basses* [Newly Invented, Fundamental Instruction . . . for the Thoroughbass]. Hamburg: 1711. Translated by George J. Buelow. Berkeley: University of California Press, 1966.

Hotteterre, Jacques. *Principles of the Flute, Recorder, and Oboe*. Translated by Paul Marshall Douglas. New York: Dover, 1983.

Kircher, Athanasius. *Musurgia Universalis*. Rome: 1650. Facsimile, Hildesheim, Germany: Olms, 1970.

Lippius, Johannes. *Synopsis Musicae Novae*. Strassburg, Austria: 1612. Translated by Benito Rivera. *Synopsis of New Music*. Colorado Springs: Colorado College Music Press, 1977.

Mattheson, Johann. *Der vollkommene Capellmeister*. Hamburg, Germany: 1739. Translated by Ernest Harris as *Johann Mattheson's "Der vollkommene Capellmeister": A Translation and Commentary*. Ann Arbor, MI: UMI Research Press, 1981.

Mersenne, Marin. *Harmonie Universelle*. Paris: 1636. Facsimile, Paris: Centre National de la Recherche Scientifique, 1963. Translated by Roger E. Chapman as *Harmonie Universelle: The Books on Instruments*. The Hague, Netherlands: Nijhoff, 1957.

Niedt. Friderich Erhard. *Musicalische Handleitung*. Part 1, *Handelt vom General-Bass*. Hamburg, Germany: 1700. Translated by Pamela Poulin and Irmgard Taylor as *The Musical Guide*. Oxford: Clarendon, 1988.

Praetorius, Michael. *Syntagma Musicum*. 3 vols. Wolfenbüttel, Germany: 1613–20. Facsimile, Kassel, Germany: Bärenreiter, 1958–59. Parts translated by David Z. Crookes as *Syntagma Musicum II: De Organographia: Parts I and II*. Oxford: Clarendon, 1986.

Quantz, Johann Joachim. *Versuch einer Anweisung, die Flöte traversiere zu spielen*. Berlin: 1752. Translated by Edward R. Reilly as *On Playing the Flute*. Boston: Northeastern University Press, 2001.

Rameau, Jean-Philippe. *Traité de l'Harmonie*. Paris: 1722. Translated by Philip Gossett as *Treatise on Harmony*. New York: Dover, 1971.

Scheibe, Johann Adolph. *Der critische Musicus*. Hamburg, Germany: 1737–40. Facsimile, Amsterdam: Antiqua, 1966.

Source Readings in Music History. Edited by Oliver Strunk. Vol. 4, *The Baroque Era*. Revised edition by Margaret Murata. New York: Norton, 1998.

Tosi, Pier Francesco. *Opinioni de' Cantori Antichi e Moderni* [Opinions of Ancient and Modern Singers]. 1723. German translation by Johann Friedrich Agricola as *Anleitung zur Singkunst*. Berlin: 1757. Translated by Julianne C. Baird as *Introduction to the Art of Singing*. Cambridge: Cambridge University Press, 1995.

Walther, Johann Gottfried. *Musicalisches Lexicon*. Leipzig, Germany: 1732. Facsimile, Kassel, Germany: Bärenreiter, 1953.

BAROQUE MUSIC ANTHOLOGIES

Antonicek, Susanne, and Günter Brosche. *Musica Imperialis: 500 Jahre Hofmusikkapelle in Wien 1498–1998: Ausstellung der Musiksammlung der Österreichischen Nationalbibliothek, 11 May–10 Nov 1998*. Tutzing, Germany: Schneider, 1998.

Denkmäler der Tonkunst in Österreich. Vols. 1–120. Graz, Austria: Akademische Druck- und Verlagsanstalt, 1974.

Silbiger, Alexander, ed. *Seventeenth-Century Keyboard Music*. 28 vols. New York: Garland, 1988–89.

Tomlinson, Gary, ed. *Florence, Italian Secular Song, 1606–1636*. Vol. 1. New York: Garland, 1986.

Walker, D. P., Federico Ghisi, and Jean Jacquot, eds. *Les Fêtes du Mariage de Ferdinand de Médicis et de Christine de Lorraine*. Vol. 1., *Musique des Intermèdes de Pellegrina, Florence, 1589*. Paris: Editions du Centre National de la Recherche Scientifique, 1963.

COLLECTED WORKS OF COMPOSERS

(listed by composer's family name)

Johann Sebastian Bachs Werke. Edited by Bach-Gesellschaft. 46 vols. Leipzig, Germany: 1851–99.

Bach, Johann Sebastian. *Neue Ausgabe sämtlicher Werke*. Edited by Johann-Sebastian-Bach-Institut Göttingen and the Bach-Archiv Leipzig. Kassel, Germany: Bärenreiter, 1954–.

Dietrich Buxtehudes Werke. Klecken, Germany: Ugrino, 1925–37; Reprint, New York: Broude Trust, 1977–.

Marc-Antoine Charpentier: Oeuvres Complètes. Paris: Minkoff, 1990–.

Corelli, Arcangelo. *Historisch-kritisch Gesamtausgabe der musikalischen Werke*. Edited by Hans Joachin Marx. Cologne, Germany: Arno Volk – Hans Gerig, 1980–.

Couperin, François. *Pièces de Clavecin*. 4 vols. Edited by Kenneth Gilbert. Paris: Heugel, 1969–72.

Frescobaldi, Girolamo. *Opere complete*. Edited by Étienne Darbellay and others. Monumenti Musicali Italiani. Milan, Italy: Suvini Zerboni, 1975–.

Froberger Johann Jacob. *Neue Ausgabe sämtlicher Clavier- und Orgelwerke*. Edited by Siegbert Rampe. Kassel, Germany: Bärenreiter, 1993–.

Gabrieli, Giovanni. *Opera Omnia*. Corpus Mensurabilis Musicae 12 (1–11). Rome: American Institute of Musicology, 1956–.

Georg Friedrich Händel's Werke. Edited by Friedrich Chrysander. Leipzig, Germany: Breitkopf und Härtel, 1858–1903.

Hallische Händel-Ausgabe. Kassel, Germany: Bärenreiter, 1955–.

Kerll, Johann Caspar. *The Collected Works for Keyboard*. Edited by C. David Harris. New York: Broude, 1995.

Locatelli, Pietro Antonio. *Opera omnia*. Edited by Albert Dunning. London: Schott, 1994.

Lully, Jean-Baptiste. *Oeuvres Complètes*. Edited by Henri Prunières. 10 vols. Paris: Édition de la Revue Musicale: 1930–39. Reprint, New York: Broude, 1966–74.

Monteverdi, Claudio. *Tutte le Opere*. Edited by G. Francesco Malipiero. 17 vols. Asola, Italy: Malipiero, 1926–42. Reprint, Vienna: Universal, 1968.

Pachelbel, Johann. *Toccaten, Fantasien, Praeludien, Fugen, Ricercare und Ciaconen für Orgel (Clavichord, Cembalo, Klavier)*. Edited by Anne Marlene Gurgel. Frankfurt, Germany: Peter, 1982–.

Pergolesi, Giovanni Battista. *Complete Works*. Edited by Barry S. Brook. New York: Pendragon, 1986–.

The Works of Henry Purcell. London: Novello, 1900–.

Rossi, Salamone. *Corpus Mensurabilis Musicae*. Edited by Don Harràn. Stuttgart: Hänssler, 1995–.

The Operas of Alessandro Scarlatti. Cambridge, MA: Harvard University Press, 1974–83.

Scarlatti, Domenico. *Sonate per Clavicembalo*. Edited by Emilia Fadini. 8 vols. Milan: Ricordi, 1978–.

———. *Sonates*. Edited by Kenneth Gilbert. 10 vols. Paris: Heugel, 1971–.

Schütz, Heinrich. *Neue Ausgabe sämtlicher Werke*. Kassel, Germany: Bärenreiter, 1955– .

———. *Sämtliche Werke*. Edited by Philipp Spitta and Arnold Schering. Wiesbaden, Germany: Breitkopf und Härtel, 1885–1927.

Telemann, Georg Philipp. *Musikalische Werke*. Kassel, Germany: Bärenreiter, 1950–.

Vivaldi, Antonio. *Edizione Critica*. Milan: Ricordi, 1982–.

———. *Opere*. Edited by Gian Francesco Malipiero. Milan, Italy: 1948–72.

BIOGRAPHIES OF MUSICIANS AND COMPOSERS AND STUDIES OF SPECIFIC WORKS

Bach, Johann Sebastian, and Family

Bach-Jahrbuch. Berlin: Evangelische Verlaganstalt, 1904–.

Bach Perspectives. Lincoln: University of Nebraska Press, 1992–.

BACH: The Quarterly Journal of the Riemenschneider Institute.

Boyd, Malcolm. *Bach.* 3rd ed. New York: Oxford University Press, 2000.

———. *Bach: The Brandenburg Concertos.* Cambridge: Cambridge University Press, 1993.

———, ed. *J. S. Bach.* Oxford Composer Companions. Oxford: Oxford University Press, 1999.

Butt, John. *Bach: Mass in B Minor.* Cambridge: Cambridge University Press, 1991.

———, ed. *The Cambridge Companion to Bach.* New York: Cambridge University Press, 1997.

Crist, Stephen A. *Bach in America.* Urbana: University of Illinois Press, 2002.

David, Hans T., and Arthur Mendel, eds. *The New Bach Reader: A Life of Johann Sebastian Bach in Letters and Documents.* Revised by Christoph Wolff. New York: Norton, 1998.

Day, James. *The Literary Background to Bach's Cantatas.* London: Dobson, 1961.

Du Bouchet, Paule. *Magnificat: Jean-Sébastien Bach, le Cantor.* Paris: Gallimard, 1991.

Dürr, Alfred, ed. *The Cantatas of J. S. Bach: With Their Librettos in German-English Parallel Text.* Oxford: Oxford University Press, 2005.

———. *Johann Sebastian Bach's St. John Passion: Genesis, Transmission and Meaning.* Translated by Alfred Clayton. Oxford: Oxford University Press, 2000.

Faulkner, Quentin. *J. S. Bach's Keyboard Technique: A Historical Introduction.* St. Louis: Concordia, 1984.

Forkel, Johann Nikolaus. *Johann Sebastian Bach: His Life, Art, and Work.* 1st. ed. 1802. Translation, New York: Da Capo, 1970.

Geck, Martin, and John Hargraves. *Johann Sebastian Bach: Life and Work.* Orlando, FL: Harcourt, 2006.

Heinze, Frauke. *Johann Sebastian Bach, Neue Ausgabe sämtlicher Werke: Gesamtregister.* Kassel, Germany: Bärenreiter, 2010.

Herz, Gerhard. *Essays on J. S. Bach.* Ann Arbor, MI: UMI Research Press, 1985.

Humphreys, David. *The Esoteric Structure of Bach's Clavierübung III.* Cardiff, UK: University College of Cardiff Press, 1983.

Jones, Richard Douglas. *The Creative Development of Johann Sebastian Bach.* Oxford: Oxford University Press, 2007.

Landmann, Ortrun. "The Dresden Hofkapelle during the Lifetime of Johann Sebastian Bach." *Early Music* XVII (1989): 17–30.

Leaver, Robin. *J. S. Bach as Preacher.* St. Louis: Concordia, 1982.

Ledbetter, David. *Bach's Well-tempered Clavier: The 48 Preludes and Fugues.* New Haven, CT: Yale University Press, 2002.

———. *Unaccompanied Bach: Performing the Solo Works.* New Haven, CT: Yale University Press, 2009.

Lester, Joel. *Bach's Works for Solo Violin: Style, Structure, Performance.* New York: Oxford University Press, 1999.

Little, Meredith, and Natalie Jenne. *Dance and the Music of J. S. Bach.* Bloomington: Indiana University Press, 1991/1998.

Marissen, Michael. *The Social and Religious Designs of J. S. Bach's Brandenburg Concertos.* Princeton, NJ: Princeton University Press, 1995.

Marshall, Robert L. *The Compositional Process of J. S. Bach*. 2 vols. Princeton, NJ: Princeton University Press, 1972.

Melamed, Daniel R. *Hearing Bach's Passions*. New York: Oxford University Press, 2005.

———. *J. S. Bach and the Oratorio Tradition*. Urbana: University of Illinois Press, 2011.

Melamed, Daniel R., and Michael Marissen. *An Introduction to Bach Studies*. New York: Oxford University Press, 1998.

Meyer, Ulrich. *Biblical Quotation and Allusion in the Cantata Libretti of Johann Sebastian Bach*. Lanham, MD: Scarecrow, 1997.

Papillon, André. *Index of Chorale Melodies in the Works of Johann Sebastian Bach*. Saint-Nicolas, QC, Canada: Les Presses de l'Université de Laval, 2006.

Parrott, Andrew. *The Essential Bach Choir*. Rochester, NY: Boydell and Brewer, 2000.

Rose, Stephen. *The Musician in Literature in the Age of Bach*. Cambridge: Cambridge University Press, 2011.

Schmieder, Wolfgang. *Thematisch-systematisches Verzeichnis der musikalischen Werke von Johann Sebastian Bach: Bach-Werke-Verzeichnis (BWV)*. Wiesbaden, Germany: 1950. 2nd ed., Wiesbaden, Germany: Breitkopf und Härtel, 1990.

Schröder, Jaap. *Bach's Solo Violin Works: A Performer's Guide*. New Haven, CT: Yale University Press, 2007.

Schulenberg, David. *The Keyboard Music of J. S. Bach*. New York: Schirmer Books, 1992.

Schulze, Hans-Joachim. *Dokumente zu Leben, Werk und Nachwirken Johann Sebastian Bachs, 1685–1800*. Kassel, Germany: Bärenreiter, 2007.

Schulze, Hans-Joachim, and Chrisoph Wolff. *Bach Compendium: Analytisch-bibliographisches Repertorium der Werke Johann Sebastian Bachs (BC)*. Frankfurt, Germany: C. F. Peters, 1985–.

Siblin, Eric. *The Cello Suites: J. S. Bach, Pablo Casals, and the Search for a Baroque Masterpiece*. New York: Atlantic Monthly, 2009.

Spitta, Philipp. *Johann Sebastian Bach: His Work and Influence on the Music of Germany*. 3 vols. Translated by Clara Bell and J. A. Fuller-Maitland. Englewood Cliffs, NJ: Dover, 1992.

Stauffer, George B. *Bach: The Mass in B Minor (The Great Catholic Mass)*. Monuments of Western Music. Edited by G. B. Stauffer. New York: Schirmer Books, 1997.

———. *J. S. Bach as Organist: His Instruments, Music, and Performance Practices*. Bloomington: Indiana University Press, 1986.

Stinson, Russell. *Bach, the Orgelbüchlein*. New York: Schirmer Books, 1996.

———. *J. S. Bach's Great Eighteen Organ Chorales*. New York: Oxford University Press, 2001.

Troeger, Richard. *Playing Bach on the Keyboard: A Practical Guide*. Pompton Plains, NJ: Amadeus, 2003.

Williams, Peter F. *J. S. Bach: A Life in Music*. Cambridge: Cambridge University Press, 2007.

———. *The Organ Music of J. S. Bach*. 1984. 2nd ed., New York: Cambridge University Press, 2004.

Wolf, Uwe. *Die neue Bach-Ausgabe 1954–2007: eine Dokumentation vorgelegt zum Abschluss von Johann Sebastian Bach Ausgabe sämtlicher Werke*. Kassel, Germany: Bärenreiter, 2007.

Wolff, Christoph. *Bach: Essays on His Life and Music*. Cambridge, MA: Harvard University Press, 1981.

———. *Johann Sebastian Bach: The Learned Musician*. New York: Norton, 2002.

———, ed. *The World of Bach Cantatas*. New York: Norton, 1997.

Wolff, Christoph, et al. *The New Grove Bach Family*. New York: Norton, 1983.

Buxtehude, Dietrich

Archbold, Lawrence. *Style and Structure in the Praeludia of Dietrich Buxtehude*. Ann Arbor, MI: UMI Research Press, 1985.

Karstädt, Georg. *Thematisch-Systematisches Verzeichnis der musikalischen Werke von Dietrich Buxtehude: Buxtehude-Werke-Verzeichnis (BuxWV)*. Wiesbaden, Germany: Breitkopf und Härtel, 1974.

Moser, Hans Joachim. *Dietrich Buxtehude: der Mann und sein Werk*. Berlin: Merseburger, 1957. Reprint, 2007.

Snyder, Kerala J. *Dietrich Buxtehude, Organist in Lübeck*. New York: Schirmer, 1987.

Webber, Geoffrey. *North German Church Music in the Age of Buxtehude*. Oxford: Oxford University Press and Clarendon, 1996.

Caldara, Antonio

Harb, Karl, and Albert F. Hartinger. *Antonio Caldara und Salzburg: Beitrag zur Musik- und Kulturgeschichte des Spätbarock*. Salzburg, Germany: Gattermair, 1981.

Kirkendale, Ursula. *Antonio Caldara: Sein Leben und seine venezianisch-römischen Oratorien*. Wiener musikwissenschaftliche Beiträge 6. Graz: Germann Böhlhaus, 1966. Translated by Warren Kirkendale as *Antonio Caldara: Life and Venetian-Roman Oratorios*. Florence, Italy: Leo S. Olschki, 2007.

Pritchard, Brian W., ed. *Antonio Caldara: Essays on His Life and Times*. Aldershot, England: Scholar, 1987.

———. "Antonio Caldara: The Cantatas Revisited." *Musical Times* CXXXIII (1992): 510–13.

———. "Caldara's *Adriano in Siria*." *Musical Times* CXXVII (1986): 379–82.

Roche, E. "Caldara and the Mass: A Tercentenary Note." *Musical Times* CXI (1970): 1101–3.

Carissimi, Giacomo

Dixon, Graham. *Carissimi*. Oxford: Oxford University Press, 1986.

Jones, Andrew V. *The Motets of Carissimi*. 2 vols. Ann Arbor, MI: UMI Research Press, 1982.

Russo, Paolo. *Musica e Drammaturgia a Roma al Tempo di Giacomo Carissimi*. Venice, Italy: Casa dell Musica, 2006.

Cavalli, Francesco

Glover, Jane. *Cavalli*. London: Batsford, 1978.
Moore, J. H. *Vespers at St Mark's: Music of Alessandro Grandi, Giovanni Rovetta and Francesco Cavalli*. Ann Arbor, MI: UMI Research Press, 1981.
Rosand, Ellen. "Aria and Drama in the Early Operas of Francesco Cavalli." In *Venezia e il Melodramma nel Seicento*. Edited by Maria Teresa Muraro, 75–96. Studi di Musica Veneta 5. Florence, Italy: Leo S. Olschki, 1976.

Charpentier, Marc-Antoine

Cessac, Catherine. *Marc-Antoine Charpentier*. Translated by E. Thomas Glasow. Portland, OR: Amadeus, 1995.
Hitchcock, Hugh Wiley. *Marc-Antoine Charpentier*. Oxford: Oxford University Press, 1990.
———. *Les Oeuvres de Marc-Antoine Charpentier: Catalogue Raisonné*. Paris: Picard, 1982.
Lowe, Robert W. *Marc-Antoine Charpentier et l'Opéra de Collège*. Paris: G. P. Maisonneuve et Larose, 1966.
Thompson, Shirley. *New Perspectives on Marc-Antoine Charpentier*. Farnham, Surrey, UK: Ashgate, 2010.

Corelli, Arcangelo

Allsop, Peter. *Arcangelo Corelli: New Orpheus of Our Times*. Oxford: Oxford University Press, 1999.
Barnett, Gregory R., and Antonella D'Ovidio, eds. *Arcangelo Corelli fra Mito e Realtà Storica*. Florence, Italy: Leo S. Olschki, 2007.
Privitera, Massimo. *Arcangelo Corelli*. Palermo, Italy: L'Epos, 2000.
Venturini, Philippe. *Arcangelo Corelli*. Paris: Fayard, 2002.

Couperin, François

Beaussant, Philippe, et al. *François Couperin*. Paris: Fayard, 2007.
Mellers, Wilfred. *François Couperin and the French Classical Tradition*. Rev. ed. London: Faber, 1987. Reprint, London: Travis and Emery, 2008.
Tunley, David. *François Couperin and "The Perfection of Music."* Aldershot, England: Ashgate, 2004.

Farinelli

Barbier, Patrick. *Farinelli: le Castrat des Lumières*. Paris: B. Grasset, 1994.

Bergeron, Katherine. "The Castrato as History." *Cambridge Opera Journal* VIII (1996): 167–84.

Burden, Michael, and Nicolas Clapton. *Farinelli*. Oxford: Voltaire Foundation, 2005.

Heartz, Daniel. "Farinelli and Metastasio: Rival Twins of Public Favour." *Early Music* XII (1984): 358–66.

———. "Farinelli Revisited." *Early Music* XVIII (1990): 430–43.

Frescobaldi, Girolamo

Hammond, Friderick. *Girolamo Frescobaldi*. Cambridge, MA: Harvard University Press, 1983.

———. *Girolamo Frescobaldi: A Guide to Research*. New York: Garland, 1988.

———. "The Influence of Girolamo Frescobaldi on French Keyboard Music." *Recercare* III (1991): 147–68.

Jackson, R. "On Frescobaldi's Chromaticism and Its Background." *Musical Quarterly* LVII (1971): 255–69.

Klein, Heribert. *Die Toccaten Girolamo Frescobaldis*. Mainz: Schott, 1989.

Silbiger, Alexander. "From Madrigal to Toccata: Frescobaldi and the Seconda Pratica." In *Critica Musica: Essays in Honor of Paul Brainard*, edited by J. Knowles, 403–28. Amsterdam: Gordon and Breach, 1996.

———. "The Roman Frescobaldi Tradition, c. 1640–1670." *Journal of the American Musicological Society* XXXIII (1980): 42–87.

Froberger, Johann Jacob

Annibaldi, Claudio. "Froberger in Rome: From Frescobaldi's Craftsmanship to Kircher's Compositional Secrets." *Current Musicology* 58 (1995): 5–27.

Schort, Howard. "Parameters of Interpretation in the Music of Froberger." *J. J. Froberger, Musicien Européen*. N.p: Klincksieck, 1998.

Siedentopf, Henning. *Johann Jakob Froberger: Drei Studien*. Tübingen, Germany: Gulde-Verlag, 1992.

———. *Johann Jakob Froberger: Leben und Werk*. Stuttgart, Germany: Stuttgarter Verlagskontor, 1977.

Silbiger, Alexander. "Tracing the Contents of Froberger's Lost Autographs." *Current Musicology* 54 (1993): 5–23.

Fux, Johann Joseph

Gruber, Gernot. *Das Wiener Sepolcro und Johann Joseph Fux*. Graz, Austria: Johann-Joseph-Fux-Gesellschaft, 1972.

Wellesz, Egon. *Fux*. London: Oxford University Press, 1965.

White, Harry, ed. *Johann Joseph Fux and the Music of the Austro-Italian Baroque.* Aldershot, England: Ashgate, 1991.

Gabrieli, Giovanni

Arnold, Denis. *Giovanni Gabrieli.* London: Oxford University Press, 1974.
———. *Giovanni Gabrieli and the Music of the Venetian High Renaissance.* London: Oxford University Press, 1979.
Charteris, Richard A. *Giovanni Gabrieli (ca. 1555–1612): A Thematic Catalogue of His Music with a Guide to the Source Materials and Translations of His Vocal Texts.* Stuyvesant, NY: Pendragon, 1996.
———. *Giovanni Gabrieli and His Contemporaries: Music, Sources and Collections.* Farnham, England: Ashgate, 2010.
———. "The Performance of Giovanni Gabrieli's Vocal Works." *Music and Letters* LXXII (1991): 170–71.

Handel, George Frideric

Bianconi, Lorenzo, ed. *I Libretti Italiani di Georg Friedrich Händel e le loro Fonti.* Florence, Italy: Leo S. Olschki, 1992–.
Burrows, Donald, ed. *The Cambridge Companion to Handel.* Cambridge: Cambridge University Press, 1997.
———. *Handel.* Master Musicians, edited by Stanley Sadie. Rev. ed. New York: Oxford University Press, 2011.
———. "Handel and the 1727 Coronation." *Musical Times* 118 (1977): 269.
———. *Handel and the English Chapel Royal.* London: Church Music Society, 1985.
———. *Handel: Messiah.* Cambridge Music Handbooks, edited by Julian Rushton. Cambridge: Cambridge University Press, 1991.
Dean, Winton. *Handel and the Opera Seria.* Berkeley and Los Angeles: University of California Press, 1969.
———. *Handel's Dramatic Oratorios and Masques.* London: Oxford University Press, 1959.
———. *Handel's Operas, 1726–1741.* Woodbridge, England: Boydell, 2006.
———, ed. *Three Ornamented Arias.* London: Oxford University Press, 1976.
Dean, Winton, and J. Merrill Knapp. *Handel's Operas, 1704–1706.* Rev. ed. Oxford: Clarendon Books, 1995.
Deutsch, Otto Erich. *Handel: A Documentary Biography.* London: Adam and Charles Black, 1955.
Eisen, Walter, and Margret Eisen. *Händel-Handbuch, herausgegeben vom Kuratorium der Georg-Friedrich-Händel-Stiftung.* 4 vols. Kassel, Germany: Bärenreiter, 1978–85.
Garner, Matthew. *Handel and Maurice Greene's Circle at the Apollo Academy: The Music and Intellectual Contexts of Oratorios, Odes and Masques.* Göttingen, Germany: V and R Unipress, 2008.

Harris, Ellen T. *Handel as Orpheus: Voice and Desire in the Chamber Cantatas.* Cambridge, MA: Harvard University Press, 2001.

Hogwood, Christopher. *Handel.* New York: Thames and Hudson, 1985.

———. *Handel: Water Music and Music for the Royal Fireworks.* Cambridge: Cambridge University Press, 2005.

Hurley, David R. *Handel's Muse: Patterns of Creation in His Oratorios and Musical Dramas, 1743–1751.* Oxford: Oxford University Press, 2001.

Keates, Jonathan. *Handel: The Man and His Music.* London: Gollancz, 1985.

Kuratorium der Georg-Friedrich-Händel-Stiftung, ed. *Händel-Handbuch.* 4 vols. Kassel, Germany: Bärenreiter, 1978–.

Landgraf, Annette. *The Cambridge Handel Encyclopedia.* Cambridge: Cambridge University Press, 2009.

Lang, Paul Henry. *George Frideric Handel.* New York: Norton, 1966.

Ledbetter, David. *Continuo Playing according to Handel.* Oxford: Oxford University Press, 1990.

Mainwaring John. *Memoirs of the Life of the Late George Frederic Handel: To which Is Added a Catalog of His Works and Observations upon Them.* 1760. Reprint, London: Travis and Emery Music Bookshop, 2007.

Mann, Alfred. *Handel: The Orchestral Music.* New York: Schirmer Books, 1996.

Meyell, Hugo Anthony. *The Art of Handel's Operas.* Lewiston, NY: Edwin Mellen, 2008.

Parker-Hale, Mary Ann. *G. F. Handel: A Guide to Research.* New York: Routledge, 2005.

Roberts, John H. "Handel and Vinci's *Didone Abbandonata*: Revisions and Borrowings." *Music and Letters* LXVII (1987): 141–50.

Rogers, Patrick John. *Continuo Realization in Handel's Vocal Music.* Rochester, NY: University of Rochester Press, 1990.

Rooke, Deborah W. *Handel's Israelite Oratorio Libretti: Sacred Drama and Biblical Exegesis.* Oxford: Oxford University Press, 2012.

Shaw, Watkins. *A Textual and Historical Companion to Handel's "Messiah."* London: Novello, 1965.

Shaw, Watkins, and Graham Dixon. "Handel's Vesper Music." *Musical Times* 126 (1985): 132.

Smith, Ruth. *Handel's Oratorios and Eighteenth-Century Thought.* Cambridge: Cambridge University Press, 1995.

Strohm, Reinhard. *Essays on Handel and Italian Opera.* Cambridge: Cambridge University Press, 1985.

Tobin, John, and Eberhard Wenzel, eds. *Hallische Händel-Ausgabe kritische Gesamtausgabe.* Kassel, Germany: Bärenreiter, 2004.

Tovey, Donald Francis. "Handel: 'Israel in Egypt.'" *Essays in Music Analysis*, vol. 5. London: Oxford University Press, 1937.

Young, Percy M. *The Oratorios of Handel.* London: Dobson, 1949.

Hasse, Johann Adolf

Landmann, Ortrun, ed. *Katalog der Dresdner Hasse-Musikhandschriften.* Munich: Saur, 1999. [CD-ROM].

Millner, Frederick L. *The Operas of Johann Adolf Hasse.* Ann Arbor, MI: UMI Research Press, 1979.

Wilson, David James. *The Masses of Johann Adolf Hasse.* Ann Arbor, MI: UMI Dissertation Services, 2005.

Keiser, Reinhard

Drauschke, Harnsjörg. *Die deutschen weltlichen Kantaten Reinhard Keisers (1674–1739).* Wilhelmshaven, Germany: F. Noetzel, Heinrichshofen Bücher, 2004.

Koch, Klaus-Peter. *Reinhard Keiser (1674–1739): Leben und Werk.* Teuchern, Germany: Förderkreis "Reinhard-Keiser-Gedenkstätte," 2000.

Roberts, John H. "Keiser and Handel at the Hamburg Opera." *Handeljahrbuch* 1990: 63–87.

Zelm, Klaus. *Die Opern Reinhard Keisers: Studien zur Chronologie, Überlieferung und Stilentwicklung.* Munich, Germany: Musikverlag Katzbichler, 1975.

Lawes, Henry and William

Ashbee, Andrew, ed. *William Lawes (1602–1645): Essays on His Life, Times and Work.* Aldershot, England: Ashgate, 1998.

Cunningham, John Patrick. *The Consort Music of William Lawes, 1602–1645.* Woodbridge, England: Boydell, 2010.

Lefkowitz, Murray. *William Lawes.* London: Routledge, 1960.

Pinto, David. *For the Violls: The Consort and Dance Music of William Lawes.* Richmond, England: Fretwork, 1995.

Spink, Ian. *Henry Lawes: Cavalier Songwriter.* Oxford: Oxford University Press, 2000.

Legrenzi, Giovanni

Fogaccia, Piero. *Giovanni Legrenzi.* Bergamo, Italy: Edizioni Orobiche, 1954.

Passadore, Francesco, and Francesco Rossi, eds. *Giovanni Legrenzi e la Cappella Ducale di San Marco.* Florence, Italy: Leo S. Olschki, 1994.

Swale, J. David. "Legrenzi's Operas: Dramatic Structures for an Autocratic Age." *Miscellanea Musicologica* XV (1988): 89–99.

Lully, Jean-Baptiste

Anthony, James R., and John Hajdu Heyer. *Jean-Baptiste Lully and the Music of the French Baroque.* Cambridge: Cambridge University Press, 1989.

Beaussant, Philippe. *Lully, ou le Musicien du Soleil*. Paris: Théâtre des Champs-Elysées, 1992.

Cooper, Kenneth, and Julius Zsako. "Georg Muffat's Observations on the Lully Style of Performance." *Musical Quarterly* LIII (1967): 220–45.

Couvreur, Manuel. *Jean-Baptiste Lully: Musique et Dramaturgie au Service du Prince*. Brussels: M. Vokar, 1992.

De La Gorce, Jérôme. *L'Opéra à Paris au Temps de Louis XIV: Histoire d'un Théatre*. Paris: Desjonquères, 1992.

Forster, Ralph Henry. *Jean-Baptiste Lully*. London: Owen, 1973.

Gustafson, Bruce, Matthew Leshinskie, and Herbert Schneider. *A Thematic Locator for the Works of Jean-Baptiste Lully*. New York: Performers' Editions, 1989.

Hajdu Heyer, John. *Lully Studies*. Edited by John Hajdu. Cambridge: Cambridge University Press, 2000.

Néraudau, Jean-Pierre. *La Tragédie Lyrique*. Paris: Théâtre des Champs-Elysées, 1991.

Prunières, Henry. *La Vie Illustre et Libertine de Jean-Baptiste Lully*. 1929. Reprint, New York: AMS Press, 1978.

Schmidt, Carl B. *The Livrets of Jean-Baptiste Lully's Tragédies Lyriques: A Catalogue Raisonée*. New York: Performers' Editions, 1995.

Schneider, Herbert. *Chronologisch-Thematisches Verzeichnis sämtlicher Werke von Jean-Baptiste Lully (LWV)*. Tutzing, Germany: Schneider, 1981.

Scott, Ralph Henry Forster. *Jean-Baptiste Lully*. London: Owen, 1973.

Stevens, Blake Christopher. *Solitary Persuasions: The Concept of the Monologue in French Opera from Lully to Rameau*. Ann Arbor, MI: Proquest/UMI, 2007.

Wood, Caroline. *Music and Drama in the "Tragédie en Musique," 1673–1715: Jean-Baptiste Lully and His Successors*. New York: Garland, 1996.

Monteverdi, Claudio

Adams, K. Gary, and Dyke Kiel. *Claudio Monteverdi: A Guide to Research*. New York: Garland, 1989.

Arnold, Denis. *Monteverdi*. 1963. 3rd edition revised by Tim Carter, London: Dent, 1990.

Arnold, Denis, and Nigel Fortune. *The New Monteverdi Companion*. London: Faber and Faber, 1985.

Carter, Tim. *Monteverdi and His Contemporaries*. Aldershot, England: Ashgate, 2000.

——. *Monteverdi's Musical Theatre*. New Haven, CT: Yale University Press, 2002.

——. "Re-Reading *Poppea*: Some Thoughts on Music and Meaning in Monteverdi's Last Opera." *Journal of the Royal Musical Association*, CXXII (1997): 173–204.

Chafe, Eric, *Monteverdi's Tonal Language*. New York: Schirmer, 1992.

Fabbri, Paolo. *Monteverdi*. 1st ed., 1985. Translated by Tim Carter, Cambridge: Cambridge University Press, 1994.

Fenlon, Iain, and Peter N. Miller. *The Song of the Soul: Understanding "Poppea."* Royal Musical Association Monographs 5. London: Royal Musical Association, 1992.

Heller, Wendy. "Tacitus Incognito: Opera as History in *L'Incoronazione di Poppea*." *Journal of the American Musicological Society* LIII (1999): 39–96.

Lax, Eva., ed. *Claudio Monteverdi: Lettere*. Florence, Italy: Leo S. Olschki, 1994.

Kurtzman, Jeffrey. *The Monteverdi Vespers of 1610: Music, Context, Performance*. New York: Oxford University Press, 1999.

Leopold, Silke. *Monteverdi: Music in Transition*. Translated by Anne Smith. Oxford: Oxford University Press, 1991.

Ridler, Anne. *The Operas of Monteverdi*. London: Calder, 1992.

Ringer, Mark. *Opera's First Master: The Musical Dramas of Claudio Monteverdi*. Pompton Plains, NJ: Amadeus, 2006.

Roche, Jerome L. *North Italian Church Music in the Age of Monteverdi*. Oxford: Oxford University Press, 1984.

Rosand, Ellen. "The Bow of Ulysses." *The Journal of Musicology* XII (1994): 376–95.

———. "Iro and the Interpretation of *Il Ritorno d'Ulisse in Patria*." *The Journal of Musicology* VII (1989), 141–64.

———. "Monteverdi's *Il Ritorno d'Ulisse in Patria* and the Power of Music." *Cambridge Opera Journal* VII (1995): 179–84.

———. "Seneca and the Interpretation of *L'Incoronazione di Poppea*." *Journal of the American Musicological Society* XXXVIII (1985): 34–71.

Solomon, J. "The Neoplatonic Apotheosis in Monteverdi's *Orfeo*." *Studi musicali* XXIV (1995), 27–47.

Stattkus, Manfred H. *Claudio Monteverdi: Verzeichnis der erhaltenen Werke (SV)*. Bergkamen, Germany: Musikverlag Stattkus, 1985.

Stevens, Denis. *Monteverdi in Venice*. Madison, NJ: Fairleigh Dickinson University Press, 2001.

———, ed. *The Letters of Claudio Monteverdi*. Rev. ed. Oxford: Oxford University Press, 1995.

Tellart, Roger. *Claudio Monteverdi*. Paris: Fayard, 1997.

Tomlinson, Gary. *Monteverdi and the End of the Renaissance*. Oxford: Oxford University Press, 1987.

Whenham, John. *Claudio Monteverdi: "Orfeo."* Cambridge: Cambridge University Press, 1985.

———. *Duet and Dialogue in the Age of Monteverdi*. Ann Arbor, MI: UMI Research Press, 1982.

———. *Monteverdi Vespers (1610)*. Cambridge: Cambridge University Press, 1997.

Pachelbel, Johann

Fairleigh, J. P. "Pachelbel's Magnificat Fugues: Models for J. S. Bach." *American Organist*, XI/6 (1980), 34–7.

Kube, Michael. "Pachelbel, Erfurt und der Orgelchoral." *Musik und Kirche* LXIV (1994): 76–82.

Perreault, Jean M. *The Thematic Catalogue of the Musical Works of Johann Pachelbel*. Lanham, MD: Scarecrow, 2004.

Thoburn, Crawford. "Pachelbel's *Christ lag in Todesbanden*: A Possible Influence on Bach's Work." New York: American Choral Foundation, 1978.

Pergolesi, Giovanni Battista

Della Corte, Andrea. *Pergolesi*. Turin: Paravia, 1936.

Paymer, Marvin E. *Giovanni Battista Pergolesi, 1710–1736: A Thematic Catalogue of the Opera Omnia with an Appendix Listing Omitted Compositions*. New York: Pendragon, 1977.

Paymer, Marvin E., and Hermine Weigel Williams. *Giovanni Battista Pergolesi: A Guide to Research*. New York: Garland, 1989.

Peri, Jacopo

Carter, Tim. *Jacopi Peri (1561–1633): His Life and Works*. New York: Garland, 1989.

———. "Jacopo Peri's *Euridice* (1600): A Contextual Study." *Music Review* LIII (1982): 83–103.

Palisca, Claude V. "Peri and the Theory of Recitative." *Studi Musicali* XV (1982): 51–61; Reprint in *Studies in the History of Italian Music and Music Theory*, edited by Claude V. Palisca, 452–66. Oxford: Clarendon, 1994.

Praetorius, Michael

Crookes, David Z., ed. *Michael Praetorius: Syntagma musicum, II: De Organographia, Parts I and II*. Oxford: Clarendon, 1986, 1991.

Forchert, Arno. *Das Spätwerk des Michael Praetorius: italienische und deutsche Stilbegegnung*. Berlin: Merseburger, 1959.

Möller-Weiser, Dietlind. *Untersuchungen zum I. Band des "Syntagma Musicum" von Michael Praetorius*. Kassel, Germany: Bärenreiter, 1993.

Unger, Robert. *Die mehrchörige Aufführungspraxis bei Michael Praetorius und die Feiergestaltung der Gegenwart*. Wolfenbüttel, Germany: G. Kallmeyer, 1941.

Purcell, Henry

Adams, Martin. *Henry Purcell: The Origins and Development of his Musical Style*. Cambridge: Cambridge University Press, 1995.

Burden, Michael. *Henry Purcell's Operas: The Complete Texts*. Oxford: Oxford University Press, 2000.

———, ed. *Performing the Music of Henry Purcell*. Oxford: Clarendon, 1996.

———, ed. *The Purcell Companion*. Portland, OR: Amadeus, 1994.

———. *Purcell Remembered*. Portland, OR: Amadeus, 1995.

Campbell, Margaret. *Henry Purcell: Glory of His Age*. London: Hutchison, 1993.

Duffy, Maureen. *Henry Purcell*. London: Fourth Estate, 1994.

Harley, John. *Music in Purcell's London: the Social Background*. London: Dobson, 1968.

Harris, Ellen T. *Henry Purcell's "Dido and Aeneas."* Oxford: Clarendon, 1987.

Herissone, Rebecca. *The Ashgate Research Companion to Henry Purcell*. Farnham, England: Ashgate, 2012.

Holman, Peter. *Henry Purcell*. Oxford: Oxford University Press, 1994.

Muller, J. *Words and Music in Henry Purcell's First Semi-Opera, "Dioclesian:" An Approach to Early Music through Early Theatre*. Lewiston, NY: Edwin Mellen, 1990.

Price, Curtis A. *Henry Purcell and the London Stage*. Cambridge: Cambridge University Press, 1984.

———, ed. *Purcell Studies*. Cambridge: Cambridge University Press, 1995.

Zimmerman, Franklin B. *The Anthems of Henry Purcell*. New York: American Choral Foundation, 1971.

———. *Henry Purcell: A Guide to Research*. New York: Garland, 1989.

———. *Henry Purcell: His Life and Times*. 2nd ed. Philadelphia: University of Pennsylvania Press, 1983.

Rameau, Jean-Philippe

Christensen, Thomas. *Jean-Philippe Rameau: The Science of Music Theory in the Enlightenment*. Cambridge: Cambridge University Press, 1993.

Dill, Charles William. *Monstrous Opera: Rameau and the Tragic Tradition*. Princeton, NJ: Princeton University Press, 1998.

Foster, Donald H. *Jean-Philippe Rameau: A Guide to Research*. New York: Garland, 1989.

Girdlestone, Cuthbert Morton. *Jean-Philippe Rameau: His Life and Work*. 1957. 2nd ed., New York: Dover, 1969.

Keane, Sister Mary. *The Theoretical Writings of Jean-Philippe Rameau*. Washington, DC: Catholic University of American Press, 1961.

Paquette, Daniel. *Jean-Philippe Rameau: Musicien Bourgignon*. Saint-Seine-l'Abbaye, France: Éditions de Saint-Seine-l'Abbaye, 1984.

Rice, Paul F. *Fontainebleau Operas for the Court of Louis XV of France by Jean-Philippe Rameau (1683–1764)*. Lewiston, NY: Edwin Mellen, 2004.

Scarlatti, Alessandro

D'Accone, Frank. *The History of a Baroque Opera: Alessandro Scarlatti's "Gli Equivoci nel Sembiante."* New York: Pendragon, 1985.

Grout, Donald J. *Alessandro Scarlatti: An Introduction to His Operas*. Berkeley: University of California Press, 1979.
Pagano, Roberto. *Alessandro and Domenico Scarlatti: Two Lives in One*. Translated by Friderick Hammond. New York: Pendragon, 2006.
Schacht-Pape, Ute. *Das Messenschaffen von Alessandro Scarlatti*. Frankfurt, Germany: P. Lang, 1993.
Vidali, Carole Franklin. *Alessandro and Domenico Scarlatti: A Guide to Research*. New York: Garland, 1993.

Scarlatti, Domenico

Boyd, Malcolm. *Domenico Scarlatti, Master of Music*. New York: Schirmer, 1987.
———. "Die Kirchenmusik von Domenico Scarlatti." *Kirchenmusikalisches Jahrbuch* XXII (1988): 117–25.
Eckersley, K. "Some Late Chamber Cantatas of Domenico Scarlatti: A Question of Style." *Musical Times* CXXXI (1990): 585–91.
Flannery, Matthew. *A Chronological Order for the Keyboard Sonatas of Domenico Scarlatti*. Lewiston, NY: Edwin Mellen, 2004.
Kirkpatrick, Ralph. *Domenico Scarlatti*. Princeton, NJ: Princeton University Press, 1953.
Sutcliffe, W. Dean. *The Keyboard Sonatas of Domenico Scarlatti and Eighteenth-Century Musical Style*. Cambridge: Cambridge University Press, 2003.

Schütz, Heinrich

Buelow, George J. *A Schütz Reader: Documents on Performance Practice*. New York: American Choral Foundation, 1985.
Civra, Ferruccio. *Heinrich Schütz*. Palermo, Italy: L'Epos, 2004.
Heinemann, Michael. *Heinrich Schütz*. Reinbek bei Hamburg, Germany: Rowohlt, 2005.
Moser, Hans Joachim. *Heinrich Schütz: His Life and Work*. Translated by Carl F. Pfatteicher. St. Louis: Concordia, 1959.
Skei, Allen B. *Heinrich Schütz: A Guide to Research*. New York: Garland, 1981.
Smallman, Basil. *The Music of Heinrich Schütz*. Leeds, UK: Mayflower, 1985.
Spagnoli, Gina Gail, trans. *Letters and Documents of Heinrich Schütz, 1656–1672: An Annotated Translation*. Ann Arbor, MI: UMI Research Press, 1990.
Varwig, Bettina. *Histories of Heinrich Schütz*. New York: Cambridge University Press, 2011.

Strozzi, Barbara

Glixon, Beth L. "More on the Life and Death of Barbara Strozzi." *Musical Quarterly* LXXXV (1999): 134–41.

——. "New Light on the Life and Career of Barbara Strozzi." *Musical Quarterly* LXXXI (1997): 311–35.

Rosand, Ellen. "Barbara Strozzi, *virtuossima cantatrice*: The Composer's Voice." *Journal of the American Musicological Society* XXXI (1978): 241–81.

Sweelinck, Jan Pierterszoon

Dirksen, Pieter. *The Keyboard Music of Jan Pieterszoon Sweelinck: Its Style, Significance and Influence*. Utrecht, Netherlands: Koninklijke Vereniging voor Nederlandse Muziekgeschiedenis, 1997.

——. *Sweelinck Studies: Proceedings of the International Sweelinck Symposium, Utrecht 1999*. Utrecht, Netherlands: STIMU, Foundation for Historical Performance Practice, 2002.

Noske, Frits. *Sweelinck*. Oxford: Oxford University Press, 1988.

Telemann, Georg Philipp

Baselt, Bernd, ed. *Telemann und seine Freunde*. Magdeburg, Germany: Zentrum für Telemann-Pflege und -Forschung, 1986.

Kleßmann, Eckart. *Georg Philipp Telemann*. Hamburg, Germany: Ellert and Richter, 2004.

——. *Telemann in Hamburg: 1721–1767*. Hamburg, Germany: Hoffmann und Campe, 1980.

Lange, Carsten. *Telemann, der musikalische Maler*. Hildesheim, Germany: Olms, 2010.

Menke, Werner. *Thematisches Verzeichnis der Vokalwerke*. Frankfurt, Germany: Klostermann, 1982–.

Neubacher, Jürgen. *Georg Philipp Telemanns Hamburger Kirchenmusik und ihre Aufführungsbedingungen (1721–1767): Organisationsstrukturen, Musiker, Besetzungspraktiken*. Hildesheim, Germany: Olms, 2009.

Petzoldt, Richard. *Georg Philipp Telemann*. Translated by Horace Fizpatrick. New York: Oxford University Press, 1974.

Ruhnke, Martin. *Georg Philipp Telemann: Thematisches-Systematisches Verzeichnis seiner Werke: Telemann-Wekverziechnis (TWV)*. Kassel, Germany: Bärenreiter, 1984–.

Zohn, Steven David. *Music for a Mixed Taste: Style, Genre, and Meaning in Telemann's Instrumental Works*. New York: Oxford University Press, 2008.

Vivaldi, Antonio

Bianconi, Lorenzo, and Giovanni Morelli, eds. *Antonio Vivaldi: Teatro Musicale, Cultura e Società*. Florence, Italy: Leo S. Olschki, 1982.

Brover-Lubovsky, Bella. *Tonal Space in the Music of Antonio Vivaldi*. Bloomington: Indiana University Press, 2008.

Heller, Karl, and David Marinelli. *Antonio Vivaldi: The Red Priest of Venice*. New York: Amadeus, 1997.

Robbins Landon, H. C. *Vivaldi: Voice of the Baroque*. London: Thames and Hudson, 1993.

Ryom, Peter. *Antonio Vivaldi: Thematisch-systematisches Verzeichnis seiner Werke (RV)*. Wiesbaden, Germany: Breitkopf and Härtel, 2007.

———. *Répertoire des Oeuvres d'Antonio Vivaldi*. Copenhagen: Engstrong and Sødering, 1986.

Sardelli, Federico Maria. *Vivaldi's Music for Flute and Recorder*. Aldershot, England: Ashgate, 2007.

Strohm, Reinhard. *The Operas of Antonio Vivaldi*. Florence, Italy: Leo S. Olschki, 2008.

Talbot, Michael. *Antonio Vivaldi: A Guide to Research*. New York: Garland, 1988.

———. *The Chamber Cantatas of Antonio Vivaldi*. Woodbridge, England: Boydell, 2006.

———. *The Sacred Vocal Music of Antonio Vivaldi*. Studi di Musica Veneta. Quaderni Vivaldiani 8. Florence, Italy: Leo S. Olschki, 1995.

———. *Venetian Music in the Age of Antonio Vivaldi*. Aldershot, England: Ashgate, 1999.

———. *Vivaldi*. 2nd ed. Oxford: Oxford University Press, 2000.

———. *Vivaldi and Fugue*. Florence, Italy: Leo S. Olschki, 2009.

———. *The Vivaldi Compendium*. Woodbridge, England: Boydell, 2011.

———. *Vivaldi, "Motezuma" and the* Opera Seria: *Essays on a Newly Discovered Work and Its Background*. Turnhout, Belgium: Brepols, 2008.

Others

Arnold, Denis. *Giovanni Gabrieli and the Music of the Venetian High Renaissance*. Oxford: Oxford University Press, 1979.

Ashbee, Andrea, and Peter Holman, eds. *John Jenkins and His Time: Studies in English Consort Music*. Oxford: Clarendon, 1996.

Augsbach, Horst. *Johann Joachim Quantz: Thematisch-systematisches Verzeichnis der Werke (QV)*. Stuttgart, Germany: Carus-Verlag, 1997.

Beckmann, Klaus, and Hans-Joachim Schulze, eds. *Johann Gottfried Walther: Briefe*. Leipzig, Germany: Deutsche Verlag für Musik, 1987.

Bizzarini, Marco. *Benedetto Marcello*. Palermo, Italy: L'Epos, 2006.

Borroff, Edith. *An Introduction to Elisabeth-Claude Jacquet de La Guerre*. Brooklyn, NY: Institute of Mediaeval Music, 1966.

Boyd, Malcolm. *Palestrina's Style: A Practical Introduction*. Oxford: Oxford University Press, 1973.

Breig, Werner. *Die Orgelwerke von Heinrich Scheidemann*. Wiesbaden, Germany: Steiner, 1967.

Brett, Ursula. *Music and Ideas in 17th-Century Italy: The Cazzati-Arresti Polemic*. New York: Garland, 1989.

Brink, Meike ten. *Die Flötenkonzerte von Johann Joachim Quantz: Untersuchungen zu ihrer Überlierferung und Form*. Hildesheim, Germany: G. Olms, 1995.

Buelow, George J., and Hans Joachim Marx, eds. *New Mattheson Studies*. Cambridge: Cambridge University Press, 1983.

Burney, Charles. *Memoirs of the Life and Writings of the Abate Metastasio*. London: 1796. Reprint, New York: Da Capo, 1971.

Careri, Enrico. *Francesco Geminiani, 1687–1762*. Oxford: Clarendon, 1994.

Cessac, Catherine. *Elisabeth Jacquet de La Guerre: Une Femme Compositeur sous le Règne de Louis XIV*. Arles, France: Actes Sud, 1995.

Chafe, Eric Thomas. *The Church Music of Heinrich Biber*. Studies in Musicology 95. Ann Arbor, MI: UMI Research Press, 1975.

Charteris, Richard. *Giovanni Gabrieli: A Thematic Catalogue of His Music*. Thematic Catalogue Series 20. Stuyvesant, NY: Pendragon, 1996.

Ciurlia, Pier Paolo. *Johann Hieronymus Kapsberger, Nobile Alemanno: una Biografia*. Padua, Italy: Armelin Musica, 2010.

Coelho, Victor Anand. "G. G. Kapsberger in Rome, 1604–1645: New Biographical Data." *Journal of the Lute Society of America* XVI (1983): 103–33.

Cusick, Suzanne. G. *Francesca Caccini at the Medici Court: Music and the Circulation of Power*. Chicago: University of Chicago Press, 2009.

Davidsson, Hans. *Matthias Weckmann: the Interpretation of his Organ Music*. Stockholm: Gehrmans Musikförlag, 1991.

Decobert, Laurence. *Henry Du Mont (1610–1684): Maistre et Compositeur de la Musique de la Chapelle du Roy et de la Reyne*. Wavre, Belgium: Mardaga, 2011.

Dennison, Peter. *Pelham Humfrey*. Oxford: Oxford University Press, 1986.

Dittrich, Raymond. *Die Messen von Johann Friedrich Fasch, 1688–1758*. Frankfurt, Germany: P. Lang, 1992.

Eynard, Marcello. *Il musicista Pietro Antonio Locatelli: un Itinerario Artistico da Bergamo a Amsterdam*. Bergamo, Italy: Circolo Lirico Mayr-Donizetti, 1995.

Farrar, Carol Reglin. *Michel Corrette and Flute Playing in the 18th Century*. Brooklyn, NY: Institute of Mediaeval Music, 1970.

Fletcher, John E., et al. *A Study of the Life and Works of Athanasius Kircher, "Germanus Incredibilis."* Leiden, Netherlands: Brill, 2011.

Gianturco, Carolyn. *Alessandro Stradella (1639–1682): His Life and Works*. Oxford: Oxford University Press, 1994.

García Ferreras, Arsenio. *Juan Bautista Cabanilles: sein Leben und sein Werk*. Regensburg, Germany: G. Bosse, 1973.

Godwin, Joscelyn. *Athanasius Kircher: A Renaissance Man and the Quest for Knowledge*. London: Thames and Hudson, 1979.

Harley, John. *Orlando Gibbons and the Gibbons Family of Musicians*. Aldershot, England: Ashgate, 1999.

Hilscher, Elisabeth Theresia, and Andrea Sommer-Mathis, eds. *Pietro Metastasio, Uomo Universale (1698–1782)*. Vienna: Verlag der Österreichischen Akademie der Wissenschaften, 2000.

Hochstein, Wolfgang. *Die Kirchenmusik von Niccolò Jommelli*. Hildesheim, Germany: Olms, 1984.

Klenz, William. *Giovanni Maria Bononcini of Modena: A Chapter in Baroque Instrumental Music*. Durham, NC: Duke University Press, 1962.

Lefkowitz, Murray. *William Lawes*. London: Routledge, 1960.

Leopold, Silke. *Stefano Landi: Beiträge zur Biographie: Untersuchungen zur weltlichen und geistlichen Vokalmusik*. Hamburg, Germany: K. D. Wagner, 1976.

Markstrom, Kurt Sven. *The Operas of Leonardo Vinci, Napoletano*. Hillsdale, NY: Pendragon, 2007.

Marvin, Clara. *Giovanni Pierluigi da Palestrina: A Guide to Research*. New York: Routledge, 2002.

Martial, Leroux. *Guillaume Bouzignac (ca. 1587–ca. 1643): Étude Musicologique*. Béziers, France: Société de Musicologie du Languedoc, 1993.

Milliot, Sylvette, and Jérôme de la Gorce. *Marin Marais*. Paris: Fayard, 1991.

Millner, Fredrick L. *The Operas of Johann Adolf Hasse*. Ann Arbor, MI: UMI Research Press, 1979.

Petrobelli, Pierluigi. *Tartini: Le Sue Idee e il Suo Tempo*. Lucca, Italy: Libreria Musicale Italiana, 1992.

Pfeiffer, Rüdiger. *Johann Friedrich Fasch, 1688–1758: Leben und Werk*. Wilhelmshaven, Germany: Noetzel, Heinrichshofen Bücher, 1994.

Pritchard, Brian W., ed. *Antonio Caldara: Essays on his Life and Times*. Aldershot, England: Scolar Press, 1987.

Reardon, Colleen. *Agostino Agazzari and Music at Siena Cathedral, 1597–1641*. Oxford: Clarendon, 1993.

Rifkin, Joshua. *North German Baroque Masters: Schütz, Froberger, Buxtehude, Purcell, Telemann*. London: Macmillan, 1985.

Sawkins, Lionel, and John Nightingale. *A Thematic Catalogue of the Works of Michel-Richard de Lalande (1657–1726)*. Oxford: Oxford University Press, 2005.

Scheibert, Beverly. *Jean-Henry D'Anglebert and the Seventeenth-Century Clavecin School*. Bloomington: University of Indiana Press, 1986.

Selfridge-Field, Eleanor. *The Music of Benedetto and Alessandro Marcello: A Thematic Catalogue with Commentary on the Composers, Works and Sources*. New York: Oxford University Press, 1990.

Shaw, Watkins. *The Services of John Blow*. Croydon: Church Music Society, 1988.

Spitz, Charlotte. *Antonio Lotti in seiner Bedeutung als Opernkomponist*. Borna-Leipzig: R. Noske, 1918.

Stevens, Denis. *Thomas Tomkins*. London: Macmillan, 1957. Reprint, New York: Dover, 1967.

Stockigt, Janice B. *Jan Dismas Zelenka (1679–1745): A Bohemian Musician at the Court of Dresden*. Oxford: Oxford University Press, 2000.

Talbot, Michael. *Benedetto Vinaccesi: A Musician in Brescia and Venice in the Age of Corelli*. Oxford: Oxford University Press, 1994.

———. *Tomaso Albinoni: The Venetian Composer and His World*. Oxford: Oxford University Press, 1990.

Timms, Colin. *Polymath of the Baroque: Agostino Steffani and His Music*. Oxford: Oxford University Press, 2003.

Vogelsänger, Siegfried. *Michael Praetorius beim Wort genommen: zur Entstehungsgeschichte seiner Werke*. Aachen: Herodot Rader Verlag, 1987.

Wollenberg, Susan. "The Keyboard Suites of Gottlieb Muffat (1690–1770)." *Proceedings of the Royal Musical Association* CII (1975–76): 83–91.

GENERIC STUDIES OF BAROQUE MUSIC

Cantata, Madrigal, and Song

Durosoir, Georgie. *Poésie, Musique et Société: L'Air de Cour en France au XVIIe Siècle*. Sprimont, Belgium: Mardaga, 2006.

Gordon-Seifert, Catherine Elizabeth. *Music and the Language of Love: Seventeenth-Century French Airs*. Bloomington: Indiana University Press, 2011.

Hill, John Walter. *Roman Monody, Cantata, and Opera from the Circles around Cardinal Montalto*. 2 vols. Oxford: Clarendon, 1997.

Jones, Edward Huws. *The Performance of English Song 1610–1670*. New York: Garland: 1989.

McGuinness, Rosamond. *English Court Odes, 1660–1820*. Oxford: Oxford University Press, 1971.

Newcomb, Anthony. *The Madrigal at Ferrara, 1579–1597*. Princeton, NJ: Princeton University Press, 1978.

Roche, Jerome. *The Madrigal*. 2nd ed. Oxford: Oxford University Press, 1990.

Samuel, Harold E. *The Cantata in Nuremberg during the Seventeenth Century*. Ann Arbor, MI: UMI Reasearch Press, 1982.

Spink, Ian. *English Song, Dowland to Purcell*. London: Batsford, 1974. Reprint: 1986.

Talbot, Michael. *Aspects of the Secular Cantata in Late Baroque Italy*. Farnham, England: Ashgate, 2009.

Thomas, R. Hinton. *Poetry and Song in the German Baroque: A Study of the Continuo Lied*. Oxford: Clarendon, 1963.

Tunley, David. *The Eighteenth-Century French Cantata*. 2nd ed. New York: Clarendon, 1997.

Concerto

Drummond, Pippa. *The German Concerto: Five Eighteenth-Century Studies*. Oxford: Oxford University Press, 1980.

Hutchings, Arthur. *The Baroque Concerto*. Rev. ed. New York: Scribner, 1979.

Keyboard Music

Bradshaw, Murray C. *The Origin of the Toccata*. Dallas: American Institute of Musicology, 1972.

Collins, Paul. *The Stylus Phantasticus and Free Keyboard Music of the North German Baroque*. Aldershot, England: Ashgate, 2005.

Douglass, Fenner. *The Language of the Classical French Organ: A Musical Tradition before 1800*. New Haven, CT: Yale University Press, 1978.

Dufourcq, Norbert. *Le Livre de l'Orgue Français, 1589–1789*. 5 vols. Paris: Picard, 1971–82.

Gustafson, Bruce. *French Harpsichord Music of the 17th Century*. Ann Arbor, MI: UMI Research Press, 1979.

Hogwood, Christopher. *The Keyboard in Baroque Europe*. Cambridge: Cambridge University Press, 2003.

Lama, Jesús Angel de la. *El Órgano Barroco Espanol*. Valladolid, Spain: Junta de Castilla y León, 1995.

Ledbetter, David. *Harpsichord and Lute Music in 17th-Century France*. London: Macmillan, 1987; Bloomington: Indiana University Press, 1988.

Parkins, Robert. "Spain and Portugal." In *Keyboard Music before 1700*, edited by Alexander Silbiger, London: Prentice Hall International, 1995.

Shannon, John R. *Organ Literature of the 17th Century: A Study of Its Styles*. Raleigh, NC: At the Sunbury, 1978.

Sharp, Ian. *The Liturgical Use of the Organ Voluntary*. Croydon, England: Royal School of Church Music, 1984.

Tilney, Colin, ed. *The Art of the Unmeasured Prelude for Harpsichord, France, 1660–1720*. 3 vols. London: Schott, 1991.

Opera and Music for the Theater

Brito, Manuel Carlos de. *Opera in Portugal in the Eighteenth Century*. New York: Cambridge University Press, 1989.

Brown, Howard Mayer. "How Opera Began: An Introduction to Jacopo Peri's *Euridice* (1600)." In *The Late Italian Renaissance*, edited by Eric Cochrane, 401–44. New York: Harper and Row, 1970. Reprint in *The Garland Library of the History of Western Music*, edited by Ellen Rosand, 1–44. Vol. 11, *Opera I: Up to Mozart*. New York: 1985.

Brown, Peter, and Suzana Ograjensek. *Ancient Drama in Music for the Modern Stage*. Oxford: Oxford University Press, 2010.

Bucciarelli, Melania. *Italian Opera and European Theatre, 1680–1720: Plots, Performers, Dramaturgies*. Turnhout, Belgium: Brepols, 2000.

Buelow, George J. "Opera in Hamburg 300 Years Ago." *Musical Times* CXIX (1978): 26–28.

Burt, Nathaniel. "Opera in Arcadia." *Musical Quarterly* 41 (1955): 145–170.

Bussey, William M. *French and Italian Influence on the Zarzeula, 1700–1770*. Ann Arbor, MI: UMI Research Press, 1982.

Charlton, David. *French Opera: 1730–1830: Meaning and Media*. Aldershot, England: Ashgate, 1999.

Coeyman, Barbara. "Theatres of Opera and Ballet during the Reigns of Louis XIV and Louis XV." *Early Music* XVIII (1990): 22–37.

Dent, Edward J. *Foundations of English Opera: A Study of Musical Drama in England during the Seventeenth Century*. Cambridge: University Press, 1928. Reprint, New York: Da Capo, 1965.

Donington, Robert. *The Rise of Opera*. London: Faber and Faber, 1981.

Fiske, Roger. *English Theatre Music in the Eighteenth Century*. 2nd ed. Oxford: Oxford University Press, 1986.

Freeman, Daniel E. *The Opera Theater of Count Franz Anton Sporck in Prague*. Stuyvesant, NY: Pendragon, 1992.

Freeman, Robert. "Apostolo Zeno's Reform of the Libretto." *Journal of the American Musicological Society* 21 (1968): 259–324.

———. *Opera without Drama: Currents of Change in Italian Opera, 1675–1725*. Ann Arbor, MI: UMI Research Press, 1981.

Gianturco, Carolyn. "Evidence for a Late Roman School of Opera." *Music and Letters* LVI (1975): 4–17.

Hammond, Friderick. *Music and Spectacle in Baroque Rome: Barberini Patronage under Urban VIII*. New Haven, CT: Yale University Press, 1994.

Hanning, Barbara Russano. *Of Music's Power: Humanism and the Creation of Opera*. Ann Arbor, MI: UMI Research Press, 1980.

Heriot, Angus. *The Castrati in Opera*. London: Secker and Warburg, 1956.

Hill, John Walter. "Florence: Musical Spectacle and Drama, 1570–1650." In *The Early Baroque Era from the Late 16th Century to the 1660s*, edited by Curtis Price, 121–45. Music and Society, edited by Stanley Sadie. New York: Prentice Hall, 1993.

Holmes, William C. *Opera Observed: Views of a Florentine Impresario in the Early Eighteenth Century*. Chicago: University of Chicago Press, 1993.

Höntsch, Winfried. *Opern-metropole Dresden: von der Festa Teatrale zum modernen Musikdrama: ein Beitrag zur Geschichte und zur Ikonographie der Dresdner Opernkultur*. Dresden, Germany: Verlag der Kunst: 1996.

Katz, Ruth. *Divining the Powers of Music: Aesthetic Theory and the Origins of Opera*. New York: Pendragon, 1986.

Kintzler, Catherine. *Poétique de l'Opéra Français de Corneille à Rousseau*. Paris: Minerve, 1991.

Knapp, J. Merrill. "Eighteenth-Century Opera in London before Handel, 1705–1710." In *British Theatre and the Other Arts, 1660–1800*, edited by Shirley Strumm Kenny, 67–91. Washington, DC: Folger Shakespeare Library, 1984.

Limon, Jerzy. *The Masque of Stuart Culture*. Newark: University of Delaware Press, 1990.

Lindgren, Lowell. "*I Trionfi di Camilla*." *Studi Musicali* 6 (1977): 89–159.

Marx, Hans Joachim, and Dorothea Schröder. *Die Hamburger Gänsemarkt Oper: Katalog der Textbücher (1678–1748)*. Laaber, Germany: Laaber Verlag, 1995.

Meyer, Ernst. *Die mehrstimmige Spielmusik des 17. Jahrhunderts in Nord- und Mitteleuropa*. Kassel, Germany: Bärenreiter, 1934. Reprint, 1982.

Meyer, Reinhart. *Die Hamburger Oper, 1678–1730: Einführung und Kommentar zur dreibändigen Textsammlung*. Reprint. Millwood, NY: Kraus: 1984.

Muraro, Maria Theresa, ed. *Venezie e il Melodramma nel Seicento*. Studi di Musica Veneta 5. Florence, Italy: Leo S. Olschki, 1976.

Murata, Margaret. *Operas for the Papal Court, 1631–1668*. Ann Arbor, MI: UMI Research Press, 1981.

Palisca, Claude V. "The 'Camerata Fiorentina': A Reappraisal." *Studi Musicali* I (1972): 203–36. Reprint in *The Garland Library of the History of Western Music*, edited by Ellen Rosand, 45–80. Vol. XI: *Opera I: Up to Mozart*. New York: 1985.

Pirrotta, Nino. *Music and Theatre from Poliziano to Monteverdi*. Translated by Karen Eales. Cambridge: Cambridge University Press, 1982.

Pitou, Spire. *The Paris Opera: An Encyclopedia of Operas, Ballets, Composers and Performers*. Westport, CT: Greenwood, 1983.

Price, Curtis A. *Music in the Restoration Theatre*. Ann Arbor, MI: UMI Press, 1979.

Rava, Arnaldo. *I teatri di Roma*. Rome: Fratelli Palombi Editori, 1953.

Robinson, Michael F. *Naples and Neapolitan Opera*. Oxford: Oxford University Press, 1972.

Rosand, Ellen. *Opera in Seventeenth-Century Venice: The Creation of a Genre*. Berkeley: University of California Press, 1991.

Rosow, Lois. "French Baroque Recitative as an Expression of Tragic Declamations." *Early Music* XI (1983): 468–77.

Schulze, W. *Die Quellen der Hamburger Oper 1678–1738: eine bibliographische-statistische Studie zur Geschichte der ersten stehenden deutschen Oper*. Hamburg-Oldenburg, Germany: G. Stalling, 1938.

Seifert, Herbert. *Die Oper am Wiener Kaiserhof im 17. Jahrhundert*. Tutzing, Germany: Schneider, 1985.

Stein, Louise. *Songs of Mortals, Dialogues of the Gods: Music and Theatre in Seventeenth-Century Spain*. Oxford: Clarendon, 1993.

Sternfeld, Friderick W. *The Birth of Opera*. Oxford: Clarendon, 1993.

———. "The First Printed Opera Libretto." *Music and Letters* LIX (1978): 121–38.

Strohm, Reinhard. *Die italienische Oper im 18. Jahrhundert*. Wilhelmshaven, Germany: Heinrichshofen, 1979.

———. Dramma per Musica: *Italian Opera Seria of the Eighteenth Century*. New Haven, CT: Yale University Press, 1997.

———. *Italienische Opernarien des frühen Settecento (1720–1730)*. Cologne: Volk, 1976.

Troy, Charles E. *The Comic Intermezzo: A Study in the History of Eighteenth-Century Italian Opera*. Ann Arbor, MI: UMI Research Press, 1979.

Walls, Peter. *Music in the English Courtly Masque, 1604–1640*. Oxford: Clarendon, 1996.

Weaver, Robert Lamar, and Norma Wright Weaver. *A Chronology of Music in the Florentine Theater: Operas, Prologues, Finales, Intermezzos, and Plays with Incidental Music*. Detroit, MI: Information Coordinators, 1978–83.

Weiss, Piero. *Opera: A History in Documents*. New York: Oxford University Press, 2002.

White, Eric Walter. *A History of English Opera*. London: Faber and Faber, 1983.

Wolff, Hellmuth Christian. *Die Barockoper in Hamburg, 1678–1738.* Wolfenbüttel, Germany: Möseler, 1957.
Wood, Caroline, and Graham Sadler. *French Baroque Opera: A Reader.* Burlington, VT: Ashgate, 2000.

Oratorio and Passion

Arnold, Denis, and Elsie Arnold. *The Oratorio in Venice.* London: Royal Musical Association, 1986.
Bianchi, Lino. *Carissimi, Stradella, Scarlatti e l'Oratorio Musicale.* Rome: De Santis, 1969.
Crowther, Victor. *The Oratorio in Bologna (1650–1730).* Oxford: Oxford University Press, 1999.
Foster, D. H. "The Oratorio in Paris in the 18th Century." *Acta Musicologica* LVII (1975): 67–133.
Hill, John Walter. *The Oratorio in Modena.* Oxford: Oxford University Press, 1992.
———. "Oratory Music in Florence." *Acta Musicologica* 51 (1979): 108–36, 246–67; 58 (1986): 129–79.
Noske, Frits. *Saints and Sinners: The Latin Musical Dialogue in the Seventeenth Century.* Oxford: Clarendon, 1992.
Smallman, Basil. *The Background of Passion Music: J. S. Bach and His Predecessors.* 1957. Reprint, New York: Dover, 1970.

Orchestral Music

Fleischhauer, Günther, and Eitelfriedrich Thom, eds. *Die Entwicklung der Ouvertüren-Suite im 17. und 18. Jahrhundert.* Michalestein, Germany: Institut für Aufführungspraxis, 1996.
Spitzer, John, and Neal Zaslaw. *The Birth of the Orchestra.* New York: Oxford University Press, 2004.

Sacred Music

Arnold, Denis. "The Solo Motet in Venice (1625–1775)." *Proceedings of the Royal Musical Association* CVI (1980): 56–68.
Brough, Delma. *Polish Seventeenth-Century Church Music with References to the Influence of Historical, Political and Social Conditions.* New York: Garland, 1989.
Carver, Anthony F. *"Cori Spezzati": The Development of Sacred Polychoral Music to the Time of Schütz.* 2 vols. Cambridge: Cambridge University Press, 1988.
Dearnley, Christopher. *English Church Music, 1650–1750: In Royal Chapel, Cathedral, and Parish Church.* New York: Oxford University Press, 1970.
Dietz, Hanns-Bertold. "Sacred Music in Naples during the Second Half of the Seventeenth Century." In *La Musica a Napoli durante il Seicento,* edited by Domenico Antonio D'Alessandro and Agostino Ziino, Miscellanea Musicologica 2. Rome: Torre d'Orfeo, 1987.

Ferraton, Yves, and Jean Mongrédien. *Le grand motet français*. Paris: Presses de L'Université de Paris-Sorbonne, 1986.

Kirwan-Mott, Anne. *The Small-Scale Sacred Concertato in the Early Seventeenth Century*. 2 vols. Ann Arbor, MI: UMI Research Press, 1981.

Krummacher, Friedhelm. *Die Choralbearbeitung in der protestantischen Figuralmusik zwischen Praetorius und Bach*. Kassel, Germany: Bärenreiter, 1978.

Laird, Paul R. *Towards a History of the Spanish Villancico*. Warren, MI: Harmonie Park, 1997.

Le Huray, Peter. *Music and the Reformation in England: 1549–1660*. New York: Oxford University Press, 1967. Reprint, Cambridge: Cambridge University Press, 1978, 1979, 1989.

Liemohn, Edwin. *The Chorale through Four Hundred Years*. Philadelphia: Muhlenberg Press, 1953.

Märker, Michael. *Die Protestantische Dialogkomposition zwischen Heinrich Schütz und Johann Sebastian Bach: Eine stilkritische Studie*. Kirchenmusikalische Studien 2. Cologne, Germany: Tank, 1990.

Moore, James H. *Vespers at St. Mark's: Music of Alessandro Grandi, Giovanni Rovetta, and Francesco Cavalli*. Ann Arbor, MI: UMI Research Press, 1981.

———. "The *Vespro delli Cinque Laudate* and the Role of *Salmi Spezzati* at St. Mark's." *Journal of the American Musicological Society* XXXIV (1981): 249–78.

Noske, Frits. *Music Bridging Divided Religions: The Motet in the Seventeenth-Century Dutch Republic*. 2 vols. Wilhelmshaven, Germany: F. Noetzel, Heinrichshofen-Books, 1989.

Saunders, Steven. *Cross, Sword, and Lyre: Sacred music at the Imperial Court of Ferdinand II of Habsburg (1619–1637)*. New York: Oxford University Press, 1995.

Stevenson, Robert Murrell. *Christmas Music from Baroque Mexico*. Berkeley: University of California Press, 1974.

———. *The Music of Colonial Spanish America*. Cambridge: Cambridge University Press, 1980/1985.

———. *Spanish Cathedral Music in the Golden Age*. Berkeley: University of California Press, 1976.

Sonata

Allsop, Peter. *The Italian "Trio" Sonata from Its Origins until Corelli*. Oxford: Clarendon, 1992.

Daniel, Thomas. *Der Choralsatz bei Bach und seiner Zeitgenossen: eine historische Satzlehre*. Cologne, Germany: Dohr, 2000.

Daverio, John. "In Search of the Sonata da Camera before Corelli." *Acta Musicologica* LVII (1985): 195–214.

Hogwood, Christopher. *The Trio Sonata*. London: British Broadcasting Corporation, 1979.

Mangsen, Susan. "The 'Sonata da Camera' before Corelli: A Renewed Search." *Music and Letters* LXXVI (1995): 19–31.

Newman, William S. *The Sonata in the Baroque Era*. 4th ed. New York: Norton, 1983.

Schmidt-Beste, Thomas. *The Sonata*. Cambridge: Cambridge University Press, 2011.

Suite and Dance

Buch, David Joseph. *Dance Music from the Ballet de Cour, 1575–1651*. New York: Pendragon, 1994.

Christout, Marie Françoise. *Le Ballet de Cour au XVIIe Siècle*. Geneva, Switzerland: Minkoff, 1987.

Cooper, Barry. *English Solo Keyboard Music of the Middle and Late Baroque*. New York: Garland, 1989.

Kant, Mario. *The Cambridge Companion to Ballet*. Cambridge: Cambridge University Press, 2007.

Mather, Betty Bang. *Dance Rhythms of the French Baroque: A Handbook for Performance*. Bloomington: Indiana University Press, 1987.

McCleave, Sahar Yuill, and Geoffrey Burgess, eds. *Dance and Music in French Baroque Theatre: Sources and Interpretations*. London: Institute of Advanced Musical Studies, King's College London, 1998.

Nevile, Jennifer. *Dance, Spectacle, and the Body Politick, 1250–1750*. Bloomington: Indiana University Press, 2008.

Silbiger, Alexander. "Passacaglia and Ciaccona: Genre Pairing and Ambiguity from Frescobaldi to Couperin." *Journal of Seventeenth-Century Music* 2 (1996).

BAROQUE MUSICAL INSTRUMENTS

Keyboard Instruments

Boalch, Donald H., Charles Mould, and Andreas H. Roth. *Makers of the Harpsichord and Clavichord, 1440–1840*. Rev. 3rd edition. Oxford: Clarendon, 1995.

Douglass, Fenner. *The Language of the Classical French Organ: A Musical Tradition before 1800*. 2nd ed. New Haven, CT: Yale University Press, 1995.

Kottick, Edward L. *A History of the Harpsichord*. Bloomington: Indiana University Press, 2003.

The New Grove Early Keyboard Instruments. New York: Norton, 1989.

The New Grove Organ. New York: Norton, 1988.

Owen, Barbara. *The Registration of Baroque Organ Music*. Bloomington: Indiana University Press, 1997.

Pollens, Stewart. *The Early Pianoforte*. Cambridge: Cambridge University Press, 1995.

Schlick, Arnolt. *Spiegel der Orgelmacher und Organisten*. Translated by Elizabeth Berry Barber. Buren, Netherlands: Frits Knuf, 1980.

Shaw, Watkins. *The Succession of Organists of the Chapel Royal and the Cathedrals of England and Wales from c. 1538*. Oxford: Clarendon, 1991.

Sumner, William Leslie. *The Organ: Its Evolution, Principles of Construction and Use.* 4th ed. New York: St. Martin's, 1981.

Thistlethwaite, Nicholas, and Geoffrey Webber, eds. *The Cambridge Companion to the Organ.* Cambridge: Cambridge University Press, 1998.

Troeger, Richard. *Technique and Interpretaion on the Harpsichord and Clavichord.* Bloomington: Indiana University Press, 1987.

Williams, Peter F. *The European Organ, 1450–1850.* 2nd ed. London: Batsford, 1978.

——. *A New History of the Organ from the Greeks to the Present Day.* Bloomington: Indiana University Press, 1980.

——. *The Organ in Western Culture.* New York: Cambridge University Press, 1993.

String Instruments

Apel, Willi. *Italian Violin Music of the Seventeenth Century.* Thomas Binkley, ed. Bloomington: Indiana University Press, 1990.

Boyden, David D. *The History of Violin Playing from Its Orgins to 1761 and Its Relationship to the Violin and Violin Music.* London: Oxford University Press, 1965.

Coelho, Victor. *The Cambridge Companion to the Guitar.* Cambridge: Cambridge University Press, 2003.

Holman Peter. *Four and Twenty Fiddlers: The Violin at the English Court, 1540–1690.* Oxford: Clarendon, 1993. 2nd ed., Oxford: Oxford University Press, 1995.

McCrickard, Eleanor F. "The Roman Repertory for Violin before the Time of Corelli." *Early Music* XVIII (1990): 563–73.

North, Nigel. *Continuo Playing on the Lute, Archlute and Theorbo.* Bloomington: Indiana University Press, 1987.

Pohlmann, Ernst. *Laute, Theorbe, Chitarrone: Die Instrumente, ihre Musik und Literatur von 1500 bis zur Gegenwart.* 5th ed. Lilienthal, Germany: Eres Ed., 1982.

Sadie, Julie A. *The Bass Viol in French Baroque Chamber Music.* Ann Arbor, MI: UMI Press, 1980.

Spring, Matthew. *The Lute in Britain: A History of the Instrument and Its Music.* Oxford: Oxford University Press, 2001.

Turnbull, Harvey. *The Guitar from the Renaissance to the Present Day.* New York: Scribner, 1974.

Tyler, James. *The Early Guitar: A History and Handbook.* London: Oxford University Press, 1980.

——. *A Guide to Playing the Baroque Guitar.* Bloomington: Indiana University Press, 2011.

Tyler, James, and Paul Sparks. *The Guitar and Its Music from the Renaissance to the Classical Era.* Oxford: Oxford University Press, 2002.

Wade, Graham. *Traditions of the Classical Guitar.* London: Calder, 1980.

Ward, John M. *Music for Elizabethan Lutes.* 2 vols. Oxford: Clarendon, 1992.

Woodfield, Ian. *The Early History of the Viol.* Cambridge: Cambridge University Press, 1984.

Wind Instruments

Addington, C. "In Search of the Baroque Flute." *Early Music* IX (1981): 307.

Baines, Anthony. *Brass Instruments: Their History and Development*. New York: Scribner, 1978.

Barclay, Robert. *The Art of the Trumpet-Maker: The Materials, Tools, and Techniques of the Seventeenth and Eighteenth Centuries in Nuremberg*. Oxford: Clarendon, 1992.

Bowers, Jane. "New Light on the Development of the Transverse Flute between about 1650 and 1770." *Journal of the Musical Instrument Society* III (1977): 5–56.

Griscom, Richard, and David Lasocki. *The Recorder: A Guide to Writings about the Instrument for Players and Researchers*. New York: Garland, 1994.

Haynes, Bruce. *The Eloquent Oboe: A History of the Hautboy, 1640–1760*. Oxford: Oxford University Press, 2001.

Kottick, Edward L. *Tone and Intonation on the Recorder*. New York: 1974.

Morgan, Friderick G. "Making Recorders Based on Historical Models." *Early Music* X (1982): 14.

Powell, Ardal. *The Flute*. New Haven, CT: Yale University Press, 2002.

Recorder and Music Magazine. London: 1963–.

Rice, Albert R. *The Baroque Clarinet*. Oxford: University Press, 1992.

Smithers, Don L. *The Music and History of the Baroque Trumpet before 1721*. London: 1973. 2nd ed., Carbondale: Southern Illinois University Press, 1988.

Solum, John. *The Early Flute*. Oxford: Oxford University Press, 1992.

Thomson, J. M. *The Cambridge Companion to the Recorder*. Cambridge: Cambridge University Press, 1995.

Vester, Frans. *Flute Music of the 18th Century: An Annotated Bibliography*. Monteux, France: Musica Rara, 1985.

PERFORMANCE OF BAROQUE MUSIC

Arnold, Frank T. *The Art of Accompaniment from a Thorough-Bass*. 2 vols. Oxford: Oxford University Press, 1932. Reprint, New York: Dover, 1965.

Brown, Howard Mayer, and Stanley Sadie, ed. *Performance Practice: Music after 1600*. New York: Norton, 1990.

Carter, Stewart. *A Performer's Guide to Seventeenth-Century Music*. New York: Schirmer, 1997.

Cyr, Mary. *Essays on the Performance of Baroque Music: Opera and Chamber Music in France and England*. Aldershot, England: Ashgate, 2008.

——. *Performing Baroque Music*. Portland, OR: Amadeus, 1992.

Dolmetsch, Arnold. *The Interpretation of Music of the 17th and 18th Centuries: Revealed by Contemporary Evidence*. London: Novello, 1915. Reprint, Seattle: University of Washington Press, 1969.

Donington, Robert. *The Interpretation of Early Music*. Rev. ed. New York: Norton, 1989.

Hansell Sven Hostrup. "Orchestral Practice at the Court of Cardinal Pietro Ottoboni." *Journal of the American Musicological Society* XIX (1966): 398–403.

Haskell, Harry. *The Early Music Revival: A History*. Mineola, NY: Dover, 1996.

Haynes, Bruce. *The End of Early Music: A Period Performer's History of Music for the Twenty-First Century*. Oxford: Oxford University Press, 2007.

Hefling, Stephen. *Rhythmic Alteration in Seventeenth- and Eighteenth-Century Music: "Notes Inégales" and Overdotting*. New York: Schirmer, 1993.

Jackson, Roland. *Performance Practice, Medieval to Contemporary: A Bibliographic Guide*. New York: Garland, 1988.

Jander, Owen. "Concerto Grosso Instrumentation in Rome in the 1660s and 1670s." *Journal of the American Musicological Society*. XXI (1968): 168–80.

Kenyon, Nicholas, ed. *Authentic and Early Music*. Oxford: Oxford University Press, 1988.

Le Huray, Peter. *Authenticity in Performance: Eighteenth-Century Case Studies*. Cambridge: Cambridge University Press, 1990.

MacClintock, Carol, ed. *Readings in the History of Music in Performance*. Bloomington: Indiana University Press, 1979.

Neumann, Friderick. *Essays in Performance Practice*. Ann Arbor, MI: UMI Research Press, 1982.

———. *Ornamentation in Baroque and Post-Baroque Music: With Special Emphasis on J. S. Bach*. Princeton, NJ: Princeton University Press, 1978.

Sanford, Sally. "A Comparison of French and Italian Singing in the Seventeenth Century." *Journal of Seventeenth-Century Music* 1 (1995).

Schnoebelen, Anne. "Performance Practices at San Petronio in the Baroque." *Acta Musicologica* XII (1969): 37–55.

Schweizer, Steven L. *Timpani Tone and the Interpretation of Baroque and Classical Music*. Oxford: Oxford University Press, 2010.

Williams, Peter. *Figured Bass Accompaniment*. 2 vols. Edinburgh, UK: Edinburgh University Press, 1970.

DISCOGRAPHIES

Bibilographic and General

A Bibliography of Discographies. Vol. 1, *Classical Music*. New York: Bowker, 1977–83.

Croucher, Trevor. *Early Music Discography: From Plainsong to the Sons of Bach*. London: Library Association, 1981.

Gray, Michael. *Classical Music Discographies, 1976–1988*. New York: Greenwood, 1989.

Schwann Opus. Santa Fe, NM: Stereophile, 1991–2001.

Specific Discographies including Baroque Music

Blyth, Alan, ed. *Choral Music on Record*. Cambridge: Cambridge University Press, 1991.

Curtis, Alan. *A Selective Monteverdi Discography*. Berkeley, CA: Curtis, 1979.

Elste, Martin. *Bachs Kunst der Fuge auf Schallplatten*. Deutsche Bibliothek deutsches Musikarchiv. Frankfurt, Germany: Buchhändler-Vereinigung GmH, 1981.

Fellers, Friderick P. *The Metropolitan Opera on Record: A Discography of the Commercial Recordings*. Westport, CT: Greenwood, 1984.

Firmage, George James. *Bach on LP: A Discography of the Vocal Works of Johann Sebastian Bach (1948–1967)*. London: Great Brook, 1968.

Kratzenstein, Marilou, and Jerald Hamilton. *Four Centuries of Organ Music: From the Robertsbridge Codex through the Baroque Era: An Annotated Discography*. Detroit: Information Coordinators, 1984.

Parsons, Charles H. *Opera Discography*. Lewiston, NY: Edwin Mellen, 1990.

———. *Recent International Opera Discography*. Lewiston, NY: Edwin Mellen, 2003. Updates: 2004, 2005–7.

Westerlund, Gunnar, and Eric Hughes. *Music of Claudio Monteverdi: A Discography*. London: British Institute of Recorded Sound, 1972.

INTERNET RESOURCES

Bach Bibliography. Compiled by Yo Tomita. http://www.qub.ac.uk/~tomita/bachbib/.

Doctoral Dissertations in Musicology. Indiana University, Thomas J. Mathiesen, director. http://www.music.indiana.edu/ddm/.

Frescobaldi Thematic Catalog Online. Alexander Silbiger, project director. http://frescobaldi.music.duke.edu/.

Index to Printed Music. http://www.ebscohost.com/academic/index-to-printed-music-ipm.

International Bibliography of Theatre and Dance with Full Text. http://www.ebscohost.com/academic/international-bibliography-of-theatre-dance-with-full-text.

Journal of Seventeenth-Century Music. http://www.sscm-jscm.org/.

Music Catalog – Library of Congress. http://www.ebscohost.com/academic/music-catalog-library-of-congress.

Music Index. http://www.ebscohost.com/academic/music-index.

Petrucci Music Library. http://imslp.org/wiki/Main_Page.

RILM Abstracts of Music Literature. http://www.ebscohost.com/academic/rilm-abstracts-of-music-literature.

RIPM Online Archive of Music Periodicals (FullTEXT). http://www.ebscohost.com/academic/ripm-online-archive-of-music-periodicals-fulltext.

RIPM: Retrospective Index to Music Periodicals. http://www.ebscohost.com/academic/ripm-retrospective-index-to-music-periodicals.

RISM: Series A/II: Music Manuscripts after 1600. http://www.ebscohost.com/academic/rism-series-a-ii-music-manuscripts-after-1600.

About the Author

Joseph P. Swain has taught music history and theory for more than 35 years. He is organist and director of music at St. Malachy's Church in Sherburne, New York, and former music director of Tapestry, the All-Centuries Singers, based in Clinton, New York. He has also written *Sacred Treasure: Understanding Catholic Liturgical Music* (Liturgical Press, 2012); *Harmonic Rhythm* (Oxford, 2002); *The Broadway Musical* (Oxford, 1990; rev. ed., Scarecrow, 2002), which won ASCAP's Deems Taylor Award in 1991; *Musical Languages* (Norton, 1997); and *Sound Judgment* (San Francisco, 1987), as well as a companion book in this series: *Historical Dictionary of Sacred Music* (Scarecrow, 2006).